P9-EDN-181

Marguerite Patten's

INTERNATIONAL COOKERY IN COLOUR

HAMLYN

LONDON · NEW YORK · SYDNEY · TORONTO

Acknowledgements

The author and publishers would like to thank the following for their help and co-operation in supplying colour pictures for this book:

Australian Gas Light Company: Pictures accompanying Recipe Nos. 31, 49.
Australian Recipe Service: Picture accompanying Recipe No. 47.
Ayds Reducing Plan: Pictures accompanying Recipe Nos. 108, 144, 284.
Belgian Chicory: Picture accompanying Recipe No. 79.
British Egg Information Service: Pictures accompanying Recipe Nos. 277, 326
Butter Information Council: Picture accompanying Recipe No. 37.
Cadbury Schweppes Food Advisory Bureau: Pictures accompanying Recipe Nos. 36, 41, 211.
California Prune Advisory Bureau: Pictures accompanying Recipe Nos. 25, 30, 32, 40, 85, 155, 171.
California Raisin Bureau: Pictures accompanying Recipe Nos. 34, 66, 112, 172.
Carnation Milk Bureau: Picture accompanying Recipe No. 94.
Cirio Company Limited: Picture accompanying Recipe No. 266.
Colman's Semolina: Pictures accompanying Recipe Nos. 175, 295.
Danish Food Centre: Pictures accompanying Recipe Nos. 285, 286, 288, 289, 291.
Dutch Dairy Bureau: Pictures accompanying Recipe Nos. 178, 243, 244, 245, 248, 252, 254.
Dutch Fruit and Vegetable Producers' Association: Pictures accompanying Recipe Nos. 4, 235, 242, 246, 247, 249, 250, 251, 253.
Eden Vale: Picture accompanying Recipe No. 129.
Flour Advisory Bureau: Pictures accompanying Recipe Nos. 20, 43.
Fruit Producers' Council: Pictures accompanying Recipe Nos. 1, 6, 9, 15, 24, 39, 53, 64, 68, 71, 87, 88, 90, 93, 100, 103, 114, 115, 116, 121, 123, 141, 142, 160, 256, 310, 318, 329.
Rich Hengstenberg Limited (Germany): Pictures accompanying Recipe Nos. 58, 232.
Herring Industry Board: Picture accompanying Recipe No. 82.
Holdorf and Richter, Gabelfisch (Germany): Picture accompanying Recipe No. 271.
International Coffee Organisation: Picture accompanying Recipe No. 101.
Italian Lemons: Picture accompanying Recipe No. 278.
Kraft Foods Limited: Picture accompanying Recipe No. 35.
Lard Information Bureau: Pictures accompanying Recipe Nos. 27, 33, 119, 126, 330, 339.
Malayan Pineapple Industry Board: Pictures accompanying Recipe Nos. 182, 183.
Meat Budget Cookery Service: Pictures accompanying Recipe Nos. 46, 158.
Nestlé Limited (Food Information Centre): Picture accompanying Recipe No. 96.
New South Wales Egg Marketing Board (Australia): Picture accompanying Recipe No. 48.
New Zealand Lamb Information Bureau: Picture accompanying Recipe No. 157.
Karl Ostmann Limited (Germany): Pictures accompanying Recipe Nos. 54, 124, 125, 127, 221, 223, 228, 229, 233, 234, 236, 238, 240, 241.
Plumrose Limited: Pictures accompanying Recipe Nos. 290, 294
Rice Council: Pictures accompanying Recipe Nos. 13, 16, 117, 134.
Rosella Foods: Picture accompanying Recipe No. 51.
Spring's Lemon Curd: Picture accompanying Recipe No. 97.
Stork Cookery Service: Pictures accompanying Recipe Nos. 84, 95, 287.
Sunsweet Prunes: Pictures accompanying Recipe Nos. 67, 340.
Swiss Cheese Union: Pictures accompanying Recipe Nos. 333, 334, 335, 336, 338.
Tabasco Pepper Sauce (Beecham Foods Limited): Pictures accompanying Recipe Nos. 11, 23.
M. Thienelt Limited (Germany): Pictures accompanying Recipe Nos. 225, 226, 231.
T. Wall and Sons Limited (Meat and Handy Foods): Picture accompanying Recipe No. 80.
White Fish Kitchen: Picture accompanying Recipe No. 195.
Wine Development Board: Picture accompanying Recipe No. 74.

Published by
The Hamlyn Publishing Group Limited
LONDON · NEW YORK · SYDNEY · TORONTO
Hamlyn House, Feltham, Middlesex, England

ISBN 0 600 34841 5

Printed in Holland by
Senefelder, Purmerend.

CONTENTS

INTRODUCTION

Like so many of you reading this book I am an inveterate traveller. I love visiting new places, seeing new sights, and meeting people in their own countries. Naturally, as cooking and writing about food has been my profession for many years, the foods and dishes of various countries fascinate me. I am fortunate in that I have been able to learn about so many recipes at first hand, and it has been a great pleasure to be taught the skills by accomplished cooks of various nationalities.

You will find recipes from all over the world in this book, with pictures to show the completed dishes. In the past it was not easy to reproduce dishes from the Far or Middle East, for some of the characteristic foods were unobtainable. Today if you wander round a good store or supermarket you will be amazed, and fascinated probably, by the wide variety of foods from other countries—both fresh and packaged—that are on sale. The recipes in this book, therefore, can be made quite easily.

I find, and hope you agree, that cooking dishes I have enjoyed while visiting other places is like a 'mini-holiday'. I recapture the exotic feeling of the East and the sophistication of the Western world.

These recipes gave me great delight to cook in my own kitchen. I trust that you and your families and friends will have equal pleasure in both preparing and eating them.

Marguerite Patten

USEFUL FACTS AND FIGURES

Weights and measures

A convenient method of converting recipe quantities is to round off gramme and millilitre measurements to the nearest unit of 25. The charts below give the exact conversion (to the nearest whole figure) of Imperial ounces and fluid ounces to grammes and millilitres, and the recommended equivalent based on the nearest unit of 25.

Solid measures

Ounces	Grammes	Recommended equivalent to nearest 25
1	28	25
2	57	50
3	85	75
4	113	100
5	142	150
6	170	175
7	198	200
8 (½ lb.)	226	225
12 (¾ lb.)	340	350
16 (1 lb.)	456	450

Liquid measures

Fluid ounces	Millilitres to nearest whole figure	Recommended equivalent to nearest 25
1	28	25
2	57	50
3	85	75
4	113	100 (1 decilitre)
5 (¼ pint)	142	150
6	170	175
7	198	200 (2 decilitres)
8	226	225
9	255	250
10 (½ pint)	283	275
15 (¾ pint)	428	425
20 (1 pint)	569	575

When converting quantities over 1 lb. or 1 pint, add together the appropriate figures in the centre column (the direct conversion) before rounding off to the nearest unit of 25.

If the nearest unit of 25 gives scant measure the liquid content in a recipe must also be reduced. For example, by looking at the Solid measures chart you will see that 1 oz. is 28 grammes to the nearest whole figure but it is only 25 grammes when rounded off to the nearest number which can be divided by 25. Therefore, if in a recipe for pouring sauce the ingredients to be converted are: 1 oz. margarine, 1 oz. flour and 1 pint (i.e. 20 fluid oz.) of milk, these conversions will have to be applied: 1 oz. margarine approximates 25 grammes; 1 oz. flour approximates 25 grammes but, even though 575 millilitres of milk is nearer to 20 fluid oz. or 1 pint, the scant measure of 550 millilitres will give a more accurate consistency. Similarly, if it so happens that the measurement of solids gives generous weight then the liquid measure used should also be generous.

Note on metric units of measurement

1 litre (1000 millilitres, 10 decilitres) equals 1·76 pints, or almost exactly 1¾ pints.
1 kilogramme (1000 grammes) equals 2·2 pounds, or almost exactly 2 pounds 3 ounces.

Note: Although using the recommended equivalent rounded off to the nearest unit of 25 will give satisfactory results in nearly all recipes, in special cases, such as delicately-balanced cake and pastry recipes, it may be better to use the more exact, but less convenient, amounts given in the centre column.

Notes for American users

Although each recipe has an American measure and ingredients column, the following list gives American equivalents or substitutes for some terms used in the book:

BRITISH	AMERICAN
Baked/unbaked pastry case	Baked/unbaked pie shell
Base	Bottom
Cocktail stick	Wooden toothpick
Cake mixture	Batter
Deep cake tin	Spring form pan
Greaseproof paper	Wax paper
Kitchen paper	Paper towels
Mixer/liquidizer	Mixer/blender
Muslin	Cheesecloth
Pastry cutters	Cookie cutters
Piping tube	Nozzle/tip
Piping bag	Pastry bag
Pudding basin	Pudding mold/ ovenproof bowl
Sandwich tin	Layer cake pan
Stoned	Pitted
Whisk	Whip/beat

Note: The British pint is 20 fluid ounces as opposed to the American pint which is 16 fluid ounces.

Where a recipe requires baking powder, use the double-acting type.

Unless otherwise stated, all tablespoons and teaspoons are level.

Chicken with fruits and wine

South Africa, one of the largest and oldest independent states in the African continent, has had plenty of time to develop national dishes. British and Dutch cooking is still very much in evidence, but many changes have been wrought on these culinary foundations.

South Africa's mild climate is ideal for growing innumerable varieties of vegetables and fruit. As well as the common root and green vegetables, popular additions to many meals are avocados, sweet corn (known as mealies) and many types of squash (of which pumpkins and marrows are the best known varieties outside South Africa). The list of fruit is even more enviable, including grenadillas (passion fruit), mangoes, pawpaws and Cape gooseberries, and an abundance of grapes, pears, oranges and peaches. Many of these delicious fruits are exported. As in many tropical countries, fruit is often incorporated into savoury dishes, like the recipe for Chicken with fruits and wine. Naturally, the wine would be South African too, for wine-making is a thriving and growing industry in this part of the world.

Meat is plentiful and of excellent quality, so it is usually prepared simply rather than in stews or casseroles which are heavy fare in a warm climate. Meat is sometimes grilled outdoors, especially in the summer at *braaivleis* which are much like American barbecues. The grilled meat, frequently steak, is often accompanied by corn-on-the-cob cooked over the same fire and several salads. Afterwards fruit salad, jelly or ice cream rounds off this ever-popular and easy way of giving a party.

The Rhodesian way of life is similar to the South African and so is much of the food. Like the South Africans, they make imaginative use of their own produce, as demonstrated in the Aubergine casserole with its unusual and exciting combination of aubergines and peanuts.

At the other end of the continent, Morocco offers a totally different cuisine, primarily Arabic but with a strong French and Spanish influence. With its Mediterranean climate and conditions, Morocco produces olives, almonds, citrus fruit and various cereals. Lamb and chicken are the most common meats, made into kebabs or cooked in a *tagine*, a type of meat and vegetable stew. Typically Mediterranean is the Moroccans' fondness for sweet pastries made with very thin pastry and various fillings, like the recipe we have included for Almond crescents.

Cooking time: 1 hr. 15 min. (see Stage 1). **Preparation time:** 15 min. (see Stage 1). **Main cooking utensils:** large saucepan, casserole, saucepan if cooking prunes. **Oven temperature:** moderate, 375°F., 190°C., Gas Mark 4–5. **Oven position:** centre.

IMPERIAL

For 4–6 people you need:
- 1 small can prunes *or* 4 oz. dried prunes and 1 oz. sugar
- 1 young roasting chicken
- $1\frac{1}{2}$ oz. flour
- seasoning
- 2–3 oz. butter *or* 2–3 tablespoons oil
- 1 red pepper
- $\frac{1}{2}$ pint white wine
- $\frac{1}{4}$ pint chicken stock (from simmering giblets) *or* use water and $\frac{1}{2}$–1 chicken stock cube
- good pinch chopped fresh rosemary *or* use dried herb
- 1 onion
- few strips lemon rind
- 2–3 firm dessert pears

AMERICAN

For 4–6 people you need:
- 1 small can prunes *or* $\frac{2}{3}$ cup dried prunes and 2 tablespoons sugar
- 1 young roasting chicken
- 6 tablespoons all-purpose flour
- seasoning
- 4–6 tablespoons butter *or* 3–4 tablespoons oil
- 1 sweet red pepper
- $1\frac{1}{4}$ cups white wine
- $\frac{2}{3}$ cup chicken stock (from simmering giblets) *or* use water and $\frac{1}{2}$–1 chicken bouillon cube
- dash chopped fresh rosemary *or* use dried herb
- 1 onion
- few strips lemon rind
- 2–3 firm dessert pears

1. If using canned prunes, drain off the syrup. If using dried prunes, add water to cover, soak for some hours or overnight. Simmer with the sugar until soft, then drain.
2. Joint the chicken, coat in half the seasoned flour. Fry until golden brown, remove from the pan.
3. Cut the pepper into strips, discarding core and seeds. Fry in butter remaining in pan, put into casserole.
4. Blend the remaining flour with wine and stock, pour into pan, cook until thickened. Add 2 tablespoons (U.S. 3 tablespoons) prune juice (more if wished, in which case use less wine) and herbs, season again.
5. Put the peeled whole onion and strips of lemon rind into liquid with peeled, cored pears, cut into thick slices (the pears *must* be firm in texture).
6. Simmer the pears for about 3 minutes (this helps to keep them a good colour). Put into the casserole with liquid, top with chicken pieces and prunes. Cover and cook for 1 hour.

To serve: Remove whole onion and lemon rind.

2

Aubergine casserole

Cooking time: 35–50 min. **Preparation time:** 25 min. **Main cooking utensils:** frying pan/skillet, shallow ovenproof casserole. **Oven temperature:** moderately hot, 400°F., 200°C., Gas Mark 5–6. **Oven position:** centre.

IMPERIAL

For 4 people you need:
2 medium-sized aubergines
seasoning
2 onions
5 oz. butter *or* peanut butter

4 oz. fresh *or* canned mushrooms (optional)
$\frac{1}{2}$ tablespoon chopped parsley *or* 1 teaspoon dried parsley
4 skinned tomatoes
3 oz. currants
4 oz. peanuts
4–5 oz. fresh breadcrumbs (white or brown)
1 oz. flour
4 oz. processed, sliced Gruyère *or* Cheddar cheese

To garnish:
parsley
paprika pepper

AMERICAN

For 4 people you need:
2 medium-sized eggplants
seasoning
2 onions
$\frac{1}{2}$ cup plus 2 tablespoons butter *or* peanut butter
1 cup fresh *or* canned mushrooms (optional)
$\frac{1}{2}$ tablespoon chopped parsley *or* 1 teaspoon dried parsley
4 skinned tomatoes
$\frac{1}{2}$ cup currants
1 cup peanuts
2–2$\frac{1}{2}$ cups fresh soft bread crumbs (white or brown)
$\frac{1}{4}$ cup all-purpose flour
$\frac{1}{4}$ lb. processed, sliced Gruyère *or* Cheddar cheese

To garnish:
parsley
paprika pepper

1. Wipe the aubergines, slice and sprinkle lightly with salt, leave for about 30 minutes. This is not essential but it does give a less bitter flavour.
2. Chop the onions finely, fry in half the butter.
3. Blend with the chopped mushrooms, if used, parsley, chopped tomatoes, currants and peanuts.
4. Stir in the coarse breadcrumbs, brown bread gives more interesting colour and flavour.
5. Put in the bottom of the casserole.
6. Coat the sliced aubergines with seasoned flour, fry for a few minutes in remaining butter; the slices need not be quite tender.
7. Arrange on top of the crumb mixture. Top with portions of cheese and bake until the cheese melts and the food is very hot, about 25 minutes.

To serve: Hot with salad, garnish with parsley and paprika pepper.

3

Kefta kebabs
Meat ball kebabs

Cooking time: 10–12 min. **Preparation time:** 15 min. **Main cooking utensils:** 4 skewers, barbecue fire or grill/broiler.

IMPERIAL

For 4 people you need:
1$\frac{1}{2}$ lb. good quality lamb (weight without bones)
2–3 small onions
sprig mint, parsley, marjoram
good pinch cayenne pepper, salt, cinnamon, ginger
3 oz. butter
little flour

To garnish:
sprigs tarragon *or* rosemary

For the sauce:
1 lb. tomatoes
1 clove garlic (optional)
sprig mint, parsley
2 tablespoons oil
1 oz. butter
seasonings and spice as above
$\frac{1}{2}$ pint water

AMERICAN

For 4 people you need:
1$\frac{1}{2}$ lb. good quality lamb (weight without bones)
2–3 small onions
sprig mint, parsley, marjoram
good dash cayenne pepper, salt, cinnamon, ginger
6 tablespoons butter
little flour

To garnish:
sprigs tarragon *or* rosemary

For the sauce:
1 lb. tomatoes
1 clove garlic (optional)
sprig mint, parsley
3 tablespoons oil
2 tablespoons butter
seasonings and spice as above
1$\frac{1}{4}$ cups water

1. Put the lamb through a mincer once or twice to give a very fine texture.
2. Mince or grate the onions, blend with the meat.
3. Chop the herbs very finely, add to the meat and onion with the spices, seasoning and 1 oz. (U.S. 2 tablespoons) melted butter.
4. Form into 8 balls or finger shapes.
5. Dip the skewers into the flour, this helps to keep the balls from breaking. Thread skewers into meat balls, allow 2 per skewer.
6. Brush with the remaining melted butter and cook over a barbecue or under a hot grill. Garnish with sprigs of tarragon or rosemary.
7. To make the sauce: skin the tomatoes, blend with the crushed garlic in a pan and the chopped herbs. Add all the other ingredients. Simmer until a thick purée. Taste and add extra seasoning if wished.

To serve: With salad or cooked rice, dip meat balls into hot sauce.

4

Salade Mireille

Ham and rice salad bowl

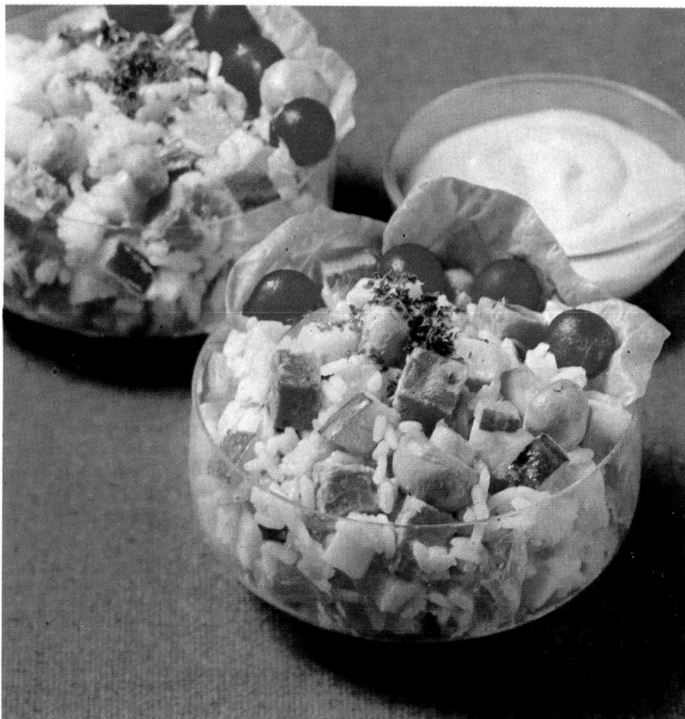

Cooking time: 15 min. **Preparation time:** 15 min. **Main cooking utensil:** saucepan.

IMPERIAL

For 4–5 people you need:
6 oz. long grain rice
pinch saffron
pinch curry powder
seasoning
12 fluid oz. ($\frac{5}{8}$ pint) ham *or* chicken stock
4 oz. small mushrooms
grated rind and juice 1 lemon
2 tablespoons mayonnaise
1 green pepper
2-inch piece cucumber
2 dessert apples
6 oz. cooked ham, cut in 1 thick slice

To garnish:
lettuce
chopped parsley
bunch radishes

AMERICAN

For 4–5 people you need:
scant 1 cup long grain rice
dash saffron
dash curry powder
seasoning
approx. $1\frac{1}{2}$ cups ham *or* chicken stock
1 cup small mushrooms
grated rind and juice 1 lemon
3 tablespoons mayonnaise
1 sweet green pepper
2-inch piece cucumber
2 eating apples
$\frac{1}{3}$ lb. cooked ham, cut in 1 thick slice

To garnish:
lettuce
chopped parsley
bunch radishes

1. Cook the rice with spices and seasoning in stock until tender. If the liquid is brought to the boil quickly, the rice added and stirred briskly, then the pan tightly covered and the rice allowed to simmer steadily for 15 minutes, it should have absorbed the liquid and be tender.
2. Add the whole or sliced mushrooms, lemon rind and juice and mayonnaise, while the rice is hot.
3. Cool, then add the diced flesh of the green pepper, discarding core and seeds, finely chopped cucumber, diced apples, peeled if wished, and the diced ham.
4. Put on a bed of lettuce and garnish with parsley and radishes.

5

Fruit jellied mould

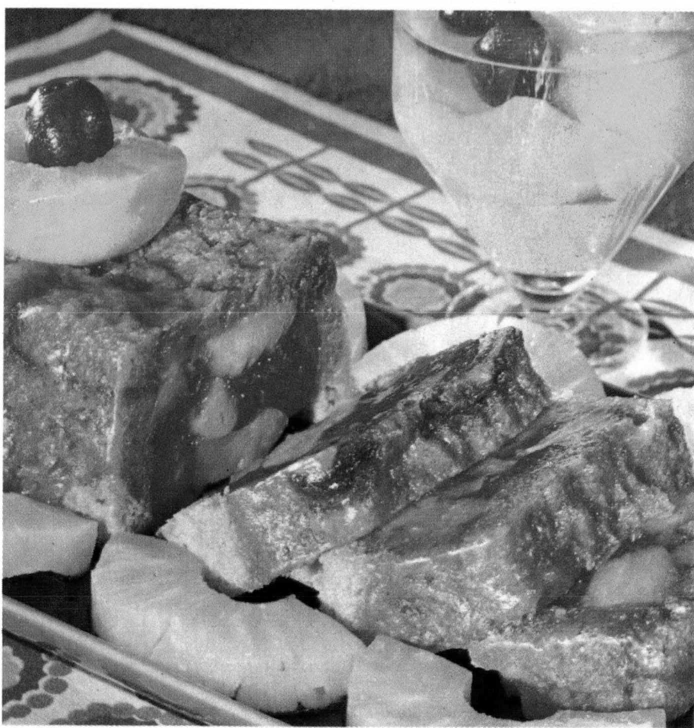

Cooking time: few min. heating only. **Preparation time:** 15 min. **Main cooking utensils:** 2-pint mould/$2\frac{1}{2}$-pint mold *or* tin, without a loose base.

IMPERIAL

For 6–8 people you need:
about 1 lb. sponge cake, *or* white bread without crusts*
1 medium-sized can pineapple rings
juice 1 orange
juice 1 lemon
6 fresh medium-sized peaches *or* 4 large**
6 fresh medium-sized pears *or* 4 large**
1 small can red cherries
$\frac{1}{2}$ oz. powder gelatine

AMERICAN

For 6–8 people you need:
about 1 lb. sponge or layer cake, *or* white bread without crusts*
1 medium-sized can pineapple rings
juice 1 orange
juice 1 lemon
6 fresh medium-sized peaches *or* 4 large**
6 fresh medium-sized pears *or* 4 large**
1 small can red cherries
2 envelopes powder gelatin

*If using bread, add little sugar to gelatine liquid.
**When fresh fruit not obtainable, use canned.

1. Cut the sponge cake into thin slices to line base and sides of the mould or tin.
2. Pour off the syrup from the can of pineapple, add the orange and lemon juice. Simmer skinned, fresh peaches and peeled, fresh pears in this for 3–4 minutes to soften them and to prevent flesh darkening.
3. Lift all the fruit out of the syrup. Measure the pineapple syrup from the pan and add enough syrup from the canned cherries to give $\frac{3}{4}$ pint (U.S. 2 cups) syrup.
4. Blend the gelatine with 2 tablespoons (U.S. 3 tablespoons) syrup, heat the rest and dissolve the gelatine in this.
5. Put aside some fruit for decoration. Chop and mix remaining fruit together and pack into the sponge-lined tin.
6. Spoon the cool jelly over the fruit. Do this slowly so the sponge cake is not 'dislodged'.
7. Put into a cool place to set.

To serve: With cream or ice cream, decorated with remaining fruit.

 6

Pear and ginger sundae

Cooking time: 15–20 min. **Freezing time:** $1\frac{1}{4}$ hr. **Preparation time:** 25 min. **Main cooking utensils:** double saucepan, saucepan.

IMPERIAL

For 6 people you need:
2 eggs
3 oz. sugar
$\frac{1}{2}$ pint milk
$\frac{1}{2}$ teaspoon powdered ginger
$\frac{1}{2}$ pint thick cream *or*
$\frac{1}{4}$ pint thick cream and
$\frac{1}{4}$ pint thin cream
4 tablespoons ginger syrup*
4–6 firm, ripe pears
3 oz. preserved ginger, sliced

To decorate:
1–2 oz. chopped *or* grated chocolate

AMERICAN

For 6 people you need:
2 eggs
6 tablespoons sugar
$1\frac{1}{4}$ cups milk
$\frac{1}{2}$ teaspoon powdered ginger
$1\frac{1}{4}$ cups whipping cream *or*
$\frac{2}{3}$ cup whipping cream and
$\frac{2}{3}$ cup coffee cream
$\frac{1}{3}$ cup ginger sirup*
4–6 firm, ripe pears
$\frac{1}{3}$ cup sliced preserved ginger

To decorate:
about $\frac{1}{3}$ cup chopped *or* grated chocolate

*This is only a small amount of liquid, so care must be taken to turn the pears round in this so they become coated and the syrup does not burn. If preferred, the syrup may be diluted with an equal amount of water.

1. Separate the egg yolks and whites, and beat the yolks with the sugar.
2. Add the warm milk, the powdered ginger and cook over hot but *not* boiling water until mixture coats back of a wooden spoon.
3. Allow to cool and thicken, stir from time to time to prevent skin forming.
4. When cold, blend with lightly whipped cream.
5. Freeze until nearly firm. Remove from freezer and whisk. Fold in stiffly beaten egg whites and re-freeze.
6. Pour ginger syrup into saucepan. In this, cook peeled sliced pears for 4–5 minutes, then cool.

To serve: Scoop ice cream into glasses. Top with pears, ginger and chocolate.

7

Kab el ghzal
Almond crescents

Cooking time: 15 min. **Preparation time:** 20 min. (or see Stage 1). **Main cooking utensil:** baking trays/sheets. **Oven temperature:** hot, 425–450°F., 220–230°C., Gas Mark 6–7. **Oven position:** just above centre.

IMPERIAL

To make about 15–16 crescents, you need:
For the almond filling:
12 oz. almonds
4 oz. sugar
1 oz. butter
$\frac{1}{2}$ tablespoon orange flower water*

For the dough:
6 oz. flour**
1 oz. butter
water to mix

AMERICAN

To make about 15–16 crescents, you need:
For the almond filling:
about $2\frac{1}{2}$ cups almonds
$\frac{1}{2}$ cup sugar
2 tablespoons butter
$\frac{1}{2}$ tablespoon orange flower water*

For the dough:
$1\frac{1}{2}$ cups all-purpose flour**
2 tablespoons butter
water to mix

*Obtainable from chemists and grocers.
**This means a very thin dough indeed, if wished use 8 oz. (U.S. 2 cups) flour plus $1\frac{1}{4}$ oz. (U.S. approx. 3 tablespoons) butter.

1. Chop, then pound the almonds until very fine indeed. They can be put through a mincer or into a blender, but pounding gives a smoother paste. If time is short, use ground almonds.
2. Add the sugar, melted butter and orange flower water to almonds. If orange flower water is not obtainable, use juice of a fresh orange, adding this drop by drop to bind.
3. Blend the flour, melted butter and water to give a pliable dough.
4. Divide the dough and almond paste into about 15 portions.
5. Roll, pull and stretch each portion of dough until wafer thin. Moroccans grease their fingers, board and rolling pin lightly.
6. Wrap round 'sausage shape' of almond paste, then form into a crescent.
7. Glaze with beaten egg if liked and bake in a hot oven.

To serve: With ordinary or mint tea.

AMERICA

The American continent has a wide range of cooking; some was brought from the Old World but much of the cookery is uniquely American.

Being in the Commonwealth, Canada has a strong British influence and there are many families who still have tea, especially at weekends. Baking is a tradition among Canadian housewives, some of their breads and scones being based on old English recipes. The maple leaf is portrayed on the Canadian flag; thus Maple prune pie is especially Canadian, using the delicious maple syrup which can also be poured over breakfast pancakes and ice cream. Finally, the French influence is evident in such dishes as Chicken pancakes, the addition of sweet corn to a filling for crêpes definitely making this a French-Canadian dish.

Since the pilgrims first landed at Plymouth in Massachusetts in 1620, many dishes have been developed which have become part of the national heritage. The pioneers were introduced to many new fruits and vegetables by the Indians: melons, cranberries, pumpkins, squash, sweet potatoes, many types of beans, and above all sweet corn, known simply as corn. Corn was eaten on the cob, cooked with beans to make succotash, and ground to make cornmeal for all sorts of breads. The oldest traditional American holiday is Thanksgiving which began as a feast to give thanks for the first harvest and continued as an unofficial celebration until 1863, when Lincoln proclaimed it a national holiday. The Thanksgiving meal is entirely American: roast turkey and cranberry sauce served with such vegetables as candied sweet potatoes and corn, and followed by pumpkin or American mincemeat pie.

The New England area has been responsible for many dishes, of which perhaps the most famous is Boston baked beans. Certain ingredients identify some dishes with particular states or areas, like Prawns Alabama, and the famous hams from Virginia. New Orleans is the centre of Creole cooking, derived from the French and Spanish who settled at the mouth of the Mississippi. New Orleans Rice fritters, called *calas*, used to be sold by vendors in the streets of the French Quarter in whose narrow streets one still finds superb French restaurants.

Some American recipes have an interesting history behind their creation. Lady Baltimore cake, for example, was created by a Mrs. Mayberry whom Owen Lister made the central character of his novel. He took *Lady Baltimore* as the title and described the delicious cake which, as a result, has remained better known than his book.

Of course many dishes belong to no particular region but have simply become part of daily American cooking. Americans are known for their delicious dips made with a basis of cream cheese or cottage cheese, which make an excellent alternative to an hors d'oeuvre. Americans are fond of salads and almost always serve one with supper, the main meal of the day. Cottage cheese pears, or indeed cottage cheese with almost any fruit, is a great favourite. For the main course, chicken and steak are among the most popular choices. The steak is particularly succulent and tender—Green pepper steak is a change from the usual grilling or frying and has an appetising oriental flavour. Americans use minced beef in many ways apart from the famous hamburger: try the Texan rice ring for a hearty, economical meal.

Pies are rivalled only by ice cream as a favourite American dessert, and best of all is a slice of pie served with ice cream, à la mode. There is an infinite variety of pies: fruit, cream, custard, meringue and chiffon. Chiffon pies and chiffon cakes are both American inventions, the name deriving from the light texture imparted by whisked egg whites. Finally, one cannot discuss American cooking without mentioning cookies. No kitchen is complete without a full cookie jar. Americans do not have afternoon tea, of course, but cookies can be eaten at almost any time: with mid-morning coffee, as an after-school snack with a glass of milk, or with ice cream as a dessert.

Mexican cuisine is a blend of Mexican Indian and Spanish cooking which, in the culinary sense, identifies it with South American rather than with the neighbouring United States. Of all Mexican specialities, tortillas are undoubtedly the best known. They are crisp fried pancakes made of cornmeal flour and they form the basis of several dishes: *tostados*, for example, are fried tortillas topped with chopped meat and vegetables as in the recipe for *Tostados de polla*. This dish uses chicken but other fillings and toppings are minced beef, pork, beans and tomatoes, often seasoned with chillies. Argentinians are fond of casseroles and *Puchero*, their national dish, is an unusual, spicy combination of lamb or beef, sausage and vegetables. *Empanadas* are fruit and meat turnovers which are well worth trying as a change from ordinary meat pies.

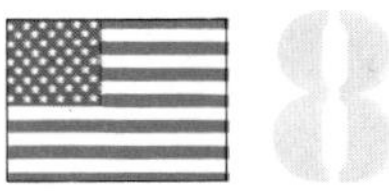

8

Piquant grapefruit cocktail

Preparation time: 10 min. **Main utensils:** sharp knife, bowl.

IMPERIAL

For 4 people you need:
2 large grapefruit
2 large pickled gherkins *or* cucumber
2 oz. small prawns *or* shrimps
¼ pint soured cream *or* yoghurt
lemon juice
seasoning
pinch sugar (optional)

To garnish:
paprika *or* cayenne pepper
parsley
grapefruit segments
sliced gherkin

AMERICAN

For 4 people you need:
2 large grapefruit
2 large sweet dill pickles *or* cucumber
⅓ cup small prawns *or* shrimp
⅔ cup sour cream *or* yoghurt
lemon juice
seasoning
dash sugar (optional)

To garnish:
paprika *or* cayenne pepper
parsley
grapefruit segments
sliced sweet dill pickle

1. Halve the grapefruit, remove pulp, discarding both pips and skin.
2. When all the pulp has been removed, cut away any skin remaining in the grapefruit shells.
3. Blend the majority of the chopped grapefruit pulp with most of the finely chopped gherkin or cucumber.
4. Add the prawns or shrimps, soured cream or yoghurt.
5. Taste the mixture, add the lemon juice and seasoning (also a pinch of sugar if wished).
6. Pile into the grapefruit shells, top with paprika or cayenne pepper, parsley, two or three grapefruit segments and slices of gherkin.

To serve: As an hors d'oeuvre.

To vary: Blend grapefruit and sliced flesh from avocado pear, bind with sweetened oil and vinegar or mayonnaise.
Just mix prawns and grapefruit segments, bind with mayonnaise.
Blend grapefruit segments with orange, sliced strawberries and cream or cottage cheese and mayonnaise.

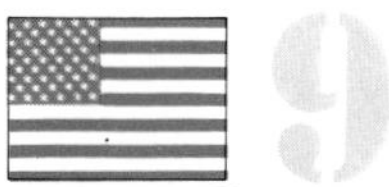

9

Cottage cheese pears

Preparation time: 10 min. **Main utensil:** bowl.

IMPERIAL

For 4 people you need:
4 firm, ripe dessert pears

For the dressing:
3 tablespoons oil
1½ tablespoons lemon juice
pinch salt, dry mustard, pepper, sugar

For the filling:
8 oz. cottage cheese
3–4 oz. lean ham
2 tablespoons mayonnaise
1–2 tablespoons chopped parsley

For the pear salad:
2 ripe dessert pears
3 large oranges

For the dressing:
4 oz. cream cheese
2 tablespoons oil
2 tablespoons lemon juice
seasoning

AMERICAN

For 4 people you need:
4 firm ripe dessert pears

For the dressing:
scant ¼ cup oil
2 tablespoons lemon juice
dash salt, dry mustard, pepper, sugar

For the filling:
1 cup cottage cheese
½–¾ cup lean ham
3 tablespoons mayonnaise
1–3 tablespoons chopped parsley

For the pear salad:
2 ripe dessert pears
3 large oranges

For the dressing:
½ cup cream cheese
3 tablespoons oil
3 tablespoons lemon juice
seasoning

COTTAGE CHEESE PEARS

1. Peel, core and halve the pears.
2. Blend the oil and lemon juice with seasonings, sprinkle this or just lemon juice over pears to keep them from discolouring.
3. Blend the cottage cheese with diced ham, mayonnaise and parsley.
4. Pile into the pear halves, place on lettuce, top with parsley.

PEAR SALAD

1. Peel and slice the dessert pears, blend with segments of fresh oranges.
2. Blend the cream cheese with the oil, lemon juice and seasoning to make a smooth thick sauce. Toss the fruit in this.

To serve: On a bed of lettuce with watercress and sliced cucumber.

10 Cucumber and mushroom dip

Preparation time: 10 min. plus time for flavour to infuse. **Main utensils:** mixing bowl, grater.

IMPERIAL

For 4 people you need:
12 oz. cottage cheese *or* 8 oz. cream cheese and 4 tablespoons thin cream
1 carton plain yoghurt
juice ½ lemon
seasoning
small portion cauliflower
2–3 oz. small, raw mushrooms
portion cucumber

To garnish:
crisp bacon (see Stage 7)
chopped chives

AMERICAN

For 4 people you need:
1½ cups cottage cheese *or* 1 cup cream cheese and ⅓ cup coffee cream
1 carton plain yoghurt
juice ½ lemon
seasoning
small portion cauliflower
½–¾ cup small, raw mushrooms
portion cucumber

To garnish:
crisp bacon slices (see Stage 7)
chopped chives

1. Sieve the cottage cheese or blend the cream cheese and cream until soft.
2. Blend with the yoghurt, lemon juice and season well.
3. Divide the cauliflower, which should be raw (or if preferred, very lightly cooked so it retains a firm texture) into tiny sprigs.
4. Wash, dry but do not peel the mushrooms, unless the skin is marked, then cut into thin slices.
5. Peel and grate the cucumber.
6. Blend the vegetables with the cheese mixture. Allow to stand for at least 30 minutes so flavours mingle.
7. Dice the bacon and fry until crisp, without using any fat. If preferred, put under a hot grill. Drain and chop into small pieces.

To serve: Pile cheese mixture in a bowl, top with chives and cold bacon. This makes an informal hors d'oeuvre or simple savoury. For a party—everyone dips potato crisps, biscuits, etc., into the cheese mixture.

11 Prawns Alabama

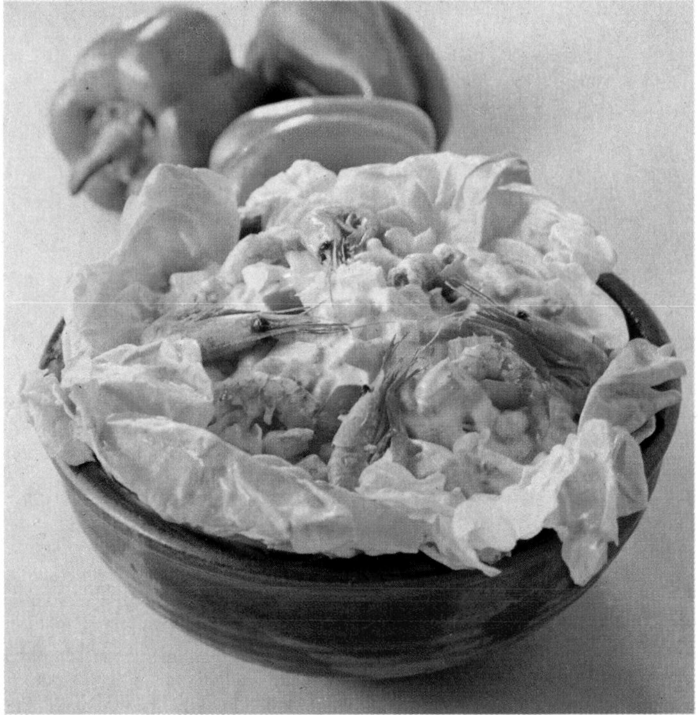

Preparation time: 15 min. **Main utensil:** mixing bowl.

IMPERIAL

For 4 people you need:
For the sauce:
½ green pepper
4 sticks celery
1 clove garlic
3 tablespoons mayonnaise
3 tablespoons thick cream
squeeze lemon juice *or* few drops wine vinegar
1 tablespoon tomato ketchup
2 teaspoons Tabasco sauce
little grated horseradish *or* horseradish cream (to taste)
seasoning

8 oz. shelled prawns*
lettuce

AMERICAN

For 4 people you need:
For the sauce:
½ sweet green pepper
4 stalks celery
1 clove garlic
scant ¼ cup mayonnaise
scant ¼ cup whipping cream
squeeze lemon juice *or* few drops wine vinegar
1 tablespoon tomato catsup
2 teaspoons Tabasco sauce
little grated horseradish *or* horseradish cream (to taste)
seasoning

1⅓ cups shelled prawns*
lettuce

*Prawns are easier to shell if put into hot water for 1 minute only.

1. Chop the pepper and the celery into neat pieces. Cover the pepper with boiling water for 2 minutes, then drain.
2. Crush garlic clove finely; adding a little salt.
3. Blend the mayonnaise with the lightly whipped cream, lemon juice, ketchup, Tabasco sauce and garlic.
4. Gradually add the horseradish and seasoning, tasting as you do so.
5. Blend the pepper, celery and the prawns with the dressing.

To serve: Pile high on a bed of crisp lettuce.

To vary: Prawns in tomato flavoured mayonnaise: Toss prawns in a sauce made with 3–4 tablespoons (U.S. 4–5 tablespoons) mayonnaise, 1 tablespoon fresh or canned tomato purée, few drops Tabasco sauce and seasoning. Serve on green salad with garnish of lemon.

Prawns with cream cheese dressing: Follow the recipe for Prawns Alabama but omit the horseradish and add 2 oz. (U.S. ¼ cup) soft cream cheese and a good teaspoon chopped chives or parsley.

 12

Tomato ham chowder with Green apple coleslaw

TOMATO HAM CHOWDER

For 6–8 people – Method 1: Put 2 large cans cream of potato soup into a pan with 1 grated onion and 1 pint (U.S. $2\frac{1}{2}$ cups) milk, heat until nearly boiling. Add 8 oz. (U.S. $1\frac{1}{3}$–$1\frac{1}{2}$ cups) finely diced ham, heat through for a few minutes, then add 3–4 skinned, diced tomatoes. Heat for 2–3 minutes, **do not boil,** and then serve. Using this method, the chowder is made in minutes.

Method 2: Grate $1\frac{1}{2}$ lb. peeled potatoes and 2 large onions into a saucepan, add 2 oz. (U.S. $\frac{1}{4}$ cup) butter and stir together until the butter has melted. Blend in 1 oz. (U.S. $\frac{1}{4}$ cup) flour and cook for several minutes, then gradually add $1\frac{1}{2}$ pints (U.S. $3\frac{3}{4}$ cups) chicken or ham stock and 1 pint (U.S. $2\frac{1}{2}$ cups) milk. Season well and cook until vegetables are tender (approximately 25 minutes). Top with ham and tomatoes as before.

GREEN APPLE COLESLAW

For 6–8 people: Choose the crisp heart of a light green cabbage (the Dutch white cabbage is not used in this particular salad). Divide into portions, then wash, dry well and shred (not too finely). Toss in a little of the dressing made with 6 tablespoons (U.S. $\frac{1}{2}$ cup) oil, 4 tablespoons (U.S. 5 tablespoons) lemon juice and plenty of seasoning. Arrange in bottom and round sides of bowl. Cut a canned or fresh red pepper and a fresh green pepper into shreds. Chop several sticks of celery finely, dice 2–3 green dessert apples (peel if wished). Blend with a few well-drained cooked or canned French or green beans and 12 oz. (U.S. 2 cups) diced chicken (the darker meat gives better flavour). Add remainder of dressing, mix well and pile into the middle of the bowl.

NOTE: Canned or cooked ham can be used in place of chicken in the salad; cooked chicken in place of ham in the chowder.

13

Green pepper steak and rice

Cooking time: 20 min. **Preparation time:** 20 min. plus time for aubergine to stand, if wished. **Main cooking utensils:** 1 *or* 2 saucepans, frying pan/ skillet.

IMPERIAL

For 6 people you need:
6 oz. long grain rice
12 fluid oz. water
salt to taste
2–3 green peppers
1 red pepper
1–2 aubergines
2 sticks celery
2–3 small leeks *or* use about
6 good-sized spring onions
4 oz. butter
$1\frac{1}{2}$–2 lb. fillet *or* rump steak
1 tablespoon stock *or* soy sauce
1 teaspoon Worcestershire sauce
seasoning

AMERICAN

For 6 people you need:
scant 1 cup long grain rice
$1\frac{1}{2}$ cups water
salt to taste
2–3 sweet green peppers
1 sweet red pepper
1–2 eggplants
2 stalks celery
2–3 small leeks *or* use about
6 good-sized scallions
$\frac{1}{2}$ cup butter
$1\frac{1}{2}$–2 lb. tenderloin steak
1 tablespoon stock *or* soy sauce
1 teaspoon Worcestershire sauce
seasoning

1. Put the rice, cold water and salt into a pan. Bring to the boil and stir briskly with a fork. Cover pan, lower heat and cook for 15 minutes.
2. Cut the flesh from the peppers into narrow strips (discard cores and seeds). If wished, blanch for 5–10 minutes in boiling, salted water to give a softer texture, drain well.
3. Cut the aubergine into narrow strips. If wished, sprinkle with salt and allow to stand for 20 minutes, to remove slightly bitter flavour.
4. Chop the celery and leeks or onion.
5. Heat the butter, toss the vegetables and steak, cut into narrow strips, in this. For underdone steak, add after the vegetables.
6. Stir in sauces and season well.

To serve: In a border of cooked rice.

NOTE: If the frying pan is small, use two, or fry vegetables then meat. Do not reverse the order as the steak should be served as soon as possible after cooking.

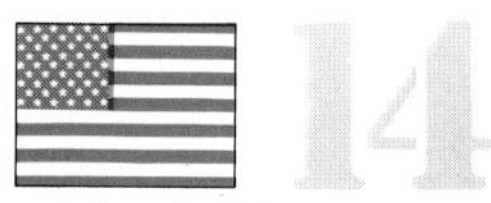

14

Virginian ham

Cooking time: as Stage 3 plus 35–40 min. in oven. **Preparation time:** 10–15 min. plus overnight soaking. **Main cooking utensils:** saucepan, roasting tin/pan. **Oven temperature:** moderately hot, 400°F., 200°C., Gas Mark 5–6. **Oven position:** centre.

IMPERIAL

For 6–8 people you need:
4 lb. joint ham *or* bacon* (if using bacon, choose gammon)

For the glaze:
4 oz. brown sugar
$\frac{1}{4}$ pint cider, *or* orange *or* pineapple juice
1 teaspoon powdered ginger (optional)
1 teaspoon dry mustard

To decorate:
cloves

To garnish:
tomatoes
parsley

AMERICAN

For 6–8 people you need:
4 lb. joint ham

For the glaze:
$\frac{1}{2}$ cup brown sugar
$\frac{2}{3}$ cup cider, *or* orange *or* pineapple juice
1 teaspoon ginger (optional)
1 teaspoon dry mustard

To decorate:
cloves

To garnish:
tomatoes
parsley

*For a cheaper meal, use forehock or collar; cook 30–35 min. per lb.

1. Unless the joint is 'sweet cure' put to soak overnight in cold water to cover.
2. Next day, put into fresh cold water in a pan, bring to the boil, remove any scum.
3. *Simmer gently* allowing 15–20 minutes per lb. and 15–20 minutes over. The difference in time is due to the type of cut and thickness; a really thick piece, as shown in picture, takes longer than a wide rather shallow piece.
4. Lift out of the water and cool sufficiently to handle.
5. Remove the skin, score fat in a neat design.
6. Mix together the ingredients for the glaze. Brush over the bacon, pressing this firmly into fat. Press cloves into the fat.
7. Roast for 35–40 minutes in oven until crisp and brown.

To serve: Hot or cold, garnished with tomatoes and parsley.

To vary: The glaze can be varied: blend 4 tablespoons (U.S. 5 tablespoons) honey with 6–8 tablespoons (U.S. $\frac{1}{2}$–$\frac{2}{3}$ cup) lemon or orange juice or syrup from cooking 8 oz. (U.S. $1\frac{1}{3}$ cups) prunes.

15

Potato and corned beef hash

Cooking time: $1\frac{1}{4}$–$1\frac{1}{2}$ hr. **Preparation time:** 15 min. **Main cooking utensils:** baking tray/sheet, frying pan/skillet. **Oven temperature:** moderate, 375°F., 190°C., Gas Mark 4–5. **Oven position:** centre.

IMPERIAL

For 4 people you need:
4 medium-sized potatoes *or* 2 really large ones
$\frac{1}{2}$–1 oz. butter *or* margarine

2 oz. shortening *or* fat
2 onions *or* equivalent in spring onions
3–4 oz. streaky bacon
12 oz. corned beef*
2 dessert apples
seasoning

AMERICAN

For 4 people you need:
4 medium-sized potatoes *or* 2 large ones
1–2 tablespoons butter *or* margarine
$\frac{1}{4}$ cup shortening *or* fat
2 onions *or* equivalent in scallions
approx. $\frac{1}{4}$ lb. bacon slices
$\frac{3}{4}$ lb. corned beef
2 eating apples
seasoning

*Corned beef, generally bought canned or sold sliced in grocers, is one of the simplest of American dishes. Just soak salted brisket for some hours, then simmer very slowly in fresh water, adding vegetables as wished. Allow nearly 1 hour per lb., keep the liquid moving slightly.

1. Wash and dry the potatoes, prick them to prevent skins breaking and brush skins with butter or margarine.
2. Put on a baking sheet, bake until soft, approximately $1\frac{1}{4}$–$1\frac{1}{2}$ hours in a moderate oven.
3. Split the potatoes through the centre and scoop out the centre pulp, trying to keep this in reasonable pieces rather than allowing it to become soft and mashed.
4. Heat the shortening or fat in pan, fry chopped onions until nearly soft. Remove from the heat and add finely chopped cooked bacon, flaked corned beef, pieces of potato and diced apple (leave peel on for extra flavour and colour). Season lightly.
5. Season the potato cases, pile mixture in these. Return to oven for about 10 minutes, to heat through.

To serve: Top with a knob of butter and a little chopped parsley. Excellent for supper or as a main dish with a green vegetable.

To vary: Add 2–3 skinned, chopped tomatoes. Flavour with 1 teaspoon curry powder.

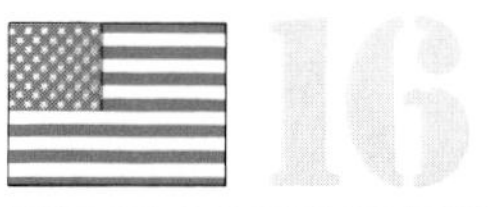 16

Texan rice ring

Cooking time: 1 hr. **Preparation time:** 30 min. plus time for the ring to stand in warm place (see Stage 7). **Main cooking utensils:** saucepan, 9-inch ring tin/pan. **Oven temperature:** moderate, 375°F., 190°C., Gas Mark 4–5. **Oven position:** centre.

IMPERIAL

For 6 people you need:
2 large onions
2–3 oz. fat
3 large tomatoes
$1\frac{1}{2}$ lb. minced beef
4 oz. breadcrumbs, preferably dark brown
1 tablespoon chopped parsley
1 red pepper, canned *or* fresh
2 eggs
seasoning
8 oz. long *or* medium grain rice

$\frac{3}{4}$ pint white stock
1 tablespoon concentrated tomato purée
8 oz. peas

To garnish:
part of a red pepper, canned *or* fresh

AMERICAN

For 6 people you need:
2 large onions
$\frac{1}{4}$–$\frac{1}{3}$ cup fat
3 large tomatoes
$1\frac{1}{2}$ lb. ground beef
2 cups soft bread crumbs, preferably dark brown
1 tablespoon chopped parsley
1 sweet red pepper, canned *or* fresh
2 eggs
seasoning
1–$1\frac{1}{4}$ cups long *or* medium grain rice
2 cups white stock
1 tablespoon concentrated tomato paste
$1\frac{1}{2}$ cups peas

To garnish:
part of a sweet red pepper, canned *or* fresh

1. Toss the chopped onions in the hot fat, then add the skinned, chopped tomatoes and minced beef.
2. Blend well together, then tip out of the pan into a mixing bowl.
3. Add the breadcrumbs, chopped parsley, diced pepper and eggs, season.
4. Put into the ring tin and cover with greased foil or greaseproof paper and bake until quite firm.
5. While the meat ring is cooking, prepare the rice topping.
6. Put the rice, stock and tomato purée into a saucepan. Bring to the boil then lower the heat, cover the pan tightly and simmer for 15 minutes, add extra seasoning if wished. Cook the peas, then drain.
7. Turn the meat ring on to hot dish, cover lightly, keep hot for 15 minutes. Put the cooked rice into the ring tin with hot cooked peas. Press down quite firmly and keep hot for 15 minutes. Invert over the meat ring so the rice and peas form topping.
8. Garnish with strips of fresh or canned red pepper.

17

New England (Boston) baked beans

Cooking time: 7 hr. **Preparation time:** 20 min. plus overnight soaking of beans. **Main cooking utensils:** saucepan, deep casserole, frying pan/skillet (optional). **Oven temperature:** cool, 250–275°F., 130–140°C., Gas Mark $\frac{1}{2}$–1. **Oven position:** centre.

IMPERIAL

For 8 people you need:
1 lb. haricot beans
about 1 lb. fat pork, cut either into 2 slices *or* dice half and slice rest
1 oz. sugar
1 tablespoon golden syrup *or* black treacle
2–3 teaspoons salt
$\frac{1}{4}$ teaspoon black pepper
$1\frac{1}{2}$ pints boiling water
3 large onions (optional)
2 tablespoons bacon fat (optional)

AMERICAN

For 8 people you need:
$1\frac{1}{2}$ cups navy beans
about 1 lb. fat back or salt pork, cut either into 2 slices *or* dice half and slice rest
2 tablespoons sugar
1 tablespoon corn sirup *or* molasses
2–3 teaspoons salt
$\frac{1}{4}$ teaspoon black pepper
$3\frac{3}{4}$ cups boiling water
3 large onions (optional)
3 tablespoons bacon fat (optional)

1. Soak the beans overnight. Drain, throw away the water in which they were soaked and put beans into a large pan.
2. Cover with fresh cold water and simmer steadily until beans are beginning to soften, about 2 hours.
3. Drain well and leave for about 10 minutes to make sure they are dry.
4. Put a layer of diced or sliced pork in the bottom of a deep casserole.
5. Blend the sugar, syrup or treacle, salt and pepper with the boiling water.
6. If using onions—which are not traditional but give an excellent flavour—toss in the bacon fat for a few minutes to brown slightly. Blend with the beans.
7. Put the beans into the casserole, pour over the liquid.
8. Cover with another slice of pork and the lid.
9. Cook for about 5 hours, stirring once or twice. Add extra water if necessary. Remove top layer of pork before serving.

To vary: To make sauce as in canned beans—sieve ingredients at Stages 5, 6 and add $1\frac{1}{2}$ lb. tomatoes, cook with 1 oz. (U.S. $\frac{1}{4}$ cup) flour, pour over beans and continue as method.

18

Puchero
Spiced casserole with corn

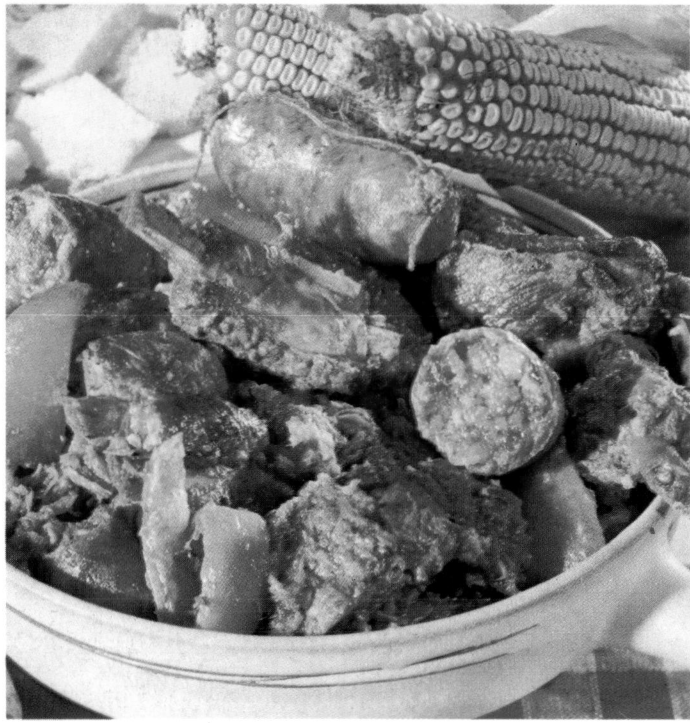

Cooking time: 2–2¼ hr. **Preparation time:** 25 min. **Main cooking utensil:** saucepan.

IMPERIAL

For 4–6 people you need:
1½ lb. lean stewing beef *or* 2 lb. loin lamb
3 oz. beef dripping *or* fat
3 large onions
1½ pints stock *or* water
seasoning
¼–½ teaspoon chilli powder (use sparingly as this is very hot)
½–1 teaspoon mixed spice
3 large tomatoes
1 medium-sized sweet potato
3 medium-sized fresh corn cobs (split down centre) *or* equivalent in small cobs
1–1½ lb. spiced *or* garlic sausages

AMERICAN

For 4–6 people you need:
1½ lb. lean beef stew meat *or* 2 lb. loin lamb
6 tablespoons beef drippings *or* fat
3 large onions
3¾ cups stock *or* water
seasoning
¼–½ teaspoon chili powder (use sparingly as this is very hot)
½–1 teaspoon mixed spice
3 large tomatoes
1 medium-sized sweet potato
3 medium-sized fresh corn cobs (split down centre) *or* equivalent in small cobs
1–1½ lb. spiced *or* garlic sausages

1. Cut the meat into neat pieces—dice beef, joint lamb.
2. Toss in hot dripping or fat with the sliced onions until golden brown. Add stock, seasoning, chilli powder and spice, cover well and cook for 1 hour.
3. Add the quartered tomatoes, peeled, sliced sweet potato, corn cobs and whole or halved sausages, check there is sufficient liquid and cover again.
4. Simmer for further 45 minutes to 1 hour; by this time the corn will probably have fallen off cobs which may be discarded.

To serve: Hot with fresh bread.

To vary: Add jointed chicken and pieces of calf's foot at Stage 2.

19

Thanksgiving dinner
Roast turkey

The traditional Thanksgiving dinner, served in the U.S.A., and by Americans throughout the world, generally includes turkey and pumpkin pie.

ROAST TURKEY

To stuff turkey
American stuffings or 'dressings' are varied and delicious. One of the most famous for this occasion is oyster stuffing; when oysters are not available, or too expensive, use chopped scallops.
For 12 lb. turkey, weight after trussing. Enough for 12–14 portions: Blend 6 oz. (U.S. 3 cups) soft breadcrumbs, 8 oz. chopped celery, few chopped celery leaves, 8 oz. (U.S. 1½ cups) chopped, cooked ham, 8–12 chopped oysters, 3 oz. (U.S. 6 tablespoons) melted butter, 8 oz. (U.S. 2 cups) sliced mushrooms, 2 tablespoons (U.S. 3 tablespoons) chopped parsley and seasoning.

To cook turkey
Put stuffing in neck end, cover with plenty of butter or fat. Weigh after stuffing, allow minimum 15 minutes per lb. and 15 minutes over in hot oven, 425°F., 220°C., Gas Mark 6–7. Reduce heat after 1½ hours if wished. Broad breasted turkeys need about 20–25 minutes per lb. as the flesh is so solid.

To serve turkey
This is often served with candied sweet potatoes; peel, cut into portions as ordinary potatoes, brush with sugar and water syrup—use 6 oz. (U.S. ¾ cup) brown sugar, ½ pint (U.S. 1¼ cups) water to 4 lb. sweet potatoes. Roast as usual round turkey or in hot fat. Ordinary roast potatoes could be substituted with green vegetables.

Cranberry sauce is the traditional accompaniment. For 12–14 portions: Simmer 1 lb. cranberries with 6–8 oz. (U.S. ¾–1 cup) sugar and ½ pint (U.S. 1¼ cups) water until berries are soft. Sieve if wished, then reheat. Two cooking apples may be cooked with the fruit, or 2–3 tablespoons (U.S. 3–4 tablespoons) redcurrant jelly added when fruit is nearly softened.

Country-style chicken casserole

Cooking time: $1\frac{1}{4}$ or $2\frac{1}{4}$ hr. (see Stage 5). **Preparation time:** 30 min. **Main cooking utensils:** 2 saucepans, 3-pint/4-pint casserole. **Oven temperature:** very moderate, 350°F., 180°C., Gas Mark 3–4. **Oven position:** centre.

IMPERIAL

For 6–8 people you need:
1 good-sized boiling fowl *or* roasting chicken
2 oz. seasoned flour
2 oz. butter
8 small onions
3 sticks celery
1 pint water
$\frac{1}{2}$–1 lemon
1 bay leaf
4–6 oz. carrots
4 oz. peas
$\frac{1}{4}$ pint soured cream

For the dumplings:
4 oz. self-raising flour
$\frac{1}{2}$ teaspoon salt
$1\frac{1}{2}$ oz. shredded suet
$\frac{1}{2}$ teaspoon powdered oregano *or* marjoram
1 tablespoon tomato purée
approx. 3 tablespoons water

AMERICAN

For 6–8 people you need:
1 good-sized stewing *or* roasting chicken
$\frac{1}{2}$ cup all-purpose seasoned flour
$\frac{1}{4}$ cup butter
8 small onions
3 stalks celery
$2\frac{1}{2}$ cups water
$\frac{1}{2}$–1 lemon
1 bay leaf
approx. 1 cup carrots
$\frac{3}{4}$ cup peas
$\frac{2}{3}$ cup sour cream

For the dumplings:
1 cup all-purpose flour, sifted with 1 teaspoon baking powder
$\frac{1}{2}$ teaspoon salt
generous $\frac{1}{3}$ cup shredded suet
$\frac{1}{2}$ teaspoon powdered oregano *or* marjoram
1 tablespoon tomato paste
scant $\frac{1}{4}$ cup water

1. Cut the fowl or chicken into joints, coat in well seasoned flour.
2. Heat butter, fry chicken until golden, then place in a casserole. Fry onions and celery and add to the chicken.
3. If any flour remains, stir into butter in the saucepan, gradually add water, bring to the boil and cook until thickened.
4. Pour over chicken. Add sliced lemon and bay leaf, cover casserole.
5. Cook a boiling fowl for about 2 hours, a roasting chicken about 1 hour.
6. While fowl or chicken is cooking, boil sliced carrots and peas in salted water. Drain and add to casserole, remove lemon slices and bay leaf and test chicken to see if tender. Stir in soured cream and top with dumplings, sprinkled with parsley.
7. For dumplings, sieve flour and salt, add suet, herbs and tomato purée. Make a soft dough with water. Form into small balls and cook in boiling, salted water until cooked, about 20 minutes . Drain.

21

Fried chicken with barbecue sauce

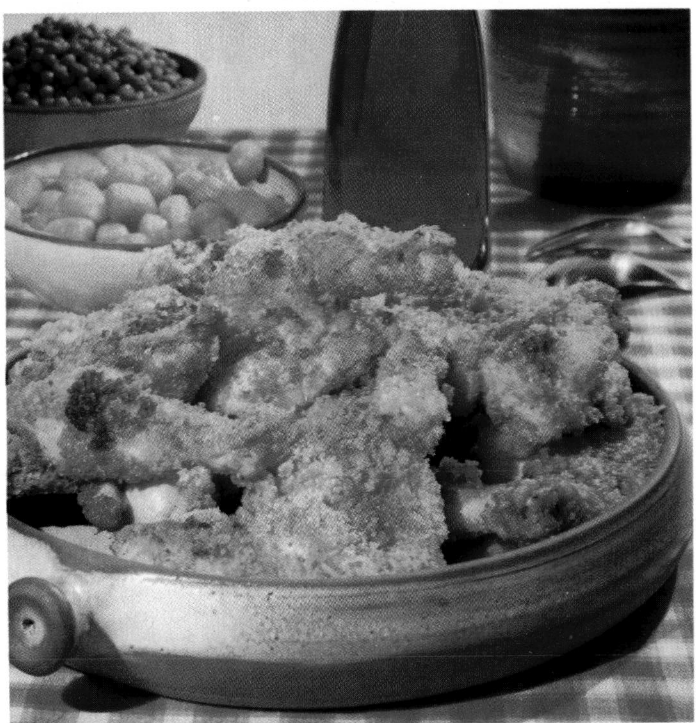

Cooking time: 15 min. **Preparation time:** 10 min. **Main cooking utensils:** pan and frying basket, absorbent paper, saucepan.

IMPERIAL

For 4 people you need:
2 small broilers*—young chickens
seasoning
1 oz. flour
1 egg
3 oz. fine soft breadcrumbs
oil or fat for frying

For the barbecue sauce:
3 oz. butter
$\frac{1}{2}$ pint water
juice 1 lemon
seasoning
good pinch each of cayenne, paprika, chilli powder, sugar
1 onion, chopped
1 clove garlic, crushed
$\frac{1}{2}$ tablespoon mustard
few drops Tabasco and Worcestershire sauces

AMERICAN

For 4 people you need:
2 small broilers
seasoning
$\frac{1}{4}$ cup all-purpose flour
1 egg
$1\frac{1}{2}$ cups fine soft bread crumbs
oil or fat for frying

For the barbecue sauce:
6 tablespoons butter
$1\frac{1}{4}$ cups water
juice 1 lemon
seasoning
dash each of cayenne, paprika, chili powder, sugar
1 onion, chopped
1 clove garlic, crushed
$\frac{1}{2}$ tablespoon mustard
few drops Tabasco and Worcestershire sauces

*Chicken fried this way is popular in the U.S.A. where broiler chickens are reared for frying or broiling (grilling).

1. Cut the chickens into neat joints. Coat in well seasoned flour.
2. Brush with beaten egg and press soft crumbs against joints. It is possible to use crisp breadcrumbs (raspings), but they can become over-cooked before the chicken joints are tender, so particular care must be taken to watch them when frying.
3. Test the temperature of the oil or fat—put in a cube of day-old bread, this should turn golden in just over $\frac{1}{2}$ minute with oil, just over 1 minute with fat. If this is any quicker, the solid chicken meat will over-brown before being cooked.
4. Fry the chicken until tender. Lift out and drain on absorbent paper.

To serve: With barbecue sauce, made by blending all ingredients together in a pan until hot. For a thick sauce, blend in 1 oz. (U.S. $\frac{1}{4}$ cup) flour.

22

Chicken pancakes

Cooking time: 30 min. **Preparation time:** 25 min. **Main cooking utensils:** frying pan/skillet, saucepan.

IMPERIAL

For 4 people you need:
For the batter:
4 oz. flour
pinch salt
2 eggs
$\frac{1}{4}$ pint milk
6 tablespoons thin cream
1 oz. butter

For the chicken mixture:
8–12 oz. cooked chicken
2 sticks celery
$\frac{1}{4}$ pint milk *or* milk and chicken stock
2 oz. butter
2–3 tablespoons cooked corn off the cob *or* canned corn
2–3 boiled potatoes
seasoning
4 tablespoons thin cream

To garnish:
quartered tomatoes
olives (optional)

AMERICAN

For 4 people you need:
For the batter:
1 cup all-purpose flour
dash salt
2 eggs
$\frac{2}{3}$ cup milk
$\frac{1}{2}$ cup coffee cream
2 tablespoons butter

For the chicken mixture:
$1\frac{1}{2}$–2 cups cooked chicken
2 stalks celery
$\frac{2}{3}$ cup milk *or* milk and chicken stock
$\frac{1}{4}$ cup butter
3–4 tablespoons cooked fresh corn off the cob *or* canned corn
2–3 boiled potatoes
seasoning
$\frac{1}{3}$ cup coffee cream

To garnish:
quartered tomatoes
olives (optional)

1. Sieve the flour and salt together, add the eggs, then gradually beat in the milk, cream and melted butter.
2. Dice the cooked chicken neatly and cut celery into thin strips.
3. Simmer the celery for about 15 minutes in the milk, or milk and stock.
4. When tender, add the butter, diced chicken, corn, diced potatoes.
5. Season well, add the cream and keep hot.
6. Heat approximately $\frac{1}{2}$–$\frac{3}{4}$ oz. butter in the frying pan for each pancake.
7. Pour in enough batter to give a wafer-thin layer.
8. Cook until golden (about 2 min.), turn and cook on second side.
9. Put some of the chicken mixture in each pancake, roll and keep hot on a dish over a pan of hot water – or cook all pancakes and keep hot as suggested, or in low oven, then fill and roll. Garnish.

23

Tostados de polla
Fried tortillas and chicken

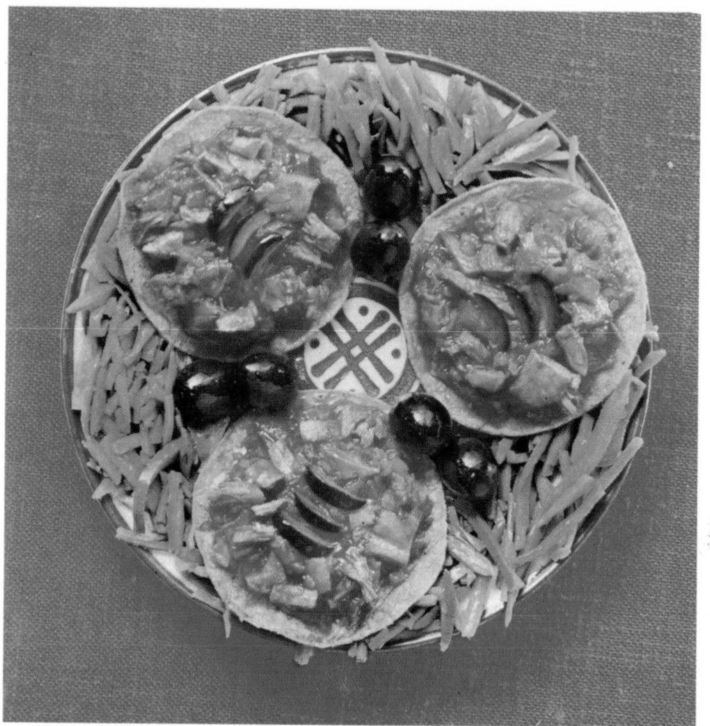

Cooking time: 15–20 min. **Preparation time:** 15 min. if tortillas already made. **Main cooking utensils:** 2 saucepans, frying pan/skillet, and griddle if making the tortillas.

IMPERIAL

For 6 people you need:
1 tablespoon oil
1 onion
6 tomatoes
3 teaspoons Tabasco sauce
6–8 oz. cooked, chopped chicken
salt to taste
6 tortillas (see below)
1 good tablespoon oil

For the topping:
3–4 oz. sliced green beans
seasoning
black olives

To make 6 tortillas:
4 oz. tortilla flour
3 oz. plain flour
$\frac{1}{2}$ teaspoon salt
$1\frac{1}{2}$ oz. lard *or* cooking fat
warm water

AMERICAN

For 6 people you need:
1 tablespoon oil
1 onion
6 tomatoes
3 teaspoons Tabasco sauce
1–$1\frac{1}{2}$ cups cooked, chopped chicken
salt to taste
6 tortillas (see below)
1 good tablespoon oil

For the topping:
approx. $\frac{1}{4}$ lb. sliced green beans
seasoning
ripe olives

To make 6 tortillas:
$\frac{3}{4}$ cup corn meal
$\frac{3}{4}$ cup all-purpose flour
$\frac{1}{2}$ teaspoon salt
3 tablespoons lard *or* cooking fat
warm water

1. Heat the oil and fry the peeled chopped onion and tomatoes until a soft pulp. Sieve if wished or put into an electric blender.
2. Return to the pan with the Tabasco sauce, chicken and salt and heat for 10–15 minutes.
3. Meanwhile fry 6 tortillas in the hot oil until crisp on each side. Drain and put on to a hot dish.
4. Cook the beans in well-seasoned water, drain.

To make tortillas: The correct flour is made from cornmeal but cornflour could be used. Sieve flours, add salt, rub in fat and bind with water. Stand for 20 minutes. Roll out very thinly. Cut into large rounds and cook on an ungreased griddle or frying pan for 1 minute on either side.

To serve: Pile the chicken mixture on the fried tortillas (known as *tostados*). Serve with the beans and olives. Top with more black olives, sliced.

24

Apple and red cabbage coleslaw

Preparation time: 20 min.

IMPERIAL

For 6–8 people you need:
For the base:
1 red cabbage
1 dessert apple
squeeze lemon juice
mayonnaise to mix

For the filling:
1 medium-sized white cabbage
2–3 dessert apples
1 green pepper
squeeze lemon juice
mayonnaise to mix

AMERICAN

For 6–8 people you need:
For the base:
1 red cabbage
1 eating apple
dash lemon juice
mayonnaise to mix

For the filling:
1 medium-sized white cabbage
2–3 eating apples
1 sweet green pepper
dash lemon juice
mayonnaise to mix

1. Cut a slice from the top of the red cabbage and carefully cut away the centre part, leaving a 'shell'. Put a small portion on one side for the base of this salad, but the remainder can be shredded and cooked for another meal.
2. Wash the small amount of red cabbage and the quartered white cabbage in cold water, drain very well and leave to dry.
3. Shred the red cabbage very finely, blend with the diced dessert apple, lemon juice and enough mayonnaise to moisten. Put this in the bottom of the red cabbage 'shell'.
4. Shred the white cabbage finely, discard any tough outer leaves. Dice the dessert apples, leaving the skins on. Cut the green pepper into thin shreds, discarding core and seeds.
5. Blend the cabbage, apple, pepper and lemon juice with the mayonnaise. Pile into the red cabbage 'shell'.

To vary: Add diced gherkin or cucumber; dried fruit and/or chopped nuts or add chopped chives or spring onions.

25

Empanadas
Prune and meat patties

Cooking time: $1\frac{3}{4}$ hr. **Preparation time:** 30 min. plus overnight soaking of prunes. **Main cooking utensils:** saucepan, baking tray/sheet. **Oven temperature:** hot, 425–450°F., 220–230°C., Gas Mark 6–7 then 375°F., 190°C., Gas Mark 4–5. **Oven position:** above centre.

IMPERIAL

For 4 people you need:
8 oz. dried prunes
water to cover
1 large onion
2 oz. butter
12 oz. raw minced beef
$\frac{1}{2}$ red pepper *or* canned pepper
2 large tomatoes
seasoning
2 teaspoons sugar
1 teaspoon cinnamon
2–3 tablespoons white wine *or* prune juice

For the pastry:
12 oz. flour, preferably plain
pinch salt
pinch powdered cinnamon
6 oz. butter
water to bind
1 egg to glaze

AMERICAN

For 4 people you need:
$1\frac{1}{3}$ cups dried prunes
water to cover
1 large onion
$\frac{1}{4}$ cup butter
$1\frac{1}{2}$ cups raw ground beef
$\frac{1}{2}$ sweet red pepper *or* canned pepper
2 large tomatoes
seasoning
2 teaspoons sugar
1 teaspoon cinnamon
3–4 tablespoons white wine *or* prune juice

For the pastry:
3 cups all-purpose flour
dash salt
dash cinnamon
$\frac{3}{4}$ cup butter
water to bind
1 egg to glaze

1. Soak prunes overnight, simmer until tender, about 1 hour. Drain.
2. Put half the prunes on one side for garnish, stone and chop remainder. Blend with chopped onion, fried lightly in hot butter.
3. Add minced meat, diced pepper, skinned, chopped tomatoes, seasoning, sugar and cinnamon.
4. Moisten with wine or prune juice.
5. Sieve flour, salt and cinnamon, rub in butter and bind with water.
6. Roll out thinly and make into 4 large squares.
7. Put fruit filling on top, fold corners into centre so they overlap.
8. Seal firmly, using trimmings of pastry to decorate. Brush with beaten egg.
9. Bake for approximately 25 minutes until pastry begins to brown, then lower heat for further 20 minutes.

To serve: Hot or cold, garnished with lettuce, prunes and prunes stuffed with red pepper.

26

Ham and egg with toasted cheese

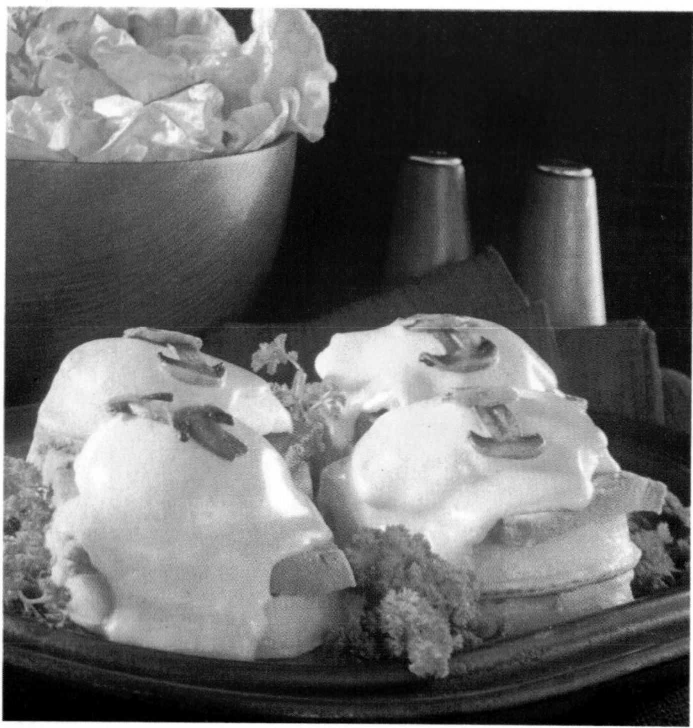

Cooking time: 10 min. **Preparation time:** 15 min. **Main cooking utensils:** frying pan/skillet, grill/broiler, 2 saucepans.

IMPERIAL

For 4 people you need:
2–3 oz. mushrooms
3 oz. butter
4 thick slices cooked ham
4 thick slices bread
4 eggs
seasoning

For the toasted cheese mixture:
1 oz. butter
½ oz. flour
1 teaspoon made mustard
1 egg yolk
6 tablespoons liquid, either milk *or* half milk and half ale
½–1 teaspoon Worcestershire sauce
4–6 oz. Cheddar *or* other good cooking cheese, finely grated

AMERICAN

For 4 people you need:
½–¾ cup mushrooms
6 tablespoons butter
4 thick slices cooked ham
4 thick slices bread
4 eggs
seasoning

For the toasted cheese mixture:
2 tablespoons butter
2 tablespoons all-purpose flour
1 teaspoon prepared mustard
1 egg yolk
½ cup liquid, either milk *or* half milk and half beer
½–1 teaspoon Worcestershire sauce
1–1½ cups finely grated Cheddar *or* other good cooking cheese

NOTE: All the various cooking processes should be done at same time, since this dish needs to be served as soon as cooked.

1. Slice the mushrooms, fry steadily in 2 oz. (U.S. ¼ cup) of the butter.
2. When nearly cooked, heat the ham in the pan and toast bread lightly, then spread with the remaining butter.
3. Break the eggs into cups, lower into very hot seasoned water and poach with water simmering steadily, moving the water around the eggs.
4. Heat butter, stir in flour, add other ingredients, *except* cheese. Blend together and cook over a very low heat until thickened. Stir cheese into the very hot mixture, remove from heat when cheese melts.

To serve: Put most of the mushrooms on the toast, top with ham, then the well-drained eggs. Coat with cheese mixture and garnish with mushrooms and parsley.

To vary: Put under the grill for 1–2 minutes to brown, if wished.

27

American mincemeat pie

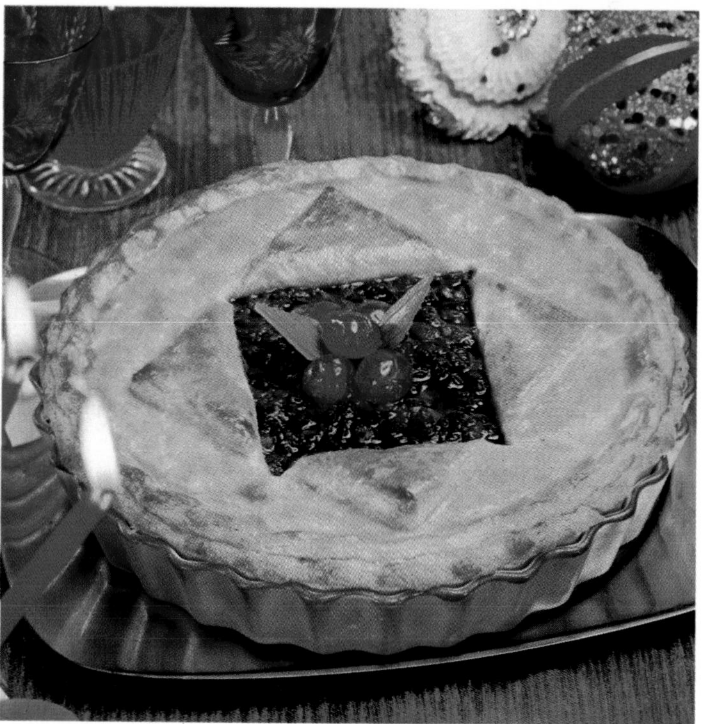

Cooking time: 30–35 min. **Preparation time:** 30 min. (including mincemeat) plus time for pastry to stand. **Main cooking utensil:** 8-inch pie plate, tin or flan dish. **Oven temperature:** moderately hot, 400°F., 200°C., Gas Mark 5–6. **Oven position:** centre.

IMPERIAL

For 4–6 people you need:
For the pastry:
12 oz. flour, preferably plain
pinch salt
6 oz. American lard
egg yolk
water to mix

For the mincemeat:
2 oz. melted American lard
2 oz. brown sugar
8 oz. dried fruit
1 apple
2 oz. glacé cherries
½ teaspoon each powdered cinnamon, spice, nutmeg
2 oz. nuts, chopped
1 tablespoon brandy

To decorate:
glacé cherries
angelica

AMERICAN

For 4–6 people you need:
For the pastry:
3 cups all-purpose flour
dash salt
¾ cup lard
egg yolk
water to mix

For the mincemeat:
¼ cup melted lard
¼ cup brown sugar
1⅓ cups dried fruit
1 apple
¼ cup candied cherries
½ teaspoon each cinnamon, spice, nutmeg
½ cup chopped nuts
1 tablespoon brandy

To decorate:
candied cherries
angelica

1. Sieve the flour and salt into a basin.
2. Rub in the lard until the mixture looks like fine breadcrumbs.
3. Bind with the egg yolk and water. Stand for 1 hour, as this is very rich. (If wishing to handle at once, use just about 5 oz. (U.S. ½ cup plus 2 tablespoons) lard.)
4. Mix the ingredients for the mincemeat together, grating peeled apple and chopping cherries.
5. Divide the pastry into two. Roll out half the pastry to line the pie plate.
6. Put the mincemeat on to the pastry.
7. Roll out the rest of the pastry. Cut a cross in the centre, by making two long cuts in the pastry.
8. Lift carefully over mincemeat. Arrange pastry as picture.
9. Seal edges, brush with the egg white and bake until crisp and golden brown. Serve hot with cream and decorate with cherries and angelica.

Baked rhubarb Betty

Cooking time: 40 min. **Preparation time:** 20 min. **Main cooking utensils:** saucepan, 2-pint/2½-pint pie dish *or* ovenproof dish. **Oven temperature:** moderate, 375°F., 190°C., Gas Mark 4–5. **Oven position:** centre.

IMPERIAL

For 4–5 people you need:
For the crumb mixture:
2 oz. butter
4 oz. sugar, brown *or* white
6 oz. fairly coarse white breadcrumbs
grated rind 1–2 oranges
½–1 teaspoon powdered cinnamon

For the rhubarb mixture:
1½ lb. rhubarb (weight after removing leaves)
juice 2 oranges
3 oz. sugar

AMERICAN

For 4–5 people you need:
For the crumb mixture:
¼ cup butter
½ cup sugar, brown *or* white
3 cups fairly coarse white bread crumbs
grated rind 1–2 oranges
½–1 teaspoon cinnamon

For the rhubarb mixture:
1½ lb. rhubarb (weight after removing leaves)
juice 2 oranges
6 tablespoons sugar

1. Melt the butter in a pan, then blend with the rest of the ingredients for crumb mixture.
2. Cut the rhubarb into neat pieces.
3. Put half the rhubarb into the dish with half the orange juice and half the sugar.
4. Press half the crumb mixture on top of the fruit, then cover with the rest of the rhubarb, orange juice and sugar.
5. Press the remainder of the crumb mixture over the top. Bake until crisp and golden brown.

To serve: It is excellent served with orange-flavoured ice cream or thick cream.

To vary: Use sliced apples instead of rhubarb.
If preferred the dessert may be steamed instead of baked. In which case, omit any liquid with the fruit, sweeten with golden syrup (U.S. corn syrup). Cover pudding well, steam for about 1½ hours over boiling water.

Prune and pineapple dessert

Cooking time: 1¼ hr. **Preparation time:** 25 min. plus time to prepare prunes. **Main cooking utensils:** 8-inch square cake tin/pan. **Oven temperature:** moderate, 375°F., 190°C., Gas Mark 4–5. **Oven position:** centre.

IMPERIAL

For 5–6 people you need:
For the glaze:
2 oz. butter
2 oz. honey
2 tablespoons pineapple syrup

For the fruit coating:
about 25 tenderized prunes
1 medium-sized can pineapple rings

For the pudding:
3 oz. butter *or* margarine
4 oz. castor sugar
3 eggs
6 oz. self-raising flour
1–2 oz. ground almonds
little milk if necessary

AMERICAN

For 5–6 people you need:
For the glaze:
¼ cup butter
3 tablespoons honey
3 tablespoons pineapple sirup

For the fruit coating:
about 25 tenderized prunes
1 medium-sized can pineapple rings

For the pudding:
6 tablespoons butter *or* margarine
½ cup granulated sugar
3 eggs
1½ cups all-purpose flour, sifted with 1½ teaspoons baking powder
¼–½ cup ground almonds
little milk if necessary

1. Cream the butter, honey and syrup and spread round the bottom and sides of the tin.
2. Arrange well-drained prunes and well-drained pineapple rings on the base and sides of the tin; see picture.
3. Cream the butter and sugar until soft and light.
4. Gradually beat in the eggs, then fold in flour and almonds, with enough milk to make a dropping consistency. Do not make too soft as the fruit coating does this.
5. Put the pudding mixture over the fruit.
6. Bake until firm to the touch*.
7. Turn out carefully on to a hot dish.

*To protect fruit round sides of tin, the outside of the tin may be wrapped in foil during cooking.

To serve: Hot with a syrup made from prune liquid and pineapple syrup.

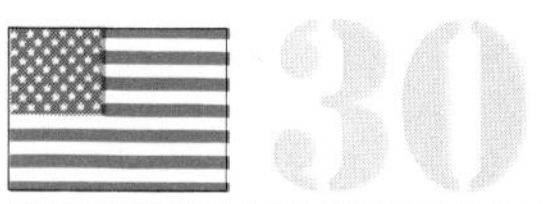

Autumn (Fall time) pie

Cooking time: 50 min. plus time to steam prunes. **Preparation time:** 20 min. plus time to soak prunes. **Main cooking utensils:** steamer, 2-pint/$2\frac{1}{2}$-pint pie dish. **Oven temperature:** 400–425°F., 200–220°C., Gas Mark 6, then 375°F., 190°C., Gas Mark 4–5. **Oven position:** centre.

IMPERIAL	**AMERICAN**
For 4–5 people you need:	For 4–5 people you need:
6 oz. flour, preferably plain	$1\frac{1}{2}$ cups all-purpose flour
pinch salt	dash salt
$1–1\frac{1}{2}$ oz. sugar	2–3 tablespoons sugar
3 oz. butter *or* shortening	6 tablespoons butter *or* shortening
cold water	cold water
For the filling:	For the filling:
1 lb. prunes	1 lb. prunes
12 oz. plums	$\frac{3}{4}$ lb. plums
sugar	sugar
$\frac{1}{3}$ pint liquid (see Stage 3)	$\frac{3}{4}$ cup liquid (see Stage 3)

1. Pour over enough water to cover prunes and leave soaking overnight. *Or* steam without water until just tender, then add liquid as Stage 3.
2. Sieve flour and salt, add sugar, rub in butter or shortening and mix to a rolling consistency with ice cold water.
3. Put the well-drained prunes, plums, sugar to taste, about $\frac{1}{3}$ pint (U.S. $\frac{3}{4}$ cup) of liquid used in soaking prunes, or use cider, water, or carefully strained weak tea, into a dish.
4. Roll out the pastry. Make a thin strip, press on damp rim of dish. Brush with water and cover with the pastry 'lid'.
5. Make the edges neat, seal together and flute or decorate neatly.
6. Bake for about 20 minutes at the higher temperature, then lower heat for further 25–30 minutes to make sure the fruit is cooked.

To serve: Top with sugar and serve with cream.

To vary: Prunes blend well with apples, pears and other fruit. Add chopped, blanched almonds to give an interesting texture.

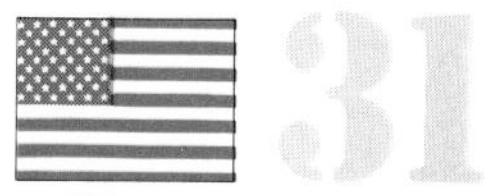

Orange chiffon pie

Cooking time: 25–30 min. **Preparation time:** 30 min. **Main cooking utensils:** 9-inch pie plate *or* flan ring, double saucepan. **Oven temperature:** moderately hot, 375–400°F., 190–200°C., Gas Mark 5–6. **Oven position:** centre.

IMPERIAL	**AMERICAN**
For 6–8 portions you need:	For 6–8 portions you need:
4 oz. butter *or* margarine	$\frac{1}{2}$ cup butter *or* margarine
3 oz. castor sugar	6 tablespoons granulated sugar
1 egg yolk	1 egg yolk
8 oz. plain flour	2 cups all-purpose flour
water if necessary	water if necessary
For the filling:	For the filling:
2 teaspoons gelatine	2 teaspoons gelatin
3 tablespoons water	scant $\frac{1}{4}$ cup water
3 eggs	3 eggs
6 tablespoons orange juice	$\frac{1}{2}$ cup orange juice
3 tablespoons lemon juice	scant $\frac{1}{4}$ cup lemon juice
4 oz. sugar	$\frac{1}{2}$ cup sugar
6 oz. cream cheese	$\frac{3}{4}$ cup cream cheese
3–4 tablespoons thick cream	$\frac{1}{4}$ cup whipping cream
To decorate:	To decorate:
1 orange	1 orange
orange *or* other green leaves	orange *or* other green leaves

1. Cream the butter and sugar until light and fluffy. Beat in the egg yolk.
2. Stir in the sieved flour until mixture is firm, using a little water if necessary. Chill well.
3. Roll out and line the pie plate, trim and flute edges.
4. Bake 'blind' until golden brown; cool.
5. Soften gelatine in the water.
6. Put egg yolks, orange and lemon juice and half of the sugar in top of a double saucepan, whisk well. Cook over hot water until mixture thickens, cool. Dissolve gelatine over heat and stir into mixture.
7. Soften cream cheese with the cream and mix into gelatine mixture. Chill until beginning to stiffen.
8. Whisk egg whites, add remaining sugar and fold into the mixture.
9. Spoon into prepared pie case, chill thoroughly. Decorate with slices of orange and leaves. Serve cold.

32

Maple prune pie

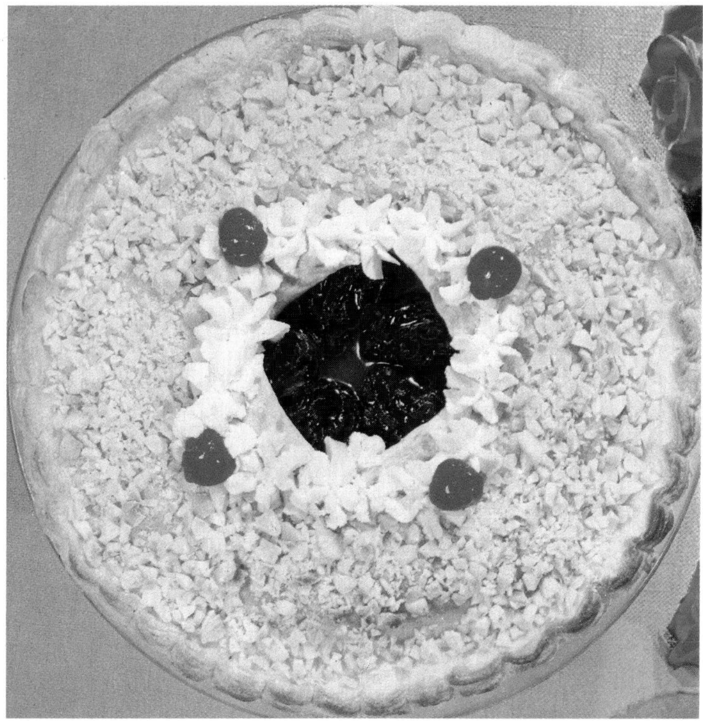

Cooking time: 35–40 min. plus time to cook prunes if necessary (see Stage 4). **Preparation time:** 30 min. plus soaking of prunes. **Main cooking utensils:** saucepan (see Stage 4), 9-inch pie plate. **Oven temperature:** moderately hot, 400°F., 200°C., Gas Mark 5–6. **Oven position:** centre.

IMPERIAL

For 5–6 people you need:
5 oz. butter
3 oz. sugar
10 oz. flour, preferably plain
pinch salt
1 egg yolk
water to bind

For the filling:
10 oz. dried prunes
rind and juice 1 lemon
$\frac{1}{2}$–1 teaspoon cinnamon
4 oz. maple syrup *or* golden syrup

For the topping:
syrup *or* jam
2–3 oz. almonds
$\frac{1}{4}$ pint thick cream
glacé cherries

AMERICAN

For 5–6 people you need:
$\frac{1}{2}$ cup plus 2 tablespoons butter
6 tablespoons sugar
$2\frac{1}{2}$ cups all-purpose flour
dash salt
1 egg yolk
water to bind

For the filling:
$1\frac{2}{3}$ cups dried prunes
rind and juice 1 lemon
$\frac{1}{2}$–1 teaspoon cinnamon
$\frac{1}{3}$ cup maple sirup

For the topping:
sirup *or* jam
approx. $\frac{1}{2}$ cup almonds
$\frac{2}{3}$ cup whipping cream
candied cherries

1. Cream the butter and sugar until soft then work in the flour and salt.
2. Bind with the egg yolk and water.
3. This is a very light pastry so it is advisable to let it stand in a cool place for about 1 hour.
4. Lift the prunes from the water in which they were soaked unless they are still very firm; if this is the case, then simmer in the water for 30 minutes, then drain.
5. Blend the prunes with the grated lemon rind and juice, cinnamon and the maple or golden syrup.
6. Roll out half the pastry and line the pie plate.
7. Put the prune mixture on top.
8. Roll out the rest of the pastry, cut a small hole out of the centre then cover the prunes with pastry.
9. Bake until crisp and golden, then allow prune pie to cool.
10. Brush the pastry with a little maple syrup or sieved apricot jam.
11. Chop blanched almonds and brown in the oven or under grill; sprinkle over pastry. Decorate with cream and glacé cherries.

33

Strawberry nut pie

Cooking time: 20–25 min. **Preparation time:** 25 min. **Main cooking utensils:** 8-inch flan ring, baking tray/sheet, saucepan. **Oven temperature:** moderately hot to hot, 400–425°F., 200–220°C., Gas Mark 6. **Oven position:** centre.

IMPERIAL

For 6 people you need:
For the pastry:
6 oz. flour, preferably plain
pinch salt
$2\frac{1}{2}$ oz. American lard
1 oz. walnuts *or* pecan nuts, chopped
egg yolk and water to mix

For the filling:
1 oz. cornflour
1 oz. flour
$\frac{1}{2}$ pint milk
2 oz. sugar
$\frac{1}{2}$ teaspoon vanilla essence
1 egg yolk
$\frac{1}{2}$ pint thick cream*
2 oz. nuts, walnuts, pecan nuts, almonds *or* a mixture
1 lb. strawberries

AMERICAN

For 6 people you need:
For the pastry:
$1\frac{1}{2}$ cups all-purpose flour
dash salt
$\frac{1}{4}$ cup plus 1 tablespoon lard
$\frac{1}{4}$ cup chopped walnuts *or* pecan nuts
egg yolk and water to mix

For the filling:
$\frac{1}{4}$ cup cornstarch
$\frac{1}{4}$ cup all-purpose flour
$1\frac{1}{4}$ cups milk
$\frac{1}{4}$ cup sugar
$\frac{1}{2}$ teaspoon vanilla extract
1 egg yolk
$1\frac{1}{4}$ cups whipping cream*
$\frac{1}{2}$ cup nuts, walnuts, pecan nuts, almonds, *or* a mixture
1 lb. strawberries

*To give a lighter cream for decoration, whisk the egg white stiffly and fold into $\frac{1}{4}$ pint (U.S. $\frac{2}{3}$ cup) of the whipped cream.

1. Sieve together the flour and salt. Rub in the lard, add the nuts and bind with egg yolk and water.
2. Roll out and line flan ring. Bake 'blind' until firm to the touch.
3. Meanwhile, blend the flours together with a little cold milk. Bring rest of the milk to the boil, add the sugar and essence.
4. Pour over flours, return to pan to thicken, stirring well.
5. Add whisked egg yolk and cook for 2 minutes *without boiling*, then allow to cool, stirring once or twice. Fold in half the whipped cream.
6. Toast nuts and scatter on the bottom of the flan case.
7. Top with the custard mixture, half the sliced strawberries and the piped cream. Decorate with whole fruit. If wished, the fruit may be sprinkled with sugar for a while before using.

34

Lady Baltimore cake

Cooking time: 25 min. for cake; see Stage 4 for frosting. **Preparation time:** cake and icing, 45 min. **Main cooking utensils:** 2 $6\frac{1}{2}$–7-inch square sandwich tins/square cake pans, saucepan. **Oven temperature:** 350–375°F., 180–190°C., Gas Mark 4–5. **Oven position:** above centre.

IMPERIAL

For 8–10 portions you need:
For the cake:
6 oz. butter *or* margarine
6 oz. castor sugar
3 large eggs
6 oz. self-raising flour

For the frosting:
8 oz. loaf *or* granulated sugar
4 tablespoons water
1 egg white
pinch cream of tartar
4 oz. seedless, plumped raisins
1–2 oz. blanched almonds
1 oz. walnuts

AMERICAN

For 8–10 portions you need:
For the cake:
$\frac{3}{4}$ cup butter *or* margarine
$\frac{3}{4}$ cup granulated sugar
3 eggs
$1\frac{1}{2}$ cups all-purpose flour, sifted with $1\frac{1}{2}$ teaspoons baking powder

For the frosting:
1 cup plus 1 tablespoon granulated sugar
$\frac{1}{3}$ cup water
1 egg white
dash cream of tartar
$\frac{3}{4}$ cup seedless, plumped raisins
approx. $\frac{1}{3}$ cup blanched almonds
$\frac{1}{4}$ cup walnuts

1. Cream the butter and sugar until soft and light. Gradually beat in the eggs, fold in the sieved flour.
2. Divide between the tins, bake until firm to touch. Oven temperatures vary considerably, so for perfect results follow manufacturer's instructions for your cooker.
3. For the frosting, put sugar and water into saucepan, stir over steady heat until sugar has dissolved.
4. Continue boiling, without stirring, until the mixture forms a soft ball when tested in a little cold water; for a soft frosting, temperature should be 238°F., for firmer frosting, 240°F. (or when weather is damp or humid).
5. Whisk the egg white until very stiff, add cream of tartar, gradually beat in syrup. Continue beating until mixture turns cloudy and thick. Add raisins, chopped almonds and walnuts. Sandwich cakes with frosting and cover top.

To vary: For a lighter and more generous topping, use double quantities of sugar and water, but add raisins and nuts to half the frosting only as a filling.

35

American cheese cake

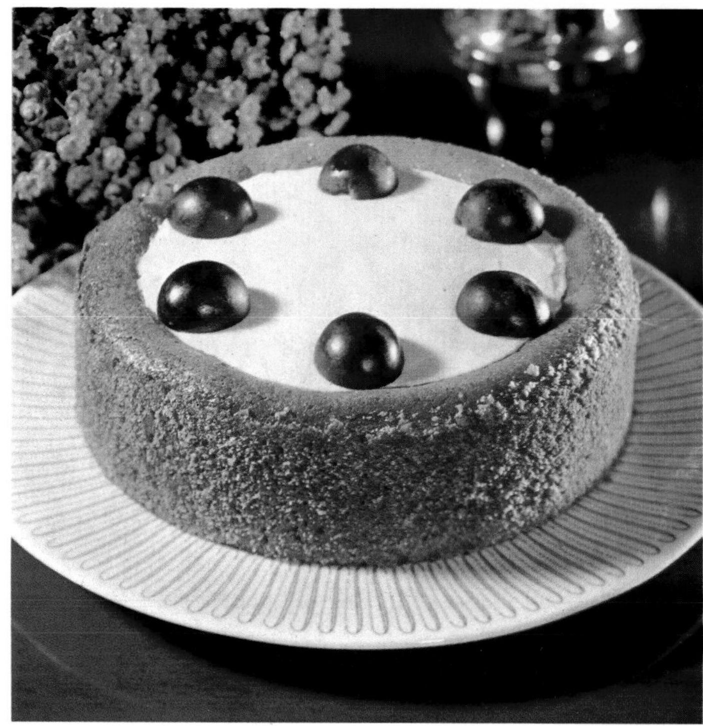

Cooking time: 1 hr. **Preparation time:** 25 min. **Main cooking utensil:** 6-inch cake tin/pan with loose base *or* ovenproof serving dish. **Oven temperature:** very moderate, 325–350°F., 170–180°C., Gas Mark 3–4. **Oven position:** centre.

IMPERIAL

For 6–8 portions you need:
For the crumb mixture:
2 oz. margarine, melted
3–4 oz. plain biscuits
1 teaspoon castor sugar
pinch powdered cinnamon
pinch grated nutmeg

For the filling:
3 small eggs
$3\frac{1}{2}$ oz. sugar
$10\frac{1}{2}$ oz. ($3\frac{1}{2} \times 3$ oz. pkts.) cream cheese
1 tablespoon lemon juice
grated rind $\frac{1}{2}$ lemon

For the topping:
2 oz. castor sugar
$4\frac{1}{2}$ oz. ($1\frac{1}{2} \times 3$ oz. pkts.) cream cheese
fresh fruit

AMERICAN

For 6–8 portions you need:
For the crumb mixture:
$\frac{1}{4}$ cup melted margarine
approx. $1\frac{1}{2}$ cups cracker crumbs
1 teaspoon granulated sugar
dash cinnamon
dash grated nutmeg

For the filling:
3 small eggs
7 tablespoons sugar
$1\frac{1}{4}$ cups plus 1 tablespoon cream cheese
1 tablespoon lemon juice
grated rind $\frac{1}{2}$ lemon

For the topping:
$\frac{1}{4}$ cup granulated sugar
$\frac{1}{2}$ cup plus 1 tablespoon cream cheese
fresh fruit

1. Brush the tin well with melted margarine.
2. Crush the biscuits until fine crumbs, mix with the sugar and spices.
3. Sprinkle the crumb mixture around sides and base of tin. Arrange a band of foil to extend 1 inch above the rim.
4. Whisk the eggs and sugar until thick.
5. Beat the cream cheese well until smooth.
6. Gradually add whisked egg mixture, lemon juice and rind to cream cheese.
7. Pour into the prepared tin and bake until just firm.
8. Remove the foil and allow to cool until cake shrinks from sides of tin.
9. Remove the cake from the tin, leaving on the metal base; do not remove cake from this.
10. Prepare the topping by beating sugar and cream cheese together. Spread over the top of the cake when cold.
11. Decorate with grapes, strawberries or other fruits.

 36

Chocolate chiffon cake

Cooking time: 50 min. **Preparation time:** 30 min. **Main cooking utensil:** 8-inch round cake tin/spring form cake pan. **Oven temperature:** very moderate, 325–350°F., 170–180°C., Gas Mark 3–4. **Oven position:** centre.

IMPERIAL

For 8 portions you need:
2 oz. cocoa powder
4 tablespoons boiling water
3 oz. self-raising flour
pinch salt
6 oz. castor sugar
3 large eggs
$1\frac{1}{2}$ oz. butter, melted
$\frac{1}{2}$ teaspoon vanilla essence

To decorate:
$\frac{1}{2}$ pint thick cream
2 oz. plain chocolate

AMERICAN

For 8 portions you need:
$\frac{1}{2}$ cup unsweetened cocoa powder
$\frac{1}{3}$ cup boiling water
$\frac{3}{4}$ cup all-purpose flour sifted with $\frac{3}{4}$ teaspoon baking powder
dash salt
$\frac{3}{4}$ cup granulated sugar
3 eggs
3 tablespoons melted butter
$\frac{1}{2}$ teaspoon vanilla extract

To decorate:
$1\frac{1}{4}$ cups whipping cream
2 oz. semi-sweet chocolate

1. Blend the cocoa with the boiling water and leave to cool.
2. Sieve the flour, salt and sugar into a bowl and add the egg yolks and melted butter.
3. Add the cocoa mixture and vanilla essence and beat until smooth.
4. Whisk the egg whites until stiff and fold them into the mixture.
5. Pour into an ungreased cake tin. Bake for approximately 50 minutes, until firm to the touch, or until a wooden cocktail stick or skewer, when inserted into the centre of the cake, comes out clean.
6. When cooked, immediately turn the tin upside down on to a wire tray, but do not remove the cake from the tin until cold.
7. To decorate, whip cream lightly, pipe over the cake and top with grated chocolate.

To serve: As a dessert or for tea.

To vary: Mocha chiffon – use strong coffee in place of water.

To store: For a very short time in the refrigerator.

37

American bride's cake

Cooking time: 8-inch cake $1\frac{1}{4}$–$1\frac{1}{2}$ hr., 9-inch cake $1\frac{3}{4}$–2 hr., 10-inch cake $2\frac{1}{4}$–$2\frac{1}{2}$ hr. **Preparation time:** 25 min. per cake. **Main cooking utensils:** 8-inch, 9-inch and 10-inch greased and floured cake tins/pans. **Oven temperature:** 325–350°F., 170–180°C., Gas Mark 3. **Oven position:** centre.

IMPERIAL

For an 8-inch cake:
8 oz. butter
8 oz. castor sugar
1 teaspoon vanilla essence
grated rind 1 lemon
4 large eggs
9 oz. self-raising flour
1 tablespoon lemon juice

AMERICAN

For an 8-inch cake:
1 cup butter
1 cup plus 1 tablespoon sugar
1 teaspoon vanilla extract
grated rind 1 lemon
4 large eggs
$2\frac{1}{4}$ cups all-purpose flour sifted with $2\frac{1}{2}$ teaspoons baking powder
1 tablespoon lemon juice

For a 9-inch middle tier: as above using half as much again, i.e. 12 oz. butter, etc. — $1\frac{1}{2}$ cups butter, etc.
For a 10-inch bottom tier: as above using twice as much, i.e. 1 lb. butter, etc. — 2 cups butter, etc.

IMPERIAL	AMERICAN
For the filling:	**For the filling:**
$1\frac{1}{2}$ lb. butter	3 cups butter
$2\frac{1}{4}$ lb. sieved icing sugar	$8\frac{3}{4}$ cups confectioner's sugar
juice 2 lemons, colouring	juice 2 lemons, coloring
To decorate:	**To decorate:**
2 lb. sieved icing sugar	$7\frac{1}{2}$ cups confectioner's sugar
vanilla essence, juice 2 lemons	vanilla extract, juice 2 lemons

1. Cream the butter, sugar, vanilla essence and lemon rind.
2. Gradually add the beaten eggs with little sieved flour.
3. Fold in the remaining flour and juice. Put into prepared tins.
4. Bake until firm to touch. The oven temperature could be lowered half way through baking if necessary. Remove from tins and cool.
5. Cream the butter and icing sugar for the filling. Add the lemon juice and a few drops of colouring. Mix well.
6. Split each cake, sandwich together with some of the butter icing. Spread base of top and middle tiers with this and put the cake together. Save the remainder for piping.
7. For decoration, mix the icing sugar, essence, lemon juice and enough water to give a flowing consistency. Pour over cakes.
8. When firm, pipe with remaining butter icing and decorate as shown.

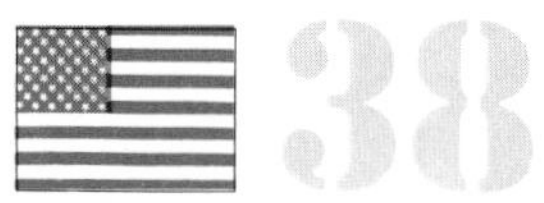

38

39

Butterscotch layer gâteau

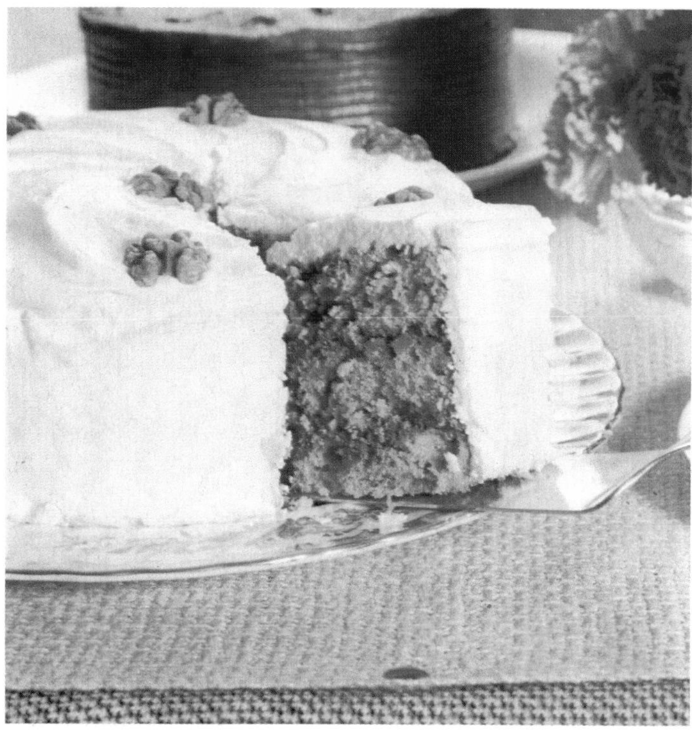

Cooking time: 30 min. **Preparation time:** 40 min. **Main cooking utensils:** three 7-inch sandwich tins/layer cake pans, saucepan. **Oven temperature:** moderate, 350°F., 180°C., Gas Mark 4–5. **Oven position:** above centre.

IMPERIAL

For 8 portions you need:
6 oz. butter *or* margarine
3 oz. soft brown sugar
3 oz. golden syrup
½ teaspoon vanilla essence
3 eggs
6 oz. self-raising flour
4 oz. walnuts, chopped

For the American frosting:
1 lb. cube or granulated sugar
¼ pint water
2 egg whites
pinch cream of tartar
7 walnut halves

AMERICAN

For 8 portions you need:
¾ cup butter *or* margarine
6 tablespoons (firmly packed) brown sugar
¼ cup corn sirup
½ teaspoon vanilla extract
3 eggs
1½ cups all-purpose flour, sifted with 1½ teaspoons baking powder
1 cup chopped walnuts

For the American frosting:
2 cups granulated sugar
⅔ cup water
2 egg whites
dash cream of tartar
7 walnut halves

1. Cream the butter, sugar, syrup and essence until soft and light.
2. Add the beaten eggs gradually, folding in a little flour if mixture shows signs of curdling.
3. Fold in the remaining sieved flour, then the nuts.
4. Divide the mixture between the well-greased tins and bake until firm to the touch.
5. Turn out carefully and cool.
6. Make the frosting by stirring sugar and water until sugar has completely dissolved.
7. Boil until the mixture reaches 238–240°F., 120°C., i.e. forms a soft ball in cold water.
8. Meanwhile whisk the egg whites until stiff, gradually blend the syrup on to these, whisking well. Add the cream of tartar.
9. Continue whisking until icing is stiff enough to hold it's shape, then sandwich cakes with some of this, if liked, and coat with remainder. Top with the nuts.

To vary: Add little melted chocolate to the frosting for a filling.

Apple bread

Cooking time: 1 hr. **Preparation time:** 15 min. **Main cooking utensil:** 2-lb. loaf tin/pan. **Oven temperature:** very moderate to moderate, 350–375°F., 180–190°C., Gas Mark 4. **Oven position:** centre.

IMPERIAL

For 10–12 slices you need:
12 oz. self-raising flour
pinch salt
½ teaspoon grated nutmeg
½ teaspoon mixed spice
3 oz. butter *or* margarine
2–3 oz. sugar
8 oz. diced cooking apples, weight when peeled and cored
4 oz. raisins *or* sultanas
2 oz. blanched almonds *or* Brazil nuts (optional), chopped
1 egg
grated rind and juice 1 lemon
little milk

For the topping (optional):
2 teaspoons sugar
1 oz. flaked almonds

AMERICAN

For 10–12 slices you need:
3 cups all-purpose flour, sifted with 3½ teaspoons baking powder
dash salt
½ teaspoon grated nutmeg
½ teaspoon mixed spice
6 tablespoons butter *or* margarine
4–6 tablespoons sugar
½ lb. diced baking apples, weight when peeled and cored
⅔ cup raisins *or* seedless white raisins
½ cup chopped blanched almonds *or* Brazil nuts (optional)
1 egg
grated rind and juice 1 lemon
little milk

For the topping (optional):
2 teaspoons sugar
¼ cup flaked *or* slivered almonds

1. Sieve the flour, salt and spices into bowl.
2. Rub in the butter or margarine until mixture resembles fine breadcrumbs.
3. Add the sugar, diced apple, dried fruit and nuts, if using, mix very well.
4. Stir in the egg and finely grated lemon rind and juice.
5. Finally stir in enough milk to give a sticky consistency; the amount will vary with the juice from the fruit, but the mixture should need a good shake to drop from a knife.
6. Put into a greased tin, top with sugar and nuts if wished.
7. Bake until firm to the touch, turn out carefully. Serve warm.

NOTE: If using a quick-mixing margarine or fat (shortening) put in all ingredients, except milk, stir briskly until blended, then add the milk.

40

Californian uncooked cookies

Preparation time: 15 min. plus overnight soaking of the prunes. **Main utensil:** 10-inch square baking tin/pan, or two 6–7-inch sandwich tins/layer cake pans.

IMPERIAL	AMERICAN
For 12–16 cookies you need:	**For 12–16 cookies you need:**
4–6 oz. prunes	approx. 1 cup prunes
water	water
10 oz. biscuit crumbs, use wholemeal biscuits *or* a mixture of wholemeal and sweet biscuits	$4\frac{1}{2}$ cups Graham cracker crumbs
4 oz. sugar	$\frac{1}{2}$ cup sugar
1 tablespoon golden syrup	1 tablespoon corn sirup
5 oz. butter	$\frac{1}{2}$ cup plus 2 tablespoons butter
few drops vanilla essence	few drops vanilla extract
To decorate:	**To decorate:**
little extra sugar	little extra sugar

1. Put the prunes into a fairly flat dish and pour over enough boiling water to *just* cover. Leave overnight.
2. Lift out of the water, spread on flat tray to dry out for a short time, then cut into convenient-sized pieces.
3. Crush the biscuit crumbs fairly finely.
4. Mix the sugar, golden syrup and butter with the vanilla essence, cream until soft, then work in the crumbs and finally add the prunes.
5. Put into the lightly greased tin and leave in a cool place to set.
6. Cut in portions with a knife dipped in hot water and shaken dry.
7. Sprinkle with sugar.

41

Brownies

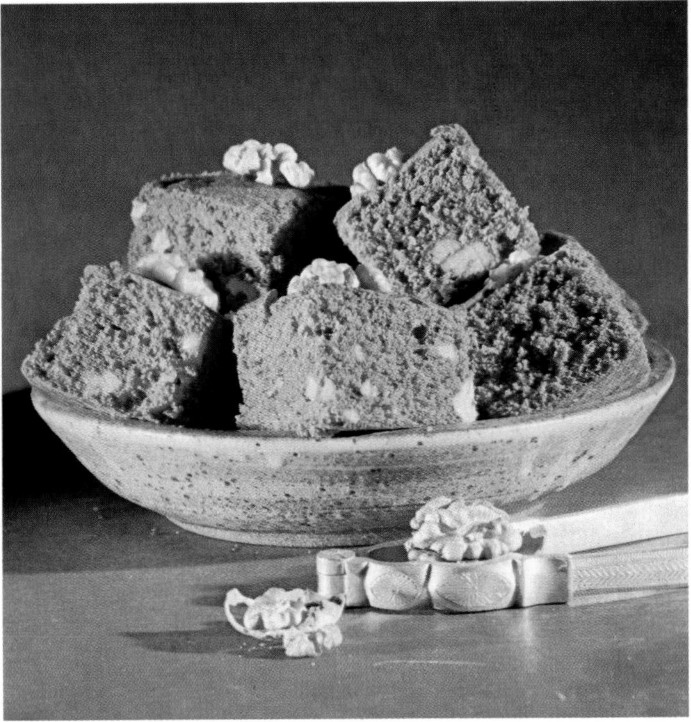

Cooking time: 45 min. **Preparation time:** 15 min. **Main cooking utensil:** 7-inch square cake tin/pan. **Oven temperature:** very moderate, 350°F., 180°C., Gas Mark 3–4. **Oven position:** centre.

IMPERIAL	AMERICAN
To make 16 cakes you need:	**To make 16 cakes you need:**
6 oz. butter *or* margarine	$\frac{3}{4}$ cup butter *or* margarine
1 oz. cocoa powder	$\frac{1}{4}$ cup unsweetened cocoa powder
6 oz. castor sugar	$\frac{3}{4}$ cup granulated sugar
2 eggs	2 eggs
2 oz. plain flour	$\frac{1}{2}$ cup all-purpose flour
2 oz. walnuts, chopped	$\frac{1}{2}$ cup chopped nuts
To decorate:	**To decorate:**
little castor sugar	little sugar
halved walnuts	halved walnuts

1. Melt 2 oz. (U.S. $\frac{1}{4}$ cup) of the butter, add cocoa. Mix well and put on one side.
2. Cream 4 oz. (U.S. $\frac{1}{2}$ cup) butter and sugar. Add the well-beaten eggs gradually.
3. Beat well, add the flour, walnuts and cocoa mixture.
4. Put into the greased tin and bake until firm. Leave to cool in the tin.
5. When cold, turn out and cut into small squares. Sprinkle with castor sugar, top with walnuts.

To serve: With coffee or tea.

To vary: Increase nuts to 4 oz. (U.S. 1 cup).
Blend 2 teaspoons instant coffee powder with the butter and cocoa at Stage 1.

To store: For 1–2 days in an airtight tin.
These cakes should have a sticky consistency when cooked, so do not over-bake otherwise it will be lost.

42

Calas
Rice fritters

Cooking time: 35 min. **Preparation time:** 20 min. plus time for mixture to 'prove'. **Main cooking utensils:** saucepan, frying pan/skillet, *or* pan for oil *or* fat, absorbent paper/paper towels.

IMPERIAL

To make approximately 18 fritters you need:
8 oz. round *or* short grain rice
$1\frac{1}{2}$ pints water
good pinch salt
$\frac{1}{2}$ oz. fresh yeast
4 oz. sugar
4 tablespoons tepid water
approx. 4 oz. self-raising *or* plain flour
2 eggs
milk if necessary

For frying:
oil *or* fat

For the coating:
sugar

AMERICAN

To make approximately 18 fritters you need:
$1\frac{1}{4}$ cups round *or* short grain rice
$3\frac{3}{4}$ cups water
dash salt
$\frac{1}{2}$ cake compressed yeast
$\frac{1}{2}$ cup sugar
5 tablespoons tepid water
approx. 1 cup all-purpose flour

2 eggs
milk if necessary

For frying:
oil *or* fat

For the coating:
sugar

Calas were sold in the streets for special feast days.

1. Cook the rice with water and salt until very soft and smooth. Watch the pan towards end of cooking time so rice does not burn; it should have absorbed all the water.
2. Cool until just tepid, then stir in the yeast creamed with 1 teaspoon of the sugar and blended with the tepid water. Either put into a warm place and allow to 'prove' quickly i.e. for about 40 minutes until well risen, or prepare dough overnight, put in storage cabinet of a refrigerator, then bring out into room temperature for about 20 minutes.
3. Blend in the flour, eggs, remaining sugar and a little milk if necessary to make a stiff batter.
4. Put again to 'prove' for 30 minutes until beginning to rise well.
5. Drop spoonfuls of the mixture into hot oil or fat. Fry until crisp and golden brown.
6. Drain well and toss in sugar. Eat hot or cold.

43

Herby scones

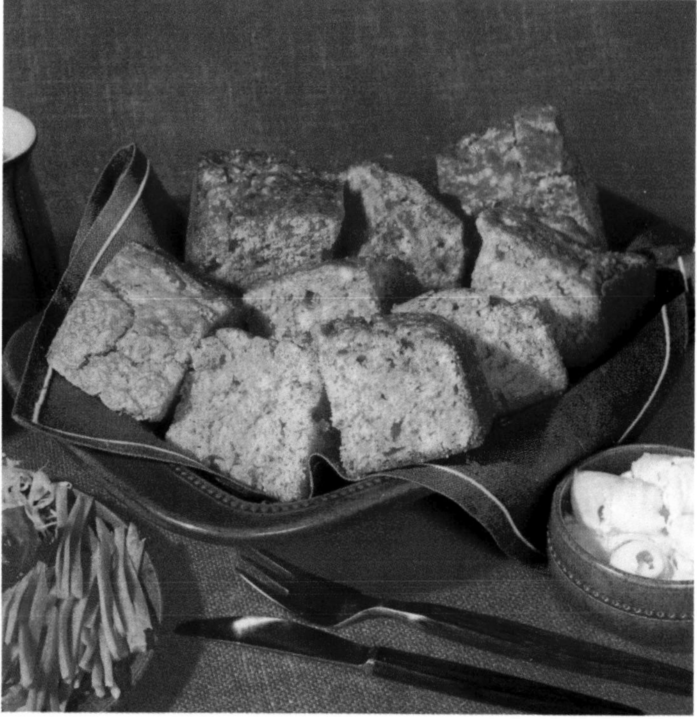

Cooking time: 45 min. **Preparation time:** 15 min. **Main cooking utensil:** 7-inch square cake tin/pan. **Oven temperature:** moderately hot, 400°F., 200°C., Gas Mark 5–6. **Oven position:** centre.

IMPERIAL

For approx. 12 scones you need:
12 oz. self-raising flour plus 1 teaspoon baking powder*

$\frac{1}{2}$ teaspoon salt
2 teaspoons sugar
3 oz. margarine
3 oz. shortening (cooking fat)
1 teaspoon mixed dried herbs
1–2 tablespoons chopped parsley
2 eggs
$\frac{1}{4}$ pint stock *or* water
2 tablespoons concentrated tomato purée
2 teaspoons Worcestershire sauce
1 tablespoon cold milk

AMERICAN

For approx. 12 scones you need:
3 cups all-purpose flour sifted with 4 teaspoons baking powder
$\frac{1}{2}$ teaspoon salt
2 teaspoons sugar
6 tablespoons margarine
6 tablespoons shortening
1 teaspoon mixed dried herbs
2–3 tablespoons chopped parsley
2 eggs
$\frac{2}{3}$ cup stock *or* water
3 tablespoons tomato paste

2 teaspoons Worcestershire sauce
1 tablespoon cold milk

**Or* plain flour with 4 level teaspoons baking power.

1. Sieve the dry ingredients into a bowl.
2. Rub in the fats until mixture resembles fine breadcrumbs.
3. Add the mixed herbs and parsley, and toss lightly to mix.
4. Beat the eggs, stock, tomato purée and Worcestershire sauce, mix well.
5. Add to the dry ingredients all at once, then mix lightly to a soft consistency with milk.
6. Turn into well-greased cake tin, and bake until firm to the touch, if necessary, reduce heat to very moderate after 25–30 minutes.
7. Turn out, cut into squares and serve warm with butter.

To serve: With salad ingredients. Top with butter and sliced cheese, or omit butter and top with a thick slice cheese or cream cheese and stiff apple purée.

To vary: Add 2–3 oz. (U.S. $\frac{1}{2}$–$\frac{3}{4}$ cup) grated cheese at Stage 2.

To store: In airtight tin for limited time, warm through in oven before serving.

Australia and New Zealand are both great farming countries and produce excellent meat, fruit and vegetables. Since so many of the people originally came from England much of the cooking is similar to the British, although with such good produce they tend to eat less starchy and more fresh food. There is always plenty of meat, particularly lamb and large tender steaks—they would consider most English steaks too small to be worthy of the name! Fruit is often cooked with grilled or roast meat, as in Apricot lamb and Orange steaks. And Duckling Nambucca, stuffed and garnished with fruit, is a delightful change from the familiar duck with orange, and makes a memorable meal.

The mild climate in Australia and New Zealand is perfect for picnics. Cold meat and salad are infinitely preferable to perpetual sandwiches. Sunrise meat loaf is easy to transport and attractive enough for a cold buffet on a hot day. Like the Americans, Australians love salads, adding variety and colour with fruit and nuts. The walnuts and apples in the Summer salad bowl, for example, transform an ordinary green salad into a delightful dish, perfect to serve with cold meats or cheese.

Of course, some Australian and New Zealand specialities depend on ingredients which are not available elsewhere. Unfortunately we can not sample swordfish steaks, Australian kangaroo tail soup, or New Zealand's *toheroas*, an expensive seafood delicacy not unlike oysters. Australia has a useful ingredient for sweet making called *copha*; it is made of vegetable fat and solidifies to just the right consistency for making delicious sweets without cooking. However, we can make most of the puddings and cakes on which both countries pride themselves. Meringue gâteau is known as Pavlova because it was created in honour of the famous Russian ballet dancer by a New Zealander. This dessert, consisting of a meringue base filled with whipped cream and passion fruit, peaches or other fruit, provides an elegant grande finale to any meal.

Australia and New Zealand are among the greatest tea drinking countries in the world and to go with it they bake many of the traditional English cakes and biscuits. Some new ones have been devised though, of which Afghans, scrumptuous rich chocolate biscuits, are especially great favourites with children.

Avocado cheese hors d'oeuvre

Preparation time: 10 min. **Main utensils:** sharp knife, bowl.

IMPERIAL

For 4 people you need:
For the mayonnaise:
1 egg yolk
good pinch, salt, pepper, dry mustard, sugar
1 tablespoon lemon juice
4 tablespoons oil

For the filling:
4 oz. Gorgonzola, Danish Blue *or* Stilton cheese
little lemon juice
seasoning, if wished

2 large ripe avocado pears
lemon juice

To garnish:
parsley

AMERICAN

For 4 people you need:
For the mayonnaise:
1 egg yolk
dash salt, pepper, dry mustard, sugar
1 tablespoon lemon juice
5 tablespoons oil

For the filling:
4 oz. Gorgonzola, Danish Blue, *or* Stilton cheese
little lemon juice
seasoning, if wished

2 large ripe avocados
lemon juice

To garnish:
parsley

1. Make the mayonnaise: this is lighter than usual as the flesh of avocado pears is so rich.
2. Blend the egg yolk, seasoning, including sugar, in a bowl. Add half the lemon juice and beat hard, gradually beat in oil until thickened slightly. Add the rest of the lemon juice.
3. Crumble the cheese into the mayonnaise and mix well.
4. Taste, add extra lemon juice and seasoning if wished.
5. Halve the pears, remove stones. If left standing, sprinkle flesh with lemon juice to prevent it turning dark.
6. Pile the cheese filling into the halved pears. Garnish with parsley.

To serve: As an hors d'oeuvre.

To vary: Fill with shellfish and mayonnaise.
Fill with an oil and vinegar dressing.
Fill with cream cheese, blended with chopped raisins, mayonnaise and chopped celery.

45

Orange steaks

Cooking time: about 10 min. **Preparation time:** 15 min. **Main cooking utensils:** string *or* metal or wooden skewers, grill pan/broiler.

IMPERIAL

For 4 people you need:
4 thick portions fillet, rump *or* sirloin steak

For the stuffing:
2 oz. butter
grated rind 1 orange and $\frac{1}{2}$ lemon
2 oz. almonds, chopped
2 oz. walnuts, chopped
2 oz. dried fruit, raisins, sultanas *or* diced, soaked and drained prunes *or* use a mixture
2 oz. breadcrumbs
seasoning
1 tablespoon orange juice

To grill:
2–3 oz. butter
juice 2 large oranges and 1 lemon

AMERICAN

For 4 people you need:
4 thick portions tenderloin *or* sirloin steak

For the stuffing:
$\frac{1}{4}$ cup butter
grated rind 1 orange and $\frac{1}{2}$ lemon
$\frac{1}{2}$ cup chopped almonds
$\frac{1}{2}$ cup chopped walnuts
$\frac{1}{3}$ cup dried fruit, *or* diced, soaked and drained prunes *or* use a mixture
1 cup soft bread crumbs
seasoning
1 tablespoon orange juice

To grill:
4–6 tablespoons butter
juice 2 large oranges and 1 lemon

1. Slit the meat halfway across to make a 'pocket'.
2. Soften the butter slightly, blend with all stuffing ingredients. Press together firmly, divide into 4 portions and insert into each 'pocket'.
3. Tie the meat or secure with small metal or wooden skewers so stuffing does not fall out.
4. Blend the melted butter for grilling with fruit juice, spoon half on to one side of the meat, put this uppermost on grid of grill pan.
5. Cook rapidly for 2–3 minutes, under a hot grill. Turn, spoon remaining butter mixture on second side. Continue cooking until the meat is as desired; remember stuffing will add to cooking time.

To serve: Pile or pipe creamed potato on to a dish, arrange meat on top. Garnish with orange slices and parsley.

NOTE: In Australia, steaks and chops are eaten for breakfast too. The fruit flavours given to meat dishes provide a change from the usual ingredients.

46

Apricot lamb

Cooking time: $2\frac{1}{2}$ hr. **Preparation time:** 25 min. plus time to soak apricots. **Main cooking utensils:** large saucepan, large covered casserole. **Oven temperature:** very moderate, 350°F., 180°C., Gas Mark 3–4. **Oven position:** centre.

IMPERIAL

For 5–7 people you need:
For the stuffing:
4 oz. dried apricots
2 oz. soft breadcrumbs
2–3 oz. cooked ham
1 egg
seasoning

For the meat and rice:
1 boned shoulder *or* best end neck lamb (latter serves 5)
2 oz. fat
5 oz. long grain rice
2 onions
1 red pepper
1 green pepper
$\frac{1}{2}$–1 tablespoon curry powder
1 stock cube
1 pint hot water

AMERICAN

For 5–7 people you need:
For the stuffing:
$\frac{2}{3}$ cup dried apricots
1 cup soft bread crumbs
approx. $\frac{1}{2}$ cup cooked ham
1 egg
seasoning

For the meat and rice:
1 rolled shoulder *or* loin roast lamb
$\frac{1}{4}$ cup fat
scant $\frac{3}{4}$ cup long grain rice
2 onions
1 sweet red pepper
1 sweet green pepper
$\frac{1}{2}$–1 tablespoon curry powder
1 bouillon cube
$2\frac{1}{2}$ cups hot water

1. First soak the apricots in water to cover, for several hours. Drain and chop (the apricot liquid could be used in place of some of the water at Stage 6).
2. Blend the apricots with the breadcrumbs, chopped ham and egg, season well.
3. Put on the meat and roll firmly, then secure with skewers or strong fine string.
4. Heat the fat in the saucepan, fry the meat until golden brown.
5. Put into the casserole, then toss rice with chopped onions, diced peppers, discarding cores and seeds, and curry powder, in any fat remaining in the saucepan.
6. Spoon into the casserole round the meat. Dissolve the stock cube in hot water (or water and apricot liquid), add and cover the casserole. Cook for $2–2\frac{1}{4}$ hours. Serve with stuffing and rice.

47

Duckling Nambucca

Cooking time: 2½ hr. **Preparation time:** 25 min. plus soaking of prunes. **Main cooking utensil:** roasting tin/pan. **Oven temperature:** very moderate, 350°F., 180°C., Gas Mark 3–4. **Oven position:** above centre.

IMPERIAL

For 4 people you need:
For the stuffing:
6 oz. prunes
4 oz. white bread (without crusts)

¼ pint milk
3 oz. blanched almonds
2 oz. stoned raisins
2 eggs
1 apple
5 lb. duck
seasoning
3 oz. honey
5 tablespoons white wine
1 teaspoon powdered ginger
5 tablespoons pineapple juice
4 tablespoons brandy

To garnish:
6 pineapple rings
6 glacé cherries
watercress sprigs

AMERICAN

For 4 people you need:
For the stuffing:
1 cup prunes
2 cups white bread (without crusts)
⅔ cup milk
⅔ cup blanched almonds
⅓ cup pitted raisins
2 eggs
1 apple
5 lb. duck
seasoning
¼ cup honey
6 tablespoons white wine
1 teaspoon ginger
6 tablespoons pineapple juice
⅓ cup brandy

To garnish:
6 pineapple rings
6 candied cherries
watercress sprigs

1. Soak the prunes overnight in cold water. Drain and stone, if necessary.
2. Soak the bread in milk for 10 minutes, then add chopped prunes, almonds, raisins and bind with the eggs. Add peeled, cored and sliced apple. Mix.
3. Put the stuffing into the duck and season very lightly with salt on the the outside. Place duck in a roasting tin; cook for 30 minutes.
4. Mix the honey, white wine, ginger, pineapple juice and half the brandy in a small bowl.
5. Add to the duck and continue roasting, basting every 30 minutes.
6. Add the pineapple rings 5 minutes before serving.

To serve: Place duck on a serving dish and garnish with pineapple rings, cherries and watercress. Pour sauce over after removing excess fat. Heat rest of brandy, pour over duck and ignite. To ignite brandy—make sure you have sufficient brandy to other liquid, i.e. 1 tablespoon brandy to each 4–5 tablespoons (U.S. 5–6 tablespoons) liquid, and heat thoroughly.

48

Sunrise meat loaf

Cooking time: 1 hr. 40 min. **Preparation time:** 20 min. **Main cooking utensils:** saucepan, 2-lb. loaf tin/pan. **Oven temperature:** very moderate to moderate, 350–375°F., 180–190°C., Gas Mark 4. **Oven position:** centre.

IMPERIAL

For 6 people you need:
7 *or* 8 eggs
2 oz. butter
3 oz. savoury biscuits, wholemeal *or* crackers, crushed
1½ lb. fresh brisket, topside *or* rump steak, *or* for economy choose minced stewing steak
4 oz. bacon
4 oz. soft white breadcrumbs
½–1 teaspoon mixed dried herbs
¼ pint milk
seasoning

Salad to serve with loaf:
2 tomatoes
lettuce
1 green pepper
1 red pepper
few spring onions
celery

AMERICAN

For 6 people you need:
7 *or* 8 eggs
¼ cup butter
generous 1 cup cracker crumbs

1½ lb. round, rump *or* chuck steak, *or* for economy choose ground beef
¼ lb. bacon or ham
2 cups soft white bread crumbs
½–1 teaspoon mixed dried herbs
⅔ cup milk
seasoning

Salad to serve with loaf:
2 tomatoes
lettuce
1 sweet green pepper
1 sweet red pepper
few scallions
celery

1. Hard-boil 6 or 7 of the eggs. Crack the shells when cooked and plunge into cold water; this prevents dark line forming round yolk.
2. Grease the sides and bottom of a tin with 1 oz. (U.S. 2 tablespoons) of the butter.
3. Crush biscuits (either in blender or on paper with a rolling pin).
4. Press two-thirds of these over the buttered surfaces.
5. Mince the beef and bacon, blend with breadcrumbs, herbs, raw egg and milk, season well. Press half the mixture into the tin.
6. Arrange 3 or 4 of the shelled eggs on this, cover with remaining meat mixture, then brush with 1 oz. (U.S. 2 tablespoons) melted butter and cover with remaining crumbs.
7. Bake for 1½ hours, lower heat if top of loaf becomes too brown.

To serve: Turn out when hot, cool, serve with salad made of remaining eggs, tomatoes, lettuce, peppers, spring onions and celery.

49

Summer salad bowl

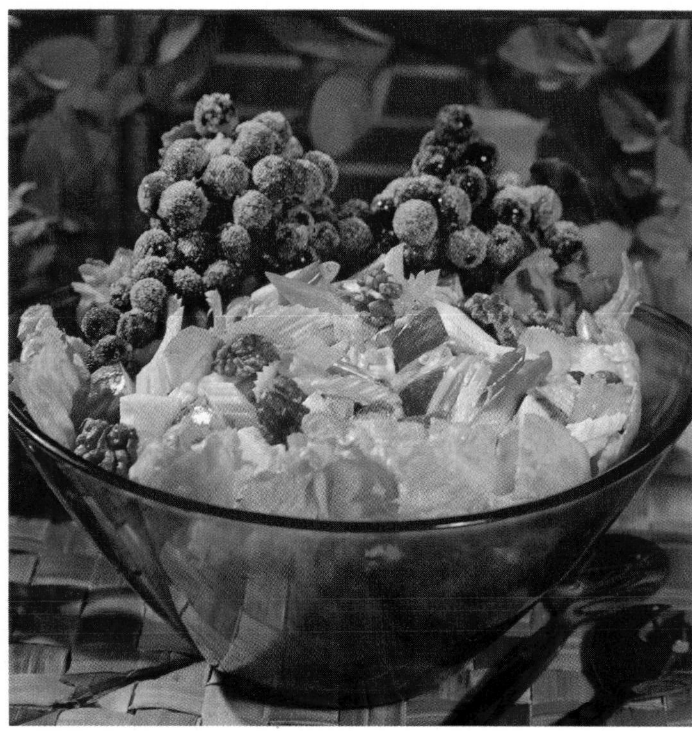

Preparation time: 15 min. **Main utensils:** screw-topped jar, salad bowl.

IMPERIAL

For 6–8 people you need:
3 eggs
1 lb. red dessert apples
juice 1 lemon
3 sticks celery
6 oz. walnut halves
8 shallots
5 tablespoons salad oil
3 tablespoons white wine
1 clove garlic
$\frac{1}{4}$ teaspoon salt
1 small lettuce

To garnish:
2 bunches grapes
1 egg white
2 oz. castor sugar

AMERICAN

For 6–8 people you need:
3 eggs
1 lb. red dessert apples
juice 1 lemon
3 stalks celery
$1\frac{1}{2}$ cups walnut halves
8 shallots
6 tablespoons salad oil
scant $\frac{1}{4}$ cup white wine
1 clove garlic
$\frac{1}{4}$ teaspoon salt
1 small lettuce

To garnish:
2 bunches grapes
1 egg white
$\frac{1}{4}$ cup granulated sugar

1. Hard boil the eggs.
2. Dice the apples and sprinkle with lemon juice to prevent them discolouring.
3. Combine in a basin with the chopped celery, walnut halves, sliced shallots and quartered eggs.
4. Place the oil, white wine, crushed garlic and the salt in a large screw-topped jar. Shake well.
5. Arrange the apple and celery mixture in a lettuce lined bowl and allow to chill.
6. Just before serving, pour over the salad dressing and toss lightly.
7. Garnish with bunches of grapes which have been brushed well with egg white and then tossed in the sugar.

To serve: This salad is delicious with rich meat such as duck, pork and ham or with cheese.

To vary: Add diced cheese, chicken, salmon, tuna or luncheon meat to the salad itself.

50

Pavlova
Meringue gâteau

Cooking time: 3–4 hr. **Preparation time:** 15 min. **Main cooking utensils:** greaseproof paper, baking tray/sheet, rose pipe/nozzle and bag/pastry bag. **Oven temperature:** see Stage 7. **Oven position:** centre *or* coolest part.

IMPERIAL

For 8–10 portions you need:
5 large egg whites
$1\frac{1}{2}$ teaspoons white vinegar
10 oz. castor sugar *or* 5 oz. castor sugar and 5 oz. sieved icing sugar
2 teaspoons cornflour

For the filling:
$\frac{1}{2}$ pint thick cream
6–8 fresh *or* canned peaches *or* $\frac{1}{2}$–$\frac{3}{4}$ pint fresh *or* canned passion fruit pulp, if available

AMERICAN

For 8–10 portions you need:
5 large egg whites
$1\frac{1}{2}$ teaspoons white vinegar
$1\frac{1}{4}$ cups sugar *or* $\frac{1}{2}$ cup plus 2 tablespoons sugar and generous 1 cup confectioners' sugar
2 teaspoons cornstarch

For the filling:
$1\frac{1}{4}$ cups whipping cream
6–8 fresh *or* canned peaches *or* $1\frac{1}{4}$–2 cups fresh *or* canned passion fruit pulp, if available

1. Whisk the egg whites until very stiff. Either use a bowl with hand or electric whisk, or a large plate with a palette knife.
2. Gradually whisk in the vinegar.
3. Blend the sugar and cornflour.
4. Gradually beat in half the sugar, then fold in remainder. There are other ways of incorporating this, it can *all* be folded in; or it can all be beaten in gradually, but beating and folding is generally the best, giving a stiff, shiny mixture.
5. Put the mixture into the bag to which the large rose pipe has been fitted.
6. Make a round of greaseproof paper, put on the tray, butter or oil lightly. Form a flan shape of meringue on this or spoon into shape.
7. Bake at the coolest temperature in the oven until firm to the touch.
8. Remove from the tray by lifting with a warmed palette knife, cool thoroughly.

To serve: Fill with whipped cream and sliced peaches or passion fruit pulp.

51

Citrus meringue gâteau

Cooking time: 2 hr. **Preparation time:** 30 min. **Main cooking utensils:** double saucepan, 8–9-inch sponge flan tin. **Oven temperature:** moderately hot, 400°F., 200°C., Gas Mark 5–6; then very cool, 200–275°F., 110°C., Gas Mark 0–$\frac{1}{4}$. **Oven position:** centre.

IMPERIAL	AMERICAN
For 6 portions you need:	For 6 portions you need:
For the curd:	For the curd:
1 large orange	1 large orange
1 large lemon	1 large lemon
8 oz. loaf sugar	generous 1 cup sugar
2 oz. butter	$\frac{1}{4}$ cup butter
2 egg yolks	2 egg yolks
For the sponge:	For the sponge:
2 eggs	2 eggs
3 oz. castor sugar	6 tablespoons granulated sugar
2 oz. self-raising flour	$\frac{1}{2}$ cup all-purpose flour, sifted with $\frac{1}{2}$ teaspoon baking powder
1 tablespoon hot water	1 tablespoon hot water
For the meringue:	For the meringue:
2 egg whites	2 egg whites
4 oz. castor sugar	$\frac{1}{2}$ cup granulated sugar

1. Rub the fruit with loaf sugar to extract zest from rind.
2. Put the fruit juice and sugar into a double saucepan and add the butter.
3. Heat well, then add beaten egg yolks and cook, without boiling, until curd coats the back of a wooden spoon.
4. Make the sponge by whisking eggs and sugar, fold in the well-sieved flour and hot water.
5. Put into a well-greased and floured sponge flan tin and bake until just firm—approximately 12 minutes; turn out carefully and cool.
6. Put the cold curd into the cold sponge. Top with the meringue made by whisking egg whites and gradually adding sugar.
7. Dry out in a very cool oven for about 1 hour.

To vary: For a soft texture, top filled flan with meringue and brown for few minutes only. Serve at once.

52

Afghans

Cooking time: 20–25 min. **Preparation time:** 20 min. **Main cooking utensils:** flat baking trays/sheets, wire rack. **Oven temperature:** very moderate to moderate, 350–375°F., 180–190°C., Gas Mark 4. **Oven position:** centre.

IMPERIAL	AMERICAN
To make about 25 biscuits you need:	To make about 25 biscuits you need:
7 oz. butter	$\frac{3}{4}$ cup plus 2 tablespoons butter
2 oz. castor sugar	$\frac{1}{4}$ cup granulated sugar
1 teaspoon vanilla essence	1 teaspoon vanilla extract
2–3 oz. dates (optional), chopped	approx. $\frac{1}{3}$ cup chopped dates (optional)
6 oz. plain flour	$1\frac{1}{2}$ cups all-purpose flour
$\frac{3}{4}$ oz. cocoa powder	scant $\frac{1}{4}$ cup unsweetened cocoa powder
1 teaspoon baking powder	1 teaspoon baking powder
2 oz. cornflakes	2 cups cornflakes
To decorate:	To decorate:
4–5 oz. icing sugar	approx. 1 cup confectioners' sugar
2 teaspoons cocoa powder	2 teaspoons unsweetened cocoa powder
water to mix	water to mix
approx. 12–13 glacé cherries	approx. 12–13 candied cherries

1. Cream the butter and sugar until soft and light, add vanilla essence and chopped dates.
2. Sieve the flour, cocoa and baking powder, crush cornflakes lightly.
3. Blend all of these into creamed butter and sugar.
4. Divide into small pieces, press hard to form into neat rounds.
5. Grease the trays well, place the biscuits on these, allowing a little room for them to spread.
6. Bake until firm to the touch, handle carefully while still warm.
7. Lift on to a wire rack when nearly cold. Allow to become quite cold before icing.
8. Blend the icing sugar, cocoa and enough water to give a soft spreading consistency.
9. Top each biscuit with a very little icing and a halved cherry.

To store: *Important* not to ice these biscuits until ready to serve, they keep well before icing, in an airtight tin.

AUSTRIA

So many dishes come to mind when one thinks of Austrian cooking that it is hard to know where to begin: soups, sweet and savoury dumplings, sausages, and probably best known of all, their beautiful rich gâteaux.

Austrians take a great interest in their food and eating ranks second only to music as a national pastime. Vienna prides itself on being the leading centre for both music and food, and great chefs like Sacher, the creator of *Sachertorte*, are almost as famous as Strauss. The great classic dish of Vienna is *Wiener Schnitzel*, tender fillets of veal expertly fried in egg and breadcrumbs. Two Viennese cakes are *Wienertorte*, a layer cake with an apricot filling, and *Wiener Marmor Gugelhupf*, a marble carnival cake baked in a special fluted *Gugelhupf* tin.

But one does not have to go to Vienna for good Austrian cooking. Throughout the country one finds all sorts of excellent dishes; there are various soups for example, often using unexpected ingredients—you will be surprised to find how delicious Beer soup and Apple soup are. Clear soups are often served, especially with dumplings. Meat dumplings in a soup or on their own make a meal in themselves, while plainer dumplings are served instead of potatoes with stews and roasts. Then there are the steamed or fried sweet dumplings filled with jam or fruit for a substantial hot dessert.

Some Austrian food is closely allied to German and Hungarian, reminiscent of the days when they were all part of the Austro-Hungarian Empire. Thus German sauerkraut and sausages are popular, as in Frankfurter and apple salad which makes an ideal hors d'oeuvre or light meal. From Hungarian cooking comes a fondness for paprika, a useful seasoning found in varying strengths. Nor do the Austrians neglect their southern neighbours, Italy and Yugoslavia: Stuffed artichokes and Stuffed pot roast of veal both bring a suggestion of the Mediterranean with their use of Parmesan cheese and anchovies.

Like the Germans, Austrians are great beer drinkers and love nothing more for an easy meal than plenty of rye bread and butter with sausages, cheese, pickled cucumbers and a generous supply of beer. For a more elegant cold meal, Ham cornets or Meat mould could be served as well. Austrian wines are world famous, ranging from full-bodied red wines to the most delicate of white wines. For special occasions, *Erdbeerbowle* or Strawberry bowl, originally made with wild strawberries from the Austrian alps, is a refreshing wine punch for the summer.

Austrians do not usually begin the day with a cooked meal but have several kinds of bread and rolls with butter and ham, and tea or coffee to drink. They will often have a biscuit or roll with their morning coffee as well and in former times this became virtually a second breakfast. Lunch always used to be the main meal of the day and in many places it still is, but with the pressures of the working day it is becoming more common to eat a light lunch and have the larger meal in the evening.

No matter what meal routine they follow, however, everyone enjoys stopping for the afternoon *jause*, the Austrian equivalent of the English tea. Sometimes this almost amounts to an entire meal, beginning with sandwiches and going on to plain cakes like *Kuchenbrot* and perhaps some small cakes like Fruit loaves or Prune-filled cakes. Last but not least there will almost invariably be one of the mouth-watering tortes or gâteaux for which Austria is so renowned. Nothing is more delightful than to go into a pâtisserie in the afternoon and choose from the vast array of beautiful cakes. A great deal of skill goes into making them but Chocolate gâteau with almonds and Viennese layer cake are not too difficult and your efforts are sure to win approval. Strudels are another Austrian delicacy which may be served in the afternoon or as a dessert. Making the paper-thin strudel pastry is quite an art but is soon mastered with a little practice. Apple strudel is the most familiar filling, but cherry, peach and cream-filled strudels are delicious variations. You will be offered tea, chocolate or coffee with whichever pastry you choose; your chocolate or coffee will probably be topped with a flourish of whipped cream and perhaps sprinkled with cinnamon or grated chocolate for that final Austrian touch.

53

Apfelsuppe
Apple soup

Cooking time: 40–45 min. **Preparation time:** 20 min. if sieving, 12–15 min. if blending. **Main cooking utensil:** saucepan.

IMPERIAL

For 4 people you need:
1 oz. butter
1 medium-sized onion
1–2 teaspoons curry powder
1 tablespoon cornflour
2 medium-sized cooking apples
1 pint clear white stock
1 tablespoon sugar
seasoning
1 lemon
2 egg yolks
$\frac{1}{4}$ pint thick cream

To garnish:
1 dessert apple
lemon juice
watercress

AMERICAN

For 4 people you need:
2 tablespoons butter
1 medium-sized onion
1–2 teaspoons curry powder
1 tablespoon cornstarch
2 medium-sized baking apples
$2\frac{1}{2}$ cups clear white stock
1 tablespoon sugar
seasoning
1 lemon
2 egg yolks
$\frac{2}{3}$ cup whipping cream

To garnish:
1 eating apple
lemon juice
watercress

1. Heat the butter, fry chopped onion until tender, but do not brown.
2. Blend in the curry powder and cornflour.
3. Cook for several minutes, then add diced apples and stock slowly.
4. Bring to the boil, stirring well until slightly thickened. Add the sugar, seasoning, grated lemon rind and juice and simmer for 30 minutes.
5. Sieve or put into a blender. Stir egg yolks, blended with the cream, into the hot soup.* Either chill or reheat gently.
6. Garnish with diced dessert apple sprinkled with lemon juice, and watercress.

*Even if serving cold, egg and cream should be cooked for a short time if soup has become cold when sieving.

To serve: Hot or chilled.

54

Biersuppe
Beer soup

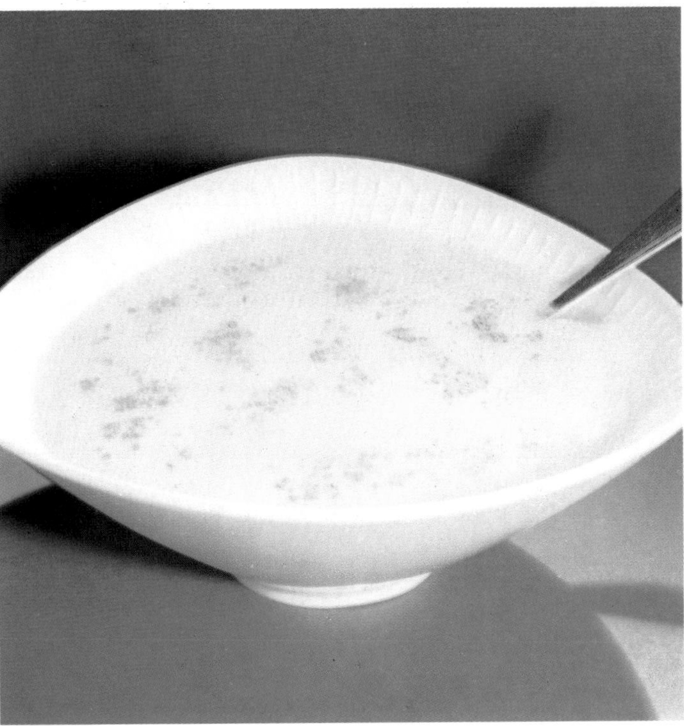

Cooking time: 20 min. The variation will take about 30 min. **Preparation time:** 10 min. **Main cooking utensil:** saucepan.

IMPERIAL

For 4 people you need:
2 oz. butter
$1\frac{1}{2}$ oz. flour
2 pints German light lager
2 eggs
$\frac{1}{2}$ lemon*
1 oz. sugar**
powdered cinnamon to taste
seasoning

To garnish:
powdered cinnamon

AMERICAN

For 4 people you need:
$\frac{1}{4}$ cup butter
6 tablespoons all-purpose flour
5 cups German light lager
2 eggs
$\frac{1}{2}$ lemon*
2 tablespoons sugar**
powdered cinnamon to taste
seasoning

To garnish:
powdered cinnamon

*Grate rind or add in strips.
**Add the sugar gradually as tastes vary and it may be too sweet if the full quantity of sugar is used, although German and Austrian beer soups are slightly sweet.

The idea of beer as a basis for a soup may be an unexpected one, but this does produce a delicious flavour. Do not use a dark beer.

1. Heat the butter in the saucepan, then stir in the flour and let the 'roux' become a golden brown. Stir well as the mixture turns colour, for the flavour is spoiled if it becomes too dark.
2. Stir in the beer and allow the soup to simmer for about 10 minutes.
3. Whisk the eggs well. Remove the soup from the heat, add the eggs, lemon juice and rind, sugar, cinnamon and any seasoning desired.
4. Heat gently for a minute only, then pour into hot soup bowls.

To serve: Garnish with a little more powdered cinnamon and serve with toast or crisp biscuits.

To vary: Use $1\frac{1}{2}$ pints (U.S. $3\frac{3}{4}$ cups) beer, $\frac{1}{2}$ pint (U.S. $1\frac{1}{4}$ cups) thin cream, 3 egg yolks, seasoning and 1–2 oz. (U.S. 2 tablespoons–$\frac{1}{4}$ cup) sugar and cinnamon to taste. Cook in the top of a double saucepan over *hot*, but not boiling, water until the soup thickens slightly.

55

Gefüllter Kalbsbraten

Stuffed pot roast of veal

Cooking time: see Stage 4 plus 15 min. to brown. **Preparation time:** 30 min. **Main cooking utensil:** large casserole. **Oven temperature:** moderate, 375°F., 190°C., Gas Mark 4–5. **Oven position:** above centre.

IMPERIAL

For 6–8 people you need:
For the stuffing:
2 onions
1 can anchovy fillets
4 oz. soft breadcrumbs
2 oz. butter
seasoning
2 egg yolks
$\frac{1}{4}$ pint soured cream

4–5 lb. boned *or* loin veal (weight before boning)
2 oz. butter
$\frac{3}{4}$ pint brown stock
3–4 onions, sliced
1 lb. young carrots
seasoning

To garnish:
parsley *or* watercress

AMERICAN

For 6–8 people you need:
For the stuffing:
2 onions
1 can anchovy fillets
2 cups soft bread crumbs
$\frac{1}{4}$ cup butter
seasoning
2 egg yolks
$\frac{2}{3}$ cup sour cream

4–5 lb. boned veal loin (weight before boning)
$\frac{1}{4}$ cup butter
2 cups brown stock
3–4 onions, sliced
1 lb. young carrots
seasoning

To garnish:
parsley *or* watercress

1. Chop the onions very finely. Blend with chopped and pounded anchovies, breadcrumbs, melted butter, seasoning, egg yolks and soured cream.
2. Form the stuffing into a neat roll, lay in the centre of the boned veal and roll tightly. Secure with skewers or string.
3. Heat the butter in a casserole, turn meat in this to brown all round, then add stock and vegetables, season well.
4. Cover the casserole and cook in a moderate oven, allowing 40 minutes per lb. and 40 minutes over.

To serve: With unthickened stock, vegetables and garnished with parsley or watercress.

To vary: Lift veal out of casserole, stir soured cream into stock. Heat but do not boil, then serve as a sauce.

56

Fleischknödel

Meat dumplings

Cooking time: 55 min. **Preparation time:** 35 min. **Main cooking utensils:** frying pan/skillet, 2 saucepans.

IMPERIAL

For 4 people you need:
5 oz. butter
2 oz. white bread, without crusts
6–8 rashers bacon (fairly fat)
3 onions
1 oz. flour
1–2 teaspoons paprika pepper
$2\frac{1}{2}$ pints stock (chicken, beef *or* ham)
$1\frac{1}{2}$ lb. tomatoes
2–3 tablespoons tomato purée
seasoning
2 teaspoons sugar
6 oz. self-raising flour

4 oz. pork, beef *or* liver, chopped
1–2 teaspoons chopped mixed fresh herbs *or* pinch dried
1 egg
water

AMERICAN

For 4 people you need:
$\frac{1}{2}$ cup plus 2 tablespoons butter
1 cup white bread, without crusts
6–8 bacon slices
3 onions
$\frac{1}{4}$ cup all-purpose flour
1–2 teaspoons paprika pepper
$6\frac{1}{4}$ cups stock (chicken, beef *or* ham)
$1\frac{1}{2}$ lb. tomatoes
3–4 tablespoons tomato paste
seasoning
2 teaspoons sugar
$1\frac{1}{2}$ cups all-purpose flour, sifted with $1\frac{1}{2}$ teaspoons baking powder
$\frac{1}{2}$ cup minced pork, beef *or* liver
1–2 teaspoons chopped mixed fresh herbs *or* dash dried
1 egg
water

1. Heat 2 oz. (U.S. $\frac{1}{4}$ cup) butter in pan, cook diced bread until golden, cool; make sure cubes of bread are not too large.
2. Fry the bacon lightly, chop 2 oz. of this for dumplings, cut remainder into fairly large pieces, keep hot or re-heat when required.
3. Add 1 oz. (U.S. 2 tablespoons) butter and fry 1 chopped onion, lift out, cool for the dumplings.
4. Heat the remainder of the butter in a saucepan, fry sliced or chopped onions for the sauce. Stir in the flour, paprika blended with $\frac{1}{2}$ pint (U.S. $1\frac{1}{4}$ cups) stock, chopped tomatoes, tomato purée, seasoning and sugar. Simmer gently for 45 minutes, sieve if wished.
5. Sieve the flour with seasoning, add finely chopped or minced meat, chopped bacon, onion and diced bread. Stir in the herbs, bind with egg, and water if necessary.
6. Press together, then spoon out 4 portions and cook steadily in remaining boiling stock for 25 minutes. Garnish with large pieces of bacon, tomato quarters and parsley. Serve on the sauce.

57

Wiener Schnitzel
Coated fried fillet of veal

Cooking time: 15 min. **Preparation time:** 10 min. **Main cooking utensil:** large frying pan/skillet.

IMPERIAL

For 4 people you need:

WIENER SCHNITZEL
4 fillets veal

To coat:
little flour, seasoning
1 egg
2–3 oz. stale, fine breadcrumbs

To fry:
3 oz. butter

RAHMSCHNITZEL
Ingredients as above, but no egg *or* crumbs

For the sauce:
$\frac{1}{2}$ pint thin cream
seasoning
paprika pepper
mustard
lemon juice to taste
1 tablespoon capers

AMERICAN

For 4 people you need:

WIENER SCHNITZEL
4 veal scallops *or* cutlets

To coat:
little flour, seasoning
1 egg
$\frac{1}{2}$–$\frac{3}{4}$ cup stale, fine bread crumbs

To fry:
6 tablespoons butter

RAHMSCHNITZEL
Ingredients as above, but no egg *or* crumbs

For the sauce:
1$\frac{1}{4}$ cups coffee cream
seasoning
paprika pepper
mustard
lemon juice to taste
1 tablespoon capers

1. Flatten the pieces of veal if wished.
2. Wash and dry, then coat in seasoned flour.
3. Blend the egg and a little water, brush meat with this; if the pieces of veal are large, 2 eggs may be needed.
4. Coat with breadcrumbs, pressing these against the meat firmly.
5. Heat butter, then fry meat on both sides until golden. Lower heat, continue cooking to make sure veal is tender. Drain.

To serve: Garnish with slices of lemon. Other garnishes used are: chopped hard-boiled egg, anchovy fillets and olives.

RAHMSCHNITZEL – Coat veal with flour only, fry in hot butter until tender, lift out. Add sauce ingredients. Heat, pour over veal.

58

Champagner-Kraut
Sauerkraut and steak party style

Cooking time: 40 min. **Preparation time:** 15 min. **Main cooking utensils:** saucepan, frying pan/skillet *or* grill pan/broil pan.

IMPERIAL

For 4 people you need:
approx. 1 lb. sauerkraut
$\frac{1}{2}$ pint champagne *or* sparkling white wine
1 medium-sized can pineapple rings
5 oz. butter
good pinch mild paprika pepper
good pinch onion seasoning *or* garlic salt
good pinch cayenne pepper
4 rump *or* fillet steaks
1 tablespoon chopped parsley *or* mixed fresh herbs

To garnish:
paprika pepper

AMERICAN

For 4 people you need:
approx. 1 lb. sauerkraut
1$\frac{1}{4}$ cups champagne *or* sparkling white wine
1 medium-sized can pineapple rings
$\frac{1}{2}$ cup plus 2 tablespoons butter
good dash mild paprika pepper
good dash onion seasoning *or* garlic salt
good dash cayenne pepper
4 tenderloin *or* sirloin steaks
1 tablespoon chopped parsley *or* mixed fresh herbs

To garnish:
paprika pepper

1. Wash the sauerkraut well, leave to drain for a short time.
2. Put into a saucepan with the wine, pineapple juice, 1 oz. (U.S. 2 tablespoons) butter and seasonings.
3. Cover and simmer gently until tender, stirring from time to time.
4. Lift the lid towards the end of the cooking time so excess liquid evaporates; but the sauerkraut should have plenty of wine and pineapple sauce.
5. Meanwhile, either grill the steaks, basting well with 2 oz. (U.S. $\frac{1}{4}$ cup) butter as they cook, or fry in the butter until tender.
6. Blend the remaining butter with parsley or mixed herbs and form into neat pats.

To serve: Cut pineapple rings in portions, arrange sauerkraut and wine sauce on dish, put pineapple round. Top with paprika pepper. Place steaks on sauerkraut and top with butter pats.

To vary: Use a little orange juice instead of pineapple juice and garnish dish with cooked vegetables. Use ordinary cabbage instead of sauerkraut, seasoning well.

59

Schweinefleisch in Teig
High domed meat pie

Cooking time: 1 hr. 25 min. **Preparation time:** 30 min. plus time for pastry to stand. **Main cooking utensils:** frying pan/skillet, 6–7-inch shallow ovenproof dish. **Oven temperature:** hot, 425–450°F., 220–230°C., Gas Mark 6–7 then 375°F., 190°C., Gas Mark 4–5. **Oven position:** centre.

IMPERIAL

For 5–6 people you need:
6 oz. fat bacon rashers
$1\frac{1}{2}$ lb. pork
8 oz. veal *or* beef
2 onions
2 oz. butter
3 oz. soft breadcrumbs
$\frac{1}{4}$ pint milk
1 tablespoon chopped parsley
seasoning
1 teaspoon French mustard
1–2 teaspoons paprika pepper

For the pastry:
8 oz. flour, preferably plain
pinch salt
1 tablespoon oil

To glaze:
1 egg

AMERICAN

For 5–6 people you need:
$\frac{1}{3}$ lb. bacon slices
$1\frac{1}{2}$ lb. pork
$\frac{1}{2}$ lb. veal *or* beef
2 onions
$\frac{1}{4}$ cup butter
$1\frac{1}{2}$ cups soft bread crumbs
$\frac{2}{3}$ cup milk
1 tablespoon chopped parsley
seasoning
1 teaspoon French mustard
1–2 teaspoons paprika pepper

For the pastry:
2 cups all-purpose flour
dash salt
1 tablespoon oil

To glaze:
1 egg

1. Remove the rind from the bacon. Put the bacon, pork and veal through a mincer.
2. Chop the onions, fry in hot butter until soft.
3. Put the breadcrumbs into a basin, add milk and leave for a short time. Beat until smooth and add to minced meat with onions.
4. Blend with parsley, seasoning, mustard and paprika pepper.
5. Sieve the flour and salt, add oil. Blend with water until an elastic dough.
6. Knead well and leave for 30 minutes if possible. Roll, pull and stretch until very thin indeed. You should be able to read a paper through the strudel pastry!
7. Roll out to a very large round, enclose meat filling in this. Gently mould until the size of the container (pastry is very pliable).
8. Grease the container, put in 'pie' and brush with beaten egg. Bake for 25 minutes in hot oven, then about 45 minutes in a moderate oven.

To serve: Cold with salad or hot with vegetables.

60

Fleischsulze
Meat mould

Cooking time: 10 min. **Preparation time:** 30 min. plus setting time. **Main cooking utensils:** 3 saucepans, 4-pint mould/5-pint mold.

IMPERIAL

For 8–10 people you need:
3 pint packets aspic jelly
$2\frac{1}{2}$ pints water *or* stock
$\frac{1}{2}$ teaspoon dried sage
$\frac{1}{2}$ teaspoon dried chervil
3 eggs
4–5 gherkins
1 green pepper
1 red pepper
1 lb. firm tomatoes
$1\frac{1}{2}$ lb. cooked ham
8 oz. cooked beef *or* pork, chopped

To garnish:
2 onions, parsley

AMERICAN

For 8–10 people you need:
4 ($\frac{1}{4}$-oz.) envelopes gelatin
$6\frac{1}{4}$ cups water *or* stock
$\frac{1}{2}$ teaspoon dried sage
$\frac{1}{2}$ teaspoon dried chervil
3 eggs
4–5 sweet dill pickles
1 sweet green pepper
1 sweet red pepper
1 lb. firm tomatoes
$1\frac{1}{2}$ lb. cooked cured ham
$1\frac{1}{3}$ cups cooked, chopped beef *or* pork

To garnish:
2 onions, parsley

To prepare a mould so that savoury jelly turns out well, brush very lightly with oil *or* rinse out in cold water and do not dry.

1. Dissolve the aspic jelly in $2\frac{1}{4}$ pints (U.S. $5\frac{2}{3}$ cups) boiling water or stock; less liquid is used as tomatoes and blanched peppers provide extra liquid.
2. Pour $\frac{3}{4}$ pint (U.S. 2 cups) into a basin, for jelly garnish round mould and add remaining $\frac{1}{4}$ pint (U.S. $\frac{2}{3}$ cup) hot liquid; allow to set.
3. Add the herbs to the hot jelly, keep liquid warm.
4. Spoon $\frac{1}{2}$ pint (U.S. $1\frac{1}{4}$ cups) into prepared mould, turn round in mould until it coats base and sides.
5. Hard-boil, shell and slice the eggs, cut gherkins in pieces. 'Blanch' the peppers in boiling salted water for 10 minutes, drain. Skin, remove seeds and chop the tomatoes.
6. Arrange the eggs, peppers and strips of ham on set jelly, brush with liquid jelly so they adhere.
7. Either continue arranging vegetables, eggs and chopped meat in layers or when the garnish is set, blend with *cold* liquid jelly and spoon carefully into the mould.
8. Turn out when set. Garnish with lightly whisked jelly, rings of raw onion and parsley.

61

Artischockenböden
Stuffed artichokes

Cooking time: 50–55 min. **Preparation time:** 20 min. **Main cooking utensils:** saucepan, ovenproof dish.

IMPERIAL

For 6 people you need:
6 large globe artichokes
seasoning
little artichoke stock
1 tablespoon olive oil
6 oz. Gruyère cheese, grated
1–2 oz. Parmesan cheese, grated
1 egg
1 can anchovy fillets
1 medium bread roll
1 tablespoon chopped parsley
grated rind 1 lemon
squeeze lemon juice

To garnish:
hard-boiled egg

For the cheese butter:
2 oz. butter
1 oz. Parmesan cheese, grated
1 oz. Gruyère cheese, grated

AMERICAN

For 6 people you need:
6 large globe artichokes
seasoning
little artichoke stock
1 tablespoon olive oil
$1\frac{1}{2}$ cups grated Gruyère cheese
$\frac{1}{4}$–$\frac{1}{2}$ cup grated Parmesan cheese
1 egg
1 can anchovy fillets
1 medium bread roll
1 tablespoon chopped parsley
grated rind 1 lemon
squeeze lemon juice

To garnish:
hard-cooked egg

For the cheese butter:
$\frac{1}{4}$ cup butter
$\frac{1}{4}$ cup each grated Parmesan and Gruyère cheese

1. Trim the tops from the artichokes, cook steadily in well seasoned water until tender. Remove the centre chokes when cool enough to handle.
2. Stand the vegetables in an ovenproof dish with a little stock in the bottom, brush sides of the artichokes with oil.
3. Blend the grated cheeses, egg, oil from can of anchovies, crumbs from the roll, parsley, lemon rind and juice together. Save 6 anchovy fillets for garnish, but any left can be chopped and added to stuffing.
4. Press the stuffing in the centre and over tops of the artichokes.
5. Bake for 20–25 minutes in oven until very hot.
6. Top with rolled anchovy fillets.
7. Garnish with sliced hard-boiled egg and pats of cheese-flavoured butter made by beating all the ingredients together until well blended.

To serve: This is excellent with poached eggs and/or mushrooms or other edible fungi or white truffles.

62

Geduenstete Gurken
Stewed cucumber

Cooking time: 20–25 min. **Preparation time:** 15 min. **Main cooking utensil:** saucepan.

IMPERIAL

For 6 people you need:
2 medium-sized cucumbers
4 large carrots
2 medium-sized onions
2 oz. butter
$\frac{1}{2}$ pint white stock *or* water and chicken stock cube
1 tablespoon lemon juice
seasoning
1 teaspoon dill seeds

AMERICAN

For 6 people you need:
2 medium-sized cucumbers
4 large carrots
2 medium-sized onions
$\frac{1}{4}$ cup butter
$1\frac{1}{4}$ cups white stock *or* water and chicken bouillon cube
1 tablespoon lemon juice
seasoning
1 teaspoon dill seeds

1. Cut the unpeeled cucumbers into slices about 1-inch in thickness.
2. Peel the carrots, cut into slices about $\frac{1}{4}$-inch thick.
3. Chop the onions very finely.
4. Toss the vegetables in the hot butter.
5. Add the stock, lemon juice, seasoning and dill seeds.
6. Simmer steadily until the cucumber is very soft and the carrot tender. Take the lid off the pan for the last 10 minutes cooking time so liquid evaporates.

To serve: With meats (especially pork).

To vary: Lift the vegetables from the pan, blend with $\frac{1}{4}$ pint (U.S. $\frac{2}{3}$ cup) soured cream and top with paprika pepper.

63

Schinkenstanitzl
Ham cornets

Cooking time: 25 min. **Preparation time:** 10 min. **Main cooking utensils:** 2 saucepans, 8 cocktail sticks/toothpicks.

IMPERIAL

For 4 people you need:
1 onion
2 tablespoons oil
5 oz. long grain rice
½ pint water
seasoning
¼ teaspoon paprika pepper
1 clove garlic
1 bay leaf
1 sprig lemon thyme
juice ½ lemon
4 oz. fresh, frozen *or* canned peas

1 green pepper
3 oz. cream cheese
8 slices pressed ham *or* use Mortadella as in picture

AMERICAN

For 4 people you need:
1 onion
3 tablespoons oil
approx. ⅔ cup long grain rice
1¼ cups water
seasoning
¼ teaspoon paprika pepper
1 clove garlic
1 bay leaf
1 sprig lemon thyme
juice ½ lemon
¾ cup fresh, frozen *or* canned peas
1 sweet green pepper
6 tablespoons cream cheese
8 slices pressed ham *or* use Mortadella as in picture

1. Grate or chop the onion very finely, cook for 5 minutes in the oil.
2. Add the rice and water, bring to the boil. Add seasoning, paprika, crushed garlic, bay leaf, lemon thyme and lemon juice.
3. Bring to the boil, stir, cover pan and lower heat, cook for 15 minutes.
4. Meanwhile cook the peas in seasoned water, drain; or drain canned peas.
5. Blend the peas and rice, cool. Add any extra seasoning, remove bay leaf and sprig of thyme.
6. Boil strips of green pepper in salted water until soft (this could be done with the peas).
7. Spread the cream cheese in centre of each slice of ham or Mortadella, top with rice mixture.
8. Insert the cocktail sticks in each slice of ham to make the shape of a 'cornet' each end. Garnish with pepper strips.

To serve: Cold with green salad or beetroot.

64

Frankfurter mit Apfelsalat
Frankfurter and apple salad

Preparation time: 10 min. **Main utensil:** mixing bowl.

IMPERIAL

For 8 people as a light hors d'oeuvre or 4 as a main course you need:
8 frankfurter sausages
3 red dessert apples
juice 1 lemon
1 lettuce

For the dressing:
4 tablespoons mayonnaise
4 tablespoons chutney
seasoning

To garnish:
1–2 onions
parsley

AMERICAN

For 8 people as a light hors d'oeuvre or 4 as a main course you need:
8 frankfurter sausages
3 red dessert apples
juice 1 lemon
1 lettuce

For the dressing:
⅓ cup mayonnaise
⅓ cup chutney *or* relish
seasoning

To garnish:
1–2 onions
parsley

Austrian salads are varied. Many include peppers and potatoes and are blended with delicious potato mayonnaise—made by blending approximately 4 oz. thinly sliced, cooked potatoes and ½ tablespoon mustard with ¼ pint (U.S. ⅔ cup) mayonnaise.

1. Cut the frankfurters into bite-sized pieces.
2. Dice the cored, unpeeled apples and toss in the lemon juice.
3. Mix the mayonnaise, chutney and seasoning for the dressing together.
4. Arrange lettuce on individual platters.
5. Pile the frankfurter pieces and apple on top.
6. Add the dressing and garnish with onion, cut into rings, and parsley.

To serve: As a light meal or hors d'oeuvre.

65

Zwetschkenknödel
Plum dumplings

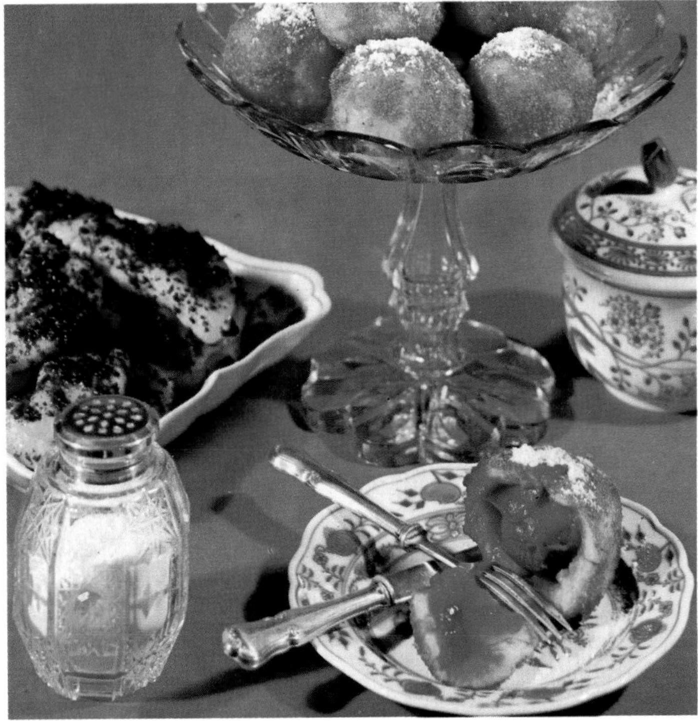

Cooking time: 10–15 min. **Preparation time:** 25 min. plus 1 hr. 15 min. to prove. **Main cooking utensils:** frying pan/skillet *or* deep fat pan.

IMPERIAL

For 10–12 dumplings you need:
¼ oz. fresh yeast
¼ pint tepid milk
2 teaspoons sugar
10 oz. plain flour
1 oz. butter

To fry:
deep fat

To coat:
sugar

To fill:
10–12 large firm plums
sugar

AMERICAN

For 10–12 dumplings you need:
¼ cake compressed yeast
⅔ cup tepid milk
2 teaspoons sugar
2½ cups all-purpose flour
2 tablespoons butter

To fry:
deep fat

To coat:
sugar

To fill:
10–12 large firm plums
sugar

1. Cream the yeast, add the milk and leave for 15 minutes in warm place.
2. Blend the sugar with the flour and rub in the butter. Add the yeast liquid and knead.
3. Cover, allow to 'prove' for 1 hour, or until double in bulk.
4. Knead well, divide into 10–12 portions and wrap round the stoned plums, adding sugar to fruit.
5. Allow to 'prove' for 15–20 minutes, then fry steadily for about 10 minutes in hot fat.
6. Drain and coat in sugar.

66

Früchtenbrot
Fruit loaves

Cooking time: 20 min. **Preparation time:** 35 min. plus time for dough to 'prove'. **Main cooking utensils:** baking trays/sheets, small saucepan. **Oven temperature:** moderate, 375°F., 190°C., Gas Mark 4–5. **Oven position:** centre.

IMPERIAL

For 10 cakes you need:
For the filling:
2 oz. walnuts and hazelnuts
1 oz. pistachio nuts *or* almonds
8 oz. seedless raisins
grated rind 1 orange
1 oz. ground almonds
2 oz. fine biscuit crumbs
2 tablespoons Kirsch
3 oz. sugar
1 tablespoon rum

For the yeast dough:
8 oz. plain flour, salt
1½ oz. sugar
½ oz. yeast *or* 1 teaspoon dried yeast, poor weight
approx. 6 tablespoons milk
1 egg yolk
1½ oz. butter
1 egg
1½–2 oz. blanched almonds, chopped

AMERICAN

For 10 cakes you need:
For the filling:
½ cup walnuts and hazelnuts
¼ cup pistachio nuts *or* almonds
1⅓ cups seedless raisins
grated rind 1 orange
¼ cup ground almonds
¾ cup fine cookie crumbs
3 tablespoons Kirsch
6 tablespoons sugar
1 tablespoon rum

For the yeast dough:
2 cups all-purpose flour, salt
3 tablespoons sugar
½ cake compressed yeast *or* 1 teaspoon dry yeast, poor weight
approx. ½ cup milk
1 egg yolk
3 tablespoons butter
1 egg
¼–½ cup chopped blanched almonds

1. Chop the nuts and raisins, mix with other filling ingredients.
2. Sieve flour and salt into a bowl, add sugar if using fresh yeast.
3. Cream yeast, add tepid milk, put into centre of the flour together with egg yolk and melted, but cooled butter. If using dried yeast, sprinkle on to the tepid milk with about a teaspoon of sugar; the remaining sugar is added to the flour.
4. Mix all these ingredients well together, then knead lightly until a smooth dough, adding any extra flour necessary.
5. Do not allow to 'prove' at this stage, but roll out until very thin. Cut into squares, put filling in the centre of each, dampen edges and seal.
6. Turn so sealed edges are underneath, put on to lightly greased trays.
7. Brush with egg yolk and leave to 'prove' for about 30 minutes.
8. Brush with egg white and scatter almonds on top. Bake.

67

Kuchen mit Backpflaumen

Prune-filled cakes

Cooking time: about 5 min. **Preparation time:** 20 min., plus time to soak prunes if necessary (see Stage 1). **Main cooking utensil:** deep fat pan.

IMPERIAL

For 12 cakes you need:
12 large prunes
little boiling water (see Stage 1)
12 blanched almonds *or*
2 oz. cream cheese

Coating for frying:
4 oz. plain *or* self-raising flour
pinch salt
1 oz. sugar
1 egg
$\frac{1}{4}$ pint milk, white wine *or* cider
fat *or* oil for frying

To decorate:
2 oz. sugar
2 oz. plain chocolate

AMERICAN

For 12 cakes you need:
12 large prunes
little boiling water (see Stage 1)
12 blanched almonds *or*
$\frac{1}{4}$ cup cream cheese

Coating for frying:
1 cup all-purpose flour
dash salt
2 tablespoons sugar
1 egg
$\frac{2}{3}$ cup milk, white wine *or* cider
fat *or* oil for frying

To decorate:
$\frac{1}{4}$ cup sugar
2 oz. semi-sweet chocolate

1. If using tenderized 'pitted' prunes, just cover with boiling water. Leave while preparing coating, and drain. Ordinary prunes should be soaked and lightly cooked, then drained and stoned.
2. Fill the prunes with almonds or cream cheese.
3. Crust for frying: Blend ingredients together to give a smooth batter. Dip the filled prunes in this, making sure they are evenly coated. Fry in hot fat or oil until crisp and golden brown. Drain on absorbent paper.
4. Roll in the sugar and sprinkle grated chocolate on top. Serve hot.

68

Apfel Strudel

Apple pastry

Cooking time: 50 min. **Preparation time:** 45 min. **Main cooking utensils:** frying pan/skillet, baking tray/sheet. **Oven temperature:** hot, 425–450°F., 220–230°C., Gas Mark 6–7, then very moderate to moderate, 350–375°F., 180–190°C., Gas Mark 4. **Oven position:** centre.

IMPERIAL

For 6–7 portions you need:
10 oz. flour, preferably plain
pinch salt
1 tablespoon oil
1 egg

For the filling:
3 oz. soft brown breadcrumbs
$3\frac{1}{2}$ oz. butter
$1\frac{1}{2}$ lb. cooking apples, weight after peeling
3 oz. sugar, preferably brown
4 oz. sultanas
3 oz. almonds, chopped, blanched
1 teaspoon cinnamon
3 oz. chopped mixed candied peel

To decorate:
1–2 oz. icing sugar
apple segments

AMERICAN

For 6–7 portions you need:
$2\frac{1}{2}$ cups all-purpose flour
dash salt
1 tablespoon oil
1 egg

For the filling:
$1\frac{1}{2}$ cups soft brown bread crumbs
scant $\frac{1}{2}$ cup butter
$1\frac{1}{2}$ lb. baking apples, weight after peeling
6 tablespoons sugar, preferably brown
$\frac{2}{3}$ cup seedless white raisins
$\frac{3}{4}$ cup chopped blanched almonds
1 teaspoon cinnamon
$\frac{1}{2}$ cup chopped mixed candied peel

To decorate:
$\frac{1}{4}$–$\frac{1}{2}$ cup confectioners' sugar
apple segments

1. Sieve the flour and salt. Add oil, egg and water to bind.
2. Leave for about 30 minutes in a covered bowl.
3. Meanwhile fry crumbs until crisp in $1\frac{1}{2}$ oz. (U.S. 3 tablespoons) butter. Peel apples and cut into wafer thin slices.
4. Put the dough on to a well-floured tea towel or board, pull and roll until a large square of paper-thin pastry.
5. Brush with a little melted butter. Put on apples and all the other filling ingredients. Fold in the ends to prevent filling falling out, then roll carefully.
6. Lift on to a baking tray, forming into horseshoe shape if wished. Brush with remaining butter.
7. Bake until firm and golden, reduce heat after 25 minutes.

To serve: Hot or cold, topped with sieved icing sugar and served with apple.

69

Wiener Marmor Gugelhupf
Viennese 'Carnival' cake

Cooking time: 45 min. **Preparation time:** 25 min. **Main cooking utensil:** 8-inch fluted ring tin/pan (Gugelhupf tin/pan). **Oven temperature:** very moderate to moderate, 350°F., 180°C., Gas Mark 4. **Oven position:** centre.

IMPERIAL

For 9–10 portions you need:
approx. $\frac{1}{2}$ oz. butter
1 oz. ground almonds
2 oz. butter and 2 oz. pure lard *or* use all butter
6 oz. sugar
4 medium eggs
10 oz. self-raising flour

grated rind 1–2 lemons
little lemon juice
approx. 6 tablespoons thin cream (see Stages 5 and 6)
3 oz. plain chocolate

To decorate:
approx. 2 oz. icing sugar

AMERICAN

For 9–10 portions you need:
approx. 1 tablespoon butter
$\frac{1}{4}$ cup ground almonds
$\frac{1}{4}$ cup butter and $\frac{1}{4}$ cup pure lard *or* use all butter
$\frac{3}{4}$ cup sugar
4 eggs
$2\frac{1}{2}$ cups all-purpose flour, sifted with $2\frac{1}{2}$ teaspoons baking powder
grated rind 1–2 lemons
little lemon juice
approx. $\frac{1}{2}$ cup coffee cream (see Stages 5 and 6)
3 squares semi-sweet chocolate

To decorate:
approx. $\frac{1}{2}$ cup confectioners' sugar

1. Grease a tin with butter, sprinkle with ground almonds, pressing gently but firmly into various 'flutes' of tin with a small palette knife. The almonds could be replaced with flour, but the flavour is excellent if the former is used.
2. Cream the butter and lard with sugar until soft and light.
3. Gradually beat in the eggs, adding a little sieved flour if mixture shows signs of curdling.
4. Fold in the flour, remove half the mixture into another bowl.
5. Blend in the grated lemon rind, take care to use only the top 'zest', and lemon juice, with just enough cream to give a soft dropping consistency.
6. Grate the chocolate finely, blend with remaining mixture, add cream as Stage 5. Put one third of the lemon mixture into tin, then chocolate mixture and finally remaining lemon mixture.
7. Bake until firm to the touch. Make sure the cake does not cook too quickly and become brown on the outside. Turn out, coat with icing sugar while warm and again when cold if wished.

70

Mandelschokoladetorte
Chocolate gâteau with almonds

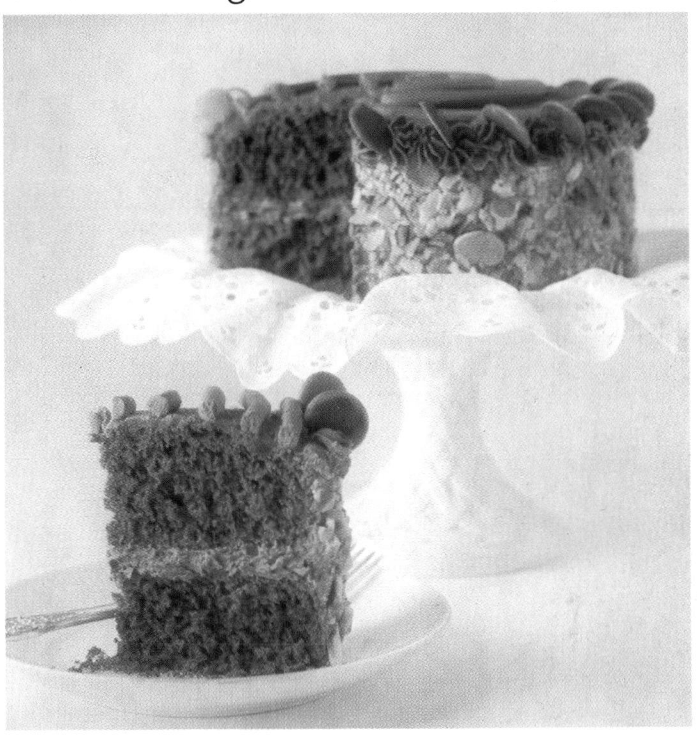

Cooking time: 50 min.–1 hr. **Preparation time:** 40 min. **Main cooking utensils:** 7–$7\frac{1}{2}$-inch cake tin/pan, double saucepan. **Oven temperature:** very moderate, 325–350°F., 170–180°C., Gas Mark 3–4. **Oven position:** centre.

IMPERIAL

For 7–8 portions you need:
6 oz. almonds*
3 eggs
4 oz. butter
5 oz. castor sugar

4 oz. self-raising flour

1 tablespoon cocoa powder

For the chocolate butter cream filling:
8 oz. plain chocolate, melted

8 oz. butter
12 oz. icing sugar, sieved

To decorate:
chocolate drops (optional)

AMERICAN

For 7–8 portions you need:
scant $1\frac{1}{4}$ cups almonds*
3 eggs
$\frac{1}{2}$ cup butter
$\frac{1}{2}$ cup plus 2 tablespoons granulated sugar
1 cup all-purpose flour, sifted with 1 teaspoon double-acting baking powder
1 tablespoon unsweetened cocoa powder

For the chocolate butter cream filling:
$\frac{1}{2}$ lb./8 squares semi-sweet chocolate, melted
1 cup butter
$2\frac{3}{4}$ cups sifted confectioners' sugar

To decorate:
chocolate drops (optional)

*Half for cake, half for decoration.

1. Blanch the almonds, dry well. Chop half of these very finely indeed. Split or chop others coarsely and brown.
2. Separate the egg yolks from whites.
3. Beat yolks until slightly thick.
4. Cream the butter and sugar until soft and light. Add the beaten egg yolks, well-sieved flour, cocoa, finely chopped almonds and finally fold in the stiffly beaten egg whites.
5. Bake in the well-greased and floured or lined tin until firm to the touch.
6. Split through the centre and fill with $\frac{1}{3}$ of the chocolate cream; made by blending the melted chocolate into the creamed butter and icing sugar.
7. Sandwich together, coat the top and sides with some of the butter cream.
8. Roll the sides in browned almonds.
9. Pipe the remainder of the butter cream on top and round the edges.

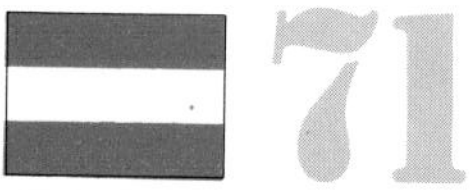

71

Feiner Gugelhupf
Madeira type cake

Cooking time: 45–50 min. **Preparation time:** 20 min. **Main cooking utensil:** a Gugelhupf mould (A deep fluted tin/pan). **Oven temperature:** moderate, 350–375°F., 180–190°C., Gas Mark 4–5. **Oven position:** centre.

IMPERIAL

For 6–8 portions you need:
2 dessert pears
juice $\frac{1}{2}$ lemon
4 oz. butter
4 oz. sugar
2 eggs
1 tablespoon treacle
7 oz. plain flour
2 oz. ground almonds
1 teaspoon ginger
1 teaspoon mixed spice
$\frac{1}{4}$ pint milk
1 teaspoon bicarbonate of soda

To decorate:
little icing sugar

AMERICAN

For 6–8 portions you need:
2 dessert pears
juice $\frac{1}{2}$ lemon
$\frac{1}{2}$ cup butter
$\frac{1}{2}$ cup sugar
2 eggs
1 tablespoon molasses
1$\frac{3}{4}$ cups all-purpose flour
$\frac{1}{2}$ cup ground almonds
1 teaspoon ginger
1 teaspoon mixed spice
$\frac{2}{3}$ cup milk
1 teaspoon baking soda

To decorate:
little confectioners' sugar

1. Peel, core and dice the pears, sprinkle with lemon juice.
2. Cream the butter and sugar, gradually beat in the eggs. Stir in the treacle.
3. Sieve the remaining dry ingredients except bicarbonate of soda.
4. Add the warmed milk to the bicarbonate of soda and add to the creamed mixture alternately with the dry ingredients.
5. Fold in the diced pear.
6. Grease the tin, put in mixture and bake until firm. Leave 5 minutes before unmoulding.

To serve: Either hot or cold, dredged with icing sugar.

To vary: Omit treacle and add 2–3 oz. (U.S. $\frac{1}{4}$–$\frac{1}{2}$ cup) raisins soaked in 2 tablespoons (U.S. 3 tablespoons) rum. Other types of Gugelhupf have no fruit added.

To store: When including fresh fruit, this must be stored in a refrigerator and preferably eaten soon after cooking.

72

Kuchenbrot
Cake bread

Cooking time: 50 min. **Preparation time:** 20 min. **Main cooking utensil:** 8-inch fluted ring tin/pan (Gugelhupf tin/pan). * **Oven temperature:** moderate, 375°F., 190°C., Gas Mark 4–5. * **Oven position:** centre.

IMPERIAL

For 14–16 thin slices you need:
4 oz. butter
3 oz. sugar
grated rind and juice 1 lemon
3 eggs
5 oz. self-raising flour and 4 oz. potato flour *or* use 6 oz. self-raising flour and 3 oz. cornflour
2 teaspoons caraway seeds
little milk

AMERICAN

For 14–16 thin slices you need:
$\frac{1}{2}$ cup butter
6 tablespoons sugar
grated rind and juice 1 lemon
3 eggs
1$\frac{1}{4}$ cups all-purpose flour, sifted with 1 teaspoon baking powder and scant 1 cup potato flour *or* use 1$\frac{1}{2}$ cups flour, sifted with 1$\frac{1}{2}$ teaspoons baking powder and approx. $\frac{2}{3}$ cup cornstarch
2 teaspoons caraway seeds
little milk

*If baking in an ordinary tin/pan instead of the ring tin/pan, use a very moderate oven 325–350°F., 170–180°C., Gas Mark 3 and bake for slightly longer.

1. Cream the butter, sugar and grated lemon rind until soft and light.
2. Separate the egg yolks from whites, beat yolks into butter mixture.
3. Sieve the flours together. Fold into the mixture with lemon juice, seeds and enough milk to make a soft dropping consistency.
4. Whisk the egg whites until very stiff, fold in carefully and slowly, until well blended.
5. Grease and flour a tin, put in the mixture, pressing down carefully.
6. Bake until firm to the touch; do not allow to become too brown. Reduce heat if necessary after 30 minutes.

To serve: Sliced thinly, spread with butter, if liked.

To vary: Another light Austrian bread called Bischofsbrot (Bishop's bread) is made in a similar way, adding slightly less liquid to give a stiffer dough. About 3 oz. plain chopped chocolate, 3 oz. (U.S. $\frac{1}{2}$ cup) raisins, 3 oz. (U.S. $\frac{3}{4}$ cup) chopped nuts and 2 oz. (U.S. $\frac{1}{4}$ cup) chopped glacé cherries are added. Bake in a ring tin in a very moderate oven for approximately 1 hour.

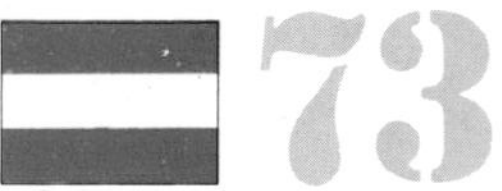

73

Wiener Torte
Viennese layer cake

Cooking time: 40 min. **Preparation time:** 25 min. **Main cooking utensils:** flat baking trays/sheets, saucepan. **Oven temperature:** very moderate, 325–350°F., 170–180°C., Gas Mark 3–4. **Oven position:** centre.

IMPERIAL

For 6–8 portions you need:
6 oz. butter
6 oz. castor sugar
4 eggs
1 egg yolk
10 oz. plain flour
2 oz. potato flour *or* cornflour
4 oz. ground almonds

To glaze:
egg white

For the filling and topping:
$1\frac{1}{4}$–$1\frac{1}{2}$ lb. ripe apricots
sugar to taste
$\frac{1}{2}$ pint thick cream
1–2 tablespoons apricot brandy
few glacé cherries

AMERICAN

For 6–8 portions you need:
$\frac{3}{4}$ cup butter
$\frac{3}{4}$ cup granulated sugar
4 eggs
1 egg yolk
$2\frac{1}{2}$ cups all-purpose flour
scant $\frac{1}{2}$ cup potato flour *or* cornstarch
1 cup ground almonds

To glaze:
egg white

For the filling and topping:
$1\frac{1}{4}$–$1\frac{1}{2}$ lb. ripe apricots
sugar to taste
$1\frac{1}{4}$ cups whipping cream
1–3 tablespoons apricot brandy
few candied cherries

1. Cream the butter and sugar until soft and light.
2. Beat in the eggs, flour, potato or cornflour and ground almonds. If the mixture is sticky, leave in a cool place to become firm.
3. Divide into three and shape into three equal-sized rounds.
4. Make a decorative edge; brush with egg white and bake until golden brown.
5. Cool on the trays.
6. Cook and sieve half the apricots with water and sugar to taste.
7. Blend with the lightly whipped cream.
8. Halve the rest of the apricots and sprinkle with apricot brandy.
9. Sandwich the cakes together with the apricot cream and the halved apricots.
10. Top with a similar mixture and decorate with cherries.

To serve: As a dessert or for tea.

To store: The crisp rounds can be kept several days in a tin before filling.

74

Erdbeerbowle
Strawberry bowl

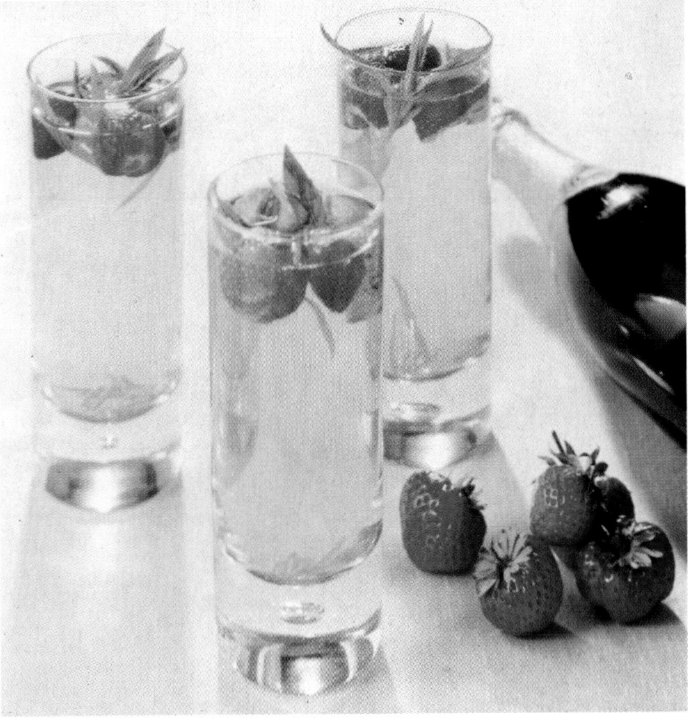

Preparation time: 15 min. **Main utensil:** large bowl.

IMPERIAL

For about 16–18 glasses you need:
2 large, fine-skinned oranges
3 oz. castor sugar
1 lb. fresh strawberries (see Stage 5)
2 bottles white wine* (sweet or dry *or* use 1 bottle sweet and 1 bottle dry)
$\frac{1}{2}$ bottle champagne *or* use $\frac{1}{2}$ bottle sparkling wine

To decorate:
borage *or* mint leaves

AMERICAN

For about 16–18 glasses you need:
2 large, fine-skinned oranges
6 tablespoons granulated sugar
1 lb. fresh strawberries (see Stage 5)
2 bottles white wine* (sweet or dry *or* use 1 bottle sweet and 1 bottle dry)
$\frac{1}{2}$ bottle champagne *or* use $\frac{1}{2}$ bottle sparkling wine

To decorate:
borage *or* mint leaves

*Choose from: Dry: Spanish Chablis, Medium: Spanish Graves, Sweet: Spanish Sauternes.

1. Pare the rind from the oranges, discarding the white pith, which could make the drink bitter.
2. Shred the orange rind very finely with a sharp knife, put into the bowl.
3. Squeeze out the juice from the oranges and strain carefully into a bowl. You need about $\frac{1}{4}$ pint (U.S. $\frac{2}{3}$ pint) orange juice, but you may like to add a little less; taste the drink and add more later.
4. Sprinkle the sugar into the bowl.
5. Wash and dry the strawberries in cold water. Halve neatly if very large, although for this purpose small really ripe fruit is best.
6. Put the strawberries into the bowl, pour over the still wine.
7. Put the bowl into the refrigerator to chill for 1 hour, a little crushed ice may be added.
8. Cool the champagne or sparkling wine. Add just before serving.

To serve: Ladle into glasses, top with mint or borage leaves.

Artichauts sauce verte
Artichoke salad with green sauce

The location of Belgium gives a good indication of its cooking, with Holland to the north and France to the south. Flemish is spoken in the northern half of the country while the southerners speak French, and this split has often led to friction. Fortunately, however, food is a matter on which there is unity, for all Belgians take a lively interest in cooking. They have combined the best of the French, Flemish and Dutch influences with the result that they have a varied and distinctive national cuisine. Brussels is renowned as a centre for sophisticated eating but the cooking throughout the country is of an exceptionally high standard; you may well sample some of the best Belgian food in a farmhouse where expert cooking is complemented by the freshest ingredients.

Even at breakfast the French and Dutch influences are evident. As in France, you will be given a large cup or bowl of cafe-au-lait with rolls and possibly croissants and butter and jam, but there will also be bread with slices of cheese and meat and sometimes grated chocolate which is typical in Holland. Like most people these days, the Belgians have a light lunch and their main meal is in the evening.

The Belgians are fond of vegetables and create delicious dishes with them for hors d'oeuvres and light main courses as well as accompaniments for meat. Artichoke salad with green sauce is a delightful way of serving this elegant French vegetable. The homely onion takes on a new lease of life with the addition of tomato, raisins, wine and seasoning in Onion and raisin hot-pot. Both these dishes can be served with cheese to make appetising light main dishes. Chicory with cheese sauce is a famous Belgian dish which is equally versatile and goes particularly well with ham.

Of the two meat dishes we have included, Chicken terrine has distinctly French overtones, a terrine being a type of pâté deriving its name from the French word for the earthenware dish in which it is traditionally cooked. The Hot-pot of meat and vegetables, however, is popular in both Holland and Belgium. This hearty dish using beef and ham can either be served with its gravy or the liquid may be strained and served as a soup to precede the main course. Like the French, the Belgians are connoisseurs of wine but they also enjoy beer, of which they produce some themselves and import the rest from Holland and Germany.

Cooking time: 25–35 min. **Preparation time:** 15 min. **Main cooking utensils:** 2 saucepans.

IMPERIAL

For 4 people you need:
4 large *or* 8 small artichokes

For the sauce:
1 tablespoon chopped parsley
2 teaspoons chopped tarragon
2 teaspoons chopped chervil
1 tablespoon chopped watercress leaves
$\frac{1}{2}$ pint thick mayonnaise
1 tablespoon cooked chopped spinach leaves (optional)

AMERICAN

For 4 people you need:
4 large *or* 8 small artichokes

For the sauce:
1 tablespoon chopped parsley
2 teaspoons chopped tarragon
2 teaspoons chopped chervil
1 tablespoon chopped watercress leaves
$1\frac{1}{4}$ cups thick mayonnaise
1 tablespoon cooked chopped spinach leaves (optional)

1. Cut the tops off the artichokes and trim the stalks at the base. Put into boiling salted water and cook for the time given. Test to see if cooked, by inserting the tip of a sharp knife or skewer into the base; the artichokes should be very tender.
2. When cool enough to handle, halve the artichokes down the centre; the centre 'choke' which is not edible, should be removed.
3. Prepare the sauce by blending together the parsley, tarragon, chervil, watercress and spinach (if used) with the mayonnaise.

To serve: Hot or cold.

To vary: 1–2 diced, cooked potatoes may be added to the mayonnaise.

76

Hutsepot met klapstuck
Hot-pot of meat and vegetables

Cooking time: $2\frac{1}{2}$–$2\frac{3}{4}$ hr. **Preparation time:** 30 min. **Main cooking utensil:** large saucepan.

IMPERIAL

For 6–7 people you need:
$1\frac{1}{4}$ lb. stewing beef
$1\frac{1}{4}$ lb. lamb *or* mutton, boned breast may be used *or* piece from top of leg *or* shoulder
seasoning
approx. 3 pints water *or* stock
$1\frac{1}{2}$ lb. potatoes, weight before peeling
1 lb. carrots
1 lb. tiny onions
4 oz. small button mushrooms
6–8 oz. cooked ham *or* use half cooked ham and half small sausages (see Stage 6)
4–6 oz. cooked *or* canned haricot *or* butter beans

To garnish:
1–2 tomatoes
about 9–10 gherkins

AMERICAN

For 6–7 people you need:
$1\frac{1}{4}$ lb. beef stew meat
$1\frac{1}{4}$ lb. lamb *or* mutton, boned breast may be used *or* piece from top of leg *or* shoulder
seasoning
approx. $7\frac{1}{2}$ cups water *or* stock
$1\frac{1}{2}$ lb. potatoes, weight before peeling
1 lb. carrots
1 lb. tiny onions
1 cup button mushrooms
about $\frac{1}{2}$ lb. cooked ham, Canadian-style bacon *or* use half cooked ham and half sausages (see Stage 6)
about 1 cup cooked *or* canned navy beans

To garnish:
1–2 tomatoes
about 9–10 sweet dill pickles

1. Cut the meat into neat pieces, put into a saucepan with plenty of seasoning and cold water or stock to cover.
2. Bring to the boil, remove any scum that appears on top of liquid. Reduce heat, cover pan and simmer for about 30 minutes.
3. Cut the potatoes and carrots into small pieces. They should become so soft in cooking that they may be beaten into the liquid as thickening.
4. Add potatoes and carrots to meats, simmer for a further 45 minutes.
5. Put in onions and mushrooms and stir vigorously so that potatoes and carrots begin to blend with the stock. Cook until meat is tender.
6. About 30 minutes before serving, add fingers of cooked ham (canned luncheon meat can be used) and/or chopped sausages and beans.

To serve: Either as shown in picture, garnished with raw tomatoes and gherkin 'fans', or strain meat with a perforated spoon, serve as main course with the liquid as soup, together with raw vegetables.

77

Oignons aux raisins secs
Onion and raisin hot-pot

Cooking time: approximately 50 min. **Preparation time:** 30 min. **Main cooking utensil:** saucepan.

IMPERIAL

For 4–5 people you need:
16–20 small even-sized onions
2–3 tablespoons olive oil
$\frac{1}{2}$ pint tomato juice *or* sieved fresh tomato purée
5–6 oz. seedless raisins
$\frac{1}{2}$ pint white wine
sprig fresh thyme *or* pinch dried thyme
seasoning
good pinch sugar

AMERICAN

For 4–5 people you need:
16–20 small even-sized onions
3–4 tablespoons olive oil
$1\frac{1}{4}$ cups tomato juice *or* sieved fresh tomato purée
1 cup seedless raisins
$1\frac{1}{4}$ cups white wine
sprig fresh thyme *or* dash dried thyme
seasoning
dash sugar

1. Peel the onions, then cook them in the saucepan in boiling salted water for about 5 minutes only and drain.
2. Heat the oil in the pan and toss the onion in this until a pale golden colour.
3. Add the tomato juice or fresh sieved purée, the seedless raisins, wine, thyme, seasoning and sugar.
4. Cover the pan and simmer for about 45 minutes then remove the lid and continue cooking for another 10 minutes, so that some of the liquid evaporates.
5. Serve hot or cold. This hot-pot is excellent by itself *or* with cheese dishes.

78

Terrine au poulet
Chicken terrine

Cooking time: 1½ hr. plus time to make stock. **Preparation time:** 30 min. plus setting time. **Main cooking utensils:** saucepan, 2-pint/2½-pint ovenproof mould *or* dish. **Oven temperature:** very moderate, 325–350°F., 170–180°C., Gas Mark 3. **Oven position:** centre.

IMPERIAL

For 5–10 people you need:*
1 roasting chicken, about 4 lb.
about 8 rashers fat bacon
8 oz. bacon rashers
½ teaspoon chopped lemon thyme *or* pinch dried herb
½ teaspoon chopped rosemary *or* pinch dried herb
8 oz. pork sausage meat
2 tablespoons sherry *or* brandy
2 eggs
4 tablespoons thick cream
seasoning

To garnish:
1 pint packet aspic jelly
3 tablespoons sherry
1 truffle *or* mushroom
parsley

AMERICAN

For 5–10 people you need:*
1 roasting chicken, about 4 lb.
about 8 bacon slices
½ lb. bacon slices
½ teaspoon chopped lemon thyme *or* dash dried herb
½ teaspoon chopped rosemary *or* dash dried herb
½ lb. pork sausage meat
3 tablespoons sherry *or* brandy
2 eggs
⅓ cup whipping cream
seasoning

To garnish:
approx. 1½ tablespoons gelatin
scant ¼ cup sherry
1 truffle *or* mushroom
parsley

*5 as a main dish, 10 as an hors d'oeuvre.

1. Remove bones from the chicken. Put bones and giblets into saucepan add 1½ pints (U.S. 3¾ cups) water, simmer for 1 hour, season and strain.
2. Cut the best pieces of chicken breast and thigh, keep on one side.
3. Line the mould or dish with fat bacon.
4. Mince the remaining chicken with bacon or ham.
5. Add the herbs, sausage meat and remaining ingredients, moisten with 4 tablespoons (U.S. ⅓ cup) chicken stock.
6. Pack the chicken forcemeat and pieces of chicken into bacon-lined mould, making sure you have a good distribution of breast and leg.
7. Cover with well buttered foil. Stand mould in tin of water to keep moist. Cook until firm, cool in mould.
8. Dissolve the aspic jelly in nearly 1 pint (U.S. 2½ cups) well strained chicken stock and sherry. Cool and allow to stiffen slightly. (If using gelatin, soak it in ½ cup liquid, then dissolve it in the remaining liquid.)
9. Put truffle or mushroom on terrine, coat with half-set jelly and allow to set. Garnish. Any aspic jelly left should be put round the terrine.

79

Witloof mornay
Chicory with cheese sauce

Cooking time: 15–20 min. **Preparation time:** 15 min. **Main cooking utensils:** saucepan, ovenproof dish. **Oven temperature:** moderate, 375°F., 190°C., Gas Mark 4–5. **Oven position:** above centre.

IMPERIAL

For 4 people you need:
4 large *or* 8 small heads chicory
seasoning
squeeze lemon juice
1 oz. butter
1 oz. flour
¼ pint milk
¼ pint chicory stock
2 tablespoons thick cream
3 oz. cheese, grated, Cheddar *or* Gruyère

For the topping:
1 oz. cheese, grated
1 tomato
parsley

AMERICAN

For 4 people you need:
4 large *or* 8 small heads Belgian endive
seasoning
squeeze lemon juice
2 tablespoons butter
¼ cup all-purpose flour
⅔ cup milk
⅔ cup endive stock
3 tablespoons whipping cream
¾ cup grated cheese, Cheddar *or* Gruyère

For the topping:
¼ cup grated cheese
1 tomato
parsley

1. Pull off outer leaves from the chicory heads.
2. Put the heads into boiling, salted water to which a squeeze of lemon juice is added. Cook for 10 minutes, do not overcook otherwise this vegetable has a slightly bitter taste.
3. Drain, keep ¼ pint (U.S. ⅔ cup) stock.
4. Put the chicory into a hot dish, keep warm. Heat the butter, stir in flour, cook for several minutes.
5. Gradually add the milk and stock, bring to the boil. Cook until thickened, then blend in cream, grated cheese, and season well.
6. Pour the sauce over chicory, sprinkle with cheese, brown under grill. Top with sliced tomato and parsley.

To serve: As a light main dish or hors d'oeuvre; or with a main dish.

BRITAIN

British cooking has a long and fascinating history behind it. The interest the English have always shown in their food is demonstrated by how much they have written about it. Chaucer frequently mentions the food his Canterbury pilgrims enjoyed on their journey, even down to the spices used for some of the strong sauces often made to disguise meat that wasn't fresh. Samuel Johnson was a great 18th century epicure who confessed to that peculiarly English addiction for tea drinking that had come into fashion when tea was introduced in the previous century. From Dickens we learn how many of today's luxuries, including such delicacies as oysters and lobsters, were everyday fare for the Victorians. Before we become too envious, however, we must remember that many imported food items we take for granted, were not generally available, and that without modern preserving methods much produce was limited to a short season.

In the past, and particularly in the 19th century, there was a terrific contrast between what the aristocracy and the working classes ate. The former had the means to procure almost anything they fancied and plenty of it, while the latter often went hungry and had very little variety in what meagre meals they did manage to scrape together. For breakfast, for example, the working classes rose early and hastily downed some bread with a bit of cheese and meat, but an upper class breakfast was a large leisurely meal served at nine or ten. Bacon and eggs were only part of the spread to be found on sideboards laden with kippers or other fish, devilled kidneys, pheasant or ptarmigan, meat or game pie, galantines and cold meats. This large meal was most freely indulged in by the men; women tended to limit themselves to a more dainty breakfast of scones and jam or honey and perhaps a boiled egg, knowing that there would be a substantial meal at mid-day. This was followed, much as today in traditional homes, by afternoon tea, a popular social occasion, and then a light supper in the evening.

The British have always enjoyed game and have developed innumerable ways of preparing it, from roasting and simple stews to elaborate game pies. Jugged hare is one of the most famous old recipes and makes a superb traditional meal. Many country dishes are economical, having been designed to make the best use of a small amount of meat when times were lean; it is a measure of their success that they remained popular even during more prosperous years. Lamb hot-pot, a favourite in the north, is a typical dish for which the quantity and quality of the lamb can vary according to what is available. Sausage meat makes a good economical meal in such dishes as Savoury sausage meat pie and the typically Irish O'Flanagan's sausage supper.

With nowhere in the British Isles more than seventy miles from the sea, it is hardly surprising that fish plays an important role in the English diet. Grilled cod with prawn and anchovy sauce is an elegant way of presenting this familiar fish. Reminiscent of the Mediterranean is the unusual Skewered herrings, an example of how Britain has been influenced by foreign cooking in recent years.

Some of the most delicious English puddings use fruit in different combinations, one of the most familiar being apples with blackberries. Blackberry and apple pie never fails to please, but for a refreshing change in the summer Apple and blackcurrant mould is a beautiful cold dessert. Toffee fruit pudding is a steamed pudding filled with a mixture of colourful summer fruits, while Brandied fruits preserves seasonal fruits to enjoy all year round.

The English use pastry for all sorts of dishes, from savoury canapés and starters, to flans and pies for main courses, and sweet pies and tarts for puddings. Lemon curd, or lemon cheese as it is known in the North, is a famous English creation which makes an appetising and convenient tart filling; for a filling with a more subtle flavour, apple purée combined with lemon curd makes a pleasant change. Many adults find treacle tart a little too sweet and cloying, but the addition of lemon and a little ginger in Lemon treacle tart adds a spicy tang to this childhood favourite.

Baking has a long tradition in Britain, including scones and yeast breads, plain everyday cakes, and rich cakes and gâteaux. From the South we have Somerset spiced bread, a moist fruity loaf served generously spread with thick cream. Baps, flat soft yeast rolls from Scotland, are equally good with butter or with a sweet or savoury filling. Coffee walnut layer gâteau is a lovely rich tea cake; it also makes a perfect dessert accompanied by a dessert wine or a good cup of coffee. Nowadays, we have all types of coffee to choose from: Turkish coffee is served in very small cups and has a distinctive flavour, and Gaelic coffee makes a really luxurious conclusion to any meal.

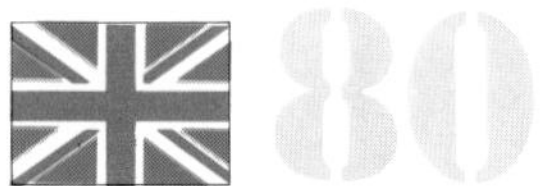

80

Sausage dips

Cooking time: 15 min. Preparation time: 15 min. Main cooking utensils: frying pan/skillet, 3 mixing bowls.

IMPERIAL

Allow about 3 sausages per person:
1 lb. small chipolata sausages

Dip A:
2 tablespoons French mustard
3 tablespoons mayonnaise
2 tablespoons tomato ketchup
few drops Worcestershire sauce

Dip B:
2–3 rings canned pineapple
3–4 spring onions
2 tablespoons mayonnaise
1 tablespoon lemon juice
grated rind 1 lemon

Dip C:
4 oz. cream cheese
2 tablespoons mayonnaise
good-sized sprigs fresh thyme, parsley, sage and chives
seasoning, made mustard

AMERICAN

Allow about 3 sausages per person:
1 lb. small link sausages

Dip A:
3 tablespoons French mustard
scant $\frac{1}{4}$ cup mayonnaise
3 tablespoons tomato catsup
few drops Worcestershire sauce

Dip B:
2–3 rings canned pineapple
3–4 scallions
3 tablespoons mayonnaise
1 tablespoon lemon juice
grated rind 1 lemon

Dip C:
$\frac{1}{2}$ cup cream cheese
3 tablespoons mayonnaise
good-sized sprigs fresh thyme, parsley, sage and chives
seasoning, prepared mustard

Fry the sausages in fat until golden brown. Put cocktail sticks into hot sausages, arrange on a hot dish with bowls of dips round.

A Blend all the ingredients together, garnish with a sprig of parsley.
B Chop the pineapple and onions finely, mix with other ingredients.
C Blend all the ingredients together. Serve sprinkled with chopped chives.

To vary: Sausage twists: Make puff pastry with 4 oz. (U.S. 1 cup) flour. Cut into 16 narrow strips. Half-cook 1 lb. chipolata sausages, twist pastry strips round. Brush with beaten egg. Bake for 12–15 minutes in a very hot oven.

Bacon sausage rolls: Fry or grill 1 lb. large sausages, cut in half and make a slit in each half. Spread with mustard or chutney, insert pieces of cheese. Derind 8 rashers bacon, cut into halves. Roll round sausages, secure with cocktail sticks. Bake, grill or fry.

81

Grilled cod with prawn and anchovy sauce

Cooking time: 15 min. Preparation time: 20 min. Main cooking utensils: grill pan/broil pan, saucepan.

IMPERIAL

For 6 people you need:
6 cod steaks
seasoning
2–3 oz. butter
juice $\frac{1}{2}$ lemon
finely grated rind $\frac{1}{2}$–1 lemon (optional)

For the sauce:
$1\frac{1}{2}$ oz. butter *or* margarine
$1\frac{1}{2}$ oz. flour
$\frac{3}{4}$ pint milk *or* milk and fish stock (see Stage 8)
$\frac{1}{2}$–1 teaspoon anchovy sauce *or* essence
seasoning
1 pint unshelled prawns *or* more if wished

AMERICAN

For 6 people you need:
6 cod steaks
seasoning
4–6 tablespoons butter
juice $\frac{1}{2}$ lemon
finely grated rind $\frac{1}{2}$–1 lemon (optional)

For the sauce:
3 tablespoons butter *or* margarine
6 tablespoons all-purpose flour
2 cups milk *or* milk and fish stock (see Stage 8)
$\frac{1}{2}$–1 teaspoon anchovy sauce *or* paste
seasoning
$2\frac{1}{2}$ cups unshelled prawns *or* more if wished

1. Dry the fish, season lightly.
2. Pre-heat grill; slow cooking dries the fish and spoils the flavour.
3. Cream or melt the butter with lemon juice and rind.
4. Put the fish on to grill pan grid, brushing this with a little butter to prevent the fish sticking.
5. Brush the fish well with the lemon flavoured butter. Cook until golden coloured, turn.
6. Brush the second side of the fish with butter, continue grilling until cooked, about 10 minutes. Keep well basted during cooking.
7. To make the sauce: heat the butter, stir in flour, cook for several minutes.
8. Gradually blend in the milk, or use half milk and half fish stock (made by simmering shells of the prawns for 15 minutes).
9. Stir until thickened. Add anchovy sauce or essence to taste, seasoning and most of the shelled prawns.

To serve: Either serve sauce separately or arrange fish and pour sauce into the dish. Garnish with unshelled prawns. Serve with jacket potatoes.

82

Skewered herrings

Cooking time: 25 min. **Preparation time:** 15 min. plus 1 hour for saffron to soak. **Main cooking utensils:** 2 saucepans, 4 strong skewers, grill pan/broil pan.

IMPERIAL

For 4 people you need:
For the rice:
$\frac{1}{2}$ teaspoon powdered saffron *or* saffron strands
1 pint water
1 oz. butter
6 oz. long grain rice
seasoning

For the kebabs:
4 small onions
4 small firm tomatoes
4 button mushrooms
4 herrings
1 oz. butter
seasoning

To garnish:
parsley

AMERICAN

For 4 people you need:
For the rice:
$\frac{1}{2}$ teaspoon powdered saffron *or* saffron strands
$2\frac{1}{2}$ cups water
2 tablespoons butter
scant 1 cup long grain rice
seasoning

For the kebabs:
4 small onions
4 small firm tomatoes
4 button mushrooms
4 herrings
2 tablespoons butter
seasoning

To garnish:
parsley

1. Soak the saffron in $\frac{1}{4}$ pint (U.S. $\frac{2}{3}$ cup) water, if using powder pour into rice liquid, if using strands, strain liquid only and use.
2. Heat the butter, toss the rice in this, add remaining cold water, saffron liquid and seasoning. Bring to the boil then lower heat. Cover pan and simmer for 15 minutes until tender.
3. Remove the lid for the last minute to 'dry out' the rice. Put on to serving dish.
4. Peel the onions, simmer in salted water for 15 minutes, drain and dry.
5. Skin the tomatoes, if wished. Remove stalks from mushrooms, wash and dry.
6. Fillet herrings, cut off heads, split down stomach, remove intestines. Put the herrings cut side down, run thumb along backbone, turn and bones come away. Cut into 2 fillets, put chopped roes on these if wished and roll firmly.
7. Put the ingredients on skewers, brush with butter and season. Cook under a hot grill, turning. Serve kebabs on the bed of rice, garnished with parsley.

83

Creamed chicken and vegetable pie

Cooking time: approx. $2\frac{1}{2}$ hr. (or see Stage 1). **Preparation time:** 30 min. **Main cooking utensils:** saucepan, 2–$2\frac{1}{2}$-pint/3–$3\frac{1}{2}$-pint pie dish/pan, baking tray/sheet. **Oven temperature:** hot, 425–450°F., 220–230°C., Gas Mark 6–7, then 375°F., 190°C., Gas Mark 4–5. **Oven position:** centre.

IMPERIAL

For 5–6 people you need:
1 small boiling fowl *or* about $1\frac{1}{4}$–$1\frac{1}{2}$ lb. cooked chicken
2 oz. chicken fat *or* butter
2 onions
$1\frac{1}{2}$ oz. flour
$\frac{1}{2}$ pint chicken stock *or* water and chicken stock cube
$\frac{1}{2}$ pint milk
pinch powdered rosemary
seasoning
4 firm tomatoes

For the pastry:
8 oz. flour, preferably plain
pinch salt
4 oz. fat *or* butter
water to mix

To glaze:
1 egg

AMERICAN

For 5–6 people you need:
1 small stewing chicken *or* about $1\frac{1}{4}$–$1\frac{1}{2}$ lb. cooked chicken
$\frac{1}{4}$ cup chicken fat *or* butter
2 onions
6 tablespoons all-purpose flour
$1\frac{1}{4}$ cups chicken stock *or* water and chicken bouillon cube
$1\frac{1}{4}$ cups milk
dash powdered rosemary
seasoning
4 firm tomatoes

For the pastry:
2 cups all-purpose flour
dash salt
$\frac{1}{2}$ cup fat *or* butter
water to mix

To glaze:
1 egg

1. Simmer the boiling fowl for 1 hour, joint. Cut the chicken into pieces, mix dark and light meat, or use light meat only.
2. Heat the chicken fat (obtain this from top of liquid from simmering fowl), toss sliced onions in this, do not allow to brown.
3. Stir in the flour, cook for several minutes. Blend in stock and milk.
4. Bring to the boil, cook until thickened, add rosemary and seasoning.
5. Mix chicken with the sauce, put half into a dish. Cover with sliced tomatoes, then remaining chicken mixture.
6. Sieve flour and salt, rub in fat or butter and bind with water. Roll out and cover chicken mixture. Decorate pie with pastry 'leaves' and glaze.
7. Stand the dish on a baking tray. Bake for approximately 40 minutes, reduce heat if necessary after 25 minutes; cooking time should be a little longer at a lower temperature if the chicken mixture was cold. Garnish with parsley. Serve hot or cold.

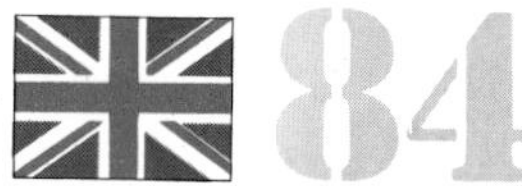

84

Potato thatched meat loaf

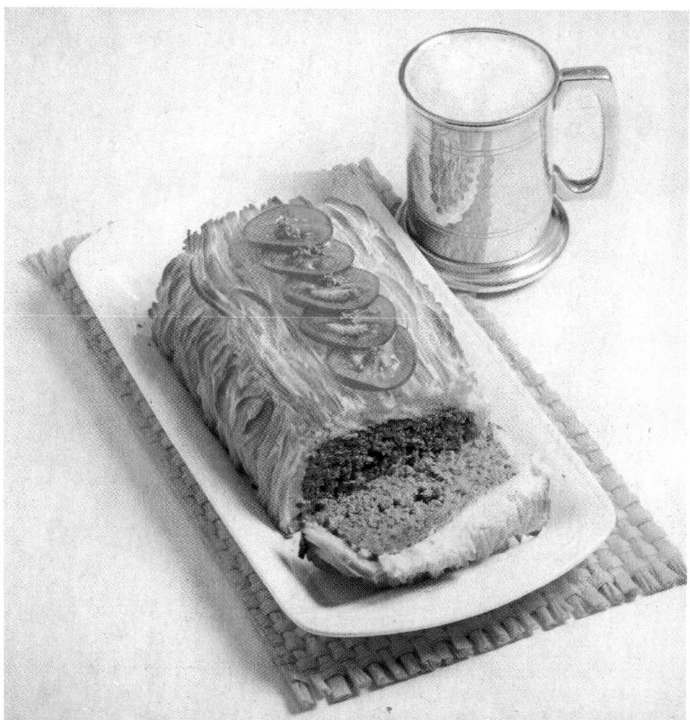

Cooking time: 1 hr. 25 min. **Preparation time:** 30 min. plus 30 min. for bread to stand. **Main cooking utensils:** saucepan, 2-lb. loaf tin/pan, ovenproof serving dish. **Oven temperature:** very moderate to moderate, 350–375°F., 190°C., Gas Mark 4. **Oven position:** centre, then nearer top.

IMPERIAL

For 6 people you need:
1 slice bread, ½-inch thick
¼ pint milk *or* stock
1½ lb. uncooked minced beef
2–3 teaspoons Worcestershire sauce
1 tablespoon tomato ketchup
2 tablespoons chutney
2 rashers streaky bacon
1 stick celery (optional)
1 egg
seasoning
2½ oz. margarine
1½ lb. potatoes, weight when peeled
2–3 tablespoons milk

To garnish:
1 tomato
few sprigs parsley

AMERICAN

For 6 people you need:
1 slice bread, ½ inch thick
⅔ cup milk *or* stock
1½ lb. uncooked ground beef
2–3 teaspoons Worcestershire sauce
1 tablespoon tomato catsup
3 tablespoons chutney
2 slices bacon
1 stalk celery (optional)
1 egg
seasoning
5 tablespoons margarine
1½ lb. potatoes, weight when peeled
3–4 tablespoons milk

To garnish:
1 tomato
few sprigs parsley

1. Soak the bread in milk or stock for 30 minutes, beat well until smooth.
2. Blend with the minced beef, sauce, ketchup, chutney and finely diced bacon and celery.
3. Bind with egg and season.
4. Grease the tin with about 1 oz. (U.S. 2 tablespoons) margarine. Press in the mixture and bake for 1 hour.
5. While meat mixture is cooking, boil potatoes in salted water. Strain, sieve or mash well, adding the remaining margarine and the milk, season.
6. Turn the meat mixture on to an ovenproof serving dish. Pour off any surplus liquid before doing this.
7. Coat with the potato and mark into a neat design. Return to the oven for a further 25 minutes.

To serve: Garnish with sliced tomato and sprigs of parsley.

85

Lamb hot-pot

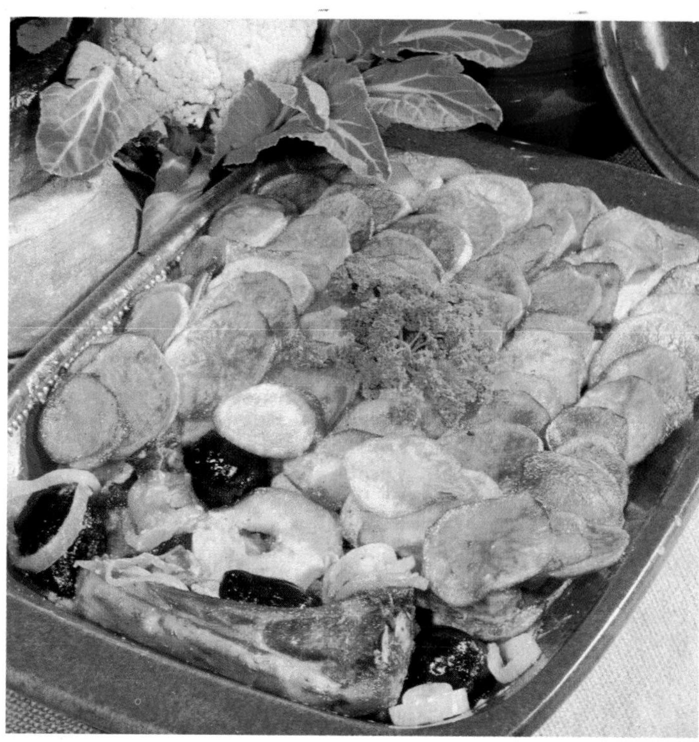

Cooking time: 2 hr. **Preparation time:** 25 min. plus time for prunes to soak (see Stages 1 and 2). **Main cooking utensil:** fairly shallow 2–3-pint/2½–3½-pint ovenproof dish with lid *or* foil. **Oven temperature:** very moderate, 325–350°F., 170–180°C., Gas Mark 3. **Oven position:** centre.

IMPERIAL

For 4–5 people you need:
4–6 oz. prunes
2 large onions .
2 large cooking apples
1½–2 lb. lamb, choose best end neck *or* loin for special occasions, scrag *or* middle neck *or* breast for economy
seasoning
1 teaspoon sugar
½ teaspoon finely chopped mint *or* pinch dried mint
½ pint stock *or* prune liquid
1–1½ lb. potatoes(weight when peeled)
1 oz. fat

To garnish:
parsley

AMERICAN

For 4–5 people you need:
⅔–1 cup prunes
2 large onions
2 large baking apples
1½–2 lb. lamb, choose loin *or* rib roast for special occasions, shanks *or* breast for economy
seasoning
1 teaspoon sugar
½ teaspoon finely chopped mint *or* dash dried mint
1¼ cups stock *or* prune liquid
1–1½ lb. potatoes (weight when peeled)
2 tablespoons fat

To garnish:
parsley

1. Prunes vary a great deal today; it is possible to buy tenderized prunes which need no soaking, or use a medium-sized can of prunes.
2. If prunes are dry, however, soak overnight. Drain and use ½ pint (U.S. 1¼ cups) of this liquid instead of stock.
3. Peel and cut the onions and apples into rings, coring the apples.
4. Arrange the prunes, onions, apples and jointed meat in the dish.
5. Blend seasoning, sugar and mint with stock. Pour over the meat.
6. Peel and slice potatoes, the amount used depends upon personal taste.
7. Arrange neatly on meat. Season, then brush with the melted fat.
8. Cover with a lid or greased foil and bake for 1½ hours.
9. Remove lid or foil to brown potatoes; garnish. Serve with green salad.

To vary: Omit apples and add halved tomatoes.

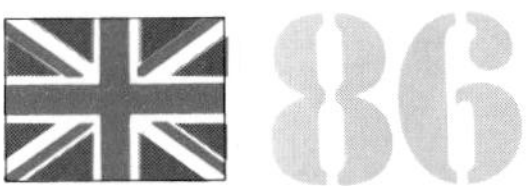

86

Jugged hare

Cooking time: 3 hr. **Preparation time:** 45 min. **Main cooking utensil:** saucepan *or* casserole. **Oven temperature:** slow to very moderate, 300–325°F., 150–170°C., Gas Mark 2–3. **Oven position:** centre.

IMPERIAL

For 6 portions you need:
1 hare, cut into joints—try to save as much blood as possible
seasoning
2 tablespoons port *or* red wine
3 onions
2 carrots
2 oz. butter
2 oz. flour
2 pints water *or* brown stock
2 tablespoons redcurrant jelly
2 tablespoons gooseberry jelly *or* sieved gooseberry jam
little lemon juice
bouquet garni

To garnish:
forcemeat balls (see method)
croûtons of bread
glacé cherries
parsley

AMERICAN

For 6 portions you need:
1 hare, cut into joints—try to save as much blood as possible
seasoning
3 tablespoons port *or* red wine
3 onions
2 carrots
$\frac{1}{4}$ cup butter
$\frac{1}{2}$ cup all-purpose flour
5 cups water *or* brown stock
3 tablespoons red currant jelly
3 tablespoons gooseberry jelly *or* sieved gooseberry jam
little lemon juice
bouquet garni

To garnish:
forcemeat balls (see method)
croûtons of bread
candied cherries
parsley

1. Soak the hare in cold water, drain, dry. Put on flat dish, cover with seasoning and wine, with one sliced onion. Marinate for 1 hour.
2. Fry onions and carrots in butter, stir in flour, blend in water or stock. Put hare's liver into sauce, simmer for at least 30 minutes.
3. Add blood, jelly, marinade from hare, lemon juice. Sieve or put into liquidizer to give smooth sauce. Add hare and bouquet garni. Cook very slowly for 3 hours in a saucepan or casserole.
4. Make forcemeat by blending 4 oz. (U.S. 2 cups) breadcrumbs, 2 oz. (U.S. scant $\frac{1}{2}$ cup) shredded suet, 1 tablespoon parsley, seasoning, 1 egg and $\frac{1}{2}$ tablespoon mixed herbs. Form into balls, bake for 20 minutes.

To serve: With forcemeat balls, croûtons, cherries, chopped parsley.

87

O'Flanagan's sausage supper

Cooking time: 25 min. **Preparation time:** 20 min. **Main cooking utensils:** 2 saucepans, grill pan/broil pan.

IMPERIAL

For 4 people you need:
$1\frac{1}{2}$–2 lb. potatoes, weight when peeled
seasoning
4 tablespoons milk
1 oz. butter
1 lb. pork sausages
2–3 oz. lard *or* fat
3 large onions
3 red skinned apples

For the sauce:
1 oz. butter
1 oz. flour
$\frac{1}{2}$ pint stock
2 tablespoons chutney

To garnish:
parsley

AMERICAN

For 4 people you need:
$1\frac{1}{2}$–2 lb. potatoes, weight when peeled
seasoning
$\frac{1}{3}$ cup milk
2 tablespoons butter
1 lb. pork link sausages
4–6 tablespoons lard *or* fat
3 large onions
3 red skinned apples

For the sauce:
2 tablespoons butter
$\frac{1}{4}$ cup all-purpose flour
$1\frac{1}{4}$ cups stock
3 tablespoons chutney

To garnish:
parsley

The Irish love of potatoes is world famous. Nothing is a better accompaniment to well-mashed potatoes than sausages, this is the kind of quick dish that one could expect to find in an Irish home.

1. Cook the potatoes in boiling, salted water until just soft, drain. Mash, beat in hot milk and butter until light and white in colour.
2. Meanwhile, prick and grill sausages (or fry if preferred).
3. Heat the lard in the pan. Cook peeled, sliced onions until nearly transparent, add cored, but unpeeled, apples, cook until tender. Keep hot.
4. Add the butter for the sauce to the pan.
5. Stir in the flour, cook for several minutes. Gradually add stock, chutney and seasoning.
6. Bring to the boil, cook until thickened.

To serve: With potatoes. Arrange sausages, onions and apples on a dish. Top with sauce, garnish with parsley.

Savoury sausage meat pie

Cooking time: 1 hr. 10 min. **Preparation time:** 25 min. **Main cooking utensils:** saucepan, 2-lb. loaf tin/pan. **Oven temperature:** hot, 425–450°F., 220–230°C., Gas Mark 6–7 then very moderate, 350°F., 180°C., Gas Mark 3–4. **Oven position:** centre.

IMPERIAL

For the hot water crust pastry:
⅜ pint water (12 tablespoons)
6 oz. fat
1 lb. flour, preferably plain
pinch salt

For the filling:
1½ lb. pork sausage meat
1 medium-sized onion
1 egg
seasoning
1 teaspoon fresh sage *or* ½ teaspoon dried sage
grated rind 1 lemon
2 dessert pears *or* apples

To glaze:
1 egg

AMERICAN

For the hot water crust pastry:
scant 1 cup water
¾ cup fat
4 cups all-purpose flour
dash salt

For the filling:
1½ lb. pork sausage meat
1 medium-sized onion
1 egg
seasoning
1 teaspoon fresh sage *or* ½ teaspoon dried sage
grated rind 1 lemon
2 eating pears *or* apples

To glaze:
1 egg

1. Heat the water and fat together until the fat has just melted.
2. Pour over flour, sieved with salt, and knead well.
3. Put one third in a warm place, this will be the 'lid' of the pie. Knead remainder. Roll out and line base and sides of tin.
4. Blend the pork sausage meat with the finely chopped onion, egg and seasoning.
5. Add the finely chopped fresh sage or dried sage and finely grated lemon rind.
6. Put one third of the sausage meat into the pastry lined tin, then one of the thinly sliced pears or apples. Cover with more sausage meat, second sliced fruit and the final layer of meat.
7. Roll out the rest of the pastry, put over the filling, sealing the edges well.
8. Cut leaves from any pastry trimmings and press on to the top of the pie.
9. Brush with beaten egg to glaze and bake until golden brown. Lower the heat after 25–30 minutes.

Beef galantine

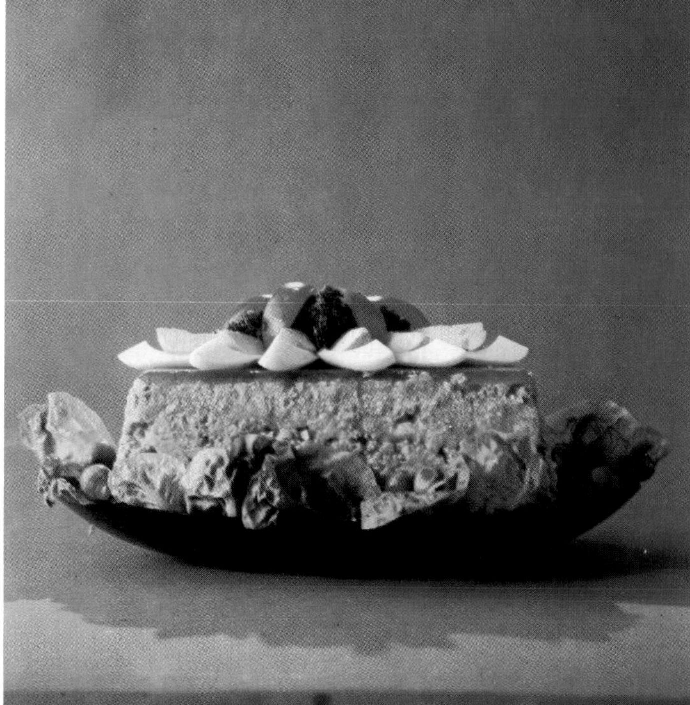

Cooking time: 2½ hr. **Preparation time:** 20 min. **Main cooking utensils:** saucepan, 2-lb. loaf tin/pan. **Oven temperature:** very moderate to moderate, 350–375°F., 180–190°C., Gas Mark 4. **Oven position:** centre.

IMPERIAL

For 6 people you need:
2 medium-sized onions
3 medium-sized tomatoes
2 oz. fat *or* butter
1 oz. flour
¼ pint stock *or* water and ½ stock cube
1½ lb. beef
12 oz. beef *or* pork sausage meat
1 egg
½–1 teaspoon mixed dried herbs
seasoning

To top:
½ pint packet aspic jelly
½ pint water *or* stock

To garnish:
lettuce
stuffed olives
2–3 hard-boiled eggs
2–3 tomatoes
watercress *or* parsley

AMERICAN

For 6 people you need:
2 medium-sized onions
3 medium-sized tomatoes
¼ cup fat *or* butter
¼ cup all-purpose flour
⅔ cup stock *or* water and ½ bouillon cube
1½ lb. beef
¾ lb. beef *or* pork sausage meat
1 egg
½–1 teaspoon mixed dried herbs
seasoning

To top:
2 teaspoons gelatin
1¼ cups water *or* stock

To garnish:
lettuce
stuffed olives
2–3 hard-cooked eggs
2–3 tomatoes
watercress *or* parsley

1. Slice the onions and skin, de-seed and chop the tomatoes.
2. Toss in the hot fat or butter until soft, then stir in the flour.
3. Cook for several minutes, then gradually add the stock. Bring to the boil and cook until thick.
4. Mince the beef, mix with the sauce, sausage meat, beaten egg and herbs, season very well.
5. Put into the greased tin, cover with greased foil and bake until firm. To give a soft outside to the galantine stand in a tin of water, for a crisp outside coat the tin with butter, then with crisp breadcrumbs and omit the tin of water. Turn out when cold and firm.
6. Meanwhile dissolve the aspic jelly in the boiling water or stock, wait until beginning to stiffen, then spread over top of galantine.

To serve: Garnish as picture and serve with salad.

90

Cheese and apple toasts

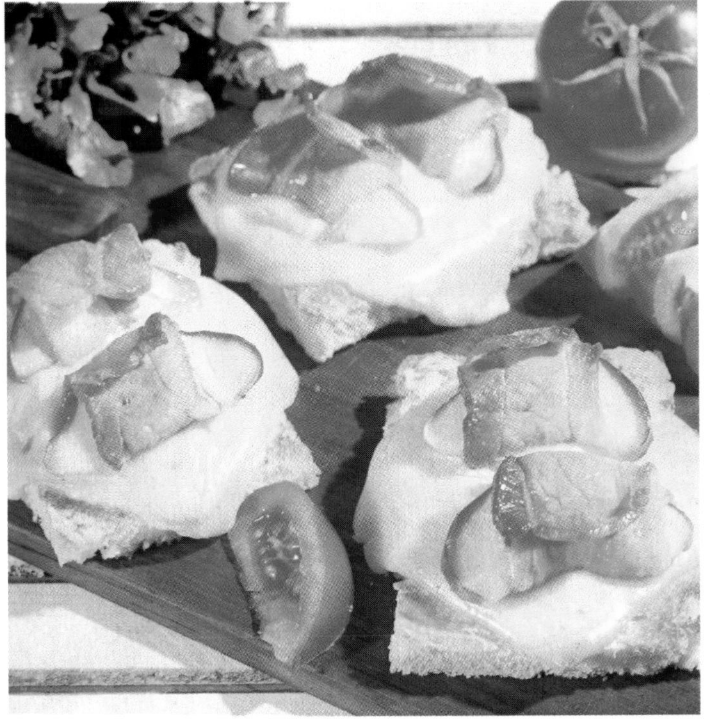

Cooking time: few min. **Preparation time:** few min. **Main cooking utensil:** grill pan/broil pan.

IMPERIAL

For 3 larger portions or 6 smaller ones you need:

A: CHEESE AND APPLE TOASTS

3 slices white bread
little butter
3 slices cheese, Gruyère, Cheddar *or* processed
6 thin rashers short back bacon
1 dessert apple

B: DEVILS ON HORSEBACK

3 slices white bread
little butter
6 cooked, drained prunes
little pâté *or* 6 blanched almonds (optional)
3 rashers long streaky bacon

AMERICAN

For 3 larger portions or 6 smaller ones you need:

A: CHEESE AND APPLE TOASTS

3 slices white bread
little butter
3 slices cheese, Gruyère, Cheddar *or* processed
6 thin lean bacon slices
1 eating apple

B: DEVILS ON HORSEBACK

3 slices white bread
little butter
6 cooked, drained prunes
little pâté *or* 6 blanched almonds (optional)
3 bacon slices

A: CHEESE AND APPLE TOASTS

1. Toast the bread, spread with butter.
2. Top with cheese and toast for 1 minute under grill.
3. Remove rind from the bacon, roll round segments of apple. Put on cheese and cook until bacon is crisp, garnish.

To serve: As a cocktail savoury, cut into fingers, or an after-dinner savoury.

B: DEVILS ON HORSEBACK

1. Toast the bread, spread with butter.
2. Remove stones from the prunes.
3. Put a little pâté or blanched almond into each prune.
4. Remove rind from the bacon, halve each rasher, roll round prunes.
5. Grill, turning once or twice, until bacon is crisp. Dust with cayenne pepper and garnish with parsley.

To serve: Put on toast. Cut into 6 fingers for light cocktail savoury, or larger portions for an after-dinner savoury.

91

Toffee fruit pudding

Cooking time: 2 hr. **Preparation time:** 20 min. **Main cooking utensils:** 2-pint/$2\frac{1}{2}$-pint basin, foil *or* greased paper to cover, steamer.

IMPERIAL

For 6–7 people you need:
1 oz. butter
1–2 oz. brown sugar

For the crust:
8 oz. self-raising flour
pinch salt
2 oz. very fine soft breadcrumbs
4 oz. shredded suet *or* melted butter
water to mix

For the filling:
$1\frac{1}{2}$–2 lb. fruit (see Stage 5)
sugar to taste
little water, if necessary

AMERICAN

For 6–7 people you need:
2 tablespoons butter
2–4 tablespoons brown sugar

For the crust:
2 cups all-purpose flour, sifted with $2\frac{1}{4}$ teaspoons baking powder
dash salt
1 cup very fine soft bread crumbs
scant 1 cup shredded suet *or* $\frac{1}{2}$ cup melted butter
water to mix

For the filling:
$1\frac{1}{2}$–2 lb. fruit (see Stage 5)
sugar to taste
little water, if necessary

1. Cover the bottom of the basin with most of the butter, use rest to grease sides lightly.
2. Sprinkle sugar over the butter at the bottom of the basin.
3. Sieve the flour and salt, add crumbs, suet or melted and cooled butter and water to mix.
4. Roll out and use two-thirds to line the basin.
5. Prepare the fruit; this pudding is delicious with a mixture of fruits as in the picture—peeled, sliced apples, gooseberries, greengages, cherries, strawberries or raspberries (canned or fresh).
6. Add sugar to taste and water, if necessary—do not use water with soft fruits.
7. Cover with a 'lid' made of remaining pastry. Seal edges, cover with greased foil or paper.
8. Steam over boiling water for at least 2 hours, fill up steamer with boiling water as necessary.

To serve: Turn out and serve with cream or custard.

Lemon treacle tart

Cooking time: 25–30 min. **Preparation time:** 20 min. **Main cooking utensil:** 8–9-inch pie plate. **Oven temperature:** hot, 425–450°F., 220–230°C., Gas Mark 6–7. **Oven position:** just above centre.

IMPERIAL

For 6–8 people you need:
8 oz. flour, preferably plain
pinch salt
4 oz. butter *or* butter and margarine *or* margarine and cooking fat
cold water

For the filling:
grated rind 2 lemons
4 oz. very fine soft breadcrumbs

1 teaspoon powdered ginger
2 tablespoons lemon juice
8 oz. golden syrup

To glaze:
1 egg white *or* beaten egg

AMERICAN

For 6–8 people you need:
2 cups all-purpose flour
dash salt
$\frac{1}{2}$ cup butter, *or* butter and margarine, *or* margarine and cooking fat
cold water

For the filling:
grated rind 2 lemons
2 cups very fine soft bread crumbs
1 teaspoon powdered ginger
3 tablespoons lemon juice
$\frac{2}{3}$ cup corn *or* maple sirup

To glaze:
1 egg white *or* beaten egg

1. Sieve the flour and salt, rub in fat. Bind with cold water.
2. Roll out the pastry, use two-thirds to line a pie plate. Stand in a cool place before baking.
3. Blend the grated lemon rind, crumbs, ginger, lemon juice and golden syrup together.
4. Prick the pastry lightly to stop the bottom rising during cooking. Cover with the syrup mixture.
5. Roll out the remaining pastry, cut into thin strips.
6. Make a design as shown in the picture. Press against sides of pastry, putting a tiny ball of pastry to cover the join.
7. Brush with egg white or egg.
8. Bake until crisp and brown; if necessary lower the heat to make sure the bottom pastry is cooked.

To serve: Hot with lemon sauce. To make: blend 2 teaspoons cornflour or arrowroot with $\frac{1}{2}$ pint (U.S. $1\frac{1}{4}$ cups) water, grated rind and juice 2 lemons, 1 tablespoon golden syrup. Boil, stirring, until thick and clear.

93

Apple and blackcurrant mould

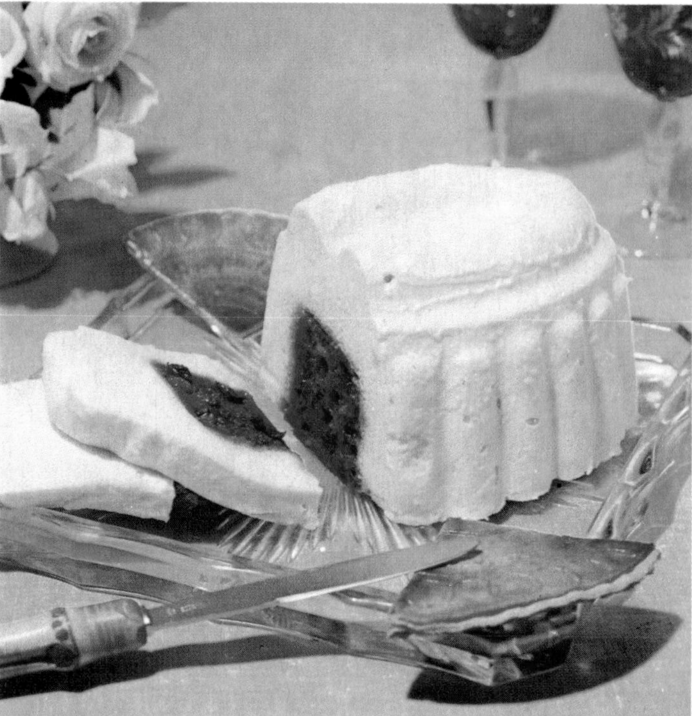

Cooking time: 20 min. **Preparation time:** 25 min. **Main cooking utensils:** double saucepan, saucepan, 2-pint/$2\frac{1}{2}$-pint mould, $\frac{3}{4}$–1-pint/$1\frac{1}{2}$-pint mould of similar shape.

IMPERIAL

For 6 people you need:
For the apple layer:
1 lb. apples
5 tablespoons water
2–3 oz. sugar
scant $\frac{1}{2}$ oz. powder gelatine
$\frac{1}{2}$ pint thick cream
1 egg white

For the blackcurrant layer:
8 oz. fresh *or* frozen blackcurrants with 2 oz. sugar and $\frac{1}{4}$ pint water, *or* 1 medium can blackcurrants

$\frac{1}{2}$ tablespoon cornflour
3 tablespoons water
1 egg yolk
scant $\frac{1}{2}$ oz. gelatine

AMERICAN

For 6 people you need:
For the apple layer:
1 lb. apples
6 tablespoons water
4–6 tablespoons sugar
2 envelopes gelatin
$1\frac{1}{4}$ cups whipping cream
1 egg white

For the blackcurrant layer:
2 cups fresh *or* frozen black currants *or* blueberries with $\frac{1}{4}$ cup sugar and $\frac{2}{3}$ cup water, *or* 1 medium can black currants
$\frac{1}{2}$ tablespoon cornstarch
scant $\frac{1}{4}$ cup water
1 egg yolk
2 envelopes gelatin

1. Peel and slice the apples, cook with 3 tablespoons (U.S. scant $\frac{1}{4}$ cup) water and sugar. A double saucepan prevents any possibility of mixture sticking. Sieve if wished, or beat until smooth.
2. Soften the gelatine in remaining water and dissolve in the very hot apple purée. Allow to cool.
3. Whip the cream until it is just stiff enough to hold its shape, then fold into apple with stiffly beaten egg white.
4. Prepare the blackcurrant mixture. Simmer fresh or frozen fruit with sugar and water until skins are very soft.
5. Blend the cornflour with 1 tablespoon water in a basin. Pour on hot blackcurrants, stirring well, return to pan and cook until smooth.
6. Add the egg yolk, simmer for 2 minutes without boiling.
7. Add the gelatine softened in 2 tablespoons (U.S. 3 tablespoons) water, stir until dissolved.
8. Insert a $\frac{3}{4}$ or 1-pint (U.S. $1\frac{1}{2}$-pint) basin or mould inside a 2-pint (U.S. $2\frac{1}{2}$-pint) mould. Firstly, either dip in cold water or brush lightly with oil. Spoon apple mixture round this, allow to set.
9. Remove the mould or basin, spoon blackcurrant mixture into space; leave this to become firm. Unmould and slice to serve.

94

Mandarin fruit ring

Cooking time: few min. heating only. **Preparation time:** 10 min. **Main cooking utensils:** saucepan, 2-pint/$2\frac{1}{2}$-pint ring mould.

IMPERIAL

For 4–5 people you need:
1 packet orange jelly (enough to set 1 pint water)
1 small can mandarin oranges
1 small can evaporated milk (approx. $5\frac{1}{2}$ fluid oz.)
few drops orange colouring

To decorate:
mandarin oranges
small bunch black grapes

AMERICAN

For 4–5 people you need:
1 (3 oz.) package orange-flavored gelatin
1 small can mandarin oranges
1 small can evaporated milk (approx. $5\frac{1}{2}$ fluid oz.)
few drops orange coloring

To decorate:
mandarin oranges
small bunch purple grapes

1. Dissolve the jelly in $\frac{1}{4}$ pint (U.S. $\frac{2}{3}$ cup) boiling water.
2. Make up to $\frac{3}{4}$ pint (U.S. scant 2 cups) with the syrup from the can of mandarin oranges, and cold water.
3. Allow this to cool.
4. Whisk the evaporated milk until thick.
5. Then, whisk the evaporated milk and jelly together and continue whisking until the mixture is thick and almost set.
6. Add enough colouring to make the mixture a pale gold.
7. Rinse out the ring mould in cold water and spoon in the mixture.
8. Leave to set.
9. When set, turn out and decorate with well-drained mandarin oranges and halved, de-seeded grapes.

NOTE: To position any jellied sweet on a serving dish, turn the mould upside-down over the dish, which should be dampened with little water, and shake so the jelly drops out. By dampening the plate, it is possible to move the jelly so it is in the centre.

To serve: With cream.

To vary: This mixture can be used as a filling for small tarts. When it is almost set at Stage 7, put into crisp tartlet cases and decorate with grapes and/or mandarin oranges.

95

Coffee walnut layer gâteau

Cooking time: 30–35 min. **Preparation time:** 40 min. **Main cooking utensils:** two 8-inch sandwich tins/layer cake pans, wire rack. **Oven temperature:** very moderate, 325–350°F., 170–180°C., Gas Mark 3. **Oven position:** above centre.

IMPERIAL

For 16 thin slices you need:
6 oz. margarine
6 oz. castor sugar
4 medium eggs
7 oz. self-raising flour
1 tablespoon coffee essence

For the icing:
6 oz. margarine
1 lb. sieved icing sugar
3 tablespoons coffee essence

To coat sides:
3 oz. walnuts, chopped

To decorate:
8 halved walnuts

AMERICAN

For 16 thin slices you need:
$\frac{3}{4}$ cup margarine
$\frac{3}{4}$ cup granulated sugar
4 eggs
$1\frac{3}{4}$ cups all-purpose flour, sifted with 2 teaspoons baking powder
1 tablespoon coffee extract

For the icing:
$\frac{3}{4}$ cup margarine
1 lb. sieved confectioners' sugar
scant $\frac{1}{4}$ cup coffee extract

To coat sides:
$\frac{3}{4}$ cup chopped walnuts

To decorate:
8 halved walnuts

1. Cream the margarine and sugar until soft and light.
2. Gradually beat in the eggs. If mixture shows signs of curdling, fold in a little sieved flour.
3. Fold in the sieved flour and coffee essence.
4. Divide the mixture equally between 2 greased and floured sandwich tins, smooth level on top.
5. Bake until firm to the touch. Turn out carefully and cool on rack. Sandwich the cakes together with some of the coffee icing, made by beating margarine and gradually beating in sieved icing sugar and coffee essence. Coat the cake round the sides with icing.
6. Chop the nuts and roll the cake in these. (The easiest way is to put nuts on a piece of greaseproof paper and roll the cake like a 'hoop'.)
7. Cover the top of the cake with remaining icing and mark a design with the prongs of a fork. Top with halved walnuts.

To serve: As a gâteau for tea or as a dessert.

 96

Somerset spiced bread

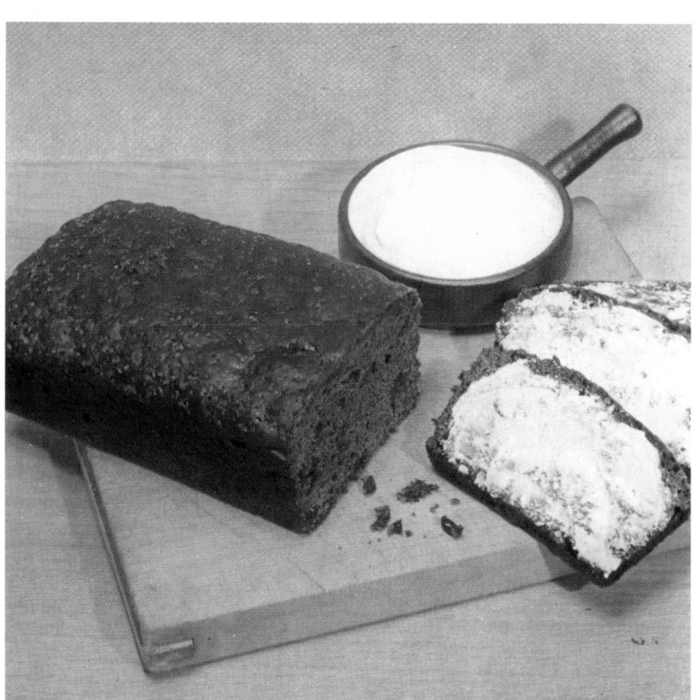

Cooking time: 2 hr. 5 min. **Preparation time:** 15 min. **Main cooking utensils:** saucepan, 2-lb. loaf tin/pan. **Oven temperature:** cool to very moderate, 300–325°F., 150–170°C., Gas Mark 2–3. **Oven position:** centre.

IMPERIAL

To give 9–10 slices you need:
- 10 oz. self-raising flour
- 4 oz. sugar, preferably demerara
- 4 oz. sultanas
- 2 oz. mixed candied peel, chopped
- 1 teaspoon mixed spice
- 1 teaspoon ground ginger
- 6 oz. black treacle
- 4 tablespoons milk
- 1 large egg, beaten
- $\frac{1}{2}$ level teaspoon bicarbonate of soda

To serve:
- butter
- 1 (6 oz.) can cream *or* $\frac{1}{4}$ pint thick cream

AMERICAN

To give 9–10 slices you need:
- $2\frac{1}{2}$ cups all-purpose flour, sifted with $2\frac{1}{2}$ teaspoons baking powder
- $\frac{1}{2}$ cup sugar, preferably brown
- $\frac{2}{3}$ cup seedless white raisins
- $\frac{1}{3}$ cup chopped, mixed candied peel
- 1 teaspoon mixed spice
- 1 teaspoon ground ginger
- $\frac{1}{2}$ cup dark molasses
- 5 tablespoons milk
- 1 large egg, beaten
- $\frac{1}{2}$ level teaspoon baking soda

To serve:
- butter
- 1 (6 oz.) can cream *or* $\frac{2}{3}$ cup whipping cream

1. Put the sieved flour, sugar, fruit and spices into a mixing bowl.
2. Warm the treacle over a low heat.
3. Mix the treacle, milk, egg and bicarbonate of soda.
4. Pour into the mixing bowl.
5. Beat thoroughly.
6. Spoon into a well-greased tin.
7. Bake in a cool oven for 2 hours, or until firm and well risen.
8. Cool on a wire tray.

To serve: Butter slices of the bread and top with thick cream.

To vary: Use chopped dates in place of sultanas, and chopped nuts in place of the peel. Substitute golden syrup for the treacle.

NOTE: Breads or cakes made by this melting method are very easy and quick.

97

Lemon curd tarts

Cooking time: A: 15 min. B: 30 min. **Preparation time:** 15–20 min. **Main cooking utensils:** A: patty tins/muffin pans. B: saucepan plus patty tins/muffin pans. **Oven temperature:** hot, 425–450°F., 220–230°C., Gas Mark 6–7. **Oven position:** above centre.

IMPERIAL

For about 12–18 tarts (depending upon size) you need:

Recipe A:
- 8 oz. flour, preferably self-raising
- pinch salt
- $1\frac{1}{2}$ oz. cooking fat
- $1\frac{1}{2}$ oz. margarine
- 2 teaspoons sugar
- little milk to mix
- about 10 oz. lemon curd

Recipe B:
- Pastry ingredients as A
- approx. 8 oz. apples (weight when peeled)
- little water
- 1 oz. sugar
- 1 oz. margarine
- about 5 oz. lemon curd

AMERICAN

For about 12–18 tarts (depending upon size) you need:

Recipe A:
- 2 cups all-purpose flour, sifted with $2\frac{1}{4}$ teaspoons baking powder
- dash salt
- 3 tablespoons cooking fat
- 3 tablespoons margarine
- 2 teaspoons sugar
- little milk to mix
- about 1 cup lemon curd

Recipe B:
- Pastry ingredients as A
- approx. $\frac{1}{2}$ lb. apples (weight when peeled)
- little water
- 2 tablespoons sugar
- 2 tablespoons margarine
- about $\frac{1}{2}$ cup lemon curd

Recipe A
1. Sieve the flour and salt, rub in the cooking fat and margarine.
2. Add sugar, bind with the milk to a firm rolling consistency.
3. Roll out and cut into rounds to fit the patty tins. Cut decorative shapes for tops.
4. Bake 'blind' for approximately 15 minutes until crisp and golden brown.
5. Fill with lemon curd. Top with pastry decorations.

Recipe B
1. Prepare the pastry as before and bake 'blind'.
2. Meanwhile simmer apples with a little, if any, water, add the sugar and margarine.
3. Almost fill the pastry cases with the apple purée, then top with lemon curd.

98

Assorted easy sweetmeats

ALMOND FONDANTS

To make 1 lb.: Ground almonds can be used in this recipe. Blanch 8 oz. almonds by putting into boiling water for few minutes, chop and finely pound until smooth. Blend with 8 oz. (U.S. scant 2 cups) sieved icing sugar and 2 egg whites. Divide mixture into three. In one portion work little green colouring and few drops peppermint essence or 1–2 teaspoons crème de menthe, plus extra icing sugar to make rolling consistency. In the second portion, add $\frac{1}{2}$–1 oz. (U.S. 2–4 tablespoons) sieved cocoa (according to personal taste); you may need to add few drops of liquid, this can be more egg white or egg yolk or few drops of Tia Maria (coffee liqueur). In the third portion, add a few drops cochineal plus raspberry essence to give a pink colour, or 1–2 teaspoons cherry brandy, plus a little extra sugar. Roll out each portion to the same size on a board coated with castor sugar. Put one on the other, press together. Dry out for 2–3 hours, cut in portions and roll in sugar.

STUFFED DATES

To make approximately $1\frac{1}{2}$–$1\frac{3}{4}$ lb.: Make almond paste as above, bind with egg yolks instead of whites. Flavour with finely grated orange rind and tint pale orange. Stone 1 lb. dates, fill with almond paste and roll in sugar if wished.

COCONUT TRUFFLES

To make nearly 1 lb.: Melt 8 oz. plain chocolate in a basin over hot water. Add 2 oz. (U.S. $\frac{2}{3}$ cup) desiccated coconut, 2 tablespoons (U.S. 3 tablespoons) condensed milk and 3 oz. (U.S. $1\frac{1}{2}$ cups) fine cake or biscuit crumbs. Leave until firm enough to handle. Roll into balls or cut into rounds. Coat in desiccated coconut and top with melted chocolate.

99

Baps

Cooking time: 15 min. **Preparation time:** 20 min. plus time for dough to 'prove'. **Main cooking utensils:** flat baking trays/sheets. **Oven temperature:** hot to very hot, 450–475°F., 230–240°C., Gas Mark 7–8. **Oven position:** above centre.

IMPERIAL

To make about 8 baps you need:

$\frac{1}{2}$ oz. yeast*
1 teaspoon sugar
12 tablespoons tepid milk and water
12 oz. plain flour**
$\frac{1}{2}$ teaspoon salt
1–$1\frac{1}{2}$ oz. lard

AMERICAN

To make about 8 baps you need:

$\frac{1}{2}$ cake compressed yeast*
1 teaspoon sugar
approx. 1 cup tepid milk and water
3 cups all-purpose flour**
$\frac{1}{2}$ teaspoon salt
2–3 tablespoons lard

*If preferred, use $1\frac{1}{2}$ teaspoons dried yeast. Dissolve sugar in tepid milk, sprinkle on the yeast, leave for a few minutes, then blend and continue as Stage 2.

**In this, and most recipes using yeast, *strong*, plain flour is advisable.

1. Cream the yeast and sugar, blend with liquid.
2. Sieve the flour and salt, rub in lard.
3. Make a well in the centre of the flour mixture and pour in yeast liquid.
4. Leave until it bubbles for 15 minutes.
5. Knead the dough until a smooth ball, cover and leave for about 1 hour to 'prove'.
6. Knead well and form into about 8 rounds or ovals, place on warm greased baking trays allowing for spreading.
7. Brush with milk, dust with flour and leave for 15 minutes.
8. Dust again with flour and press tops firmly.
9. Bake until firm to the touch. Serve hot or cold with butter.

To vary: This may also be turned into a fruit bap. Add 6–8 oz. (U.S. 1–$1\frac{1}{3}$ cups) dried fruit and 2 oz. (U.S. $\frac{1}{4}$ cup) chopped glacé cherries at Stage 2 after rubbing in lard. Continue until Stage 6, then form into a very large round or oval. Fold as shown in the picture, brush with beaten egg and continue as recipe, but bake 25–30 minutes, reducing heat to moderate after 15 minutes.

Brandied fruits

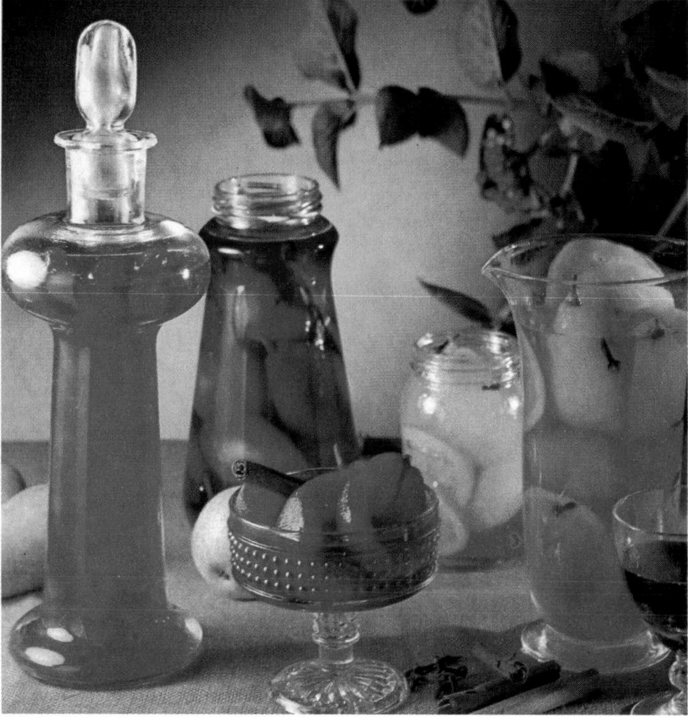

Cooking time: approx. 10–15 min. (dependent on fruit). **Preparation time:** dependent on fruit. **Main cooking utensil:** large saucepan.

IMPERIAL

To make 2 lb. brandied fruits:

2 lb. ripe, prepared fruit, halved or whole (see Stage 2)
$1\frac{1}{2}$ pints water
1 lb. sugar
little cochineal *or* 2 tablespoons redcurrant jelly
$\frac{1}{2}$ pint brandy *or* other spirit such as rum

AMERICAN

To make 2 lb. brandied fruits:

2 lb. ripe, prepared fruit, halved or whole (see Stage 2)
$3\frac{3}{4}$ cups water
1 lb. sugar
little red food coloring *or* 3 tablespoons red currant jelly
$1\frac{1}{4}$ cups brandy *or* other spirit such as rum

1. First prepare the fruit; pears, apples, peaches, apricots and other soft fruit are delicious.
2. Peel the apples or pears, try to keep them whole but remove cores. To keep apples and pears white before using, put in brine made with 1 teaspoon kitchen salt to 1 pint (U.S. $2\frac{1}{2}$ cups) water. Peaches should be lowered into boiling water for about 30 seconds, then put into cold water and skins removed. Plums and other stone fruits may be halved or left whole, cherries may be stoned.
3. Put the water and sugar in a pan over low heat until sugar has dissolved.
4. Put the fruit into the syrup, simmer for a few minutes only. If wishing to colour white fruit, add either cochineal or jelly.
5. Lift fruit out of syrup and put into jars.
6. Add brandy to the syrup, bring *just to boiling point*.
7. Pour over fruit in jars and cover.

To serve: Cold with cream.

To store: These will last as other preserves if kept in cool place. To ensure perfect storage, put into bottling jars and seal well.

101

British, Turkish and Gaelic coffee

To make good coffee remember: Coffee should be freshly purchased at regular intervals and stored in air-tight jars. The right quantity of ground coffee must be used—for ordinary coffee allow 2 heaped tablespoons (U.S. 3 heaped tablespoons) *or* 4 level tablespoons (U.S. 5 level tablespoons) to each 1 pint (U.S. $2\frac{1}{2}$ cups) *freshly drawn* water. The milk should be cold or hot, but never boiled. Cream is often served with coffee.

BRITISH COFFEE

Jug method: Measure correct amount of coffee, as above, into a warmed jug. Pour on freshly boiling water, stir well. Stand for 3–4 minutes in a warm place, put lid on jug or cover with clean cloth. Draw a spoon across the surface to skim coffee grounds. Leave for a further minute. Serve the coffee by pouring gently, preferably through a strainer, into cups or into another warmed jug.

TURKISH COFFEE

This must be made with a special, very finely ground coffee (obtainable from specialist shops)—or use an electric blender or grinder. For each person, measure 1 tiny cup of cold water into pan. Boil water over medium heat. For each cup, add at least 1 teaspoon castor sugar (Turkish coffee is very sweet). Return to the pan to dissolve. Add 1 heaped (2 level) teaspoons pulverised coffee for each cup. Stir well and allow to boil up three times. Between each boiling, the pan should be lifted from the heat until the froth on the top subsides. Remove from heat, spoon some of the creamy foam into each cup, then pour out the coffee. In an Ibrik, shown in the picture (a special coffee pot used in Turkey), the method is the same.

GAELIC COFFEE (Often called Irish coffee)

Put whiskey into warmed glasses, the amount depends on personal taste. Add coffee (made in the usual way) and sugar, stir vigorously. Very slowly pour thick cream over the back of a spoon on to the coffee to form a good layer.

It is hardly surprising that some of the early explorers who landed in the West Indies thought they had discovered Utopia. The beautiful islands set in a sparkling clear sea must have been an unbelievable vision to the weary voyagers from the Old World. And when they stepped on shore and found the profusion of lush vegetation bearing exotic fruits, vegetables and nuts, it must have seemed a true paradise.

To define any particular trends or influences in Caribbean cookery is very difficult because the islands have had such different histories. The English, French, Spanish, Indians, Dutch and many other nationalities brought their recipes with them to be adopted and changed by the West Indians. The Spanish and Indian love of spices has been imparted to the West Indians, especially curry and hot chilli and cayenne pepper. Thus one finds such recipes as Curried soup and Spiced chicken legs, the latter served cold on a bed of rice mixed with some of the most popular West Indian ingredients: green pepper, raisins and ginger.

As one would expect, the islanders are expert in preparing fish, especially the superb Caribbean shellfish. Dressed crab makes a delicious first course or light main course dish and Grapefruit, prawn and pepper cocktail is an unusual, surprisingly good way of serving prawns. Fruit features in many dishes, of course, for with an abundance of fruit always available, the West Indians have learned to use it in endless different ways. They don't hesitate to combine meat with bananas, pineapples and even mangoes, and all sorts of fruit appear in hors d'oeuvres and salads. Pineapples are used in Orange rice salad and Pineapple ham slaw, tart fresh pineapples being infinitely preferable to the syrupy canned fruit. Limes have a distinctive flavour that goes particularly well with seafood, but they can of course be replaced by lemons.

The best rum is made in the Caribbean, many islands specialising in a certain type, and many cooling summer drinks are made with rum and various fruits. Pineapple rum dessert from the Bahamas is a pudding using rum, which resembles an American upside down cake. Coconut is the basis for several delectable cakes and puddings, like Coconut ring cake, and the popular rich sweet Coconut cream pie. As you can see from these recipes, the West Indians love sweet things, and luscious sweets like Coconut raisin candy are great favourites.

Grapefruit, prawn and pepper cocktail

Preparation time: 15 min

IMPERIAL

For 4 people you need:
4 medium-sized grapefruit
4 oz. shelled prawns *or* shrimps
1 large green pepper
pieces preserved ginger
ripe mango, canned pineapple *or* 2–3 grapes *or* other fruit

For the dressing:
1 egg yolk
good pinch salt, pepper
dry mustard *or* $\frac{1}{2}$ teaspoon French mustard
sugar
1 tablespoon lemon juice
up to $\frac{1}{4}$ pint olive oil
few drops chilli sauce *or* pinch chilli powder
few drops Worcestershire sauce
lettuce (optional)

AMERICAN

For 4 people you need:
4 medium-sized grapefruit
$\frac{2}{3}$ cup peeled prawns *or* shrimp
1 large sweet green pepper
pieces preserved candied ginger
ripe mango, canned pineapple, *or* 2–3 grapes *or* other fruit

For the dressing:
1 egg yolk
dash salt, pepper
dry mustard *or* $\frac{1}{2}$ teaspoon French mustard
sugar
1 tablespoon lemon juice
up to $\frac{2}{3}$ cup olive oil
few drops chili sauce *or* dash chili powder
few drops Worcestershire sauce
lettuce (optional)

1. Cut a slice from the top of each grapefruit, make sure the fruit stands steady.
2. Remove the pulp from fruit slices, decorate edges of grapefruit skin.
3. Spoon the pulp from the remainder of grapefruit and cut into neat segments, discard skin, pith and pips.
4. Put the grapefruit segments in one bowl and juice in a second bowl. Mix prawns with the grapefruit. Cut pepper into pieces, discarding core and seeds, add to grapefruit with ginger, mango or fruit.
5. Make the mayonnaise by blending the egg yolk with seasonings and sugar, *gradually* whisk in lemon juice, oil and sauces. Add remaining lemon juice and enough grapefruit juice to give a very sharp, piquant dressing.
6. Put a good portion into bottom of grapefruit shells, with shredded lettuce, if wished. Put fruit on top, cover with fresh grapefruit juice to keep moist, serve very cold. Serve the remainder of the mayonnaise separately.

Curried soup

Cooking time: 15 min. **Preparation time:** 15 min. **Main cooking utensils:** saucepan, electric blender *or* sieve.

IMPERIAL

For 4–6 people you need:
2 oz. butter
2 large onions
1 pint chicken stock
1 tablespoon curry powder
1 tablespoon cornflour
2 egg yolks
$\frac{1}{4}$ pint thin cream
1 eating apple
seasoning
juice $\frac{1}{2}$ lemon

To garnish:
watercress*
1–2 rashers bacon, grilled

AMERICAN

For 4–6 people you need:
$\frac{1}{4}$ cup butter
2 large onions
$2\frac{1}{2}$ cups chicken stock
1 tablespoon curry powder
1 tablespoon cornstarch
2 egg yolks
$\frac{2}{3}$ cup coffee cream
1 eating apple
seasoning
juice $\frac{1}{2}$ lemon

To garnish:
watercress*
1–2 bacon slices, broiled

*Green pepper is more usual in Jamaica.

1. Melt the butter, add chopped onions. Cook until soft, but not brown.
2. Stir in chicken stock and curry powder.
3. Add the cornflour mixed with a little water. Bring to the boil, simmer for 8 minutes.
4. Beat the egg yolks into the cream, stir this mixture gradually into hot soup.
5. Remove from the heat at once, transfer mixture to an electric blender with peeled, cored and sliced apple.
6. Blend until smooth. If pressing through a sieve, the apple should be cooked with soup *before* adding egg yolks and cream.
7. Season to taste and add lemon juice.
8. Either reheat gently or chill.

To serve: Garnish with watercress and grilled, chopped bacon.

To vary: Add half a chopped, fresh mango to onions. A more interesting flavour can be obtained if peanut butter is used instead of ordinary butter.

104

Orange rice salad

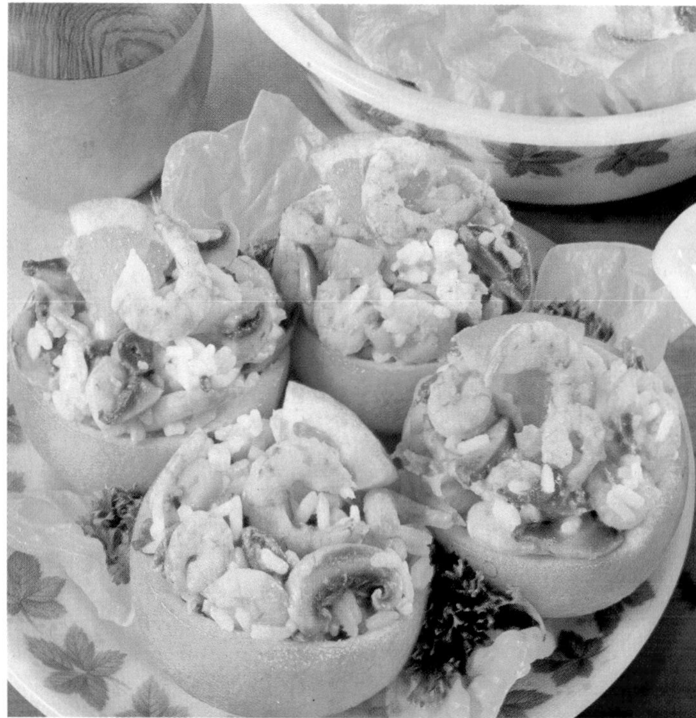

Cooking time: 15–20 min. **Preparation time:** 15 min. **Main cooking utensil:** large saucepan.

IMPERIAL

For 4 people you need:
2 oz. long grain rice
seasoning
4 large firm oranges
4 oz. shelled prawns *or* shrimps
1 mango (2 oz. mushrooms can be used instead)
slice fresh *or* canned pineapple

For the dressing:
1 small onion
$\frac{1}{2}$ clove garlic (optional)
few drops tomato purée
1 teaspoon brown sugar
2 tablespoons olive oil
2 tablespoons fresh lime *or* lemon juice
seasoning

To garnish:
lettuce
parsley

AMERICAN

For 4 people you need:
$\frac{1}{3}$ cup long grain rice
seasoning
4 large firm oranges
$\frac{2}{3}$ cup peeled prawns *or* shrimp
1 mango ($\frac{1}{2}$ cup mushrooms can be used instead)
slice fresh *or* canned pineapple

For the dressing:
1 small onion
$\frac{1}{2}$ clove garlic (optional)
few drops tomato paste
1 teaspoon brown sugar
3 tablespoons olive oil
3 tablespoons fresh lime *or* lemon juice
seasoning

To garnish:
lettuce
parsley

1. Put the rice into 1 pint (U.S. $2\frac{1}{2}$ cups) boiling, seasoned water, cook until just tender.
2. While the rice is cooking, prepare all the other ingredients and sauce.
3. Cut a slice from oranges, leave stalk end intact to make sure they balance.
4. Cut four triangles off one slice for garnish.
5. Take the pulp out of the orange cases, discarding pips and skin.
6. Mix with shelled fish, peeled diced mango or washed, sliced mushrooms (they need not be skinned) and well-drained, diced pineapple.
7. To make the dressing, chop or grate onion and crush garlic and blend with the other ingredients.
8. Drain the rice, toss in the dressing. Add the other ingredients to the warm rice and pile into the orange cases. Stand on lettuce and garnish with parsley.

105

Dressed crab

Shellfish, in particular crab, are plentiful in the West Indies and are a favourite food.

DRESSED CRAB

For 2 people: Open the body of a medium-sized crab, discard stomach bag and 'dead man's fingers' (grey fingers). Put white meat into one basin, dark meat into another. Crack large claws, remove meat from these. Blend a few drops Tabasco sauce, about 2 tablespoons (U.S. 3 tablespoons) fresh soft breadcrumbs and good squeeze lemon or lime juice with the white meat, and 1 tablespoon sherry, good shake cayenne pepper and 2 chopped hard-boiled egg whites with the dark meat. Clean out the shell, oil outside if wished. Arrange dark meat in shell, top with light meat. Garnish with 2 sieved, hard-boiled egg yolks, lines of chopped parsley and capers and a shaking of cayenne or paprika pepper.

BAKED CRAB

For 2 people: Prepare crab as above, but add a little Worcestershire sauce, as well as Tabasco sauce. Coat crab meat with crisp breadcrumbs and a little melted butter. Bake for about 15 minutes in a hot oven, 425–450°F., 220–230°C., Gas Mark 6–7.

CRAB, CRAWFISH OR LOBSTER CREOLE

For 4 people: Open 2 medium-sized crabs, lobsters or crawfish. Remove all flesh from shells, discarding stomach bag etc. as in crabs, above, and intestinal vein and 'lady's fingers' in crawfish or lobster. Blend meat with 2 oz. (U.S. 1 cup) soft breadcrumbs. Fry crushed clove garlic and 1 medium, finely chopped red pepper in 2 oz. (U.S. $\frac{1}{4}$ cup) butter. Blend with the fish, together with few drops Tabasco sauce, shake cayenne pepper, squeeze lemon juice and little chopped parsley. Press back into oiled shells and heat for about 15 minutes in hot oven.

106

Spiced chicken legs

Cooking time: about 1 hr. **Preparation time:** 20 min. plus 1 hr. marinating time. **Main cooking utensils:** grill/broiler *or* frying pan/skillet (see Stage 3) *or* saucepan.

IMPERIAL

For 4 people you need:
2 lemons *or* limes
1 clove garlic
2 teaspoons chopped red chilli pepper *or* $\frac{1}{4}$ teaspoon chilli powder
$\frac{1}{2}$–1 teaspoon powdered ginger
4 plump chicken legs
4 oz. butter
1 medium-sized onion
1 red pepper *or* red chilli pepper

6 oz. long grain rice
12 fl. oz. water
seasoning
1 green pepper
1–2 oz. seedless raisins
1–2 oz. sliced stem ginger

AMERICAN

For 4 people you need:
2 lemons *or* limes
1 clove garlic
2 teaspoons chopped red chili pepper *or* $\frac{1}{4}$ teaspoon chili powder
$\frac{1}{2}$–1 teaspoon powdered ginger
4 plump chicken legs
$\frac{1}{2}$ cup butter
1 medium-sized onion
1 sweet red pepper *or* red chili pepper
scant 1 cup long grain rice
scant 2 cups water
seasoning
1 sweet green pepper
$\frac{1}{3}$ cup seedless raisins
$\frac{1}{4}$ cup sliced stem ginger

1. Blend the juice from the lemons or limes with the crushed garlic clove, chopped red chilli pepper or powder (add this very gradually as it is hot) and powdered ginger.
2. Put on a flat dish and turn the chicken legs in this. These may be boned first, if wished. Leave the legs in the marinade for 1 hour.
3. Either cook the chicken under a grill or over a barbecue, brush well with 3 oz. (U.S. 6 tablespoons) melted butter; or fry in a pan.
4. Chill thoroughly.
5. Chop the onion and red pepper or red chilli pepper and fry in the remaining butter for a few minutes.
6. Stir in the rice, seasoning and water. Bring to the boil, stir briskly. Cover the pan and simmer for 15 minutes until just soft.
7. Chop the green pepper, add to the rice with the seedless raisins and/or the sliced stem ginger. Allow to cool.
8. If wished the rice may then be tossed in a little oil and lemon juice.
9. Put the cold rice on a bed of crisp lettuce leaves and top with the chicken legs.

Jellied whole chicken

Cooking time: approx. $1\frac{1}{2}$ hr. (see Stage 4). **Preparation time:** 10 min. **Main cooking utensil:** large saucepan.

IMPERIAL

For 4–6 people you need:
1 roasting chicken, about $3\frac{1}{2}$ lb.
1 clove garlic
seasoning
$\frac{1}{2}$ lemon
2 bay leaves
either aspic jelly to set $1\frac{1}{2}$ pints liquid *or* $\frac{3}{4}$ oz. powder gelatine
1 tablespoon Worcestershire sauce (if using aspic jelly, reduce amount of sauce to $\frac{1}{2}$ tablespoon)

AMERICAN

For 4–6 people you need:
1 roasting chicken, about $3\frac{1}{2}$ lb.
1 clove garlic
seasoning
$\frac{1}{2}$ lemon
2 bay leaves
2 tablespoons gelatin

$\frac{1}{2}$–1 tablespoon Worcestershire sauce

1. Wash the chicken, put into a saucepan rubbed round with a clove of garlic. For a stronger flavour, make a slit in the skin on each side of chicken and insert half a clove of garlic.
2. Add the seasoning, water to cover, lemon and 1 bay leaf.
3. The giblets may be added, the liver gives a more bitter flavour, however, it is quite pleasant.
4. Bring the water to boil, remove any scum. Lower heat and cook gently for 15 minutes per lb. and 15 minutes over.
5. When the chicken is cooked, lift out of stock and cover with foil or paper so it does not become dry.
6. Boil the liquid in the pan without a lid until reduced to $1\frac{1}{2}$ pints (U.S. $3\frac{3}{4}$ cups). Dissolve the aspic jelly or gelatine in this and add Worcestershire sauce.
7. Put the chicken in a deep dish, pour over jelly mixture. Add second bay leaf and put cutlet frills on legs.

To serve: Lift out of the dish as a mould. Serve with salad made by shredding pepper, cabbage, pineapple, carrots and mixing with mayonnaise and lemon juice.

108

Pineapple ham slaw

Preparation time: 10 min. **Main utensil:** mixing bowl.

IMPERIAL

For 4 people you need:
For the dressing:
$1\frac{1}{4}$ teaspoons made mustard
$\frac{1}{2}$ teaspoon salt
$\frac{1}{4}$ teaspoon black pepper
1 teaspoon sugar
4 tablespoons white vinegar

$\frac{1}{2}$ small firm white cabbage (about 12 oz.)
2 medium-sized carrots
1 small fresh pineapple (about 10 oz.) *or* 4 canned pineapple rings
8 oz. cooked ham

To garnish:
2 green eating apples
pineapple

AMERICAN

For 4 people you need:
For the dressing:
$1\frac{1}{4}$ teaspoons prepared mustard
$\frac{1}{2}$ teaspoon salt
$\frac{1}{4}$ teaspoon black pepper
1 teaspoon sugar
$\frac{1}{3}$ cup white vinegar

$\frac{1}{2}$ small firm white cabbage (about $\frac{3}{4}$ lb.)
2 medium-sized carrots
1 small fresh pineapple (about 10 oz.) *or* 4 canned pineapple rings
$\frac{1}{2}$ lb. cooked ham

To garnish:
2 green eating apples
pineapple

1. Make the dressing by combining all the ingredients together in a screw-topped jar.
2. Shred the cabbage very finely, coarsely grate carrots, dice pineapple and slice ham into narrow strips.
3. Core the apples, but retain the peel, and cut into rings. Dip the rings in the dressing to prevent them turning brown.
4. Mix the cabbage, carrots, ham and pineapple together, saving a few pineapple pieces for garnish.
5. Pile into the dish and garnish with pineapple pieces and the apple rings.

To serve: Excellent with cheese or as a light meal.

To vary: Omit pineapple, use soaked well-drained prunes and a few chopped nuts. Blend a little curry paste with dressing.

109

Pineapple rum dessert

Cooking time: 1¼ hr. **Preparation time:** 25 min. **Main cooking utensil:** 7-inch square *or* 8-inch round cake tin/pan *or* ovenproof dish. **Oven temperature:** moderate, 375°F., 190°C., Gas Mark 4–5. **Oven position:** centre.

IMPERIAL

For 5–6 people you need:
1 medium-sized fresh pineapple *or* 1 medium can pineapple
1 oz. butter
2 oz. moist brown *or* white sugar
1–2 tablespoons rum

For the pudding:
6 oz. self-raising flour
3 oz. butter
4 oz. castor sugar
2 eggs
pineapple (see Stages 3 and 5)
1 tablespoon rum

AMERICAN

For 5–6 people you need:
1 medium-sized fresh pineapple *or* 1 medium can pineapple
2 tablespoons butter
¼ cup brown *or* white sugar
1–3 tablespoons rum

For the pudding:
1½ cups all-purpose flour, sifted with 1½ teaspoons baking powder
6 tablespoons butter
½ cup granulated sugar
2 eggs
pineapple (see Stages 3 and 5)
1 tablespoon rum

1. Skin, slice and chop fresh pineapple or drain canned pineapple very thoroughly.
2. Brush the bottom of the tin or dish with melted butter and sprinkle over soft moist brown or white sugar.
3. Put half the pineapple at the bottom of the tin or dish.
4. Sprinkle with rum and leave for a while before topping.
5. Sieve flour, rub in butter; add sugar, beaten eggs, rest of the pineapple and the rum. Pour into the dish.
6. Bake until firm to the touch.
7. Turn out on to a hot dish.

To serve: Sliced while hot, with cream or with a rum butter made by creaming 2 oz. (U.S. ¼ cup) butter, 3 oz. (U.S. ¾ cup) sieved icing sugar and 2 tablespoons (U.S. 3 tablespoons) rum (this should be chilled thoroughly before serving).

To store: Although any dessert left could be eaten cold, it is inclined to become heavy as it cools, so use while fresh if possible.

110

Coconut cream pie

Cooking time: 35–40 min. **Preparation time:** 30 min. **Main cooking utensils:** 8-inch flan ring, baking tray *or* tin/baking sheet *or* pan. **Oven temperature:** moderately hot, 400°F., 200°C., Gas Mark 5–6, then very moderate 325–350°F., 170–180°C., Gas Mark 3. **Oven position:** centre.

IMPERIAL

For the pastry:
3 oz. butter
2 oz. sugar
6 oz. flour, preferably plain
1 egg yolk
little cold water

For the filling:
2 oz. butter
grated rind and juice 1 lemon
8 tablespoons condensed milk
2 tablespoons cream
6 oz. coconut, freshly grated
½ teaspoon mixed spice
1 egg yolk
2 egg whites

To decorate:
2 oz. coconut, freshly grated
glacé cherries

AMERICAN

For the pastry:
6 tablespoons butter
¼ cup sugar
1½ cups all-purpose flour
1 egg yolk
little cold water

For the filling:
¼ cup butter
grated rind and juice 1 lemon
⅔ cup condensed milk
3 tablespoons cream
approx. 2 cups freshly grated coconut
½ teaspoon mixed spice
1 egg yolk
2 egg whites

To decorate:
approx. ⅔ cup freshly grated coconut
candied cherries

1. Cream the butter and sugar, add flour, egg yolk and water to bind.
2. Roll out to fit an 8-inch flan ring or tin and bake 'blind' until just golden, but not too brown.
3. Cream the butter with grated lemon rind and juice. Add condensed milk, cream, coconut, spice and egg yolk, then fold in stiffly beaten egg whites.
4. Put into the flan case and return to oven, lowering the heat.
5. Cook for a further 20 minutes. Top with coconut and glacé cherries.

To serve: Hot with ice cream or can be eaten cold.

To store: Can be kept in a cool place.

111

Coconut ring cake

Cooking time: 25 min. **Preparation time:** 20 min. **Main cooking utensils:** baking tray/sheet *or* 9-inch shallow cake tin/shallow cake pan, double saucepan *or* basin over saucepan of hot water. **Oven temperature:** 425–450°F., 220–230°C., Gas Mark 6–7. **Oven position:** above centre.

IMPERIAL

For 12 portions you need:
10 oz. self-raising flour
5 oz. butter *or* margarine
6 oz. sugar
5–6 oz. fresh coconut
4 oz. candied orange peel, chopped
1 orange
2 eggs
little coconut milk

For the topping:
4–5 oz. plain chocolate
2 teaspoons coconut milk
few pieces crystallized rose petals, 1 silver ball

AMERICAN

For 12 portions you need:
$2\frac{1}{2}$ cups all-purpose flour, sifted with $2\frac{3}{4}$ teaspoons baking powder
$\frac{1}{2}$ cup plus 2 tablespoons butter *or* margarine
$\frac{3}{4}$ cup sugar
about $\frac{1}{3}$ lb. fresh coconut
$\frac{2}{3}$ cup chopped, candied orange peel
1 orange
2 eggs
little coconut milk

For the topping:
$\frac{2}{3}$–$\frac{3}{4}$ cup semi-sweet chocolate
2 teaspoons coconut milk
few pieces crystallized rose petals, 1 silver ball

1. Put the sieved flour into bowl, rub in the butter or margarine until mixture resembles fine breadcrumbs.
2. Add the sugar, finely grated coconut, orange peel and finely grated orange rind.
3. Bind with eggs and coconut milk, or use orange juice.
4. There are 2 ways of preparing this cake:
Method 1: Form into a 9-inch round, put on baking tray or into lightly greased tin, mark into 12 portions.
Method 2: (shown in picture) Divide mixture into 12 triangular pieces, press these into tin.
5. Bake until firm (reduce heat after 15 minutes if wished), allow to cool.
6. Melt chocolate in the top of a double saucepan or basin over hot water, add coconut milk.
7. Pour over cake, decorate with the rose petals and silver ball.

To vary: When fresh coconut is not available, use 9 oz. (U.S. $2\frac{1}{4}$ cups) flour and 7 oz. (U.S. approx. $1\frac{1}{2}$ cups) desiccated coconut and bind with orange juice. Add orange juice or ordinary milk to the chocolate.

112

Coconut raisin candy and Sunny raisin fudge

Cooking time: see Stages 2 and 3, 1 and 2. **Preparation time:** 10–15 min. each. **Main cooking utensils:** *strong* saucepans.

IMPERIAL

For $1\frac{1}{2}$ lb. you need:

A: COCONUT RAISIN CANDY
1 lb. granulated sugar
$\frac{1}{4}$ pint water
1 tablespoon rum (optional)
6 oz. fresh coconut, grated *or* 4 oz. desiccated coconut
6 oz. seedless raisins
few drops cochineal

B: SUNNY RAISIN FUDGE
2 oz. butter
1 lb. granulated sugar
4 tablespoons water
8 tablespoons sweetened condensed milk
2 tablespoons clear honey
3–4 oz. seedless raisins
1–2 oz. nuts, chopped

AMERICAN

For $1\frac{1}{2}$ lb. you need:

A: COCONUT RAISIN CANDY
4 cups granulated sugar
$\frac{2}{3}$ cup water
1 tablespoon rum (optional)
generous 1 cup grated fresh coconut *or* 1 cup shredded coconut
1 cup seedless raisins
few drops red food coloring

B: SUNNY RAISIN FUDGE
$\frac{1}{4}$ cup butter
4 cups granulated sugar
$\frac{1}{3}$ cup water
$\frac{2}{3}$ cup sweetened condensed milk
3 tablespoons clear honey
$\frac{2}{3}$ cup seedless raisins
$\frac{1}{4}$–$\frac{1}{2}$ cup chopped nuts

A: COCONUT RAISIN CANDY

1. Put the sugar and water into pan, stir until sugar has dissolved, add rum.
2. Boil steadily until mixture forms a soft ball when tested in cold water, 238°F.
3. Add the coconut, continue boiling for a few minutes until mixture reaches 240°F. (slightly firmer ball).
4. Add the raisins, beat for few minutes. Pour half into a well oiled or buttered tin, quickly tint remainder pink, pour on top and leave to set. Cut into squares.

B: SUNNY RAISIN FUDGE

1. Butter the pan, put the sugar and water into pan, stir until sugar has dissolved. Add the remaining butter, milk and honey.
2. Continue boiling, stir from time to time until mixture starts to thicken, (238°F.), then add raisins and chopped nuts.
3. Beat until slightly cloudy. Pour into a buttered tin and allow to set. Cut into squares.

Chinese food has become increasingly popular in the Western world with the appearance of so many Chinese restaurants, but only recently have housewives begun to realise that Oriental dishes can easily be made at home. Many recipes do not call for particularly unusual or exotic ingredients, and such items as bean sprouts, water chestnuts and soy sauce are available in most well-stocked supermarkets. Chinese food has several advantages for entertaining. Most dishes require only a few minutes cooking once the ingredients have been prepared, so the meat and vegetables can be cut up ahead of time and the cooking can be done later in a short time. Another advantage for the hostess is that Chinese meals are not eaten in courses; a large bowl of fluffy white rice and all the different dishes are placed on the table at once. The hostess is then free to sit down at the table with her guests and doesn't have to return to the kitchen, except for China tea and perhaps a simple dessert like fruit salad.

Deep-fried Pancake rolls, filled with chopped meat, prawns and bean sprouts, are a famous Chinese delicacy which are sometimes served as an hors d'oeuvre but can also be one of the dishes of the main meal.

Sweet and sour dishes are always popular, vinegar and sugar or honey being the essential ingredients to achieve the sweet-sour flavour. Veal sweet and sour is unusual with its use of citrus fruit and Beef with cauliflower in sweet-sour sauce is made particularly colourful with the addition of tomato purée. Lobster balls are a sophisticated Chinese speciality and, as in Pork with pepper and pineapple, the use of pineapple gives the sauce a distinctive sweet flavour.

Fried chicken with vegetables is typical of many Chinese dishes made with meat and various vegetables chopped and cooked together quickly so the vegetables retain some of the crispness. This recipe, like the sweet and sour recipes may be varied by using a different type of meat or substituting other vegetables. Rice is the most common accompaniment to Chinese food but noodles are also frequently served. They may be boiled but an attractive way of cooking fine noodles is to deep fry them, making Crispy noodles.

The Chinese do not usually have a dessert after their meals but they are very fond of sweet pastries which they eat as snacks. If you want to serve a sweet, lychees, guavas or fruit salad and perhaps small sweet biscuits are suitable. Alternatively, Chinese toffee apples make a delicious dessert.

Loong har kow and Tan tsu
Sweet and sour lobster balls

Cooking time: 10–15 min. **Preparation time:** 25 min. **Main cooking utensils:** saucepan, pan for oil, absorbent paper/paper towels.

IMPERIAL

For 4 people you need:
For the lobster balls:
1 small lobster *or* 1 medium-sized can lobster
3 oz. self-raising flour
seasoning
pinch Chinese 'taste' powder
1 egg
$\frac{1}{4}$ pint water
1 tablespoon flour *or* cornflour

For the sauce:
$\frac{1}{2}$ small green pepper
1 tablespoon honey
about 8 pineapple cubes
few canned lychees (optional)
2 teaspoons cornflour
2 tablespoons vinegar
1 tablespoon soy sauce
seasoning
$\frac{1}{4}$ pint water

AMERICAN

For 4 people you need:
For the lobster balls:
1 small lobster *or* 1 medium-sized can lobster
$\frac{3}{4}$ cup all-purpose flour, sifted with 1 teaspoon baking powder
seasoning
dash Chinese 'taste' powder
1 egg
$\frac{2}{3}$ cup water
1 tablespoon flour *or* cornstarch

For the sauce:
$\frac{1}{2}$ small sweet green pepper
1 tablespoon honey
about 8 pineapple cubes
few canned lychees (optional)
2 teaspoons cornstarch
3 tablespoons vinegar
1 tablespoon soy sauce
seasoning
$\frac{2}{3}$ cup water

1. Remove flesh from the lobster and cut into tiny pieces. If using canned lobster where the flesh is less firm, mix with a fork. Form into about 20 tiny balls.
2. Make the batter by mixing the flour, seasoning, taste powder, well beaten egg and water to a smooth consistency.
3. Coat the lobster with flour or cornflour, but do not coat in batter until ready to fry; it is advisable to prepare sauce before doing this.
4. Chop flesh of green pepper and blend all ingredients for sauce.
5. Put into the saucepan, cook until thickened, stirring, keep hot.
6. Dip the lobster in batter, fry for 2–3 minutes only in hot oil; this is the correct temperature when a cube of day-old bread turns golden brown in 30 seconds.
7. Put the well-drained lobster balls into a hot serving bowl, top with sauce. Serve at once with cooked rice.

Chin chiao niu jou szu
Pork with pepper and pineapple

Cooking time: 15 min. **Preparation time:** 20 min. **Main cooking utensil:** frying pan/skillet *or* shallow saucepan.

IMPERIAL

For 4 people you need:
8–10 oz. very lean tender pork
2 teaspoons cornflour
seasoning, pinch sugar
2 tablespoons oil
1 small red pepper
1 small green pepper

For the sauce:
3 rings pineapple
1 dessert apple *or* pear
2 teaspoons cornflour
$\frac{1}{4}$ pint chicken stock
1 tablespoon sherry
1 tablespoon soy sauce
1 tablespoon sugar
2 tablespoons vinegar
pinch Chinese 'taste' powder
4 tablespoons pineapple syrup

To serve:
6 oz. long grain rice

AMERICAN

For 4 people you need:
$\frac{1}{2}$–$\frac{2}{3}$ lb. very lean tender pork
2 teaspoons cornstarch
seasoning, dash sugar
3 tablespoons oil
1 small sweet red pepper
1 small sweet green pepper

For the sauce:
3 rings pineapple
1 eating apple *or* pear
2 teaspoons cornstarch
$\frac{2}{3}$ cup chicken stock
1 tablespoon sherry
1 tablespoon soy sauce
1 tablespoon sugar
3 tablespoons vinegar
dash Chinese 'taste' powder
$\frac{1}{3}$ cup pineapple sirup

To serve:
scant 1 cup long grain rice

1. Cut the meat into neat pieces, it must be smaller than shown in the picture if you are to find it easy to pick up with chop-sticks.
2. Blend the cornflour, seasoning and sugar and roll the meat in this.
3. Fry in hot oil for about 5 minutes, then add the diced red and green pepper, discarding the core and seeds.
4. Continue cooking for several minutes.
5. Cut each ring of pineapple into several pieces.
6. Core, slice, but do not peel the apple or pear.
7. Blend the cornflour with all the other ingredients.
8. Add to the meat with the fruit, bring to the boil and cook until thickened and very hot. Serve with boiled rice.

To vary: Add sliced bamboo shoots, bean sprouts and sliced water chestnuts to the pork with finely chopped spring onions and cucumber.

115

Hua chiano jou wantze
Meat balls

Cooking time: few min. to brown nuts. **Preparation time:** 15 min. **Main utensil:** mixing bowl.

IMPERIAL

For 4 people you need:
12 oz. cooked pork
1 large dessert apple
1–2 teaspoons powdered sage
2 tablespoons chopped bean sprouts
2 teaspoons chopped parsley
1 tablespoon chopped spring onions
grated rind $\frac{1}{2}$ lemon
1–2 teaspoons soy sauce
1–2 teaspoons tomato ketchup
seasoning

To coat:
4 oz. blanched almonds

To garnish:
parsley

AMERICAN

For 4 people you need:
$\frac{3}{4}$ lb. cooked pork
1 large eating apple
1–2 teaspoons powdered sage
3 tablespoons chopped bean sprouts
2 teaspoons chopped parsley
1 tablespoon chopped scallions
grated rind $\frac{1}{2}$ lemon
1–2 teaspoons soy sauce
1–2 teaspoons tomato catsup
seasoning

To coat:
scant 1 cup blanched almonds

To garnish:
parsley

1. Mince the pork and the apple.
2. Mix with the sage, bean sprouts, parsley, spring onions, lemon rind, soy sauce, ketchup and seasoning.
3. Chill mixture for 30 minutes.
4. Form into about 8–12 even-sized balls.
5. Chop the almonds and brown under the grill.
6. Roll each ball in the chopped nuts. Garnish with parsley.

To vary: This is an adaptation of a Chinese meat ball and may be varied in a number of ways. The apple could be omitted and finely diced preserved ginger added.
The meat balls could be coated in a batter made with 3 oz. self-raising flour (U.S. $\frac{3}{4}$ cup all-purpose flour, sifted with 1 teaspoon baking powder), $\frac{1}{4}$ pint (U.S. $\frac{2}{3}$ cup) water, seasoning and one stiffly beaten egg white. The balls should be formed as Stage 4, dipped in the batter, fried in hot oil until crisp and golden brown. They may then be served either hot or cold.

116

Gu lo yuk
Veal sweet and sour

Cooking time: 20–25 min. **Preparation time:** 20 min. **Main cooking utensils:** frying pan/skillet, saucepan.

IMPERIAL

For 4 people you need:
1 lb. veal
½ oz. flour
seasoning
6 tablespoons oil
4 shallots *or* 2 onions
2 apples
1 orange
1 grapefruit

For the sauce:
1 tablespoon cornflour
½ pint chicken stock
½–1 tablespoon soy sauce
3 tablespoons vinegar
2 tablespoons honey

AMERICAN

For 4 people you need:
1 lb. veal
2 tablespoons all-purpose flour
seasoning
½ cup oil
4 shallots *or* 2 onions
2 apples
1 orange
1 grapefruit

For the sauce:
1 tablespoon cornstarch
1¼ cups chicken stock
½–1 tablespoon soy sauce
scant ¼ cup vinegar
3 tablespoons honey

1. Cut the veal into 1-inch cubes.
2. Coat in seasoned flour.
3. Heat the oil and fry the veal until lightly browned. Lower heat.
4. Add the skinned, halved shallots or sliced onions, cook for 5 minutes.
5. Add cored and thinly sliced apples, skinned orange and grapefruit segments.
6. Continue cooking over a very low heat for 10 minutes, or until meat is tender.
7. To make the sauce: blend cornflour with chicken stock.
8. Put into the pan with the rest of the ingredients and bring to boil, cook until thick and clear.

To serve: With boiled rice.

To vary: Use pork, chicken, prawns or shrimp.

117

Char gee ngow yuk
Beef with cauliflower

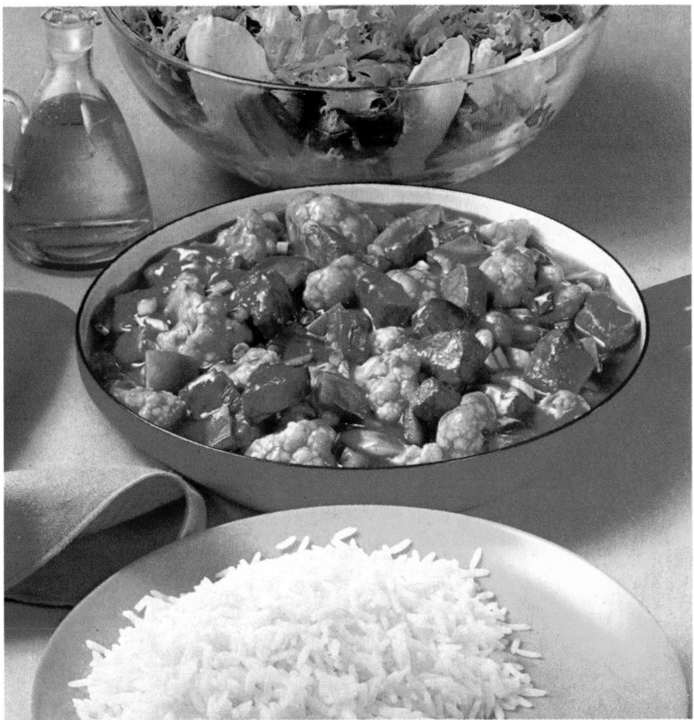

Cooking time: 25 min. **Preparation time:** 25 min. **Main cooking utensils:** 2 saucepans.

IMPERIAL

For 4 people you need:
6 oz. long grain rice
seasoning
12 oz.–1 lb. fillet *or* rump steak
1 medium-sized cauliflower
1 green pepper
small piece cucumber
4 oz. bean sprouts *or* green beans
1 clove garlic
½ oz. cornflour
seasoning
2 tablespoons oil

For the sauce:
½ oz. cornflour
½ pint brown stock
2 tablespoons vinegar
½ tablespoon soy sauce
1 tablespoon honey
2 tablespoons mustard pickles
½ tablespoon tomato purée

AMERICAN

For 4 people you need:
scant 1 cup long grain rice
seasoning
¾–1 lb. fillet *or* other good quality steak
1 medium-sized cauliflower
1 sweet green pepper
small piece cucumber
2 cups bean sprouts *or* green beans
1 clove garlic
2 tablespoons cornstarch
seasoning
3 tablespoons oil

For the sauce:
2 tablespoons cornstarch
1¼ cups brown stock
3 tablespoons vinegar
½ tablespoon soy sauce
1 tablespoon honey
3 tablespoons mustard pickles
½ tablespoon tomato paste

1. Cook the rice.
2. Cut the steak into neat pieces.
3. Divide the cauliflower into small sprigs (flowerets) and cook for 10 minutes only in well seasoned water; drain.
4. Divide the flesh of the green pepper into cubes, discarding core and seeds, peel and dice cucumber and chop the green beans into neat pieces (bean sprouts may be left whole).
5. Crush the garlic and blend with cornflour and seasoning.
6. Roll the meat in this and brown lightly in hot oil.
7. Add the sauce, made by blending cornflour with stock, vinegar, soy sauce, honey, chopped pickles and tomato purée.
8. Bring to the boil and cook until thickened. Add drained cauliflower, pepper, cucumber, bean sprouts or beans and continue cooking for about 10 minutes.

Chao chi ting
Fried chicken with vegetables

Cooking time: 20 min. **Preparation time:** 25 min. plus time to soak mushrooms (see Stage 6). **Main cooking utensils:** 2 saucepans, frying pan/skillet.

IMPERIAL

For 4 people you need:
$\frac{1}{2}$ swede *or* 2 carrots
seasoning
1 small frying chicken *or* part of a larger one (young bird)
3 tablespoons oil
1 red pepper
1 green pepper
few sticks celery
1 small can bean sprouts
6–8 water chestnuts
part of a bamboo shoot
3 tablespoons chicken stock (made from simmering gibiets)
1 tablespoon soy sauce
3–4 oz. mushrooms *or* 1 oz. dried

To serve:
12 oz. cooked rice

AMERICAN

For 4 people you need:
$\frac{1}{2}$ rutabaga *or* 2 carrots
seasoning
1 small frying chicken, *or* part of a larger one (young bird)
scant $\frac{1}{4}$ cup oil
1 sweet red pepper
1 sweet green pepper
few stalks celery
1 small can bean sprouts
6–8 water chestnuts
part of a bamboo shoot
scant $\frac{1}{4}$ cup chicken stock (made from simmering giblets)
1 tablespoon soy sauce
1 cup mushrooms *or* 1 oz. dried

To serve:
approx. 6 cups cooked rice

This is typical of any easy-to-prepare Chinese meal, all the ingredients may be prepared, covered with polythene or foil, then cooked at the last minute.

1. Dice the peeled swede or carrots, simmer in boiling, seasoned water until just soft.
2. Dice the chicken flesh neatly, toss for a few minutes in hot oil.
3. Dice the flesh from red and green peppers, discarding cores and seeds. If wished to be 'crisp' in texture, add to the chicken; for a softer texture, cook for 5 minutes only with the swede or carrots, drain, then add to the chicken.
4. Dice the celery (see Stage 3 for peppers, in the picture it has *not* been partially boiled).
5. Continue cooking until the chicken is tender, then add the drained swede or carrots, bean sprouts, sliced chestnuts, bamboo shoot, stock and sauce.
6. Heat with the sliced mushrooms (if using dried mushrooms, cover with cold water, leave for 1 hour, drain, chop and cook). Serve with rice.

119

Chen guin
Pancake rolls

Cooking time: 15–20 min. **Preparation time:** 15 min. **Main cooking utensils:** frying pan/skillet, small saucepan, deep fryer and basket.

IMPERIAL

For 4 people you need:
For the batter:
4 oz. plain flour
2 oz. cornflour
pinch salt
$\frac{3}{4}$ pint water

For frying:
lard

For the filling:
1 onion
1 oz. lard
4 oz. raw pork *or* cooked beef
3 oz. prawns, shelled
1 (4 oz.) can bean sprouts
seasoning
few drops soy sauce

AMERICAN

For 4 people you need:
For the batter:
1 cup all-purpose flour
scant $\frac{1}{2}$ cup cornstarch
dash salt
scant 2 cups water

For frying:
lard

For the filling:
1 onion
2 tablespoons lard
$\frac{1}{4}$ lb. raw pork *or* cooked beef
$\frac{1}{2}$ cup shelled prawns *or* shrimp
1 (4 oz.) can bean sprouts
seasoning
few drops soy sauce

1. Make a thin batter with flour, cornflour, salt and water.
2. Heat the pan, brush base and sides with melted lard.
3. Pour in sufficient batter to just cover the base, cook on one side only until quite dry, but not golden in colour.
4. Peel the pancake away with fingers and place on a clean tea towel.
5. Repeat, using most of the remaining batter, making 6–8 pancakes.
6. Fry the onion in lard until transparent, add minced meat and 2 oz. (U.S. $\frac{1}{3}$ cup) chopped prawns, cook for 1–2 minutes.
7. Add the drained bean sprouts, seasoning and soy sauce, cook for further 2 minutes. Drain off excess liquid.
8. Spread 2 tablespoons (U.S. 3 tablespoons) of the mixture on each pancake.
9. Fold ends over and roll up pancakes, sealing edges with remaining batter. Allow to dry thoroughly. Fry until golden brown in deep lard at 375°F., 190°C. (At this temperature, a 1-inch cube of stale bread will brown in 40–50 seconds).

To serve: Top with remainder of prawns.

120

Jar min
Crispy noodles

Cooking time: 4 min. **Preparation time:** few min. unless making noodles. **Main cooking utensils:** pan for oil with frying basket, absorbent paper/paper towels.

IMPERIAL

For 4 people you need:
6 oz. noodles
approx. $1\frac{1}{2}$ pints peanut oil

For vegetable and prawn mixture:
3 large Pacific prawns
1 bamboo shoot
1 water chestnut
small pieces cucumber
2 spring onions
2 tablespoons oil
1 teaspoon cornflour
$\frac{1}{2}$ pint chicken stock
1 teaspoon soy sauce
seasoning

To garnish:
spring onions

AMERICAN

For 4 people you need:
$\frac{1}{3}$ lb. noodles
approx. $3\frac{3}{4}$ cups peanut oil

For vegetable and prawn mixture:
3 large Pacific prawns
1 bamboo shoot
1 water chestnut
small pieces cucumber
2 scallions
3 tablespoons oil
1 teaspoon cornstarch
$1\frac{1}{4}$ cups chicken stock
1 teaspoon soy sauce
seasoning

To garnish:
scallions

Noodles are a usual and popular accompaniment to Chinese dishes.

1. Chinese noodles are already shaped into a nest shape, but ordinary fine noodles should be shaped at Stage 2.
2. Turn the raw noodles into small frying basket to fill this neatly and completely.
3. Heat the oil, test if correct temperature, a cube of day-old bread should turn golden brown in 30 seconds. Make sure the pan is not more than half full.
4. Lower the basket of raw noodles into the oil, fry steadily until golden and drain on absorbent paper.

To serve: With any dish. The picture shows them on a mixture of vegetables and prawns. Fry chopped prawns and vegetables in oil for 1–2 minutes, then add cornflour, blended with stock and sauce. Season and allow to thicken. Garnish with spring onions.

121

Chinese toffee apples

Cooking time: 10 min. **Preparation time:** 15 min. plus time for apples to stand. **Main cooking utensils:** large shallow saucepan, or frying pan/skillet, pan for oil, absorbent paper/paper towels.

IMPERIAL

For 4 people you need:
For the syrup:
2 oz. sugar
2 tablespoons honey
$\frac{1}{4}$ pint water
juice 1 large lemon

4 good-sized cooking apples
3 oz. flour, plain *or* self-raising
pinch salt
2 teaspoons sugar
2 eggs
$\frac{1}{4}$ pint water

To fry:
oil

To top:
castor *or* sieved icing sugar

1 lemon

AMERICAN

For 4 people you need:
For the sirup:
$\frac{1}{4}$ cup sugar
3 tablespoons honey
$\frac{2}{3}$ cup water
juice 1 large lemon

4 good-sized baking apples
$\frac{3}{4}$ cup all-purpose flour
dash salt
2 teaspoons sugar
2 eggs
$\frac{2}{3}$ cup water

To fry:
oil

To top:
granulated *or* sifted confectioners' sugar
1 lemon

In China small crab apples are often used for this delicacy, but segments of cooking apples would be equally good, and this has been used in the picture.

1. Make the syrup of sugar, honey, water and lemon juice.
2. Peel the apples, divide into thick segments and put into hot syrup; do not heat again, as they will become too soft. Leave for about 1 hour, turning round in the syrup from time to time.
3. Sieve the flour and salt, add the sugar, the egg yolks, water and finally the stiffly whisked egg whites.
4. Lift the apple segments from the syrup, drain for a moment over a sieve, then coat in the batter.
5. Fry in hot oil until crisp and golden brown and drain on absorbent paper, then top with sugar and serve with lemon.

To vary: Segments of potato are sometimes cooked in the same way and, although not a typical Chinese dessert, sharp plums are excellent.

EASTERN EUROPE

Eastern Europe is not often acknowledged in the West as having interesting food. This is a great pity because many excellent recipes come from this part of the world, particularly for hearty soups and casseroles, dumplings and pancakes, and rich cakes.

Czechoslovakia is the westernmost European country which accounts for the popularity of such German and Austrian specialities as sausages, sauerkraut and dumplings. Beef in paprika shows a resemblance to recipes from neighbouring Hungary and is especially good served with pickled cucumbers. The Slovak celebration menu includes recipes that are equally popular in the other Eastern European countries. This selection of homely warming food makes a good buffet for a cold winters day, to be accompanied by tea, beer or a robust red wine, depending on your guests and the time of day. If you want to add something sweet to the menu, a good choice would be *Bukhty*, small filled yeast cakes or *Babovka*, a marbled chocolate and nut cake.

One cannot think of Hungarian cooking without thinking of paprika and sweet red peppers which appear in so many dishes. Pepper soup uses both and is an exceptionally colourful, well-seasoned vegetable soup. Other favourite recipes using paprika are Veal stew paprika and Hungarian savoury fish steaks. However, one must be careful not to insult the Hungarians by assuming that the use of paprika and peppers is the only distinctive characteristic of their cuisine. They are renowned for sustaining soups and casseroles of all kinds, including Butter bean soup, an excellent economical stand-by that is virtually a meal in itself. Like Austria and Czechoslovakia, Hungary has a Germanic addiction to sausages and the Farmhouse sausage selection shows a typical country meal of sausages, sauerkraut, brown bread and beer.

All Eastern European countries have their own baked specialities and Hungary is no exception. Morello cherry cake, a far cry from an ordinary cherry cake, uses the sharp Morello cherries that grow so well in Hungary. Most Continental countries do not have the British type of fruit cake for Christmas but make a rich, fruity yeast cake. The Czechs make a simple dough which is rolled up like a Swiss roll with a filling of dried fruit and plenty of nuts.

Poland is a wonderfully hospitable country and visitors are always generously catered for. Cold meats and pâtés, like Veal pâté, are kept on hand for unexpected guests and are often served as a main course. The Poles excel in pancake making and have some delicious savoury ways of filling them. They are often stuffed with vegetables and served with sausages, or stacked with layers of meat filling for an unusual and attractive main dish. A well-known Polish dish is Hunter's stew, so named because it was a sustaining one-dish meal that hunters could take with them and reheat at any time. The Poles have some original ideas for sausages, Sausages and chestnuts being sophisticated enough to serve at a supper party.

Czarist Russia was a country with a vast peasant population ruled by a small select aristocracy. Although this feudal system was done away with by the revolution, Russian cooking still reflects its past. Peasants relied heavily on bread, porridge and soups, especially in the bleak winter months, and these remain the staples of Russian cooking today. Red cabbage pot-au-feu derived from such simple peasant origins as these.

When we think of Russia we tend to forget how far it extends, reaching from Europe to the Far East, from the Arctic down to the Black Sea. Thus we would not be surprised to find Middle Eastern and Oriental influences in Russian cooking. *Shashlik*, for example, is a version of the Turkish kebabs and *Piroshki* are like Chinese pancake rolls with a different filling. Rice is almost as common as potatoes, as one might expect with China on the southern border.

Perhaps the most famous Russian speciality of all is Boeuf Stroganoff, a rich luxurious dish with strips of tender steak in cream sauce. Soured cream is preferable to cream in this recipe for it is a favourite ingredient in Russia and throughout Eastern Europe. Almost any vegetable benefits from the addition of soured cream, particularly potatoes and aubergines which are rather dull on their own. Soured cream is also used in desserts like *Pashka*, a traditional Easter Cream cheese moul

Yugoslavian cooking is difficult to categorise because it belongs almost as much to the Eastern Mediterranean as to Eastern Europe. They often grill their meat and we have included a recipe for the popular combination of grilled meat with cheese.

122

Vajbab leves
Butter bean soup

Cooking time: 2 hr. **Preparation time:** 15 min. plus overnight soaking of beans. **Main cooking utensil:** large saucepan.

IMPERIAL

For 5–6 people you need:
8 oz. butter beans

approx. 4 pints water *or* stock (ham, bacon and chicken stock are all excellent)
seasoning (be sparing with salt, if using ham stock)
1 medium-sized onion
bunch parsley *or* good pinch dried parsley
2 oz. butter *or* fat
2 oz. flour

To garnish:
2–3 oz. bacon

To serve:
$\frac{1}{4}$ pint soured cream

AMERICAN

For 5–6 people you need:
approx. $1\frac{1}{4}$ cups dried fava *or* lima beans
approx. 5 pints water *or* stock (ham, bacon and chicken stock are all excellent)
seasoning (be sparing with salt, if using ham stock)
1 medium-sized onion
bunch parsley *or* dash dried parsley
$\frac{1}{4}$ cup butter *or* fat
$\frac{1}{2}$ cup all-purpose flour

To garnish:
4–6 bacon slices

To serve:
$\frac{2}{3}$ cup sour cream

1. Soak the beans overnight in water or stock to cover.
2. Add seasoning and cook in this liquid until tender, about $1\frac{1}{2}$ hours.
3. Towards the end of the cooking time add chopped onion and parsley.
4. Rub through a sieve, saving a few beans for garnish.
5. Heat the butter or fat in a pan. Stir in the flour and cook for several minutes then gradually blend in the bean stock.
6. Bring to the boil and cook until thickened.
7. The pieces of bacon may be fried until crisp and added to the soup just before serving, or put into the mixture as it comes to the boil and cooked until tender.

To serve: Garnish with the whole beans and serve with soured cream or top the soup with soured cream and paprika.

To vary: 2 teaspoons paprika may be added to the beans at Stage 2.

123

Czerwona kapusta
Red cabbage pot-au-feu

Cooking time: approx. 1 hr. **Preparation time:** 25 min. **Main cooking utensils:** saucepan, frying pan/skillet, 2–3-pint/$2\frac{1}{2}$–$3\frac{1}{2}$-pint ovenproof dish. **Oven temperature:** very moderate to moderate, 350–375°F., 180–190°C., Gas Mark 4. **Oven position:** centre.

IMPERIAL

For 4–5 people you need:
1–2 tablespoons vinegar *or* lemon juice (depending upon personal taste)
seasoning
1 pint water
1 small red cabbage
2 large onions
3 oz. butter
12 oz. streaky bacon
4 dessert apples
1–2 oz. brown sugar (depending upon personal taste)

AMERICAN

For 4–5 people you need:
1–3 tablespoons vinegar *or* lemon juice (depending upon personal taste)
seasoning
$2\frac{1}{2}$ cups water
1 small red cabbage
2 large onions
6 tablespoons butter
$\frac{3}{4}$ lb. bacon slices
4 eating apples
2–4 tablespoons brown sugar (depending upon personal taste)

1. Put the vinegar and a little seasoning into the pan of boiling water.
2. Shred the cabbage, discarding outer leaves and core, and add gradually to the boiling water, then cook until just tender. It is better to under-cook this at this stage, as cabbage loses colour and flavour if too soft.
3. Meanwhile peel and cut the onions into rings, fry in half the butter until just tender, lift out of the pan.
4. Add another $\frac{1}{2}$ oz. (U.S. 1 tablespoon) butter and fry the chopped bacon until tender, together with the cored, sliced, unpeeled apples.
5. One method of cooking this pot-au-feu is to blend the cabbage with the onions, bacon, apples, extra butter, sugar and more seasoning and to continue cooking until very tender, lifting lid so extra liquid evaporates.
6. Another method is to put the strained cabbage in layers in a casserole with onions etc. then to top with extra butter and sugar, cover and cook for approximately 45 minutes.

124

Paprika leves
Pepper soup

Cooking time: 30 min. (little longer if not using quick-cooking rice, see Stage 4). **Preparation time:** 20 min. **Main cooking utensil:** saucepan.

IMPERIAL

For 5–6 people you need:
4 oz. rice, preferably quick-cooking*
$\frac{1}{2}$–1 tablespoon soup seasoning*
good pinch Hungarian goulash seasoning* *or* paprika pepper
3 pints water *or* white stock
salt
1 large *or* 2 small red peppers
1 large *or* 2 small green peppers *or* use all red *or* all green
2 leeks
2–3 sticks celery
2 carrots
2 tomatoes
$\frac{1}{4}$ pint white wine

To garnish:
chopped fresh *or* dried parsley

AMERICAN

For 5–6 people you need:
generous $\frac{1}{2}$ cup rice, preferably quick-cooking*
$\frac{1}{2}$–1 tablespoon soup seasoning*
dash Hungarian goulash seasoning* *or* paprika pepper
$7\frac{1}{2}$ cups water *or* white stock
salt
1 large *or* 2 small sweet red peppers
1 large *or* 2 small sweet green peppers *or* use all red *or* all green
2 leeks
2–3 stalks celery
2 carrots
2 tomatoes
$\frac{2}{3}$ cup white wine

To garnish:
chopped fresh *or* dried parsley

*Many food shops sell these, including '5-minute' rice.

1. Put the rice, soup seasoning and goulash seasoning or paprika into the water or stock, bring to the boil.
2. Add salt to taste, and chopped peppers, removing cores and seeds.
3. Shred the leeks finely, chop celery, chop or grate the peeled carrots and skin and chop the tomatoes. Add to the rice liquid.
4. Simmer steadily until the vegetables are tender and the rice so soft it has almost blended with the liquid.
5. Add the white wine and reheat, then taste and add extra seasoning if necessary.

To serve: With crisp toast or rusks, garnished with parsley. Allow dried parsley to simmer in the soup for a few minutes.

125

Borsch
Beetroot pot-au-feu

Cooking time: $2\frac{1}{2}$ hr. **Preparation time:** 35 min. **Main cooking utensils:** 2 saucepans.

IMPERIAL

For 6–8 people you need:
1 lb. beef bones
1 lb. brisket of beef
8 oz. lean bacon
3 pints water
1 tablespoon soup seasoning
salt
$1\frac{1}{2}$ oz. butter
3 onions, finely chopped
2 leeks
several sticks celery
8 oz. potatoes
1 very large raw beetroot
2 medium-sized carrots
$\frac{1}{2}$ small cabbage
3 medium-sized tomatoes
$\frac{1}{4}$ teaspoon caraway seeds
$\frac{1}{4}$ teaspoon paprika pepper
pinch garlic seasoning *or* salt
2 bay leaves

To serve:
soured cream
$\frac{1}{4}$ teaspoon dill tips *or* chopped parsley

AMERICAN

For 6–8 people you need:
1 lb. beef bones
1 lb. shank knuckle of beef
$\frac{1}{2}$ lb. lean bacon
$7\frac{1}{2}$ cups water
1 tablespoon soup seasoning
salt
3 tablespoons butter
3 onions, finely chopped
2 leeks
several stalks celery
$\frac{1}{2}$ lb. potatoes
1 very large raw beet
2 medium-sized carrots
$\frac{1}{2}$ small cabbage
3 medium-sized tomatoes
$\frac{1}{4}$ teaspoon caraway seeds
$\frac{1}{4}$ teaspoon paprika pepper
dash garlic seasoning *or* salt
2 bay leaves

To serve:
sour cream
$\frac{1}{4}$ teaspoon dill tips *or* chopped parsley

1. Simmer bones, beef and bacon with 2 pints (U.S. 5 cups) water, soup seasoning and salt for $2\frac{1}{2}$ hours; after 1 hour remove bacon.
2. Heat butter in another pan, toss onions and leeks in this.
3. Add remaining water, chopped celery, peeled, diced potatoes, grated, raw beetroot and grated, peeled carrots.
4. Simmer for 30 minutes, then add shredded cabbage, skinned, chopped tomatoes, and remainder of ingredients, except the cream.
5. Simmer for 30 minutes, add the strained liquid from the beef and the meat itself, which should be finely diced and added to the vegetable mixture. If preferred, the meat could be served at another meal.
6. Put soup into a hot dish, top with soured cream, dill or parsley and sliced re-heated bacon from Stage 1.

126

Kouli biaka s siemgoi
Salmon pie

Cooking time: 50 min. **Preparation time:** 35 min. plus time for pastry to stand. **Main cooking utensils:** 2 saucepans, 7–8-inch square baking tin/pan. **Oven temperature:** hot, 425–450°F., 220–230°C., Gas Mark 6–7. **Oven position:** centre.

IMPERIAL

For 4–6 people you need:
For rough puff pastry:
10 oz. flour, preferably plain
pinch salt
6 oz. lard

For the filling:
3 oz. long grain rice
seasoning
1¼–1½ lb. fresh salmon *or* equivalent in canned salmon
juice 1 lemon
sprig fennel *or* parsley
1 onion, finely grated
2–3 tablespoons soured cream

To glaze:
1 beaten egg

To garnish:
slice lemon
parsley

AMERICAN

For 4–6 people you need:
For rough puff pastry:
2½ cups all-purpose flour
dash salt
¾ cup lard

For the filling:
scant ½ cup long grain rice
seasoning
1¼–1½ lb. fresh salmon *or* equivalent in canned salmon
juice 1 lemon
sprig fennel *or* parsley
1 onion, finely grated
3–4 tablespoons sour cream

To glaze:
1 beaten egg

To garnish:
slice lemon
parsley

1. Sieve the flour and salt, add lard cut in pieces. Blend with water to an elastic rolling consistency.
2. Roll out the pastry, fold in 3, seal ends, 'rib' and re-roll. Give a total of 5 rollings and foldings, putting pastry into a cool place between rollings.
3. Cook the rice in boiling salted water, drain.
4. Poach the salmon for approximately 10 minutes only, in well-seasoned water, adding lemon juice and fennel, drain and flake.
5. Blend salmon and rice, onion, soured cream and seasoning.
6. Roll out half the pastry to a neat square, and put in baking tin.
7. Top with the salmon mixture and a second square of pastry.
8. Seal edges, brush with egg. Bake until crisp and brown, about 30 minutes.

To serve: Hot or cold, garnished with lemon and parsley, with sliced cucumber fried in butter.

127

Hungarian savoury fish steaks

Cooking time: 30 min. **Preparation time:** 25 min. **Main cooking utensils:** frying pan/skillet, ovenproof dish. **Oven temperature:** moderately hot, 400°F., 200°C., Gas Mark 5–6. **Oven position:** just above centre.

IMPERIAL

For 6 people you need:
6 portions white fish, fillets *or* steaks
1 teaspoon mild paprika pepper
1 lemon
4 oz. butter *or* margarine
seasoning
4 oz. bacon
2 large onions
shake dried parsley *or* little chopped fresh parsley
½ pint soured cream *or* thin cream and 1 tablespoon lemon juice
1 tablespoon flour
2–3 tablespoons concentrated tomato purée
1–2 teaspoons French mustard
2–3 oz. cheese, grated
2 oz. soft breadcrumbs

AMERICAN

For 6 people you need:
6 portions white fish, fillets *or* steaks
1 teaspoon mild paprika pepper
1 lemon
½ cup butter *or* margarine
seasoning
¼ lb. bacon *or* ham
2 large onions
shake dried parsley *or* little chopped fresh parsley
1¼ cups sour cream *or* coffee cream and 1 tablespoon lemon juice
1 tablespoon all-purpose flour
3–4 tablespoons concentrated tomato paste
1–2 teaspoons French mustard
½–¾ cup grated cheese
1 cup soft bread crumbs

1. Season pieces of fish with paprika and lemon juice, then fry for 2–3 minutes only in 3 oz. (U.S. 6 tablespoons) hot butter or margarine.
2. Lift into an ovenproof dish, season lightly.
3. Chop the bacon and onions finely, fry in butter remaining in pan until nearly soft. Add parsley, soured cream, blended with flour and cook *without boiling* for 2–3 minutes.
4. Blend tomato purée with the mustard, spread on top of the fish, then cover with onion and bacon mixture. Any remaining may be put round the fish in the dish.
5. Top the fish portions with cheese and crumbs and the remaining butter and bake for approximately 20 minutes in the oven.

128

Shashlik
Lamb or mutton on skewers

Cooking time: 10 min. **Preparation time:** 10 min. plus time for meat to stand in the marinade. **Main cooking utensils:** skewers, grill pan/broil pan, saucepan.

IMPERIAL

For 4–5 people you need:
For the marinade:
½ teaspoon pepper
1 teaspoon salt
pinch dry mustard
1 teaspoon chopped fresh herbs
1–2 crushed cloves garlic
1 tablespoon oil
¼ pint vinegar

1¼ lb. lamb
bay leaves
fresh bread
6 oz. thinly cut pork *or* thick rashers bacon

To serve:
cooked rice

AMERICAN

For 4–5 people you need:
For the marinade:
½ teaspoon pepper
1 teaspoon salt
dash dry mustard
1 teaspoon chopped fresh herbs
1–2 crushed cloves garlic
1 tablespoon oil
⅔ cup vinegar

1¼ lb. lamb
bay leaves
fresh bread
⅓ lb. thinly cut pork *or* thick bacon slices

To serve:
cooked rice

1. Blend the ingredients for the marinade in a shallow bowl; stir well.
2. Cut the meat into pieces, put into marinade and leave for 1–2 hours.
3. Lift the meat out of the liquid.
4. Put on to the skewers with the other chosen ingredients. The picture shows bay leaves, slices of fresh bread, pieces of pork or bacon, but vegetables are often chosen. They can be young marrow or cucumber, cut into slices; aubergine, sliced and left sprinkled with seasoning for 30 minutes; tomatoes, halved or whole; onions, green peppers etc., cut into pieces or rings.
5. Cook over a charcoal fire or under a grill until the meat is tender, basting with marinade.

To serve: With rice or fresh bread.

129

Borjupaprikas
Veal stew paprika

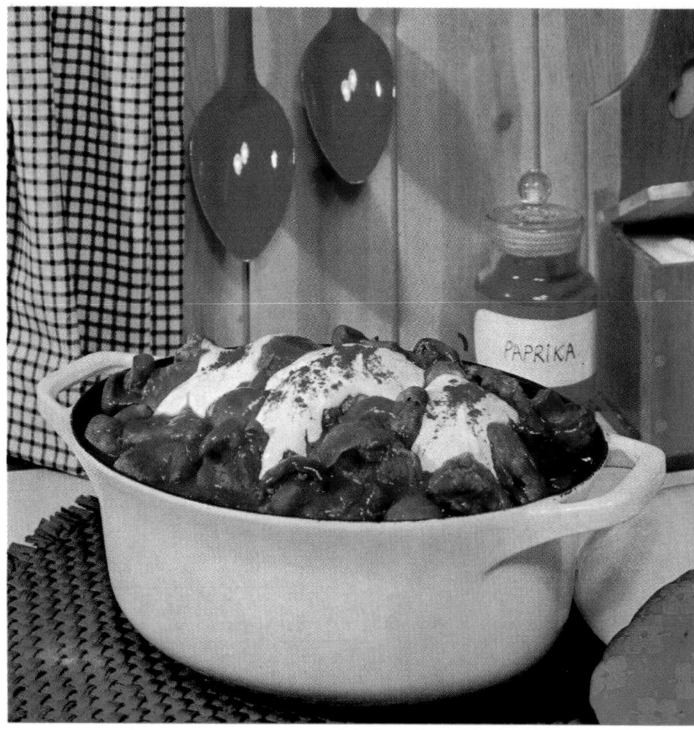

Cooking time: 2–2½ hr. **Preparation time:** 25 min. **Main cooking utensil:** tightly-covered pan.

IMPERIAL

For 4 people you need:
1–1¼ lb. stewing veal
1 oz. lard
8 oz. onions
1 clove garlic (optional)
4 oz. button mushrooms
1 tablespoon paprika pepper
1 tablespoon plain flour
½–¾ pint stock *or* water
3 tablespoons tomato purée
seasoning
¼–½ pint plain yoghurt *or* soured cream (or use fresh thin cream blended with ½–1 tablespoon lemon juice)

To garnish:
paprika pepper

AMERICAN

For 4 people you need:
1–1¼ lb. stewing veal
2 tablespoons lard
½ lb. onions
1 clove garlic (optional)
1 cup button mushrooms
1 tablespoon paprika pepper
1 tablespoon all-purpose flour
1¼–2 cups stock *or* water
scant ¼ cup tomato paste
seasoning
⅔–1¼ cups plain yoghurt *or* sour cream (or use fresh coffee cream blended with ½–1 tablespoon lemon juice)

To garnish:
paprika pepper

1. Cut the meat into 1-inch cubes and brown quickly in the hot lard.
2. Remove the meat and fry lightly the sliced onions, crushed garlic and sliced mushrooms.
3. Add the paprika and flour and stir over a low heat.
4. Pour in the stock and bring slowly to boil, stirring all the time.
5. Return the meat, add tomato paste and seasoning. Simmer gently for 1½–2 hours.
6. Just before serving, stir in the yoghurt, or soured cream.

To serve: With buttered noodles or mashed potatoes and sauerkraut, garnished with paprika pepper.

To vary: Diced pork can be used instead of veal.

130

Znojemsky gulás
Beef in paprika with pickles

Cooking time: A: 1 hr. 10 min. B: 1 hr. 20 min. **Preparation time:** A: 15 min. B: 15 min. plus time for cucumbers to soak. **Main cooking utensils:** frying pan/skillet, saucepan.

IMPERIAL

For 6 people you need:
A: BEEF IN PAPRIKA
$1\frac{1}{2}$–2 lb. sirloin steak *or* rump steak
2 oz. flour
salt
black pepper, cayenne pepper
4 oz. butter
3–4 onions, chopped
1–2 tablespoons paprika pepper
$1\frac{1}{2}$ pints brown stock
3 tablespoons tomato purée
1–2 old potatoes

B: PICKLED CUCUMBERS
2 lb. small pickling cucumbers
4 oz. kitchen salt
2 pints water
2 pints pure malt brown *or* white vinegar
2 tablespoons mixed pickling spices

AMERICAN

For 6 people you need:
A: BEEF IN PAPRIKA
$1\frac{1}{2}$–2 lb. sirloin steak
$\frac{1}{2}$ cup all-purpose flour
salt
black pepper, cayenne pepper
$\frac{1}{2}$ cup butter
3–4 onions, chopped
1–3 tablespoons paprika pepper
$3\frac{3}{4}$ cups brown stock
scant $\frac{1}{4}$ cup tomato paste
1–2 old potatoes

B: PICKLED CUCUMBERS
2 lb. small pickling cucumbers
$\frac{1}{3}$ cup salt
5 cups water
5 cups pure malt brown *or* white vinegar
3 tablespoons mixed pickling spices

A: BEEF IN PAPRIKA

1. Cut the beef into neat pieces, coat in flour, salt and peppers.
2. Fry in hot butter for 5–6 minutes.
3. Lift out of the pan, fry chopped onions in remaining fat.
4. Stir in paprika blended with stock, bring to boil, thicken.
5. Add tomato purée and diced, peeled potatoes and cook for 30 minutes. For a smooth sauce, sieve or put into electric blender, return to pan.
6. Add pieces of diced meat and simmer for 15–25 minutes.

To serve: With pickled cucumbers, salad and rice.

B: PICKLED CUCUMBERS

Put unpeeled cucumbers in brine (made by mixing salt and water) for 48 hours, lift out, rinse in cold water. Dry, pack in jars. Cover with *cold* strained, spiced vinegar made by boiling vinegar and spices together.

131

Kielbasa I kasztany
Sausages and chestnuts

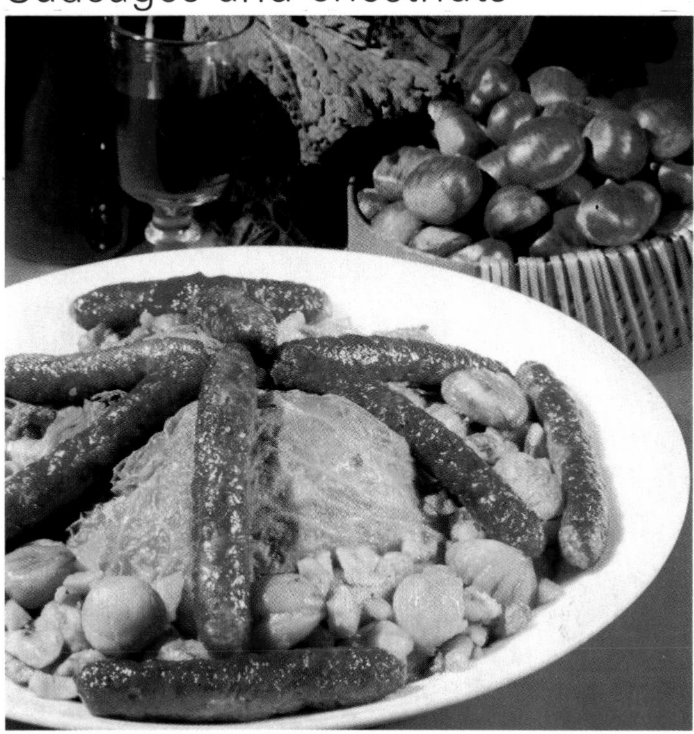

Cooking time: 35 min. **Preparation time:** 30 min. **Main cooking utensils:** 2 saucepans, baking tray/sheet if used, grill pan/broil pan, *or* frying pan/skillet. **Oven temperature:** moderately hot, 400°F., 200°C., Gas Mark 5–6 (see Stage 2). **Oven position:** above centre.

IMPERIAL

For 4–6 people you need:
2 lb. chestnuts, weight before shelling
2 pints good white stock *or* water and 3–4 chicken stock cubes
seasoning
1 lb. pork chipolata sausages
1 cabbage
$\frac{1}{4}$ pint white wine
1 large onion
1–2 bay leaves
sprig thyme
1–2 oz. butter

AMERICAN

For 4–6 people you need:
2 lb. chestnuts, weight before shelling
5 cups good white stock *or* water and 3–4 chicken bouillon cubes
seasoning
1 lb. pork sausages
1 cabbage
$\frac{2}{3}$ cup white wine
1 large onion
1–2 bay leaves
sprig thyme
2–4 tablespoons butter

1. First prepare the chestnuts. Slit the skins slightly, this prevents any possibility of the nuts 'bursting' during cooking.
2. Either simmer steadily in very hot water for 10 minutes or put on tray in a moderately hot oven for approximately 12–15 minutes.
3. Shell while still warm, this means both the inner and outer skins can be removed without trouble.
4. If the chestnuts are overcooked, they are difficult to remove from the shells.
5. Continue cooking the chestnuts in 1 pint (U.S. $2\frac{1}{2}$ cups) hot stock until tender, seasoning well.
6. Grill or fry the sausages and cook the quartered cabbage in wine and remaining stock with whole onion, seasoning and herbs.
7. Strain the nuts and cabbage, remove onion, toss both in any fat remaining in the grill or frying pan, add butter.

To serve: Arrange on serving dish and top with sausages.

132

Kaduckievap

Grilled meats with cheese

Cooking time: 15 minutes. **Preparation time:** about 10 min. **Main cooking utensil:** grill/broil pan.

IMPERIAL

For each person allow:
pinch chopped fresh herbs; fennel, thyme, bay leaf, tarragon and/*or* rosemary and parsley
1 oz. butter *or* 1 tablespoon oil

seasoning
1 teaspoon finely chopped red *or* green chilli pepper
1 pork *or* veal chop and/*or* lamb cutlet
1 small piece steak
1 portion liver
2 thin rashers streaky bacon
1 frankfurter sausage
1 oz. Cheddar *or* Gruyère cheese
1 oz. cream cheese

AMERICAN

For each person allow:
dash chopped fresh herbs; fennel, thyme, bay leaf, tarragon, and/*or* rosemary and parsley
2 tablespoons butter *or* 1 tablespoon oil
seasoning
1 teaspoon finely chopped red *or* green chili pepper
1 pork *or* veal chop and/*or* lamb cutlet
1 small piece steak
1 portion liver
2 thin bacon slices
1 frankfurter sausage
1 oz. Cheddar *or* Gruyère cheese
2 tablespoons cream cheese

1. Blend the finely chopped herbs with the butter or oil to be used to baste the meat during cooking, reserving a few herbs for the end, and season well. Add the chopped red or green chilli pepper if wished.
2. Place the meats on the grill pan and brush with the herb mixture on one side.
3. Grill until brown.
4. Then, brush on the other side and continue cooking until tender.
5. Before serving slit the cooked frankfurter and insert small pieces of the Cheddar or Gruyère cheese.
6. Top the steak with some butter or a little of the cream cheese.
7. Blend the remaining herbs with the rest of the cream cheese and put this on top of the liver.
8. Heat for 1–2 minutes, until the cheese begins to melt, then serve.

133

Bigos

Hunter's stew

Cooking time: minimum 2 hr. **Preparation time:** 20 min. **Main cooking utensils:** large pan, fireproof casserole.

IMPERIAL

For 5–6 people you need:
$2\frac{1}{4}$ lb. sauerkraut
2 oz. lard
1 onion
2 tablespoons flour
few tablespoons meat glaze*
2 tablespoons tomato purée
3 tablespoons vodka
$\frac{1}{4}$ pint red *or* white wine
8–10 oz. mixed *cooked* game, meat and poultry
4–8 oz. smoked pork sausages
2 oz. gammon, diced
1–2 apples

AMERICAN

For 5–6 people you need:
$2\frac{1}{4}$ lb. sauerkraut
$\frac{1}{4}$ cup lard
1 onion
$\frac{1}{4}$ cup all-purpose flour
few tablespoons meat glaze*
3 tablespoons tomato paste
scant $\frac{1}{4}$ cup vodka
$\frac{2}{3}$ cup red *or* white wine
$\frac{1}{2}$–$\frac{3}{4}$ lb. mixed *cooked* game, meat and poultry
$\frac{1}{4}$–$\frac{1}{2}$ lb. smoked pork sausages
$\frac{1}{4}$ cup diced bacon *or* cured ham
1–2 apples

*This is the jelly that forms under the fat when meat or poultry is roasted; meat stock could be substituted, if it were boiled until reduced to thick jelly and concentrated in flavour.

This traditional dish is extremely popular in every part of Poland. The flavour is often better when the dish is reheated.

1. Wash the sauerkraut, blanch in boiling water and drain.
2. Melt the lard, then fry chopped onion until brown, adding flour.
3. Add the meat glaze, tomato purée, vodka and wine. Bring to the boil.
4. Put a layer of sauerkraut in a fireproof casserole or saucepan, followed by a layer of the meats, sliced sausages, gammon and sliced apples.
5. Moisten with a little meat glaze and wine mixture.
6. Continue these layers until all the ingredients are used up.
7. Cover and simmer over a low heat for 2 hours.
8. The casserole should be given an occasional gentle shake during the cooking period.

134

Boeuf stroganoff

Beef in cream sauce

Cooking time: 10–15 min. **Preparation time:** 15 min. **Main cooking utensils:** frying pan/skillet, saucepan.

IMPERIAL

For 4 people you need:
$1–1\frac{1}{4}$ lb. fillet steak
seasoning, including little mustard
little powdered nutmeg
little powdered mace
2 medium-sized onions
4 oz. mushrooms
3 oz. butter
6 tablespoons brown stock
1–2 tablespoons tomato purée (optional)
$\frac{1}{2}$ pint soured cream *or* use $\frac{1}{2}$ pint thin cream and 1 tablespoon lemon juice

For the savoury rice:
$\frac{1}{2}$–1 green pepper
$\frac{1}{2}$–1 red pepper
6 oz. long grain rice
12 fluid oz. ($\frac{5}{8}$ pint) water
salt

AMERICAN

For 4 people you need:
$1–1\frac{1}{4}$ lb. tenderloin steak
seasoning, including little mustard
little powdered nutmeg
little powdered mace
2 medium-sized onions
1 cup mushrooms
6 tablespoons butter
$\frac{1}{2}$ cup brown stock
1–3 tablespoons tomato paste (optional)
$1\frac{1}{4}$ cups sour cream *or* use $1\frac{1}{4}$ cups coffee cream and 1 tablespoon lemon juice

For the savoury rice:
$\frac{1}{2}$–1 sweet green pepper
$\frac{1}{2}$–1 sweet red pepper
scant 1 cup long grain rice
scant 2 cups water
salt

1. Cut the steak into neat strips–it gives a better texture if cut across the grain of the meat.
2. Season well and sprinkle with nutmeg and mace.
3. Chop the onions very finely and slice the mushrooms.
4. Heat half the butter in a large pan, fry the mushrooms for a few minutes, lift out.
5. Add the rest of the butter and fry the onions and meat until tender.
6. Add the stock, tomato purée, if wished, and soured cream. Heat thoroughly, stirring well. Taste and re-season if necessary. Stir in the mushrooms.

To serve: With savoury rice made by tossing diced, chopped peppers, or other vegetables, with rice cooked gently in the boiling, salted water.

135

Piroshki

Fried pancake rolls

Cooking time: 30 min. **Preparation time:** 25 min. **Main cooking utensils:** 2 saucepans, small frying pan/skillet, pan for deep frying.

IMPERIAL

For 6 people you need:
For the batter:
6 oz. flour, preferably plain
pinch salt
2 eggs
scant $\frac{3}{4}$ pint milk *or* milk and water
2–3 oz. butter

For the filling:
2 oz. rice
$1\frac{1}{2}$ lb. spinach
10 oz. cooked chicken
2 hard-boiled eggs
seasoning
1 egg

To coat:
2 eggs
little water
3 oz. crisp breadcrumbs (raspings)

AMERICAN

For 6 people you need:
For the batter:
$1\frac{1}{2}$ cups all-purpose flour
dash salt
2 eggs
scant 2 cups milk *or* milk and water
4–6 tablespoons butter

For the filling:
$\frac{1}{3}$ cup rice
$1\frac{1}{2}$ lb. spinach
$\frac{2}{3}$ lb. cooked chicken
2 hard-cooked eggs
seasoning
1 egg

To coat:
2 eggs
little water
$\frac{3}{4}$ cup fine dried bread crumbs

Although the word Piroshki often describes small pies, it can also be a pancake filled, coated in more batter or egg and crumbs and fried.

1. Mix together all the ingredients, except butter, for the batter.
2. Fry the pancakes in the hot butter.
3. Cook the rice in salted water until tender. Cook and chop spinach, chop or mince chicken (or other meat or game).
4. Put the chicken into a basin, add chopped hard-boiled eggs, cooked rice, 3 tablespoons (U.S. 4 tablespoons) of the spinach and seasoning; bind with the fresh egg.
5. Put on to the pancakes and roll firmly, secure with tiny wooden cocktail sticks if wished.
6. Coat with eggs, beaten with a little water, and crumbs. Fry in hot fat until crisp and golden.

To serve: With the remaining spinach and lemon wedges.

136

Disnotors hurka kolbasz
Farmhouse sausage selection

Cooking time: about 50 min. **Preparation time:** 15 min. **Main cooking utensils:** 2 saucepans *or* frying pan/skillet *or* grill pan/broil pan.

IMPERIAL

For 4–6 people you need:
2 onions
2 apples (optional)
2 oz. butter
either 1 small cabbage *or* 1–1½ lb. sauerkraut
2 lb. various sausages: frankfurters, blood sausage, spiced sausage
8 oz. fairly thick rashers streaky bacon

AMERICAN

For 4–6 people you need:
2 onions
2 apples (optional)
¼ cup butter
either 1 small head cabbage *or* 1–1½ lb. sauerkraut
2 lb. various sausages: frankfurters, blood sausage, spiced sausage
½ lb. fairly thick bacon slices

1. Slice the onions and apples. Heat butter in a pan and fry them in this.
2. Shred the cabbage, cook in boiling salted water till just tender and drain. Or, drain the sauerkraut, rinse well and cook until tender in water with plenty of pepper, drain.
3. Mix the cabbage with the onions and apples, and pile into the centre of a dish. Keep warm.
4. Heat the frankfurters thoroughly in their own brine or stock.
5. Prick the spiced sausage and grill or fry in a very little fat.
6. Cook the bacon in a pan.
7. Cut the blood sausage into thick slices and heat through in the bacon fat.
8. Arrange all on the cabbage.

To serve: With brown or black bread, boiled potatoes or baked potatoes in their jackets and beer.

137

Nalésniki
Stuffed pancakes

Cooking time: 20–25 min. **Preparation time:** 20 min. plus time for batter to stand. **Main cooking utensils:** saucepan, frying pan/skillet.

IMPERIAL

For 4–6 people you need:
For the pancake batter:
8 oz. flour, preferably plain
½ pint milk
½ pint water
pinch sugar
1 oz. butter, melted
1 tablespoon brandy
2 large eggs
pinch salt
good pinch fresh *or* dried yeast (this could be omitted, but gives a light texture)

For the filling:
1–1½ lb. spinach
seasoning
1 oz. butter
soured cream (optional, see Stage 4)

To cook pancakes:
4 oz. butter

AMERICAN

For 4–6 people you need:
For the pancake batter:
2 cups all-purpose flour
1¼ cups milk
1¼ cups water
dash sugar
2 tablespoons melted butter
1 tablespoon brandy
2 large eggs
dash salt
dash fresh *or* dried yeast (this could be omitted, but gives a light texture)

For the filling:
1–1½ lb. spinach
seasoning
2 tablespoons butter
sour cream (optional, see Stage 4)

To cook pancakes:
½ cup butter

1. Mix all the ingredients, except the egg whites, together for the batter. Let this stand for about 3–4 hours.
2. Meanwhile prepare the filling, in this case it is spinach.
3. Put the well-washed spinach into a saucepan with seasoning and a little, if any, water.
4. Cook steadily, stirring once or twice so it does not burn, until tender, strain well. Sieve, if wished, or chop on a board and blend with the butter (1–2 tablespoons soured cream could be added).
5. Reheat. Fold in the stiffly beaten egg whites to the batter mixture.
6. Heat the butter and cook the pancakes. Keep hot over a pan of hot water, do not cover.

To serve: When all the pancakes are cooked, put in the spinach, roll or fold and serve with heated frankfurter sausages.

Slovak celebration menu

Slovak food is very varied, but the picture shows a simple, economical, yet interesting menu that could be served for a celebration.

Soft cream or curd cheese is made into a mould and served topped with caraway seeds. Garnished with butter slices (to put on the rye or black bread), sliced green pepper, paprika (which is served as the usual seasoning with salt), large caraway seeds and sliced raw onion.

NACHINKOY KASCHA

This is made with buckwheat flour, but ordinary flour could be used. Put 12 oz. (U.S. 3 cups) flour into a large pan and heat *very gently* until just golden. Blend with seasoning, 1 oz. (U.S. 2 tablespoons) butter, and put into a dish with enough water to bind. Stand in another dish of water and heat steadily for about 2 hours in a very cool oven; it becomes like a crumbly 'bread'. Cut into strips and cover with thin strips of fried pork or bacon. Serve very hot, with soured cream or cottage cheese.

VARENNIKI

These are little 'pies' that are boiled, rather than baked. Make a pastry dough using 8 oz. (U.S. 2 cups) plain flour sieved with seasoning and bind with an egg and water. Roll out thinly, cut into small, fluted rounds. Put small amount of cream cheese, blended with a little soured cream and seasoning on to each round. Fold over, seal edges and simmer steadily in salted water for 15 minutes. Drain, toss in melted butter and top with fried fat pork.

SLOVAK 'PANCAKES'

Make a thick pancake batter with 8 oz. (U.S. 2 cups) flour, seasoning, 2 eggs, $\frac{1}{2}$ pint (U.S. $1\frac{1}{4}$ cups) milk and 3 tablespoons (U.S. scant $\frac{1}{4}$ cup) thin cream. Add diced, cooked meat or poultry and fry in hot fat until brown on either side.

139

Baklajany y smetane
Aubergines and soured cream

Cooking time: 15 min. **Preparation time:** 10 min. plus time for aubergines to stand if desired. **Main cooking utensils:** frying pan/skillet, absorbent paper.

IMPERIAL

For 4 people you need:
2 medium-sized aubergines, sliced
seasoning
1 oz. flour (optional)
3 oz. butter *or* fat
1–2 cloves garlic
$\frac{1}{4}$–$\frac{1}{2}$ pint soured cream (depending on personal taste)
1–2 teaspoons paprika pepper

To garnish:
chopped parsley *or* chopped chives

AMERICAN

For 4 people you need:
2 medium-sized eggplants, sliced
seasoning
$\frac{1}{4}$ cup all-purpose flour (optional)
6 tablespoons butter *or* fat
1–2 cloves garlic
$\frac{2}{3}$–$1\frac{1}{4}$ cups sour cream (depending on personal taste)
1–2 teaspoon paprika pepper

To garnish:
chopped parsley *or* chopped chives

1. Slice the aubergines thinly, do not peel; if wishing to avoid the slightly bitter flavour on skin, sprinkle with salt, leave for about 20 minutes.
2. Season well, or coat with seasoned flour for a crisper coating.
3. Heat the butter or fat, then fry finely chopped or crushed garlic and aubergines, for 2–3 minutes on each side.
4. Top with hot or cold soured cream, paprika and parsley or chives.

To serve: With toast or bread and butter.

140

Makaron krajany
Noodles with tomato sauce

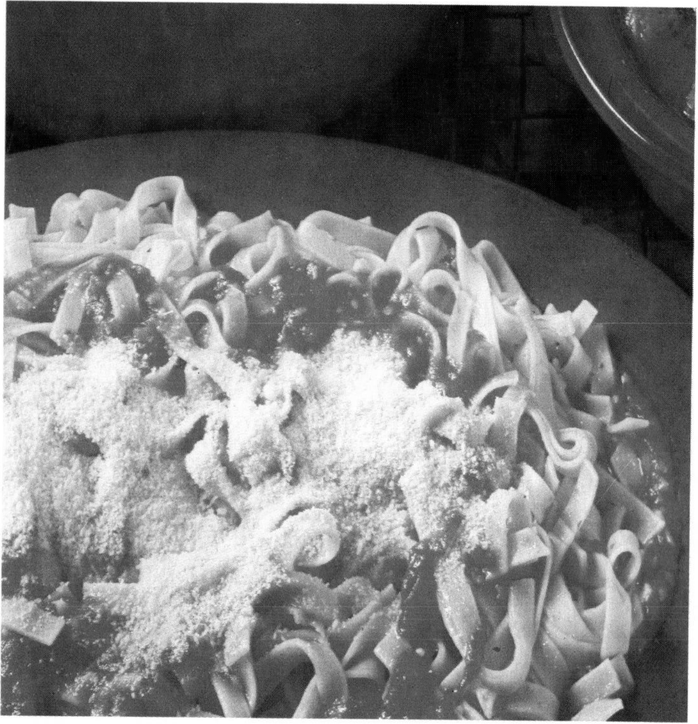

Cooking time: 30 min. **Preparation time:** 10 min. **Main cooking utensil:** saucepan.

IMPERIAL

For 4–6 people you need:
5–6 pints water *or* white stock

12 oz. noodles
$1\frac{1}{2}$ lb. tomatoes
2 oz. butter
1 pint stock
2 teaspoons sugar
seasoning
1 oz. flour
1 teaspoon chopped dill
6 oz. ham, finely chopped (optional)
1 oz. Gruyère *or* Parmesan cheese, grated

AMERICAN

For 4–6 people you need:
$6\frac{1}{4}$–$7\frac{1}{2}$ pints water *or* white stock
$\frac{3}{4}$ lb. noodles
$1\frac{1}{2}$ lb. tomatoes
$\frac{1}{4}$ cup butter
$2\frac{1}{2}$ cups stock
2 teaspoons sugar
seasoning
$\frac{1}{4}$ cup all-purpose flour
1 teaspoon chopped dill
1 cup finely chopped cured ham (optional)
$\frac{1}{4}$ cup grated Gruyère *or* Parmesan cheese

1. Bring the stock or water to the boil, season and add the noodles. Cook till tender, 10–12 minutes, drain and keep warm.
2. Skin and chop the tomatoes. Melt the butter in a saucepan and toss the tomatoes in this.
3. Add $\frac{3}{4}$ pint (U.S. 2 cups) stock, the sugar and seasoning. Simmer till the tomatoes are soft, about 15 minutes.
4. Blend the flour with the remaining $\frac{1}{4}$ pint (U.S. $\frac{1}{2}$ cup) stock and add to the sauce with the chopped dill and ham if used. Cook until thickened.
5. Pour over the noodles and sprinkle with grated cheese.
6. For a more substantial meal, serve with chopped, crisply fried bacon and sliced, fried mushrooms.

141

Paszteciki z pieczenia
Savoury pancake stack

Cooking time: 25 min. **Preparation time:** 25 min. **Main cooking utensils:** frying pan/skillet, foil, 2 saucepans.

IMPERIAL

For 4–6 people you need:
For the pancakes:
4 oz. flour, preferably plain
seasoning
1 egg
$\frac{1}{2}$ pint milk

For the filling:
3 onions
1 oz. lard *or* dripping
1 oz. butter
1 oz. flour
$\frac{1}{4}$ pint milk
12 oz. cooked meats
1 large cooking apple
few drops Worcestershire sauce
2–3 tablespoons soured cream

To garnish:
onion rings (see Stage 5)
parsley

AMERICAN

For 4–6 people you need:
For the pancakes:
1 cup all-purpose flour
seasoning
1 egg
$1\frac{1}{4}$ cups milk

For the filling:
3 onions
2 tablespoons lard *or* drippings
2 tablespoons butter
$\frac{1}{4}$ cup all-purpose flour
$\frac{2}{3}$ cup milk
$\frac{3}{4}$ lb. cooked meats
1 large baking apple
few drops Worcestershire sauce
3–4 tablespoons sour cream

To garnish:
onion rings (see Stage 5)
parsley

1. Sieve the flour with seasoning and blend with egg. Gradually blend in the milk until a smooth pouring batter.
2. Heat a little oil in the pan, pour in enough batter to form a thin coating. Cook until brown, turn and cook on second side. Remove and add more oil.
3. Continue cooking all the mixture; always adding small quantity of oil before each pancake is cooked.
4. Keep pancakes hot on a dish covered with foil, over pan of hot water.
5. Slice the onions thinly, fry in hot lard or dripping until tender. Put a little onion on one side for garnish and add butter to pan.
6. Heat, stir in flour, cook for 1–2 minutes. Blend in milk and bring to the boil, cook until a thick sauce.
7. Add the minced meat, diced apple, sauce and seasoning.
8. Heat together, add soured cream but *do not boil*.

To serve: Sandwich pancakes with meat mixture, garnish and serve hot.

142

Pasztet
Veal pâté

Cooking time: $1\frac{1}{2}$–$1\frac{3}{4}$ hr. **Preparation time:** 30 min. plus setting time. **Main cooking utensil:** 7–8-inch cake tin/pan (without loose base) *or* $2\frac{1}{2}$-pint/3-pint mould. **Oven temperature:** very moderate, 325–350°F., 170–180°C., Gas Mark 3. **Oven position:** centre.

IMPERIAL

For 6–12 people you need:*
- $1\frac{1}{2}$ lb. stewing veal
- 12 oz. belly pork
- 3 oz. calf's *or* pig's liver
- 8 oz. streaky bacon
- 1 large onion
- 1 tablespoon chopped parsley
- 1–2 teaspoons chopped sage *or* $\frac{1}{2}$ teaspoon dried sage
- 1 lemon
- 1 egg
- seasoning
- 4 tablespoons thick cream (optional, see Stage 3)
- 1 bay leaf

To garnish:
- $\frac{1}{2}$ pint packet aspic jelly
- 1 tablespoon sherry
- $\frac{1}{2}$ pint clarified brown stock**
- 2 dessert pears
- parsley

AMERICAN

For 6–12 people you need:
- $1\frac{1}{2}$ lb. stewing veal
- $\frac{3}{4}$ lb. fresh picnic shoulder pork
- 3 oz. calf *or* pork liver
- $\frac{1}{2}$ lb. bacon slices
- 1 large onion
- 1 tablespoon chopped parsley
- 1–2 teaspoons chopped sage *or* $\frac{1}{2}$ teaspoon dried sage
- 1 lemon
- 1 egg
- seasoning
- $\frac{1}{3}$ cup whipping cream (optional, see Stage 3)
- 1 bay leaf

To garnish:
- scant 1 tablespoon gelatin
- 1 tablespoon sherry
- $1\frac{1}{4}$ cups clarified brown stock**
- 2 eating pears
- parsley

*Six as a main dish, 12 as an hors d'oeuvre.
**To clarify stock, heat and strain through muslin once or twice.

1. Mince the veal, belly of pork, liver and bacon finely.
2. Lastly put the peeled onion through the mincer.
3. Blend together with parsley, sage, grated lemon rind, egg, seasoning and lemon juice to taste. This is a firm pâté, but if a softer texture is required, add up to 4 tablespoons (U.S. $\frac{1}{3}$ cup) cream.
4. Put the bay leaf at the bottom of the tin, cover with veal mixture.
5. Stand in a tin of water, cover with buttered foil.
6. Bake until firm. Cool in the tin.
7. Make up the aspic jelly with the sherry and stock, cool.
8. Peel, core and slice dessert pears, brush with half-set aspic jelly.
9. Turn out pâté, coat top only with aspic. Garnish with pears and parsley.

143

Kerti borso es piros paprika
Garden peas and red peppers

Cooking time: 30 min. **Preparation time:** 20 min. **Main cooking utensils:** strong saucepan with tight-fitting lid.

IMPERIAL

For 4–6 people you need:
- 4 oz. bacon (optional)
- 2 medium-sized onions
- 2 oz. butter
- 2 lb. fresh peas *or* equivalent in frozen peas
- 3–4 tablespoons water
- seasoning
- 1 teaspoon sugar
- 2–3 red peppers, depending on size
- 2 teaspoons chopped parsley

AMERICAN

For 4–6 people you need:
- $\frac{1}{4}$ lb. bacon (optional)
- 2 medium-sized onions
- $\frac{1}{4}$ cup butter
- 2 lb. fresh peas *or* equivalent in frozen peas
- 4–5 tablespoons water
- seasoning
- 1 teaspoon sugar
- 2–3 sweet red peppers, depending on size
- 2 teaspoons chopped parsley

1. Chop the bacon and onions finely, fry in butter in pan.
2. Shell the peas, put into pan, toss in butter with bacon and onions.
3. Add the water, cook for 10 minutes, season well and add the sugar. Cover the pan, shake from time to time so there is no fear of the peas burning.
4. Meanwhile prepare the red peppers. Cut a slice from round the stalk, the flesh round this should be sliced.
5. Pull out the centre core and seeds, discard. Cut the remaining flesh in rings.
6. Add to the peas, turn in butter and water mixture; if liquid has evaporated, add a little more.
7. Continue cooking for 15 minutes, shaking pan from time to time.
8. Top with chopped parsley.

To serve: As a light dish or accompaniment to a main dish.

144

Russki salat
Russian salad

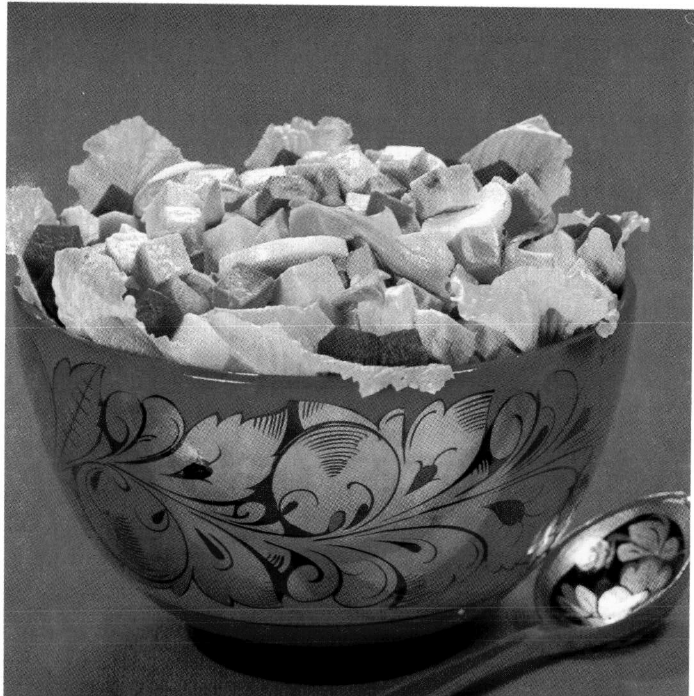

Cooking time: 15 min. **Preparation time:** 20 min. **Main cooking utensils:** 2 saucepans.

IMPERIAL

For 4 people you need:
1 medium-sized carrot
1 small turnip
2 oz. peas
2 oz. sliced green beans
1 egg
4 oz. cooked ham
4 oz. cooked chicken

For the dressing:
1 teaspoon made mustard
$\frac{1}{4}$ teaspoon sugar
$\frac{1}{4}$ teaspoon salt
pinch pepper
2 tablespoons oil
$1\frac{1}{2}$ tablespoons white wine *or* vinegar
1 teaspoon mayonnaise

To garnish:
1 small cooked beetroot
small lettuce leaves

AMERICAN

For 4 people you need:
1 medium-sized carrot
1 small turnip
$\frac{1}{3}$ cup peas
approx. $\frac{1}{2}$ cup sliced green beans
1 egg
$\frac{1}{4}$ lb. cooked ham
$\frac{1}{4}$ lb. cooked chicken

For the dressing:
1 teaspoon prepared mustard
$\frac{1}{4}$ teaspoon sugar
$\frac{1}{4}$ teaspoon salt
dash pepper
3 tablespoons oil
2 tablespoons white wine *or* vinegar
1 teaspoon mayonnaise

To garnish:
1 small cooked beet
small lettuce leaves

A true Russian salad is a combination of vegetables, cooked meat, chicken and eggs, and is therefore a complete dish. The modern version has become a mixed vegetable salad to serve with meat or fish.

1. Put the vegetables into boiling salted water and cook until just soft, drain— mixed frozen vegetables could be used instead.
2. While the vegetables are cooking, hard-boil and shell the egg.
3. Mix the hot, well-strained vegetables with diced meat and chicken and dressing, made by blending all the ingredients (except mayonnaise) together.
4. Allow to cool, then add the mayonnaise and sliced egg.
5. Garnish with diced beetroot and small lettuce leaves.

145

Salata po polsku ze smietana
Salads with sour cream dressing

Cooking time: 10 min. **Preparation time:** 20 min. **Main cooking utensil:** saucepan.

IMPERIAL

For 6 people you need:
2 eggs
$\frac{1}{2}$ pint soured cream
1 teaspoon sugar
1 tablespoon lemon juice
seasoning

For the mixed salad:
1 green pepper
1 red pepper
4 oz. mushrooms
about 12 black olives

For the stuffed tomatoes:
6 large firm tomatoes
2–3 medium-sized cooked potatoes
6 black olives
endive *or* lettuce

AMERICAN

For 6 people you need:
2 eggs
$1\frac{1}{4}$ cups sour cream
1 teaspoon sugar
1 tablespoon lemon juice
seasoning

For the mixed salad:
1 sweet green pepper
1 sweet red pepper
1 cup mushrooms
about 12 ripe olives

For the stuffed tomatoes:
6 large firm tomatoes
2–3 medium-sized cooked potatoes
6 ripe olives
curly endive *or* lettuce

1. Boil the eggs. When hard plunge into cold water, cracking shells.
2. Shell, halve and remove the yolks (the whites could be added to salads).
3. Put the yolks into a bowl, gradually blend in the soured cream.
4. Stir in the sugar, lemon juice and seasoning.
5. The mixed salad is made with slices of green and red pepper, sliced raw mushrooms and black olives.
6. The tomatoes are stuffed with diced, cooked potatoes, blended with the soured cream dressing.
7. To stuff the tomatoes, cut into 6 segments almost to the base.
8. Press the stuffing into the centres, press the segments of tomato firmly round.
9. Top with black olives and put on bed of crisp endive or lettuce.

To serve: These salads are delicious as a separate course or with cold meats.

146

Pashka
Cream cheese mould

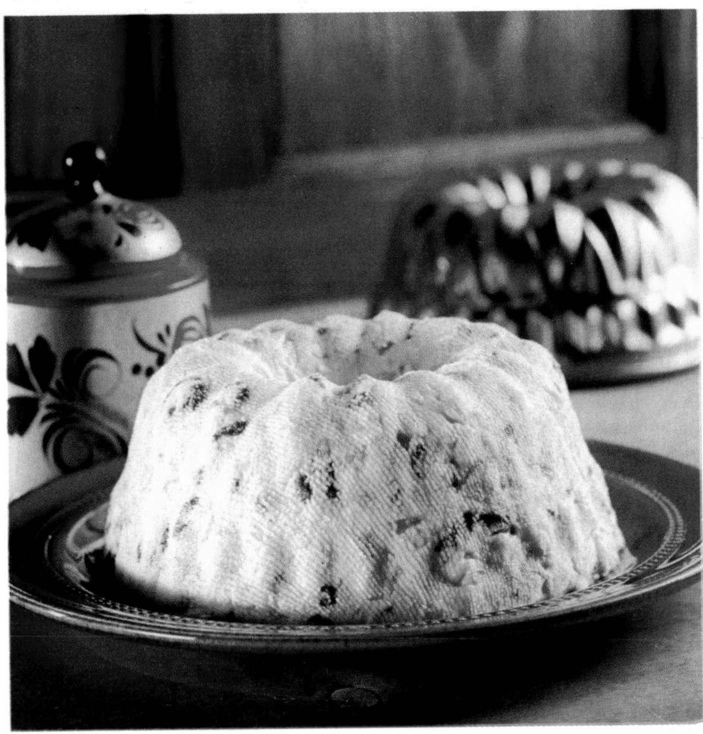

Preparation time: 20 min. plus time for mixture to stand (see Stage 5).
Main utensils: 2–3-pint/2½–3½-pint fancy mould, muslin/cheesecloth.

IMPERIAL

For 8–10 people you need:
1 lb. cream cheese
4 oz. unsalted butter
5 oz. sugar
¼ pint soured cream *or* thin cream with ½ tablespoon lemon juice
6 oz. almonds, blanched

4 oz. chopped, mixed candied peel
12 oz. large raisins *or* seedless raisins

AMERICAN

For 8–10 people you need:
1 lb. cream cheese
½ cup sweet butter
½ cup plus 2 tablespoons sugar
⅔ cup sour cream *or* coffee cream with ½ tablespoon lemon juice
generous 1 cup blanched almonds
⅔ cup chopped, mixed candied peel
2 cups large raisins *or* seedless raisins

This mould has long been a traditional dessert in Russia for Easter time. It takes a little while to make, but it really is most delicious. In the old days a Turk's head mould was generally used.

1. Sieve the cream cheese, this makes it easier to handle.
2. Blend with the creamed butter, sugar, soured cream, blanched almonds, chopped or flaked, if wished.
3. Beat together very thoroughly.
4. Add the candied peel and stoned or seeded raisins.
5. Line the mould with muslin (this absorbs surplus moisture), put in mixture. Put muslin over the top of the mould with a weight on top, leave for at least half a day in a cool place. This mould improves in flavour if it is kept in a cool place for another day before serving.
6. Turn out, serve with soured cream and sugar, or a yeast cake.

147

Plombir
Ice cream and cream dessert

Cooking time: 2–3 min. **Freezing time:** 1 hr. **Preparation time:** 15 min.
Main cooking utensils: 2 basins, saucepan.

IMPERIAL

For 4–5 people you need:
For the ice cream:
2 large eggs
3–4 oz. sieved icing sugar

¼ pint milk
1 vanilla pod
1 teaspoon powder gelatine, *or* enough to set ¼ pint
1 tablespoon water
½ pint thick cream

¼ pint thick cream *or* use a mixture of thick and thin cream
2–3 oz. walnuts, hazelnuts *or* blanched almonds*
wafer biscuits

AMERICAN

For 4–5 people you need:
For the ice cream:
2 large eggs
approx. ¾ cup sieved confectioners' sugar
⅔ cup milk
1 vanilla bean
1 teaspoon powder gelatin, *or* enough to set ⅔ cup
1 tablespoon water
1¼ cups whipping cream

⅔ cup whipping cream *or* mixture of whipping and coffee cream
approx. ½ cup walnuts, hazelnuts *or* blanched almonds*
wafers

*The almonds may be put in the oven or under the grill to brown.

1. Turn the indicator on the refrigerator to the coldest setting, 30 minutes before putting the mixture into the freezing compartment.
2. Whisk the egg yolks and sugar together until thick and fluffy.
3. Heat the milk with the vanilla pod for 2–3 minutes.
4. Soften the gelatine in the cold water, then stand basin in a saucepan of boiling water until dissolved.
5. Remove the vanilla pod and blend the gelatine with the milk.
6. Pour on to the whisked egg yolks then let this mixture stand, cool and begin to thicken very slightly.
7. Fold the lightly whipped cream and stiffly whisked egg whites into the egg yolk mixture.
8. Freeze until quite firm.
9. Whip the cream, blend with the ice cream. Some of the nuts may be added or all put on top. Serve with wafers.

To vary: If liked, a peach or apricot half may be placed in the glass, and covered with Plombir, as in picture.

148

Dios es makos beigli
Christmas cake

Cooking time: 45 min. **Preparation time:** 35 min. plus time for dough to 'prove'. **Main cooking utensils:** saucepan, baking tray/sheet. **Oven temperature:** moderately hot, 400°F., 200°C., Gas Mark 5–6. **Oven position:** centre.

IMPERIAL

For 12 portions you need:
$\frac{3}{4}$ oz. fresh yeast
$1\frac{1}{2}$ oz. sugar
approx. $\frac{1}{4}$ pint milk
12 oz. flour, preferably plain
pinch salt
4 oz. butter
1 egg

For the filling:
8 oz. almonds
4 oz. walnuts *or* hazelnuts
3 tablespoons thick cream *or* 1 egg yolk and little milk
8–10 oz. sugar
4 oz. sultanas
2 oz. butter

To glaze:
1 egg white

AMERICAN

For 12 portions you need:
$\frac{3}{4}$ cake compressed yeast
3 tablespoons sugar
approx. $\frac{2}{3}$ cup milk
3 cups all-purpose flour
dash salt
$\frac{1}{2}$ cup butter
1 egg

For the filling:
generous $1\frac{1}{2}$ cups almonds
1 cup walnuts *or* hazelnuts
scant $\frac{1}{4}$ cup whipping cream *or* 1 egg yolk and little milk
$1–1\frac{1}{4}$ cups sugar
$\frac{2}{3}$ cup seedless white raisins
$\frac{1}{4}$ cup butter

To glaze:
1 egg white

1. Cream the yeast with a teaspoon sugar. Add $\frac{1}{4}$ pint (U.S. $\frac{2}{3}$ cup) tepid milk, sprinkling of flour and put in warm place until surface is covered with bubbles.
2. Sieve the flour and salt, rub in butter, add remaining sugar, blend with yeast liquid and egg.
3. Knead lightly to a firm rolling consistency, if necessary add extra milk.
4. Cover dough, 'prove' for 1 hour in a warm place till double its original size.
5. Knead again and divide in half.
6. Roll each half thinly to an oblong.
7. Prepare the filling; chop, then pound unskinned nuts (or put in blender or mixer), mix with other ingredients; cream the butter.
8. Spread half of the filling on one rectangle of dough, put second piece on top and remaining filling.
9. Roll like Swiss roll and allow to 'prove' for 25 minutes.
10. Glaze and bake until firm. Dust with sugar before serving.

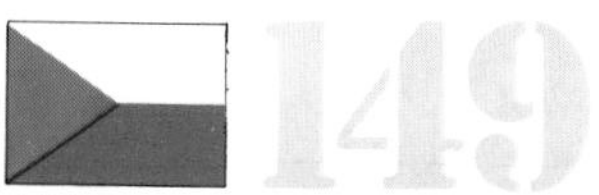

149

Babovka
Chocolate and nut gâteau

Cooking time: $1–1\frac{1}{4}$ hr. **Preparation time:** 35 min. **Main cooking utensil:** 8–9-inch cake tin/spring form cake pan. **Oven temperature:** very moderate, 325–350°F., 170–180°C., Gas Mark 3. **Oven position:** centre.

IMPERIAL

For 8–10 portions you need:
8 oz. butter *or* margarine
8 oz. castor sugar
6 eggs
12 oz. flour, preferably plain with $1\frac{1}{2}$ teaspoons baking powder

6 oz. blanched almonds *or* use mixture of nuts
milk to mix
2 tablespoons rum *or* brandy
3 oz. cocoa powder

AMERICAN

For 8–10 portions you need:
1 cup butter *or* margarine
generous 1 cup granulated sugar
6 eggs
3 cups all-purpose flour, sifted with $3\frac{1}{2}$ teaspoons double-acting baking powder
scant $1\frac{1}{4}$ cups blanched almonds *or* use mixture of nuts
milk to mix
3 tablespoons rum *or* brandy
$\frac{3}{4}$ cup unsweetened cocoa powder

This is one of the celebrated festive cakes in Czechoslovakia.

1. Cream the butter or margarine with the sugar until soft and light.
2. Separate the egg yolks and whites, gradually beat yolks into the butter mixture.
3. Sieve the flour and baking powder well, fold into the butter mixture with chopped nuts and enough milk to make a soft consistency.
4. Divide this mixture in half, add rum to one half; very well sieved cocoa to second half, together with a little extra milk so it returns to the original consistency.
5. Whisk the egg whites until very stiff, then fold equally into the two mixtures.
6. Fill the cake tin with alternate spoonfuls of rum and chocolate mixtures.
7. Bake until firm to the touch.

150

Meggy-lepény
Morello cherry cake

Cooking time: 45–55 min. **Preparation time:** 25–30 min. **Main cooking utensil:** 7–8-inch cake tin/spring form cake pan. **Oven temperature:** very moderate to moderate, 350–375°F., 180–190°C., Gas Mark 4. **Oven position:** centre.

IMPERIAL

For 8–9 portions you need:
5 oz. butter
5 oz. sugar
3 eggs
7 oz. self-raising flour
8 oz. Morello cherries (weight before stoning)

To decorate:
2 oz. icing sugar

AMERICAN

For 8–9 portions you need:
$\frac{1}{2}$ cup plus 2 tablespoons butter
$\frac{1}{2}$ cup plus 2 tablespoons sugar
3 eggs
1$\frac{3}{4}$ cups all-purpose flour, sifted with 2 teaspoons baking powder
$\frac{1}{2}$ lb. Morello cherries (weight before pitting)

To decorate:
$\frac{1}{2}$ cup confectioners' sugar

1. Cream the butter and sugar until soft and light.
2. Gradually beat in the eggs, adding a little sieved flour if the mixture shows signs of curdling.
3. Mix about 1 oz. (U.S. $\frac{1}{4}$ cup) flour with two-thirds of the stoned cherries. To stone the cherries; insert the bent end of a very fine new hairpin into the fruit, gently ease out the stone.
4. Fold the remainder of the flour into the egg and butter mixture.
5. Add the floured cherries to the cake mixture, stir thoroughly.
6. Grease and flour the cake tin or line with greased and floured greaseproof paper. Put in cake mixture.
7. Put remaining cherries on top of the cake, but spread the cake mixture lightly over the fruit to prevent cherries browning during cooking.
8. Bake until firm to the touch. (The smaller, deeper cake requires the longer baking time, and heat may have to be reduced slightly, look after 30 minutes baking.)
9. Turn out carefully and, when cold, sprinkle lavishly with the sugar. This cake must be eaten fresh.

To vary: Other *firm* cherries could be used.

151

Bukhty
Small filled cakes

Cooking time: 15 min. **Preparation time:** 25 min. plus time for dough to 'prove'. **Main cooking utensils:** saucepan, preferably 9–10-inch square tin or flat baking tray/sheet. **Oven temperature:** moderately hot, 400°F., 200°C., Gas Mark 5–6. **Oven position:** just above centre.

IMPERIAL

For 12–16 cakes you need:
$\frac{3}{4}$ oz. fresh yeast
2 oz. sugar
approx. 12 tablespoons milk
12 oz. plain flour
pinch salt
1$\frac{1}{2}$ oz. butter
$\frac{1}{2}$ teaspoon vanilla essence
grated rind 1 lemon
1 egg
1 oz. fat

For the filling:
8 oz. cottage cheese
1 tablespoon cream
1 oz. butter
little grated lemon rind
2 oz. sugar
2 oz. dried fruit

For the topping:
2 oz. vanilla *or* ordinary sugar

AMERICAN

For 12–16 cakes you need:
$\frac{3}{4}$ cake compressed yeast
$\frac{1}{4}$ cup sugar
approx. 1 cup milk
3 cups all-purpose flour
dash salt
3 tablespoons butter
$\frac{1}{2}$ teaspoon vanilla extract
grated rind 1 lemon
1 egg
2 tablespoons fat

For the filling:
1 cup cottage cheese
1 tablespoon cream
2 tablespoons butter
little grated lemon rind
$\frac{1}{4}$ cup sugar
$\frac{1}{3}$ cup dried fruit

For the topping:
$\frac{1}{4}$ cup vanilla *or* ordinary sugar

1. Cream the yeast with a teaspoon of sugar.
2. Add approximately 8 tablespoons (U.S. $\frac{2}{3}$ cup) tepid milk and a sprinkling of flour, leave until surface is covered with bubbles.
3. Sieve the flour and salt. Rub in butter and add remaining sugar.
4. Blend vanilla essence and lemon rind with the yeast mixture, add to flour with egg. Add remaining milk gradually as flour varies in absorbtion.
5. Knead lightly but firmly until a smooth dough. Cover, put into a warm place, allow to 'prove' (rise) until double its original size, about 1 hour. Knead again and divide into portions.
6. Flatten each one, put cottage cheese filling, jam or fruit purée in centre, re-form into rounds or squares.
7. Grease a baking tin or tray well, brush sides of buns with a little melted fat and 'prove' for 20 minutes.
8. Bake until firm and sprinkle with sugar while hot.
9. To make the cottage cheese filling, blend all the filling ingredients.

EASTERN MEDITERRANEAN

The Eastern Mediterranean countries have widely differing political and social histories but in culinary matters they have a common bond in their location on the Mediterranean. The vegetation and agriculture, and consequently the food, are very largely determined by the Mediterranean climate. Tomatoes, aubergines and courgettes are the most common vegetables; beef is popular but lamb, chicken and fish are cheaper for everyday meals, and since goats thrive better than cows, goat's milk and cheese are often used.

Egypt and the Lebanon share Arabic traditions in cooking. Spiced lamb stew is an Egyptian recipe served with dumplings or rice. The Beirut celebration menu includes several Arabic specialities, of which the most famous is *Cous-cous*, steamed crushed millet or other cereal served with a stew of lamb or chicken.

Greece has a fascinating and distinctive cuisine. It is closer to Italy than the other Eastern Mediterranean countries and this is reflected in dishes like Artichokes with eggs and sauce using Parmesan cheese. But there are plenty of dishes that definitely belong to Greece and will be found in virtually every home or restaurant one enters. Potato omelettes, for example, are served everywhere—in fact, it is often easier to get an omelette with potatoes than without. A dish which is so popular that it might be considered a national dish is Moussaka, a lamb casserole with cheese topping. *Souvlaki* are small kebabs of herbed meat sold as snacks at souvlaki stalls; a more sophisticated variation on these is *Arni souvla,* marinated kebabs of lamb and courgettes which are ideal for a summer barbecue. Needless to say, fish is excellent in Greece. An original method of cooking fish is to bake it in paper; this not only seals in the flavour but makes washing up much easier.

The classic conclusion to a Greek meal is a syrupy pastry or cake with which one sips a small cup of thick strong Turkish coffee made with lots of sugar—if you want your coffee without sugar you must say so or it will be put in automatically. *Baklava* is an exquisite creation made with layers of special paper-thin pastry, for which puff pastry is an approximate substitute, filled with chopped nuts and soaked in a sugar or honey syrup. *Halvas* is a cake also soaked in syrup, the addition of semolina giving it an unusual texture. Most Greek bread is plain but there is

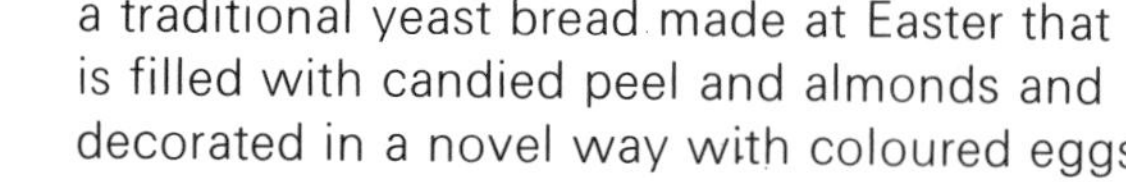

a traditional yeast bread made at Easter that is filled with candied peel and almonds and decorated in a novel way with coloured eggs.

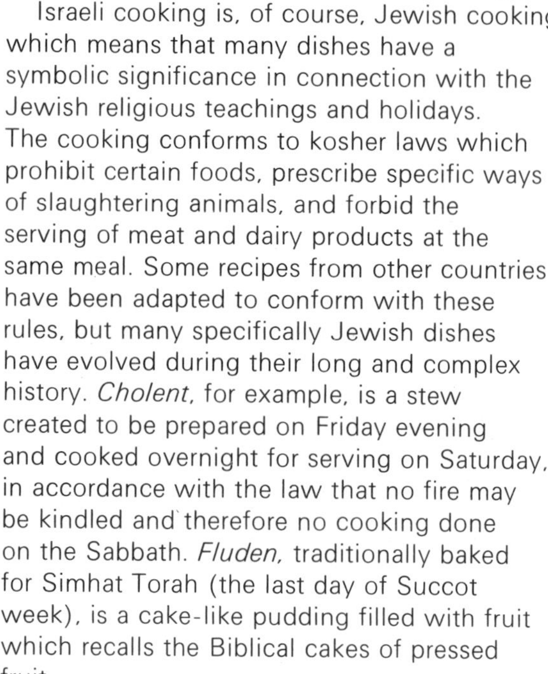

Israeli cooking is, of course, Jewish cooking which means that many dishes have a symbolic significance in connection with the Jewish religious teachings and holidays. The cooking conforms to kosher laws which prohibit certain foods, prescribe specific ways of slaughtering animals, and forbid the serving of meat and dairy products at the same meal. Some recipes from other countries have been adapted to conform with these rules, but many specifically Jewish dishes have evolved during their long and complex history. *Cholent*, for example, is a stew created to be prepared on Friday evening and cooked overnight for serving on Saturday, in accordance with the law that no fire may be kindled and therefore no cooking done on the Sabbath. *Fluden,* traditionally baked for Simhat Torah (the last day of Succot week), is a cake-like pudding filled with fruit which recalls the Biblical cakes of pressed fruit.

It is difficult to separate Syrian cooking from neighbouring Turkey for the cooking of these countries is very similar. However, Syria is the home of a chicken casserole with haricot beans and tomatoes and *Tadjun ahmar*, a colourful hot-pot of meat and vegetables topped with soured cream, which can be made quickly for a party dish.

Turkish cooking has close affinities with the Greek and the two countries both claim to have originated several famous dishes. However, no-one will dispute the fact that kebabs are a Turkish invention, usually with lamb and such Mediterranean vegetables as tomatoes, onions, green peppers or aubergines. Rice is used in many dishes, often with diced meat and vegetables in a pilaff; we have included a recipe for *Sayadiah,* a fish and rice dish. A type of flan or pie called *börek* is made in Turkey with layers of very thin pastry and various sweet and savoury fillings. *Peynirli börek* has a cheese filling for which we suggest a white cheddar; sieved cottage cheese can also be used and in Turkey the filling would probably be a crumbly goat cheese. The Turks love sweet things as much as the Greeks and of course they too serve them with strong, sweet Turkish coffee. Their most famous confection is Turkish delight but Semolina cakes are a delicious lesser-known delicacy which are really sweets rather than cakes.

152

Sayadiah
Fish and rice

Cooking time: 25 min. **Preparation time:** 20 min. **Main cooking utensil:** large saucepan. **Oven temperature:** very cool to keep food warm (Stage 3).

IMPERIAL

For 4–6 portions you need:
2 medium-sized onions
$1\frac{1}{2}$ lb. fish—use a mixture of white fish and tuna fish
4 tablespoons olive oil
4 tomatoes, skinned
$1\frac{1}{2}$ pints water
6 oz. long grain rice
seasoning
good pinch powdered nutmeg
good pinch cinnamon

To garnish:
shellfish
chopped hard-boiled eggs

AMERICAN

For 4–6 portions you need:
2 medium-sized onions
$1\frac{1}{2}$ lb. fish—use a mixture of white fish and tunafish
$\frac{1}{3}$ cup olive oil
4 tomatoes, skinned
$3\frac{3}{4}$ cups water
scant 1 cup long grain rice
seasoning
dash powdered nutmeg
dash cinnamon

To garnish:
shellfish
chopped hard-cooked eggs

1. Cut the onions into neat slices and fish into tiny portions.
2. Fry both for a short time in the oil, then add tomatoes.
3. When tender, lift out of the pan on to a plate, cover and keep warm.
4. Put the water in a pan, bring to the boil, add rice and season.
5. Cook steadily, without a lid on the pan, until rice is tender. Stir well towards end of cooking time using a fork. Add spices.
6. Put layers of fish mixture and well-drained rice in a dish.
7. Garnish with shellfish and chopped hard-boiled eggs.

To serve: As a hot hors d'oeuvre or light savoury dish.

To vary: The cooked fish and onions may be allowed to cool and tossed in a little oil and lemon juice. The rice may also be tossed in well-seasoned oil and lemon juice, and the dish served cold.

153

Psari sto harti
Fish cooked in paper

Cooking time: 35 min. **Preparation time:** 20 min. **Main cooking utensils:** 4 sheets greaseproof paper, baking tray/sheet. **Oven temperature:** moderately hot, 375–400°F., 190–200°C., Gas Mark 5. **Oven position:** just above centre.

IMPERIAL

For 4 people you need:
4 fish—red mullet, mackerel *or* trout are ideal
seasoning
little lemon juice
2 tablespoons olive oil

For the topping:
1–2 cloves garlic
seasoning
1 onion
$\frac{1}{2}$ small cucumber
1–2 tablespoons chopped parsley
1–2 tablespoons olive oil
grated rind and juice 1 lemon

To garnish:
1 lemon

AMERICAN

For 4 people you need:
4 fish—mullet, mackerel *or* trout are ideal
seasoning
little lemon juice
3 tablespoons olive oil

For the topping:
1–2 cloves garlic
seasoning
1 onion
$\frac{1}{2}$ small cucumber
1–3 tablespoons chopped parsley
1–3 tablespoons olive oil
grated rind and juice 1 lemon

To garnish:
1 lemon

1. Remove the heads from the fish and clean well.
2. Dry thoroughly and season lightly, then flavour with lemon juice.
3. Lay the pieces of paper on the flat baking sheet.
4. Oil this very thoroughly.
5. Lift fish on to the paper, wrap carefully and bake for approximately 25–30 minutes, depending on the size of the fish.
6. Open parchment and either bake or grill for a few minutes until the fish is brown.
7. Crush the garlic with a little salt.
8. Mix the garlic with finely diced onion and peeled, diced cucumber. Add the chopped parsley, oil, lemon rind and juice and season.

To serve: Top the fish with the vegetable mixture, garnish with lemon and serve hot or cold.

To vary: Other vegetables and ingredients may be added to form an interesting topping; chopped tomatoes, marjoram, chopped olives.

154

Garithes mythia pilafi
Shrimp and mussel pilaff

Cooking time: 35 min. **Preparation time:** 20 min. **Main cooking utensils:** 2 saucepans.

IMPERIAL

For 6 people you need:
3 pints mussels
6 onions
$1\frac{1}{2}$ pints water
seasoning
3 tablespoons olive oil
9 oz. long *or* medium grain rice

generous $\frac{1}{4}$ pint white wine
1 large green pepper
1 small red pepper
$1\frac{1}{2}$ pints unshelled shrimps *or* prawns
6–10 oz. cooked chicken (optional)

To garnish:
few unshelled prawns
cooked mussels in shells

AMERICAN

For 6 people you need:
4 pints mussels
6 onions
$3\frac{3}{4}$ cups water
seasoning
scant $\frac{1}{4}$ cup olive oil
generous $1\frac{1}{3}$ cups long *or* medium grain rice
generous $\frac{2}{3}$ cup white wine
1 large sweet green pepper
1 small sweet red pepper
$3\frac{3}{4}$ cups unshelled shrimp *or* prawns
1–2 cups cooked chicken (optional)

To garnish:
few unshelled prawns *or* shrimp
cooked mussels in shells

1. Scrub the mussels. If any are open, tap sharply, if shells do not close, discard these.
2. Put into a pan with 1 chopped onion, water and seasoning; cook until mussels open. Cool, enough to handle, remove shells and 'beard'. Keep a few mussels on half a shell only for garnish. Strain mussel liquid.
3. Chop the remaining onions very finely, fry in oil for few minutes. Add rice, turn in oil and onion mixture, add mussel stock and wine.
4. Cook steadily for about 15–18 minutes until rice is tender, leave lid off pan so liquid gradually evaporates.
5. Add the diced green and red pepper during cooking, or towards end of cooking if a firmer texture is required, season.
6. Shell the shrimps or prawns, keeping a few unshelled for garnish, add to rice mixture with mussels and chicken.

To serve: Turn on to a serving dish and garnish with a few unshelled prawns and mussels in their shells.

155

Cholent mit flohmen simmes
Beef ragoût with fruit

Cooking time: $2\frac{1}{2}$ hr. **Preparation time:** 25 min. plus time to soak prunes. **Main cooking utensils:** saucepan *or* casserole, 2 small saucepans. **Oven temperature:** slow to very moderate, 300–325°F., 150–170°C., Gas Mark 2. **Oven position:** centre.

IMPERIAL

For 5–6 people you need:
1 lb. prunes
$1\frac{1}{2}$–2 lb. fresh brisket of beef
8–12 oz. turnips *or* carrots
1 lb. potatoes *or* sweet potatoes
seasoning
grated rind and juice 1 lemon
2 oz. brown sugar *or* honey

juice from prunes and water

To garnish:
prunes (see Stage 6)
puff pastry shapes
cooked peas

AMERICAN

For 5–6 people you need:
1 lb. prunes
$1\frac{1}{2}$–2 lb. fresh beef brisket
$\frac{1}{2}$–$\frac{3}{4}$ lb. turnips *or* carrots
1 lb. potatoes *or* sweet potatoes
seasoning
grated rind and juice 1 lemon
$\frac{1}{4}$ cup brown sugar *or* $\frac{1}{8}$ cup honey
juice from prunes and water

To garnish:
prunes (see Stage 6)
puff paste shapes
cooked peas

1. Put the prunes to soak for few hours in water to cover.
2. Cut the beef and vegetables into neat pieces. Put into a saucepan or casserole with seasoning, most of the drained prunes (keep few for garnish), lemon rind and juice.
3. Blend the brown sugar with most of the juice from prunes, pour over the meat.
4. Add enough water to cover, stir well to mix ingredients.
5. Cover, cook until meat is tender.
6. Meanwhile simmer rest of the prunes in liquid left and reheat pastry.

To serve: Put cooked peas round ragoût, top with prunes and pastry.

156

Holishkes

Stuffed cabbage rolls

Cooking time: $1\frac{1}{4}$–$1\frac{1}{2}$ hr. **Preparation time:** 25 min. **Main cooking utensils:** saucepan, colander, sieve, frying pan/skillet, casserole. **Oven temperature:** very moderate, 350°F., 180°C., Gas Mark 3–4. **Oven position:** centre.

IMPERIAL

For 5–6 people you need:
1 lb. raw minced beef
3 oz. cooked rice
4 oz. mushrooms
2 medium-sized onions
3 medium-sized carrots
seasoning
1 egg
10–12 large, young cabbage leaves

For the sauce:
1 tablespoon lemon juice
2 oz. brown sugar
$\frac{1}{4}$ pint water
1 lb. ripe tomatoes

To fry:
2 oz. chicken fat

AMERICAN

For 5–6 people you need:
1 lb. raw ground beef
$\frac{1}{2}$ cup cooked rice
1 cup mushrooms
2 medium-sized onions
3 medium-sized carrots
seasoning
1 egg
10–12 large, young cabbage leaves

For the sauce:
1 tablespoon lemon juice
$\frac{1}{4}$ cup brown sugar
$\frac{2}{3}$ cup water
1 lb. ripe tomatoes

To fry:
$\frac{1}{4}$ cup chicken fat

1. Blend the minced meat, rice, chopped mushrooms, grated onions and carrots. Season well. Add egg.
2. Put the cabbage leaves into boiling salted water and cook for 3–4 minutes. Drain.
3. Put the stuffing on to each leaf and roll firmly. Secure with wooden cocktail sticks if wished.
4. Blend the lemon juice, sugar, water and sieved, skinned tomatoes.
5. Heat the fat in a pan and turn the cabbage rolls in this until slightly browned on the outside.
6. Transfer to a casserole, putting some of the sauce underneath and the rest on top.
7. Cover tightly and cook for $1\frac{1}{4}$–$1\frac{1}{2}$ hours.

To serve: With green salad or cooked beans.

To vary: Add raisins to the sauce.

157

Moussaka

Cheese-topped casserole

Cooking time: 45 min. **Preparation time:** 35 min. **Main cooking utensils:** large frying pan/skillet, $2\frac{1}{2}$-pint/3-pint ovenproof dish. **Oven temperature:** moderately hot, 400°F., 200°C., Gas Mark 5–6. **Oven position:** centre.

IMPERIAL

For 4–5 people you need:
1 lb. lean cooked lamb (weight without bone)
$1\frac{1}{2}$ oz. butter
$1\frac{1}{2}$–2 tablespoons oil
1 good-sized onion
seasoning
1 small can tomato purée
8 oz. potatoes (weight when peeled)
1–2 aubergines
1 clove garlic
8 oz. skinned tomatoes

For the sauce:
1 oz. butter
1 oz. flour
$\frac{1}{2}$ pint milk
3–4 oz. cheese, grated

For the topping:
2–3 oz. cheese, grated
parsley

AMERICAN

For 4–5 people you need:
1 lb. lean cooked lamb (weight without bone)
3 tablespoons butter
2–3 tablespoons oil
1 good-sized onion
seasoning
1 small can tomato paste
$\frac{1}{2}$ lb. potatoes (weight when peeled)
1–2 eggplants
1 clove garlic
$\frac{1}{2}$ lb. skinned tomatoes

For the sauce:
2 tablespoons butter
$\frac{1}{4}$ cup all-purpose flour
$1\frac{1}{4}$ cups milk
$\frac{3}{4}$–1 cup grated cheese

For the topping:
$\frac{1}{2}$–$\frac{3}{4}$ cup grated cheese
parsley

1. Mince or dice the meat, then heat butter and oil. Fry the chopped onion until tender, mix with meat, seasoning and tomato purée, put into dish and keep hot.
2. Slice the potatoes and aubergines, and crush garlic; fry until tender, add sliced de-seeded tomatoes, heat, then put on the meat.
3. Top with the cheese sauce. This is made by heating the butter, add the flour and mix away from the heat. Gradually add the milk over the heat and stir to a smooth sauce. Add the cheese just before adding to the dish.
4. Top with grated cheese, and brown for approximately 20 minutes in the oven. Garnish with parsley.

158

Arron bilruz
Meat ball meal

Cooking time: 35 min. **Preparation time:** 15–30 min. **Main cooking utensils:** 2 saucepans.

IMPERIAL

For 4–5 people you need:
1 lb. raw minced beef
2 oz. coarse oatmeal
1 teaspoon made mustard
1 small onion
1 teaspoon Worcestershire sauce
seasoning
1 egg

To coat:
1–1$\frac{1}{2}$ oz. flour, seasoned

To fry and for the sauce:
3 oz. butter, oil *or* fat
1 onion
approx. 12 oz. mixed, diced vegetables
$\frac{1}{2}$–1 teaspoon marjoram
$\frac{1}{2}$ pint fresh tomato pulp *or* canned tomato soup
$\frac{1}{2}$ pint stock *or* beef stock cube and water

To serve:
8 oz. noodles

AMERICAN

For 4–5 people you need:
1 lb. raw ground beef
scant $\frac{1}{2}$ cup coarse oatmeal
1 teaspoon prepared mustard
1 small onion
1 teaspoon Worcestershire sauce
seasoning
1 egg

To coat:
4–6 tablespoons flour, seasoned

To fry and for the sauce:
6 tablespoons butter, oil *or* fat
1 onion
approx. $\frac{3}{4}$ lb. mixed, diced vegetables
$\frac{1}{2}$–1 teaspoon marjoram
1$\frac{1}{4}$ cups fresh tomato pulp *or* canned tomato soup
1$\frac{1}{4}$ cups stock *or* beef bouillon cube and water

To serve:
$\frac{1}{2}$ lb. noodles

1. Blend the meat, oats, mustard and very finely chopped onion together.
2. Add the sauce, seasoning to taste and bind with beaten egg.
3. Form into small balls, roll in seasoned flour.
4. Heat the butter, fry meat balls until golden brown, lift out of pan.
5. Slice the peeled onion, fry in butter remaining in pan, together with diced vegetables.
6. Add the marjoram, tomato pulp and stock, season and bring to the boil. Return meat balls to pan, simmer for 20 minutes.
7. Meanwhile, boil the noodles in 4 pints (U.S. 5 pints) salted water until tender, drain.

To serve: Arrange noodles in dish, top with meat balls and sauce.

159

Roulo me makaronia
Beef roll and noodles

Cooking time: 1$\frac{1}{4}$–1$\frac{1}{2}$ hr. *or* about 30 min. (see Stages 1 and 8). **Preparation time:** 15 min. **Main cooking utensils:** roasting tin/pan, 2 saucepans. **Oven temperature:** moderately hot, 400°F., 200°C., Gas Mark 5–6. **Oven position:** above centre.

IMPERIAL

For 4–5 people you need:
1$\frac{3}{4}$–2 lb. lean beef
1–2 cloves garlic
grated rind and juice 1 lemon
1 oz. flour
seasoning
small head celery *or* several sticks celery
pinch dried marjoram *or* 1 teaspoon chopped fresh herbs
3 oz. butter
$\frac{1}{2}$ pint brown stock *or* $\frac{1}{4}$ pint brown stock and $\frac{1}{4}$ pint red wine
1–2 bay leaves
8 oz. tomatoes
8 oz. noodles
1–2 oz. butter

To garnish:
1 lb. carrots, parsley

AMERICAN

For 4–5 people you need:
1$\frac{3}{4}$–2 lb. lean beef
1–2 cloves garlic
grated rind and juice 1 lemon
$\frac{1}{4}$ cup all-purpose flour
seasoning
small head celery *or* several stalks celery
dash dried marjoram *or* 1 teaspoon chopped fresh herbs
6 tablespoons butter
1$\frac{1}{4}$ cups brown stock *or* $\frac{2}{3}$ cup brown stock and $\frac{2}{3}$ cup red wine
1–2 bay leaves
$\frac{1}{2}$ lb. tomatoes
$\frac{1}{2}$ lb. noodles
2–4 tablespoons butter

To garnish:
1 lb. carrots, parsley

1. The meat may be cooked as one large roll or 4–5 smaller ones.
2. For one roll, flatten meat with rolling pin, for small rolls cut into portions and flatten.
3. Cut the garlic in wafer-thin slices, insert in the cuts in the meat.
4. Mix the lemon rind with flour and seasoning.
5. Chop celery finely (use enough to cover slice or slices of meat), sprinkle with marjoram. Roll firmly and tie, coat in flour.
6. Heat the butter in roasting tin and cook the meat for 10–15 minutes in this, turning.
7. Add stock, bay leaves, lemon juice and skinned and sieved tomatoes.
8. Cook for a further 20 minutes for small rolls or 1–1$\frac{1}{4}$ hours for a large roll, basting from time to time.
9. Meanwhile cook the noodles in boiling salted water. Drain, mix with the butter. Cook the carrots for garnish.

To serve: Arrange rolls (slice large one) and sauce with noodles and garnish with carrots and parsley.

160

Sefrito

Spiced lamb stew

Cooking time: $1\frac{1}{2}$ hr. **Preparation time:** 25 min. **Main cooking utensil:** saucepan.

IMPERIAL

For 4 people you need:
$1\frac{1}{2}$–2 lb. diced lean lamb
1 oz. flour
seasoning
grated rind 1 lemon
6 small onions *or* shallots
2 cloves garlic
2–3 tablespoons oil
$1\frac{1}{2}$ pints stock
good pinch coriander seeds
good pinch powdered cinnamon
2–3 medium-sized tomatoes
2–3 dessert apples

To garnish:
4 oz. self-raising flour
2 oz. butter
water to mix
chopped mint
chopped parsley

AMERICAN

For 4 people you need:
$1\frac{1}{2}$–2 lb. diced lean lamb
$\frac{1}{4}$ cup all-purpose flour
seasoning
grated rind 1 lemon
6 small onions *or* shallots
2 cloves garlic
3–4 tablespoons oil
$3\frac{3}{4}$ cups stock
dash coriander seeds
dash powdered cinnamon
2–3 medium-sized tomatoes
2–3 eating apples

To garnish:
1 cup all-purpose flour, sifted with 1 teaspoon baking powder
$\frac{1}{4}$ cup butter
water to mix
chopped mint
chopped parsley

1. Coat the lamb with flour, mixed with seasoning and grated lemon rind.
2. Peel and chop the onions and crush cloves of garlic.
3. Toss the floured meat, then onions and garlic in hot oil, gradually blend in stock. Bring to the boil, cook until thickened, adding coriander seeds, cinnamon, and skinned, de-seeded, chopped tomatoes.
4. Lower heat, simmer steadily for 1 hour.
5. Add the diced apples and dumplings about 20 minutes before the end of cooking.
6. For the dumplings, sieve flour and seasoning, rub in the butter, bind with water. Form into small balls and cook in the boiling liquid for about 15–20 minutes. Chopped mint and/or parsley can be added to the dough as well as being a garnish.

161

Kebabs

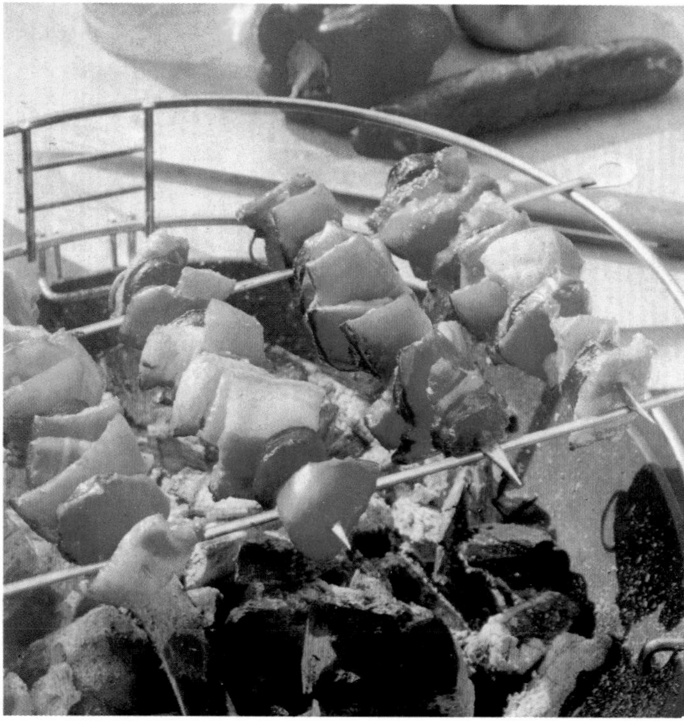

Cooking time: approximately 6–7 min. **Preparation time:** 10 min. **Main cooking utensils:** 4 skewers (see Stage 5).

IMPERIAL

For 4 people you need:
4–6 fairly thick rashers streaky bacon
4 medium-sized ripe firm tomatoes
1 green pepper
3–4 blood *or* other sausages
oil *or* melted butter
seasoning

AMERICAN

For 4 people you need:
4–6 fairly thick bacon slices
4 medium-sized ripe firm tomatoes
1 sweet green pepper
3–4 blood *or* other sausages
oil *or* melted butter
seasoning

1. Cut the rinds from the bacon and divide into portions.
2. Quarter the tomatoes.
3. Discard core and seeds of the green pepper and cut the flesh into portions. If wished these may be blanched in boiling water for 2–3 minutes. This gives a softer texture.
4. Slice the sausages.
5. Thread the food on to the skewers then brush with oil or melted butter, and season the tomatoes and pepper lightly.
6. Cook over a hot barbecue fire or under a hot grill for 6–7 minutes, turning several times and brushing with the oil or butter.

To serve: With hot rolls or cooked rice.

162

Tadjin ahmar
Sour cream-topped hot-pot

Cooking time: 30 min. **Preparation time:** 20 min. **Main cooking utensil:** saucepan.

IMPERIAL

For 6 people you need:
$1\frac{1}{2}$ lb. lean, tender beef, rump steak, veal *or* lamb*
3 oz. butter
1 large aubergine
1–2 green peppers
4 medium-sized potatoes
4 new carrots
4 medium-sized tomatoes
good pinch turmeric
good pinch saffron
good pinch cinnamon
seasoning
$\frac{1}{2}$ pint stock
squeeze lemon *or* lime juice
$\frac{1}{4}$–$\frac{1}{2}$ pint soured cream *or* yoghurt

AMERICAN

For 6 people you need:
$1\frac{1}{2}$ lb. lean, tender beef, veal *or* lamb*
6 tablespoons butter
1 large eggplant
1–2 sweet green peppers
4 medium-sized potatoes
4 new carrots
4 medium-sized tomatoes
dash turmeric
dash saffron
dash cinnamon
seasoning
$1\frac{1}{4}$ cups stock
squeeze lemon *or* lime juice
$\frac{2}{3}$–$1\frac{1}{4}$ cups sour cream *or* yoghurt

*The latter two meats are more often used in Syrian cooking.

1. Cut the meat into neat pieces, toss in butter for 5 minutes.
2. Meanwhile peel the aubergine (this prevents it being too dominating in flavour) and cut into pieces.
3. Cut the green pepper into small strips, discard core and seeds.
4. Peel and dice the potatoes and carrots fairly finely.
5. Toss the aubergine, most of the pepper, potatoes and carrots in butter with meat, add 2 skinned, chopped tomatoes.
6. Blend turmeric, saffron and cinnamon with well-seasoned stock and juice, pour over meat and vegetables. Simmer for 20 minutes or until tender. Add remainder of pepper, quartered tomatoes, and heat for a further 5 minutes. Top with soured cream or yoghurt.

To vary: Herbs, such as mint, chives or parsley, may be added or 2–4 oz. (U.S. $\frac{1}{2}$–1 cup) nuts, walnuts, almonds or pistachio nuts, and a few dates or currants.

163

Arni souvla
Lamb brochettes

Cooking time: 10 min. **Preparation time:** 15 min. plus time to marinate. **Main cooking utensils:** 4–6 strong skewers, barbecue fire *or* grill/broiler.

IMPERIAL

For 4–6 people you need:
For the marinade:
finely grated rind and juice 1 lemon
2 teaspoons curry powder (more if wished)
1 clove garlic, crushed
3 tablespoons olive oil
$\frac{1}{4}$ pint white wine
seasoning

1 lb. lean lamb, cut in one thick slice from the leg
1 lb. courgettes
little extra oil

AMERICAN

For 4–6 people you need:
For the marinade:
finely grated rind and juice 1 lemon
2 teaspoons curry powder (more if wished)
1 clove garlic, crushed
scant $\frac{1}{4}$ cup olive oil
$\frac{2}{3}$ cup white wine
seasoning

1 lb. lean lamb, cut in one thick slice from the leg
1 lb. small zuchinnis
little extra oil

1. Blend the ingredients for the marinade together, put into the shallow dish.
2. Cut the lamb into neat dice, drying this thoroughly after washing.
3. Leave in the marinade for several hours, turning once or twice.
4. Wash and dry the courgettes, cut into $\frac{1}{2}$-inch slices, but do not peel.
5. Put cubes of meat and slices of courgette on to the skewers, allow to stand for a short time, so any marinade may drip back into the bowl. Brush the courgettes with a little oil. Either cook under a hot grill or over a hot barbecue, turning and basting with the marinade as they cook.

To serve: With any marinade left as a sauce and with either cooked rice or crusty rolls.

164

Kouneli riyanato
Roasted rabbit with marjoram

Cooking time: 1½ hr. see Stage 4. **Preparation time:** 15 min. plus time for rabbit to soak and marinate. **Main cooking utensil:** roasting tin/pan. **Oven temperature:** moderately hot, 400°F., 200°C., Gas Mark 5–6. **Oven position:** above centre.

IMPERIAL

For 4–6 people you need:
1 young rabbit *or* young hare
seasoning
2 lemons
4 tablespoons oil
½–1 tablespoon chopped marjoram
1 onion

To garnish:
sauté potatoes
tomatoes
chopped marjoram *or* parsley

AMERICAN

For 4–6 people you need:
1 young rabbit *or* young hare
seasoning
2 lemons
⅓ cup oil
½–1 tablespoon chopped marjoram
1 onion

To garnish:
sauté potatoes
tomatoes
chopped marjoram *or* parsley

1. Soak the rabbit or hare in cold water and salt for 30 minutes to whiten.
2. Grate rind from lemons, squeeze out juice and put on to a shallow dish with oil, seasoning, marjoram and finely chopped onion.
3. Put the dried rabbit into this, turn once or twice, and leave for 1½ hours.
4. Put the rabbit into the roasting tin, roast for 20 minutes per lb. and 20 minutes over. If the rabbit seems to be dry, baste with a little oil.

To serve: Make stock with the liver of the rabbit or hare. Blend a little flour in the fat in the roasting tin. Blend in stock and cook until thickened.

To garnish: Garnish rabbit with sauté potatoes, cut into neat dice, baked tomatoes and chopped marjoram or parsley.

165

Pilafi me domates
Rice with tomato, chicken *or* fish

Cooking time: 35 min. **Preparation time:** 15 min. **Main cooking utensils:** 3 saucepans.

IMPERIAL

For 4 people you need:
4 tablespoons olive oil
10 oz. long *or* medium grain rice
1 lemon
2 pints beef *or* chicken stock
seasoning
1 clove garlic
3 skinned tomatoes
2 tablespoons tomato purée
4–6 oz. soft *or* grated cheese
4–6 oz. shelled prawns
portions of cooked chicken *or* fish
1 red pepper

AMERICAN

For 4 people you need:
⅓ cup olive oil
scant 1½ cups long *or* medium grain rice
1 lemon
5 cups beef *or* chicken stock
seasoning
1 clove garlic
3 skinned tomatoes
3 tablespoons tomato paste
½–¾ cup soft cheese *or* 1–1½ cups grated cheese
⅔–1 cup shelled prawns
portions of cooked chicken *or* fish
1 sweet red pepper

1. Heat 2 tablespoons (U.S. 3 tablespoons) of oil in pan, toss rice in this together with grated lemon rind.
2. When all the grains of rice are coated with oil, add stock, bring to boil, add squeeze lemon juice and seasoning.
3. Simmer steadily until rice is tender and stock has been absorbed, about 20–25 minutes, lift lid towards end of cooking.
4. Meanwhile, crush the garlic, fry with skinned tomatoes until soft, in 1 tablespoon oil, add tomato purée and half the rice. Heat thoroughly.
5. Either serve this in a separate dish or put at the bottom of a large bowl, top with cheese.
6. Toss the prawns, diced chicken or fish and red peppers, cut into strips, in remaining tablespoon of oil. Add remaining rice, heat gently and either serve in second bowl or pile over tomato and cheese pilaff.

To vary: Onions may be fried in oil with the rice; shrimps and mussels are other fish used in pilaff. Dried sultanas are often added, together with pine nuts.

166

Dfina
Eastern stew

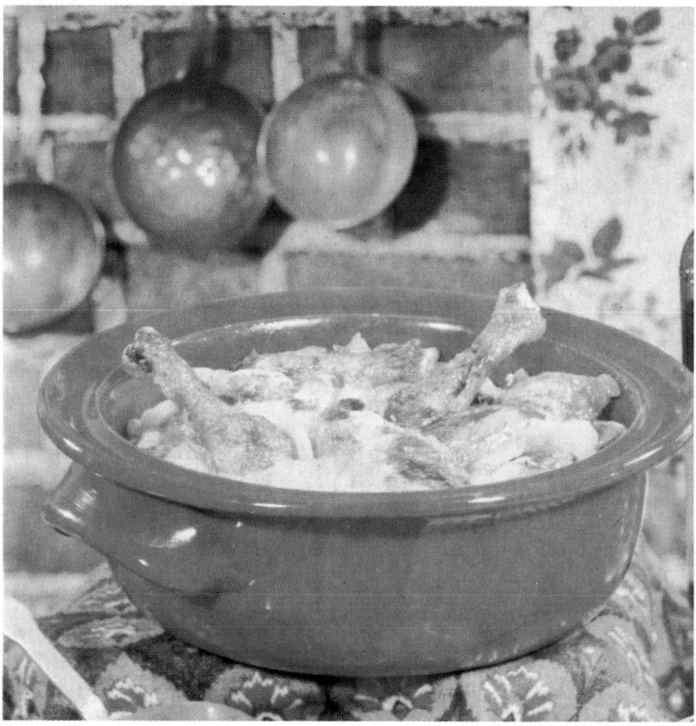

Cooking time: 2 hr. **Preparation time:** 25 min. **Main cooking utensil:** strong saucepan.

IMPERIAL

For 4 people you need:
about 8 joints chicken *or* lamb *or* veal chops*
1 oz. butter
1–2 aubergines *or* tomatoes
about 8 small onions
juice 1–2 lemons
1 tablespoon chopped mint
seasoning
good pinch powdered cinnamon, nutmeg and ginger
water
4 oz. mushrooms, thinly sliced
8 oz. curd cheese *or* use grated cheese

AMERICAN

For 4 people you need:
about 8 joints chicken *or* lamb *or* veal chops*
2 tablespoons butter
1–2 eggplants *or* tomatoes
about 8 small onions
juice 1–2 lemons
1 tablespoon chopped mint
seasoning
dash powdered cinnamon, nutmeg and ginger
water
1 cup thinly sliced mushrooms
1 cup curd cheese *or* use grated cheese

*Young mutton is the most likely meat in Arab countries.

1. Trim away any surplus fat from the chops, then brown meat in pan for a few minutes, heating any fat removed from meat at the same time.
2. Lift the meat from the pan, add butter, then fry sliced aubergines and onions.
3. Lift out surplus pieces of fat, return meat with lemon juice and all the other ingredients except the mushrooms and cheese. Add just enough water to cover the meat.
4. Cover the pan tightly and simmer until tender.
5. Add mushrooms and remove lid for last 30 minutes so the liquid evaporates and the flavour becomes more concentrated.
6. Put into hot serving dish, cover with a layer of cheese. The dish may then be put under a grill or in the oven for a few minutes if wished.

To serve: With boiled rice.

To vary: Soaked dried apricots, raisins or sliced apples can be added for extra flavour.

167

Casserole of baby chickens and beans

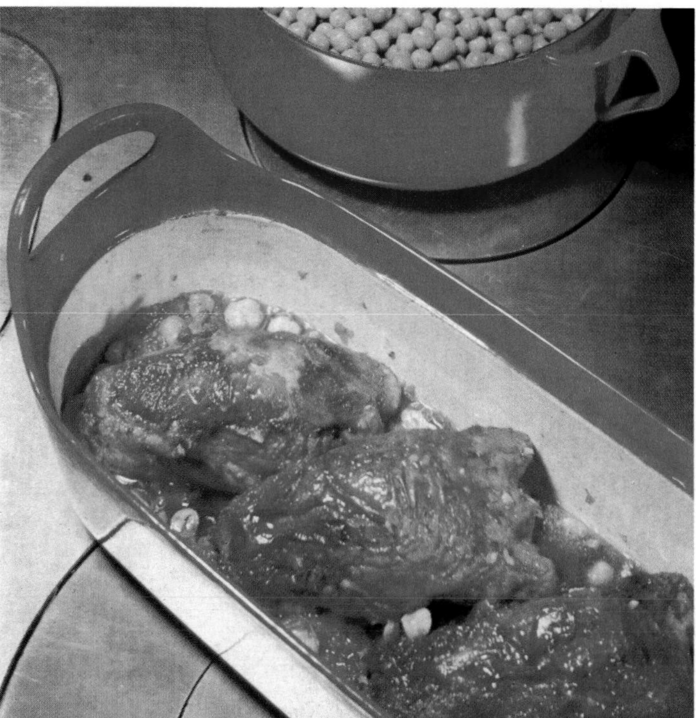

Cooking time: $1\frac{1}{2}$ hr. **Preparation time:** 25 min. **Main cooking utensils:** saucepan, ovenproof dish. **Oven temperature:** very moderate to moderate, 350–375°F., 180–190°C., Gas Mark 4. **Oven position:** centre.

IMPERIAL

For 4 people you need:
4 small spring chickens *or* use 4 joints from a large roasting chicken
1 oz. flour
seasoning
grated rind and juice 1 lemon
2–3 tablespoons oil
2 onions
4 tomatoes
1 clove garlic (optional)
$\frac{1}{2}$ pint stock (made from chicken giblets, see Stage 1)
8–10 oz. fresh haricot beans*

AMERICAN

For 4 people you need:
4 small broiler chickens *or* use 4 joints from a large roaster
$\frac{1}{4}$ cup all-purpose flour
seasoning
grated rind and juice 1 lemon
3–4 tablespoons oil
2 onions
4 tomatoes
1 clove garlic (optional)
$1\frac{1}{4}$ cups stock (made from chicken giblets, see Stage 1)
generous $\frac{1}{2}$ lb. fresh navy beans*

*If using dried haricot beans, allow about 3–4 oz. (U.S. $\frac{1}{2}$ cup), soak overnight in cold water, simmer for 1 hour, then proceed as Stage 6.

1. Remove the giblets from the chickens or chicken and simmer with about $\frac{3}{4}$ pint (U.S. 2 cups) water to give a good stock.
2. Meanwhile, coat the chickens or joints of chicken with the flour, blended with seasoning and grated lemon rind.
3. Fry the chickens or joints in the hot oil until golden.
4. Put on to a plate.
5. Meanwhile, chop the onions finely and toss in the oil, together with the skinned, chopped tomatoes and crushed garlic.
6. Gradually blend in the lemon juice and chicken stock, then add the beans, season well.
7. Simmer for 15 minutes, stirring from time to time.
8. Put the sauce into a casserole with the beans and arrange the chickens or joints on top. Cover the dish and cook for 45 minutes.

To serve: With cooked peas and rice.

168

Beirut celebration menu

ARABIC HORS D'OEUVRE

For 4–5 people: Arrange a selection of foods; radishes (both pink and white), pickled cucumbers, sliced onion, olives, oranges and other fruit and vegetables. Top with well-seasoned olive oil and lemon juice. Serve with yoghurt and fried nuts.

ARABIC WHITE SOUP

Soak and cook 6 oz. (U.S. $\frac{2}{3}$ cup) haricot beans until tender. Blend with 4 oz. (U.S. 1 cup) blanched, chopped almonds and crushed clove garlic, then gradually blend in 2 tablespoons (U.S. 3 tablespoons) olive oil and enough water to make the consistency of a thick soup. Season well, stir in soft breadcrumbs if wished and add freshly chopped mint and parsley. Serve cold.

COUS-COUS

Made with a coarse semolina or millet, obtainable in shops specialising in Arabic food; rice could be used instead. It is served with various meats (mostly mutton or chicken). The semolina or rice is put into a steamer or sieve with *very fine* holes. Seasoned well, covered with a cloth, then brush with flour and water paste of very soft consistency, and steamed until tender, about 45 minutes, over a mutton stew, *see below*. A pinch of saffron can be added to the seasoning, so giving a slightly yellow tinge to the semolina. Top with pine nuts, fried in oil and a large piece of mutton.

MUTTON STEW

Dice 2 lb. lean mutton finely, leaving 1 large piece for topping cous-cous. Brown in 3 oz. (U.S. 6 tablespoons) hot butter and lift out. Fry 2 chopped onions and 2 sliced aubergines (eggplants) until onions are transparent. Replace meat, add few soaked prunes, few fine shreds of lemon rind and seasoning, including pinch cayenne pepper, powdered ginger and cumin. Add 1 pint (U.S. $2\frac{1}{2}$ cups) water and cover with a lid for part of the time, then the steamer of cous-cous, see cous-cous recipe. In the picture, the stew is served in a crisp pastry shell.

169

Omeletta me patates

Potato omelette

Cooking time: 25 min. **Preparation time:** 15 min. **Main cooking utensils:** saucepan, omelette *or* frying pan/skillet.

IMPERIAL

For 2 people you need:
2 large potatoes
seasoning
2 tablespoons oil
1 green pepper
4 eggs
grated rind 1 lemon
1 oz. butter

To garnish:
parsley

AMERICAN

For 2 people you need:
2 large potatoes
seasoning
3 tablespoons oil
1 sweet green pepper
4 eggs
grated rind 1 lemon
2 tablespoons butter

To garnish:
parsley

In Mediterranean countries cooked beans or fried, sliced aubergines are often used as fillings for omelettes.

1. Peel, dice and cook the potatoes in salted water until just tender, drain.
2. Heat the oil in a pan, fry diced potato until golden brown.
3. Cut the green pepper into strips, discard seeds and core, add to the potatoes when nearly brown.
4. Tip the vegetables out of the pan.
5. Beat the eggs, add seasoning and grated lemon rind.
6. Heat the butter in a pan and pour in eggs. Allow to set then tilt pan and allow liquid egg to run underneath.
7. When nearly set, add hot potatoes and pepper. Fold omelette away from handle, tip on to a hot dish. Serve at once with sliced tomatoes or a green salad. Garnish with chopped or sprig parsley.

To vary: Oven baked omelettes: Fry potatoes and pepper or use fried aubergines or cooked beans. Put into well buttered, ovenproof dish. Pour well seasoned eggs on top, bake until set. Serve with yoghurt or soft cream cheese. The advantage of these omelettes is that you can cook a large quantity at one time.

Anginares me avga
Artichokes with eggs and sauce

Cooking time: 30 min. **Preparation time:** 25 min. **Main cooking utensils:** 4 saucepans.

IMPERIAL

For 6 people you need:
6 globe artichokes
seasoning
6 eggs

For the creamed cheese sauce:
2 oz. butter
2 oz. flour
$\frac{1}{2}$ pint milk
little artichoke stock
4 oz. Parmesan cheese, grated
3 tablespoons thick cream
little grated nutmeg

For the tomato sauce:
2 oz. butter *or* olive oil
1 small onion
1 clove garlic
4 large tomatoes
seasoning, pinch sugar
1 tablespoon concentrated tomato purée (optional)

AMERICAN

For 6 people you need:
6 globe artichokes
seasoning
6 eggs

For the creamed cheese sauce:
$\frac{1}{4}$ cup butter
$\frac{1}{2}$ cup all-purpose flour
$1\frac{1}{4}$ cups milk
little artichoke stock
1 cup grated Parmesan cheese
scant $\frac{1}{4}$ cup whipping cream
little grated nutmeg

For the tomato sauce:
$\frac{1}{4}$ cup butter *or* olive oil
1 small onion
1 clove garlic
4 large tomatoes
seasoning, dash sugar
1 tablespoon concentrated tomato paste (optional)

1. Cut the tops off the artichokes and cook in well seasoned water until tender. Pull out the centre chokes if possible, as they are not edible, then halve the artichokes.
2. Hard-boil, shell and halve the eggs.
3. While the vegetables and eggs are cooking, prepare the two sauces.
4. Heat the butter, stir in the flour and cook for several minutes, then gradually add the milk and about 3 tablespoons (U.S. scant $\frac{1}{4}$ cup) artichoke stock.
5. Bring to the boil and cook until thickened. Stir in the cheese, seasoning, cream and nutmeg.
6. Heat the butter in another pan. Fry the chopped onion and crushed garlic, add peeled, skinned and de-seeded tomatoes, simmer until tender, then sieve if wished. Re-heat with seasoning and sugar, a tablespoon concentrated purée can be added, if liked. Arrange the artichokes and eggs on a hot dish, top with the sauces.

171

Peynirli börek
Cheese flan

Cooking time: 45 min. **Preparation time:** 35 min. plus time to stand. **Main cooking utensils:** 8–9-inch flan ring, baking tray/sheet, frying pan/skillet. **Oven temperature:** moderate to moderately hot, 375–400°F., 190–200°C., Gas Mark 5. **Oven position:** centre.

IMPERIAL

For 4–6 people you need:
For the pastry:
10 oz. flour
pinch salt
2 oz. butter
2 eggs
water

For the filling:
2 oz. butter
10 oz. cheese, very finely grated (very white Cheddar is used in the picture)
2 eggs
seasoning
$\frac{1}{4}$ teaspoon powdered cinnamon
1 onion
1 tablespoon oil
cayenne and paprika pepper

To garnish:
bacon rolls
cooked prunes

AMERICAN

For 4–6 people you need:
For the pastry:
$2\frac{1}{2}$ cups all-purpose flour
dash salt
$\frac{1}{4}$ cup butter
2 eggs
water

For the filling:
$\frac{1}{4}$ cup butter
$2\frac{1}{2}$ cups very finely grated cheese (very white Cheddar is used in the picture)
2 eggs
seasoning
$\frac{1}{4}$ teaspoon powdered cinnamon
1 onion
1 tablespoon oil
cayenne and paprika pepper

To garnish:
bacon rolls
cooked prunes

1. Sieve the flour and salt, rub in butter. Bind with eggs and water, stand for 30 minutes then knead.
2. Roll out until paper-thin. Cut into 3 thin 8–9-inch rounds.
3. Put one round into the flan ring, brush with melted butter. Cover with quarter of the filling, made by blending grated cheese, eggs, seasoning, powdered cinnamon and finely chopped onion, fried in oil.
4. Cover with a second round, melted butter and filling, then final round. Save about half the filling for the topping.
5. Bake for 30 minutes, remove from the oven. Top with remaining filling and dusting of cayenne or paprika, return to oven for 15 minutes.
6. Meanwhile grill bacon rolls, drain cooked prunes and garnish.

172

Fluden

Fruit layer pudding

Cooking time: 1 hr. 20 min. **Preparation time:** 20 min. **Main cooking utensils:** large ovenproof dish. **Oven temperature:** very moderate, 325–350°F., 170–180°C., Gas Mark 3–4. **Oven position:** centre.

IMPERIAL

For 5–6 portions you need:
10 oz. self-raising flour

pinch salt
5 oz. sugar

1 egg, 1 egg yolk
3 tablespoons cooking oil *or* melted margarine

For the filling:
2 cooking apples
1 oz. sugar
6 tablespoons apricot jam
6 oz. seedless raisins
2 oz. desiccated coconut
4 oz. nuts, chopped
$\frac{1}{2}$ teaspoon mixed spice
$\frac{1}{2}$ teaspoon powdered cinnamon

For the topping:
1 egg white
little sugar, spice

AMERICAN

For 5–6 portions you need:
$2\frac{1}{2}$ cups all-purpose flour, sifted with $2\frac{1}{2}$ teaspoons baking powder
dash salt
$\frac{1}{2}$ cup plus 2 tablespoons sugar
1 egg, 1 egg yolk
scant $\frac{1}{4}$ cup cooking oil *or* melted margarine

For the filling:
2 baking apples
2 tablespoons sugar
$\frac{1}{2}$ cup apricot jam
1 cup seedless raisins
$\frac{2}{3}$ cup shredded coconut
1 cup chopped nuts
$\frac{1}{2}$ teaspoon mixed spice
$\frac{1}{2}$ teaspoon powdered cinnamon

For the topping:
1 egg white
little sugar, spice

1. Sieve the flour and salt. Add sugar, beaten egg and egg yolk, then two thirds of the oil or margarine.
2. Mix thoroughly, add enough water to give a firm rolling consistency.
3. Knead very lightly until smooth.
4. Grease dish well with the rest of the oil or margarine.
5. Take half the dough, roll out to fit the bottom and sides of the dish.
6. Roll out the rest of the dough, cut into 3 pieces the size of the dish.
7. Slice apples thinly and mix the filling ingredients together.
8. Put a third into the dish, cover with a piece of dough.
9. Put in a second layer of filling, then second piece of dough.
10. Add the last of the filling, top with dough.
11. Brush with egg white, sprinkle with sugar and spice and bake until golden. Slice to serve.

173

Baklava

Puff pastry sweet

Cooking time: 30–35 min. **Preparation time:** 45 min. plus time for pastry to stand. **Main cooking utensils:** flat baking tray/sheet, saucepan. **Oven temperature:** hot, 450–475°F., 230–240°C., Gas Mark 7–8, then 350–375°F., 180–190°C., Gas Mark 4–5. **Oven position:** centre.

IMPERIAL

For 10–12 portions you need:
For the syrup:
8 oz. sugar *or* honey

$\frac{1}{2}$ pint water
1 tablespoon lemon juice
2 teaspoons orange flower water
12 oz. puff pastry, see method

For the filling:
12 oz. nuts (use either all one kind *or* a mixture of almonds, pine nuts and pistachio nuts)

1 teaspoon cinnamon
4 oz. butter
1 oz. sugar *or* honey
2 teaspoons lemon juice
2 teaspoons orange flower water

AMERICAN

For 10–12 portions you need:
For the sirup:
generous 1 cup sugar *or* $\frac{2}{3}$ cup honey
$1\frac{1}{4}$ cups water
1 tablespoon lemon juice
2 teaspoons orange flower water
$\frac{3}{4}$ lb. puff paste, see method

For the filling:
approx. 3 cups nuts (use either all one kind *or* a mixture of almonds, pine nuts and pistachio nuts)
1 teaspoon cinnamon
$\frac{1}{2}$ cup butter
2 tablespoons sugar *or* honey
2 teaspoons lemon juice
2 teaspoons orange flower water

1. Make the syrup by boiling all ingredients together, allow to cool.
2. To make puff pastry: sieve 12 oz. (U.S. 3 cups) plain flour with pinch salt, mix to rolling consistency with water. Roll out to oblong shape, put 12 oz. (U.S. $1\frac{1}{2}$ cups) butter on this. Fold in 3, turn, seal edges; 'rib', then roll out. Give total of 7 rollings and 7 foldings, keeping cool.
3. Roll out until almost paper-thin, cut into 4 equal-sized oblongs.
4. Blanch the nuts.
5. Chop and blend with other filling ingredients, beating butter until soft, but not oily.
6. Put a layer of pastry on a board, spread with $\frac{1}{3}$ of the filling, cover with pastry. Continue in this way until all filling is used, finishing with pastry.
7. Cut into diamond-shaped pieces, leave in a cool place before baking.
8. Cook for about 10–15 minutes at the higher temperature, then lower heat for remainder of the time, until crisp and golden.
9. Pour syrup over pastries.

174

Halvas tou fournou
Syrup soaked cake

Cooking time: 1 hr. **Preparation time:** 25 min. **Main cooking utensils:** 8-inch ring tin/pan, saucepan. **Oven temperature:** moderate, 375°F., 190°C., Gas Mark 4–5. **Oven position:** centre.

IMPERIAL

For 4–6 people you need:
4 oz. butter
4 oz. sugar
grated rind 2 lemons *or* 1 small grapefruit
3 small *or* 2 large eggs
3 oz. semolina
4 oz. plain flour
2 teaspoons baking powder
2 oz. blanched almonds
3 tablespoons brandy, lemon *or* grapefruit juice

For the syrup:
6 oz. sugar
$\frac{1}{4}$ pint water
$\frac{1}{4}$ pint lemon *or* grapefruit juice
piece cinnamon
little brandy

To decorate:
grapefruit *or* lemon
glacé cherries

AMERICAN

For 4–6 people you need:
$\frac{1}{2}$ cup butter
$\frac{1}{2}$ cup sugar
grated rind 2 lemons *or* 1 small grapefruit
3 small *or* 2 large eggs
$\frac{1}{2}$ cup semolina flour
1 cup all-purpose flour
2 teaspoons baking powder
$\frac{1}{2}$ cup blanched almonds
scant $\frac{1}{4}$ cup brandy, lemon *or* grapefruit juice

For the sirup:
$\frac{3}{4}$ cup sugar
$\frac{2}{3}$ cup water
$\frac{2}{3}$ cup lemon *or* grapefruit juice
piece cinnamon
little brandy

To decorate:
grapefruit *or* lemon
candied cherries

1. Cream the butter and sugar until soft and light, add grated rind.
2. Gradually beat in egg yolks, semolina, sifted flour and baking powder and chopped almonds.
3. Fold in the brandy or fruit juice and stiffly beaten egg whites.
4. Put into a well-greased and floured tin, bake until firm to touch.
5. When the Halvas is nearly cooked, prepare the syrup.
6. Boil the sugar, water and fruit juice with a small piece of cinnamon. When sugar has dissolved remove cinnamon.
7. Add the brandy, heat but do not boil.
8. Turn the Halvas out of the tin. Prick, soak in the syrup and decorate with segments of fresh grapefruit or lemon and cherries.

To serve: Hot as a dessert or cold as a cake

175

Halva
Semolina cakes

Cooking time: 20–30 min. **Preparation time:** 20 min. **Main cooking utensils:** strong saucepan, 7-inch tin/pan.

IMPERIAL

To make approx. $1\frac{1}{2}$ lb. you need:
$\frac{1}{2}$ pint water
squeeze lemon juice *or* few drops orange flower water (optional)
1 lb. sugar
3 oz. semolina
4 oz. raisins
nuts (optional), these could be 3–4 oz. almonds *and/or* 3–4 oz. hazelnuts *and/or* 2–3 oz. pistachio nuts

To serve:
4 oz. blanched almonds
1–2 oz. angelica
1–2 oz. glacé cherries

AMERICAN

To make approx. $1\frac{1}{2}$ lb. you need:
$1\frac{1}{4}$ cups water
squeeze lemon juice *or* few drops orange flower water (optional)
generous 2 cups sugar
$\frac{1}{2}$ cup semolina flour
$\frac{2}{3}$ cup raisins
nuts (optional), these could be $\frac{3}{4}$ cup almonds *and/or* $\frac{3}{4}$ cup hazelnuts *and/or* $\frac{3}{4}$ cup pistachio nuts

To serve:
generous $\frac{3}{4}$ cup blanched almonds
$\frac{1}{4}$–$\frac{1}{3}$ cup candied angelica
approx. $\frac{1}{4}$ cup candied cherries

1. Put the water, lemon juice or orange flower water into the saucepan with the sugar. Stir until sugar is dissolved, then shower the semolina gradually into the boiling syrup.
2. Cook together, stirring very frequently, until the mixture begins to thicken.
3. Add the raisins. If these are dry, they could be 'plumped' by pouring over boiling water and allowing to stand for 5 minutes, then drain.
4. Continue cooking until stiff. Add the nuts at the last minute so they remain crisp.
5. Blanch the almonds and pistachio nuts by putting them into boiling water for a few minutes, draining, then peeling away the skins.
6. Press the mixture into a buttered tin. Allow to cool and set, then cut into neat pieces.
7. Serve on a dish with blanched almonds, leaves of angelica and glacé cherries.

To store: These become very sticky on contact with the air, so keep well covered.

176

Melomakarona
Shortbreads

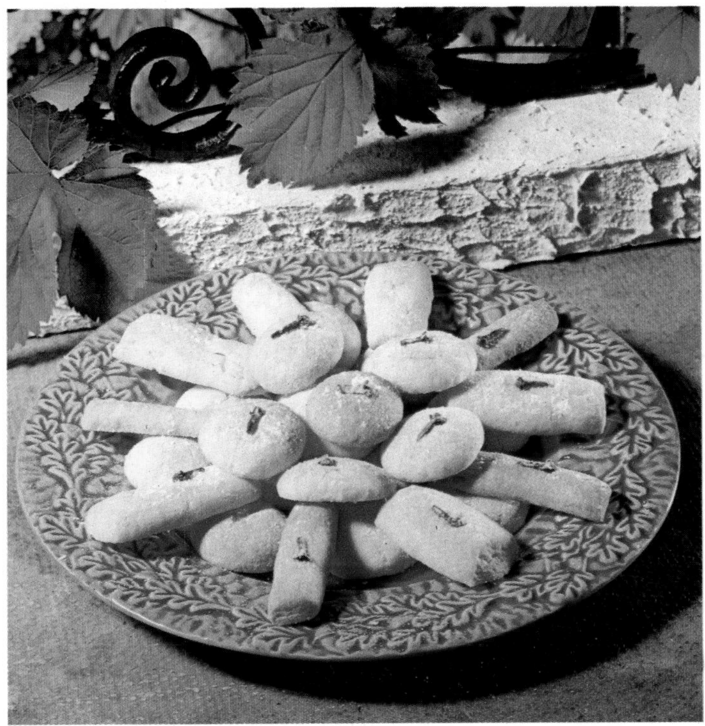

Cooking time: 25–30 min. **Preparation time:** 20 min. **Main cooking utensil:** baking tray/sheet. **Oven temperature:** slow to very moderate, 300–325°F., 150–170°C., Gas Mark 2–3. **Oven position:** just above centre.

IMPERIAL

For about 18–20 portions you need:
8 oz. butter
6 oz. castor *or* sieved icing sugar

1–2 egg yolks
few drops rose water (optional)
14 oz. flour, preferably plain
$\frac{1}{2}$ teaspoon baking powder
little brandy (in Greece, ouzo is used)
2 oz. blanched almonds
about 10 cloves

To coat:
3 oz. sieved icing sugar

AMERICAN

For about 18–20 portions you need:
1 cup butter
$\frac{3}{4}$ cup granulated sugar *or* scant $1\frac{1}{2}$ cups sifted confectioners' sugar
1–2 egg yolks
few drops rose water (optional)
$3\frac{1}{2}$ cups all-purpose flour
$\frac{1}{2}$ teaspoon baking powder
little brandy (in Greece, ouzo is used)
$\frac{1}{2}$ cup blanched almonds
about 10 cloves

To coat:
$\frac{3}{4}$ cup sifted confectioners' sugar

1. Cream the butter and sugar until soft.
2. Add 1 egg yolk, rose water, and beat well.
3. Gradually work in well sieved flour and baking powder, brandy (or ouzo). The mixture should be a firm rolling consistency, if too stiff add part of a second egg yolk.
4. If too sticky, which is unlikely except in very hot weather, work in a little extra flour. In hot weather, allow dough to stand in a cool place before proceeding.
5. Divide mixture into two halves. Into one half add chopped nuts, half the almonds could be browned if wished.
6. Form the biscuit dough into shapes or fingers, either by patting out rounds, or rolling and cutting fingers.
7. Top plain dough rounds or fingers with a clove.
8. Bake until firm, allow to cool on tin.
9. Roll in icing sugar. For a more sticky outside, top with icing sugar while warm, cool and roll in more sugar.

177

Lambropsomo
Easter bread

Cooking time: 40–45 min. **Preparation time:** 25 min. plus time for dough to 'prove'. **Main cooking utensils:** saucepan, baking tray/sheet. **Oven temperature:** hot, 425–450°F., 220–230°C., Gas Mark 6–7, then moderate, 375°F., 190°C., Gas Mark 4–5. **Oven position:** centre.

IMPERIAL

For 5 large or 10 small portions you need:
good $1\frac{1}{2}$ oz. fresh yeast
6 oz. sugar
approx. $\frac{1}{2}$ pint milk *or* milk and water
$1\frac{1}{2}$ lb. plain flour
4 oz. butter *or* margarine
4 egg yolks
pinch salt
8 oz. chopped, mixed candied peel
3 oz. blanched almonds, chopped
5 eggs
red food colouring
2 tablespoons honey
2 tablespoons water

AMERICAN

For 5 large or 10 small portions you need:
$1\frac{1}{2}$ cakes compressed yeast
$\frac{3}{4}$ cup sugar
approx. $1\frac{1}{4}$ cups milk *or* milk and water
6 cups all-purpose flour
$\frac{1}{2}$ cup butter *or* margarine
4 egg yolks
dash salt
$1\frac{1}{3}$ cups chopped, mixed candied peel
$\frac{3}{4}$ cup chopped, blanched almonds
5 eggs
red food coloring
3 tablespoons honey
3 tablespoons water

1. Cream the yeast with 1 teaspoon sugar, add *tepid* milk and sprinkling of flour.
2. Leave in a warm place to rise for about 20 minutes until surface is covered with little bubbles.
3. Cream the butter and remaining sugar, add egg yolks.
4. Work in the flour, sieved with salt, and yeast liquid, until a soft but pliable mixture.
5. Add the peel, knead until a smooth dough.
6. Return to the bowl, cover with cloth and leave in warm place for 1 hour until dough is double its original size.
7. Knead again, form into 3 long equal sized strips, plait *loosely* (to allow dough to rise).
8. Lift on to a warm, greased baking tray, cover with chopped almonds.
9. Allow to rise ('prove') for approximately 20 minutes, making 5 indentations for the eggs as picture.
10. Bake for 40–45 minutes, reducing heat after first 20–25 minutes.
11. Meanwhile, hard-boil eggs in a pan of water, adding colouring to tint. Put eggs into the bread before serving. Brush with honey, diluted with a little water, if wished.

Nasi goreng
Fried pork and rice

Far Eastern cookery is so diverse that one cannot hope to do it justice in a single volume, let alone in a few recipes. Many Westerners think of Far Eastern cooking as Indian and Chinese, forgetting how many other countries there are with lesser-known but equally distinctive cuisines.

Indonesia, made up of many islands, has been a melting pot for several nationalities which have all contributed their culinary ideas. China is the most obvious influence but India, Malaya and of course the Dutch settlers, have all added to the cuisine. A popular and versatile everyday dish is *Nasi goreng,* fried pork and rice garnished with shredded omelette; the vegetables and meat for this dish can be varied and shrimps make a pleasant addition, for a special occasion meal.

The cooking of Malaysia, which includes Malaya and part of Borneo, is not unlike the Indonesian; they have similar climates and depend a great deal on rice, fish and tropical fruit. Singapore is sophisticated and cosmopolitan, dominated by the large Chinese population, but the rest of the country is rural and the food relatively simple. As in many Asian countries, there are a number of vegetarian religious groups so meatless but interesting dishes like Eggs in pineapple sauce are often served.

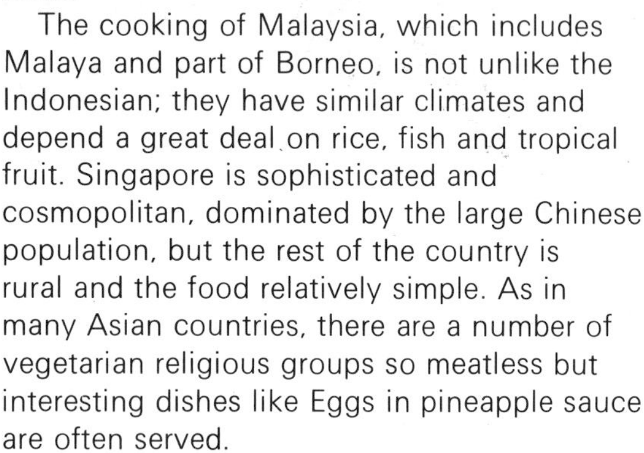

Of all Far Eastern cookery, Japanese is probably the most alien to Western palates. The Japanese attitude to food is quite different from the European, laying greater emphasis on the presentation and freshness of the ingredients than on the actual cooking. They cook most food very briefly so as to preserve an attractive appearance and the best flavour, and some vegetables and fish are often served raw.

Korean cooking combines Chinese and Japanese influences but several national dishes are becoming more widely known. The Koreans are hearty eaters, preferring rich, robust food to the elegant dainty Japanese and subtle Chinese dishes. Chicken pot stew and Korean sweet-sour meat, both highly seasoned dishes with plenty of meat, are typical casseroles that go well with rice or noodles. Like other Far Eastern countries, they usually serve only a simple dessert of fruit, if any at all. Koreans share the Chinese fondness for sweet pastries like Fried honey cakes; delicious tiny cakes covered in chopped nuts.

Cooking time: 45 min. **Preparation time:** 20 min. **Main cooking utensils:** saucepan, sieve, omelette pan, frying pan/skillet *or* ovenproof dish.

IMPERIAL

For 4 people you need:
8 oz. Patna (long grain) rice
3–4 pints water
2 teaspoons salt
8 oz. onions
12 oz. shoulder pork
4 oz. butter
12 oz. mixed cooked vegetables
2 tablespoons soy sauce
1 teaspoon curry powder
seasoning

To garnish:
omelette, made with 1 egg and $\frac{1}{2}$–1 oz. butter
2 tomatoes

AMERICAN

For 4 people you need:
generous 1 cup Patna (long grain) rice
$7\frac{1}{2}$–10 cups water
2 teaspoons salt
$\frac{1}{2}$ lb. onions
$\frac{3}{4}$ lb. shoulder pork
$\frac{1}{2}$ cup butter
$\frac{3}{4}$ lb. mixed cooked vegetables
3 tablespoons soy sauce
1 teaspoon curry powder
seasoning

To garnish:
omelette, made with 1 egg and 1–2 tablespoons butter
2 tomatoes

1. Cook the rice in boiling salted water for approximately 12 minutes. Turn into a sieve and separate the grains by holding under running cold water until all the surplus starch is removed; drain.
2. Slice the onions, cut the pork in cubes and fry in 2 oz. (U.S. $\frac{1}{4}$ cup) butter for 20 minutes, browning slowly.
3. Add the remainder of the butter, rice, mixed vegetables, soy sauce, curry powder and seasoning. Blend well over the heat until piping hot.
4. Turn into a frying pan or ovenproof dish and garnish with strips of omelette made by cooking the seasoned egg in butter. Arrange small wedges of tomato round the edge. Flash under a hot grill for a few moments.

To serve: Immediately with peanuts, shrimp crisps and a green salad.

179

Juhn-kol
Korean sweet-sour meat

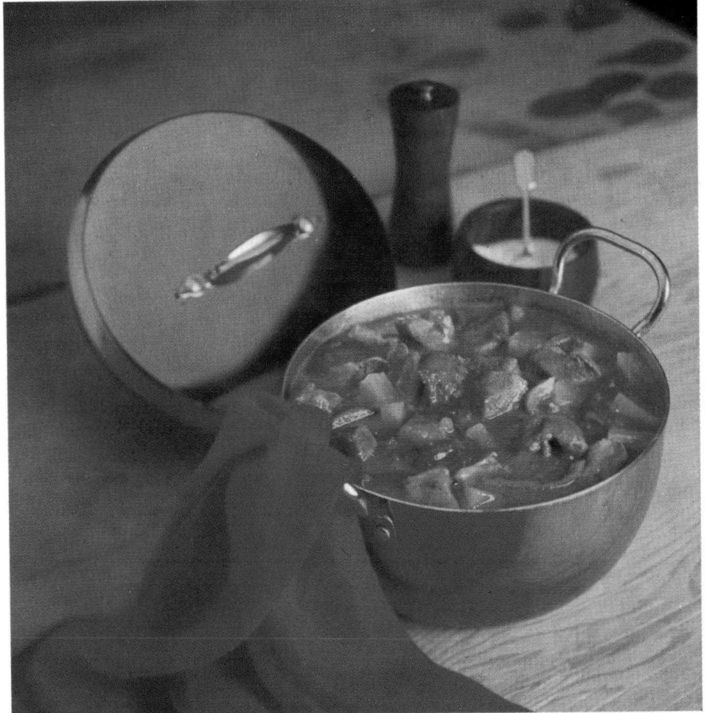

Cooking time: 1 hr. **Preparation time:** 25 min. **Main cooking utensil:** large saucepan *or* flameproof dish.

IMPERIAL

For 4–6 people you need:
3 large onions
small head celery
3 carrots
1 bamboo shoot *or* swede
1 green pepper
1 lb. good quality fresh brisket *or* topside of beef
1–2 spring onions (optional)
1 clove garlic
seasoning
pinch powdered sesame seeds
1½ tablespoons sugar
2 tablespoons oil
1½ oz. flour
1 pint beef stock *or* water and 2 stock cubes
1 tablespoon soy sauce
2 tomatoes (optional)
2 oz. pine nuts
3–4 rings pineapple, fresh *or* canned

AMERICAN

For 4–6 people you need:
3 large onions
small bunch celery
3 carrots
1 bamboo shoot *or* rutabaga
1 sweet green pepper
1 lb. good quality fresh beef
1–2 scallions (optional)
1 clove garlic
seasoning
dash powdered sesame seeds
2 tablespoons sugar
3 tablespoons oil
6 tablespoons all-purpose flour
2½ cups beef stock *or* water and 2 beef bouillon cubes
1 tablespoon soy sauce
2 tomatoes (optional)
½ cup pine nuts
3–4 rings pineapple, fresh *or* canned

1. Peel and slice the onions, chop celery, grate or chop the carrots very finely so they almost 'disappear' during cooking.
2. Slice the bamboo shoot or dice or slice swede, together with the flesh of the pepper.
3. Cut the meat in neat squares. Press finely chopped spring onions (chop green as well as white part) into this, together with crushed garlic, plenty of seasoning, sesame and some of the sugar.
4. Fry the meat in hot oil for 5 minutes, take care it does not burn. Remove from pan.
5. Blend the flour and remaining sugar with stock and soy sauce, put in the pan with vegetables prepared at Stages 1 and 2. Bring to boil, cook until thickened.
6. Add the meat, sliced, skinned tomatoes and pine nuts, simmer for approximately 55 minutes. Stir chopped pineapple into the mixture before serving with rice or noodles.

180

Tahk pok-kum
Chicken pot stew

Cooking time: 2 hr. 10 min. **Preparation time:** 25 min. **Main cooking utensil:** large saucepan.

IMPERIAL

For 5–6 people you need:
1 young roasting chicken
1 pint water
seasoning
2 tablespoons oil
about 10–12 small onions
1 crushed clove garlic
3 tablespoons soy sauce
1 tablespoon sugar
4 oz. mushrooms
1–2 chilli peppers, skinned, sliced tomatoes *or* red pepper
2 teaspoons sesame seeds*
½ teaspoon powdered ginger
2 oz. pine nuts (optional)

AMERICAN

For 5–6 people you need:
1 young roasting chicken
2½ cups water
seasoning
3 tablespoons oil
about 10–12 small onions
1 crushed clove garlic
scant ¼ cup soy sauce
1 tablespoon sugar
1 cup mushrooms
1–2 chilis, skinned, sliced tomatoes *or* sweet red pepper
2 teaspoons sesame seeds*
½ teaspoon powdered ginger
½ cup pine nuts (optional)

*These seeds are browned in a pan with a little salt then mashed to a powder.

1. Cut the chicken into 2-inch pieces, remove bones and put these into a pan with the water and seasoning, simmer for 1 hour.
2. Strain off ½ pint (U.S. 1¼ cups) stock.
3. Heat the oil, toss onions, garlic and chicken in this until chicken is golden brown.
4. Add the stock, simmer for 30 minutes. Stir in soy sauce, sugar, sliced mushrooms, sliced pepper or tomatoes, sesame, seasoning, powdered ginger and pine nuts.
5. Continue cooking for 25–30 minutes until chicken is tender.

To serve: Although not accurate for a Korean dish, a garnish of fried bread blends well.

To vary: Add bamboo shoots and chestnuts.

181

Yosenabe
Vegetable, chicken and fish stew

Cooking time: 35 min. Preparation time: 20 min. plus time for dried mushrooms to soak. Main cooking utensil: saucepan.

IMPERIAL

For 4 people you need:
8 oz. uncooked chicken, dark meat only, weight after removing bones
12 oz. white fish
3 tablespoons oil
3 medium-sized onions
1 green pepper
1–2 oz. dried mushrooms* *or* 4 oz. fresh mushrooms
4 medium-sized tomatoes**
$\frac{1}{2}$ pint chicken stock
1 tablespoon sake *or* sherry
1 teaspoon sugar
seasoning
2 bay leaves**

AMERICAN

For 4 people you need:
$\frac{1}{2}$ lb. uncooked chicken, dark meat only, weight after removing bones
$\frac{3}{4}$ lb. white fish
scant $\frac{1}{4}$ cup oil
3 medium-sized onions
1 sweet green pepper
approx. $\frac{1}{4}$ cup dried mushrooms* *or* 1 cup fresh mushrooms
4 medium-sized tomatoes**
$1\frac{1}{4}$ cups chicken stock
1 tablespoon sake *or* sherry
1 teaspoon sugar
seasoning
2 bay leaves**

*Cover with water and soak for 1 hour.
**Tomatoes and bay leaf, while not traditionally Japanese, add flavour and interest.

1. Cut the chicken into small pieces or strips and fish into fingers.
2. Heat the oil, fry chicken and very thinly sliced onions until transparent, take care they do not brown.
3. De-seed the pepper and cut the flesh into thin pieces, add to the onions and chicken with fish and chopped, dried or fresh mushrooms.
4. Add the remaining ingredients, skinning and de-seeding tomatoes. Simmer steadily for 20 minutes or until chicken is tender, and liquid evaporated. Remove the bay leaves.

To serve: This is delicious with lychees, but when not available use fairly sharp plums, and shrimp-flavoured crisps often served with Indonesian dishes. When these are not available, use ordinary potato crisps.

182

Telor dalam ketchup nanas
Eggs in pineapple sauce

Cooking time: 25 min. Preparation time: 25 min. Main cooking utensils: 3 saucepans.

IMPERIAL

For 4–6 people you need:
8 oz. long grain rice
just over $\frac{3}{4}$ pint water
seasoning
small bunch spring onions
1 tablespoon oil
1 (12 oz.) can pineapple cubes
2 teaspoons vinegar
1 tablespoon cornflour
2 teaspoons soy sauce
$\frac{1}{4}$ teaspoon powdered ginger
2 large tomatoes
6 eggs

AMERICAN

For 4–6 people you need:
generous 1 cup long grain rice
2 cups water
seasoning
small bunch scallions
1 tablespoon oil
1 (12 oz.) can pineapple cubes
2 teaspoons vinegar
1 tablespoon cornstarch
2 teaspoons soy sauce
$\frac{1}{4}$ teaspoon powdered ginger
2 large tomatoes
6 eggs

1. Put the rice with cold water and seasoning into a pan.
2. Bring to the boil, stir, cover pan tightly, then lower heat and simmer for 15 minutes until all liquid is absorbed.
3. Chop finely all but 4 onions, toss in hot oil until really brown; prepare remainder for garnish, see below.
4. Drain the pineapple, cut each cube in half, blend vinegar, cornflour and syrup from can of pineapple.
5. Pour into the pan with the onion, simmer gently for 10 minutes. Add the soy sauce, ginger, pineapple and de-seeded skinned, chopped tomatoes.
6. Meanwhile, boil the eggs for 10 minutes, plunge in cold water and remove shells.

To prepare garnish: Use bottom 3 inches of spring onions, cut downwards into thin strips to within $\frac{3}{4}$ inch from bottom. Put in ice-cold water for at least 15 minutes, longer if possible.

To serve: Arrange rice on a flat dish, the method of cooking described in Stages 1 and 2 means all liquid is absorbed and no straining is necessary. Top with halved eggs and sauce, garnish with onions.

183

Mafi nanas
Pineapple rice

Cooking time: 20 min. **Preparation time:** 20 min. plus time for coconut to stand. **Main cooking utensils:** large saucepan, 2-pint/$2\frac{1}{2}$-pint ring mould.

IMPERIAL

For 6 people you need:
2 oz. desiccated coconut*
2 pints water*
6 oz. round grain rice
1 (16 oz.) can pineapple cubes
juice $\frac{1}{2}$ lemon
$\frac{1}{2}$–1 oz. sugar

To decorate:
$\frac{1}{4}$ pint thick cream
2 oz. toasted coconut**

AMERICAN

For 6 people you need:
$\frac{2}{3}$ cup shredded coconut*
5 cups water*
scant 1 cup short grain rice
1 (16 oz.) can pineapple cubes
juice $\frac{1}{2}$ lemon
1–2 tablespoons sugar

To decorate:
$\frac{2}{3}$ cup whipping cream
$\frac{2}{3}$ cup shredded coconut, toasted**

*Or use 6 oz. shredded fresh coconut, and milk from coconut made up to 2 pints (U.S. 5 cups) with water.
**To toast coconut, put on flat baking tray in oven or under grill to brown.

1. Sprinkle the coconut into the water.
2. Leave to stand for about 10 minutes, and strain, the coconut can then be discarded, or added at Stage 6.
3. Cook the rice in 'coconut milk' for 10 minutes.
4. Drain, rinse with hot water and return to the pan with pineapple juice, lemon juice and sugar.
5. Cook until the rice is tender and the liquid absorbed.
6. Stir in half the pineapple cubes, cut into four, and coconut, if using.
7. Spoon the mixture into an oiled ring mould and chill.
8. Turn out and fill the centre with remaining pineapple.
9. Decorate with whipped cream and toasted coconut.

184

Yak kwa
Fried honey cakes

Cooking time: 8–10 min. **Preparation time:** 25 min. **Main cooking utensils:** saucepan, deep fat pan *or* frying pan/skillet (see Stage 3).

IMPERIAL

For about 26–30 cakes you need:
For the first honey syrup:
2 tablespoons honey
4 tablespoons water
1 oz. sugar

For the cakes:
approx. 1 lb. self-raising flour
1 tablespoon oil
honey syrup, above
little extra water *or* milk

For frying: oil *or* fat

For the second honey syrup:
6 tablespoons honey
12 tablespoons water
juice 1 lemon *or* 1 teaspoon vanilla essence

For the topping:
3 oz. pine nuts *or* almonds
little powdered cinnamon

AMERICAN

For about 26–30 cakes you need:
For the first honey sirup:
3 tablespoons honey
$\frac{1}{3}$ cup water
2 tablespoons sugar

For the cakes:
4 cups all-purpose flour, sifted with 5 teaspoons baking powder
1 tablespoon oil
honey sirup, above
little extra water *or* milk

For frying: oil *or* fat

For the second honey sirup:
$\frac{1}{2}$ cup honey
1 cup water
juice 1 lemon *or* 1 teaspoon vanilla extract

For the topping:
$\frac{3}{4}$ cup pine nuts *or* almonds
little powdered cinnamon

1. Make the first syrup by heating the ingredients for 1 minute only until the sugar has dissolved.
2. Blend the flour, oil, cooled honey syrup and just enough water or milk to make the dough firm enough to handle. Form the mixture into tiny balls.
3. Heat the oil or fat (it is advisable to use a deep pan, although if the balls are very small a frying pan could be used). Oil should be about 375°F., or when a cube of bread turns golden in about 30 seconds.
4. Fry for about 5 minutes only, drain on absorbent paper for 1 minute then put into the second honey syrup, made by boiling the ingredients together then allowing to cool. Lift out after 2–3 minutes.
5. Sprinkle with shredded or chopped nuts, or nuts mixed with cinnamon.

FRANCE

Many housewives are daunted by the thought of French cooking, imagining it to be far beyond the capabilities of all but the most highly skilled chef. But one must not forget that elaborate haute cuisine is only one aspect of French cooking and the ordinary housewife does not aspire to such heights. French provincial cooking, while less complicated, is of an equally high standard, for the French consider all cooking an art and just because a dish is simple there is no reason for taking less care. Perhaps the most important rule in French cooking is to use only the best and freshest ingredients—good butter (never margarine) and the most perfect vegetables—then even ordinary dishes will aquire an unlooked for elegance.

You need not even cook to begin getting an idea of the excellence of French food. Have a picnic with French bread, cheeses like Camembert and Brie, and wine and you will soon understand why eating in France is a serious national pastime. Add a pâté, a rough country pâté or the classic *Pâté de foie gras,* and you have a veritable banquet. Pâtés, always popular as hors d'oeuvres served on buttered toast, are a boon to the hostess because they are easy to make and can be prepared well in advance. The French are very fond of mussels and Creamed mussel soup or Mussels in sauce are other luxurious ways to start a meal.

Volumes could be written on French egg dishes; far from being a lowly breakfast food that is hastily boiled, fried or scrambled, eggs are held in great esteem as the basis of an infinite variety of dishes. On them depend some of the most famous French creations, from soufflés, quiches and omelettes to crêpes and choux pastry. Quiches originated in Lorraine and the old recipe specified a pastry case dotted with butter and filled with a mixture of thick cream and eggs. There are innumerable variations on this, of course, with the addition of cheese, meat or vegetables, and the combination of cheese and mushrooms is particularly delicious.

The French take great care in preparing their fish dishes, using only the freshest fish and being careful, above all, not to let it get dry by cooking it too long. Many fish recipes from the south of France have a Mediterranean flavour as belied by such titles as *Coquilles à la Portugaise*. Along the French Riviera you will find fish cooked with tomatoes, olives and herbs, like Fried fresh sardines and the tangy Fish ragoût. A classic French method for cooking fish is with browned butter, a simple but perfect sauce for bringing out the flavour of any white fish.

Many people think that cooking with wine is synonymous with French cooking and while this is far from true, as we have already seen, many French dishes do include wine. Undoubtedly the most famous of these is *Coq au vin,* using a pint of wine and also a little brandy. The French have several elegant and unusual ways of cooking game: pheasant, for example, is prepared with the delicious and unusual accompaniments of grapes and walnuts.

The French realise that good quality meat cannot be improved by elaborate preparation and is best if carefully seasoned and cooked in a straightforward manner until it is just rare. Roast lamb with herbs and Steak in pastry, typical of this method, are excellent examples of French provincial cooking. Pot roast of beef is cooked for a long time, however, because it is designed to achieve a flavourful, tender roast with a less expensive cut of beef.

Béarnaise sauce, perhaps the most highly praised of all French sauces, is sometimes said to have been invented in Béarn, the country of the Basques which borders on Spain. Others say it originated in the court of King Henry IV, who was known as the Great Béarnais. But which ever story you believe, it remains a superb sauce with steak or other grilled meat.

If you have had a rich first and main course, or even more than two courses if you are being entertained in France, you may be happy to conclude with a little fruit and cheese. French cuisine does not neglect desserts, however, and has many delectable concoctions to finish off a meal. Among the desserts based on eggs are Caramel cream and Jam omelettes, the latter being ideal for unexpected guests since they are made at the last minute with everyday ingredients. *Babas au rhum* are small yeast cakes generously soaked in rum syrup which were supposedly named after Ali Baba, the hero of their Polish creator. They were introduced to Paris in the early 19th century when they immediately became a very fashionable sweet.

Pâté de foie gras
Goose liver pâté

Cooking time: 10–15 min. **Preparation time:** 15 min. **Main cooking utensil:** frying pan/skillet with a lid.

IMPERIAL

For 4–6 people you need:
liver 1 goose
3 oz. butter
$\frac{1}{4}$ pint stock
1 teaspoon made mustard
pinch salt, pepper
pinch powdered nutmeg
1 tablespoon brandy
1 tablespoon cream

To cover:
2 oz. melted butter

To garnish:
lemon
parsley

AMERICAN

For 4–6 people you need:
liver 1 goose
6 tablespoons butter
$\frac{2}{3}$ cup stock
1 teaspoon prepared mustard
dash salt, pepper
dash powdered nutmeg
1 tablespoon brandy
1 tablespoon cream

To cover:
$\frac{1}{4}$ cup melted butter

To garnish:
lemon
parsley

1. Cut the liver into neat slices. Toss in hot butter and cook for several minutes gently, so liver does not harden.
2. Add the stock, cover pan, simmer gently for 25 minutes (until liver is just tender), do not overcook. If any liquid remains towards end of cooking time, lift lid so it evaporates.
3. Mince or pound until fine.
4. Add the other ingredients, continue mixing until very smooth.
5. Put into a buttered dish and, if storing, top with melted butter.

To serve: With hot toast and butter, garnished with lemon and parsley.

To vary: Add 1–2 beaten eggs to mixture, set in a cool oven for a while, standing in dish of water to prevent hardening on outside. Flavour with herbs, onion, garlic, gherkins.
Use other poultry or calf's liver.

186

Oeufs en cocottes
Eggs baked with cream

Cooking time: 10 min. **Preparation time:** 10 min. **Main cooking utensils:** 5 ovenproof individual soufflé dishes *or* cocotte dishes *or* tiny casseroles. **Oven temperature:** moderate, 375°F., 190°C., Gas Mark 4–5. **Oven position:** just above centre.

IMPERIAL

For 5 people you need:
2 oz. butter
$\frac{1}{4}$–$\frac{1}{2}$ pint single cream
seasoning
5–10 eggs (see Stage 3)

For flavouring:
cooked ham, prawns, cooked asparagus *or* grated Gruyère cheese

To garnish:
truffle (optional)

AMERICAN

For 5 people you need:
$\frac{1}{4}$ cup butter
$\frac{2}{3}$–$1\frac{1}{4}$ cups coffee cream
seasoning
5–10 eggs (see Stage 3)

For flavoring:
cooked cured ham, prawns, cooked asparagus *or* grated Gruyère cheese

To garnish:
truffle (optional)

1. Butter small cocotte dishes well, using half the butter.
2. Put a tablespoon cream at the bottom of each, season lightly.
3. Break an egg (or 2 if wished) on top of the cream—take care in doing this for if the yolks break, the eggs will become hard in cooking and they should always be soft and creamy.
4. Top carefully with a little diced, cooked ham, prawns, asparagus, or grated cheese.
5. Pour 1–2 tablespoons (U.S. 1–3 tablespoons) cream over the eggs and flavouring, season well.
6. Top with a little butter, then a small amount of grated cheese if wished, and a small piece of truffle if available.
7. Bake until just set, serve at once.

To serve: With crisp toast or Melba toast and butter. Serve with a teaspoon. This simple dish makes a delicious hors d'oeuvre.

Salade Italienne
A pot-au-feu served cold

Cooking time: approx. 45 min. **Preparation time:** 15 min. **Main cooking utensil:** large saucepan.

IMPERIAL

For 4–5 people you need:
2–3 tablespoons oil
about 8–10 small onions *or* shallots
$\frac{1}{2}$ pint dry white wine* *or* water and 1–2 chicken stock cubes

4–5 small green peppers
2–3 yellow peppers (green ones turning yellow can be used)

2–3 red peppers
8–12 oz. carrots
heart of head of celery
seasoning
bouquet garni

To garnish:
chopped parsley

To serve:
lemon

*Choose a really cheap wine.

AMERICAN

For 4–5 people you need:
3–4 tablespoons oil
about 8–10 small onions *or* shallots
$1\frac{1}{4}$ cups dry white wine* *or* water and 1–2 chicken bouillon cubes
4–5 small sweet green peppers
2–3 sweet yellow peppers (green ones turning yellow can be used)
2–3 sweet red peppers
$\frac{1}{2}$–$\frac{3}{4}$ lb. carrots
heart of a bunch of celery
seasoning
bouquet garni

To garnish:
chopped parsley

To serve:
lemon

1. Heat the oil in the pan, toss peeled onions or shallots in this.
2. Add the wine or water and stock cubes.
3. Prepare the vegetables, then put in the pan; the peppers should be cored and de-seeded, they may be left whole or cut into large portions. Slice carrots and cut celery into neat pieces, some of the leaves could be chopped and added to the liquid. Add seasoning and bouquet garni.
4. Cover the pan and simmer gently until vegetables are very tender. Most of the wine will have evaporated, but keep any left in the pan.
5. Allow to cool, then remove bouquet garni and top with chopped parsley.

To vary: Skinned, chopped tomatoes may be added to the oil with the onions and 1–2 crushed cloves garlic. Omit carrots, add sliced mushrooms and sliced courgettes.

188

Moules à la crème
Creamed mussel soup

Cooking time: 25 min. **Preparation time:** 20 min. **Main cooking utensils:** 1–2 saucepans, grill/broiler.

IMPERIAL

For 4 people you need:
approx. 3 pints mussels
6 shallots *or* small onions
good-sized sprig thyme
1–2 bay leaves
2–3 finely chopped sticks celery
1 pint cheap white wine *or* use half wine and half water
seasoning
$1\frac{1}{2}$ oz. butter
$1\frac{1}{2}$ oz. flour
$\frac{1}{2}$ pint thin cream

For the topping:
1–2 oz. cheese, finely grated

AMERICAN

For 4 people you need:
approx. 4 pints mussels
6 shallots *or* small onions
good-sized sprig thyme
1–2 bay leaves
2–3 finely chopped stalks celery
$2\frac{1}{2}$ cups cheap white wine *or* use half wine and half water
seasoning
3 tablespoons butter
6 tablespoons all-purpose flour
$1\frac{1}{4}$ cups coffee cream

For the topping:
$\frac{1}{4}$–$\frac{1}{2}$ cup finely grated cheese

1. Scrub the mussels well, discard any that do not shut when tapped sharply, for this means the fish could already be dead, stale and therefore harmful.
2. Put the mussels into pan with onions, finely chopped if wished, thyme, bay leaves, celery and half the liquid, season lightly.
3. Heat steadily until mussels open, allow to cool sufficiently to handle.
4. Lift out the mussels and remove from shells.
5. Return to the liquid; this can be strained or if onions were chopped, simply remove thyme and bay leaves.
6. Heat the butter, stir in the flour, cook for several minutes. Gradually blend in wine mixture from cooking the mussels and remaining wine. Bring to the boil, cook until thickened. Add the mussels and cream, heat gently, season well.
7. Top with the cheese and brown lightly for a few minutes under a hot grill.

To vary: If wished, canned or bottled mussels may be used for this soup; in which case, heat wine with onions, herbs and seasoning to give a good flavour, strain, add to the mussels and cream and proceed as Stage 6.

Sardines frites
Fried fresh sardines

Cooking time: 5 min. **Preparation time:** few min. **Main cooking utensils:** deep pan, frying basket.

IMPE

For 4 pe
about 1
use
little m
season
1–2 te
herb
che
mi
gooc
gr
abo

To
oil

To
1

AMERICAN

For 4 people you need:
about $1\frac{1}{2}$ lb. fresh sardines* *or* use fresh smelt
little milk
seasoning
1–2 teaspoons freshly chopped herbs (tarragon, parsley, fennel chervil; choose one herb or a mixture)
dash mixed spice *or* grated nutmeg
about $\frac{1}{4}$ cup all-purpose flour

To fry:
oil or fat

To garnish:
1 tomato

h is becoming very rare.

em well, then pat dry.
wet.
our and coat the fish very lightly

d should turn golden in about
fat.
ntil tender.
hot plate.

ck, or main meal.

mbs as in the picture.
our, pinch salt, 1 egg, $\frac{1}{2}$ pint
love of garlic. Coat sardines in
weet fennel and green salad.

190

Coquilles à la Portugaise
Scallops in tomato onion sauce

Cooking time: 30 min. **Preparation time:** 25 min. **Main cooking utensils:** 2 large saucepans *or* frying pans/skillets.

IMPERIAL

For 4 people you need:
1 large onion
2 medium-sized carrots
small sprig thyme (preferably lemon thyme) *or* pinch dried thyme
1 bay leaf
seasoning
12 tablespoons dry white wine
10 oz. tomatoes
2 oz. mushrooms
3 oz. butter
juice 1 lemon
4 large *or* 8 small scallops

To garnish:
parsley

AMERICAN

For 4 people you need:
1 large onion
2 medium-sized carrots
small sprig thyme (preferably lemon thyme) *or* dash dried thyme
1 bay leaf
seasoning
generous 1 cup dry white wine
6 medium-sized tomatoes
$\frac{1}{2}$ cup mushrooms
6 tablespoons butter
juice 1 lemon
4 large *or* 8 small scallops

To garnish:
parsley

1. Put the chopped onion, sliced carrots, thyme, bay leaf and seasoning in the saucepan with the wine.
2. Simmer steadily for 15 minutes then sieve or put into the blender to make a smooth purée.
3. Meanwhile skin and de-seed the tomatoes and slice the mushrooms thinly.
4. Fry the mushrooms and tomatoes in the butter until very soft, adding the lemon juice.
5. Simmer the scallops in sieved wine mixture for 10 minutes or until just tender. Do *not* over-cook or the fish will become tough.
6. Lift the scallops on to the hot shells.
7. Blend the tomato and mushroom mixture with the white wine sauce. Taste and season again if wished. Coat the scallops with this and top with parsley.

To vary: Sprinkle 2 oz. (U.S. $\frac{1}{2}$ cup) coarsely grated Gruyère cheese on top of the sauce and heat under the grill for a few minutes only.

191

Moules à la marinière
Mussels in sauce

Cooking time: 20 min. **Preparation time:** 20 min. **Main cooking utensils:** 2 saucepans.

IMPERIAL

For 4–6 people you need:
3–4 pints mussels
1 onion
bouquet garni
½ pint water
¼ pint white wine
seasoning

For the sauce:
2 oz. butter
1½ oz. flour
mussel stock
½ pint milk
2 tablespoons thick cream

To garnish:
chopped parsley

AMERICAN

For 4–6 people you need:
4–5 pints mussels
1 onion
bouquet garni
1¼ cups water
⅔ cup white wine
seasoning

For the sauce:
¼ cup butter
6 tablespoons all-purpose flour
mussel stock
1¼ cups milk
3 tablespoons whipping cream

To garnish:
chopped parsley

1. Scrub the mussels very hard with a brush and wash in several lots of cold water, until this is no longer sandy.
2. If any mussel shells are open, tap sharply and if they do not close, then these should be discarded, as the mussels could be dead and therefore stale and harmful.
3. Put the mussels with whole or finely chopped onion, herbs, liquid and seasoning into a large pan. Heat steadily until the shells open—about 8 minutes. Allow to cool enough to handle. Strain the liquid and retain this.
4. Remove mussels from the pan, pull away one shell, leaving fish on second shell. Cut off the weed-like growth.
5. Heat the butter, stir in flour, cook for several minutes.
6. Gradually blend in the mussel stock, this should be just over ½ pint (U.S. 1¼ cups), and milk. Bring to the boil, cook until thickened, stir in cream and extra seasoning. Add the mussels on their shells, heat gently.

To serve: As a soup or fish course topped with parsley.

NOTE: In this particular recipe, which is delicious, the fish is served in a creamy sauce—in other recipes it is put into the clear liquid from cooking the mussels.

192

Turbot meunière
Turbot in browned butter

Cooking time: 10–15 min. **Preparation time:** few min. **Main cooking utensil:** large frying pan/skillet.

IMPERIAL

For 6 people you need:
6 portions (slices) turbot*

4 oz. butter
seasoning
juice 1 large lemon
2 oz. fine crisp breadcrumbs (optional) see Stage 5

To garnish:
1 lemon
parsley
3 medium-sized tomatoes

AMERICAN

For 6 people you need:
6 portions (slices) turbot *or* halibut*
½ cup butter
seasoning
juice 1 large lemon
½ cup fine dry bread crumbs (optional) see Stage 5

To garnish:
1 lemon
parsley
3 medium-sized tomatoes

*Other fish may be cooked in the same way: sole, plaice or whiting, for the butter gives a moist texture and delicious flavour to good white fish.

1. Wash and dry the fish, then heat the butter in a pan.
2. Fry the seasoned fish steadily until tender.
3. Lift out. Add the lemon juice and extra seasoning to the butter remaining in the pan.
4. Continue cooking this until it turns golden brown.
5. Pour over the fish and top with the crumbs or, when the butter has turned brown, toss the crumbs in this for a few minutes, then sprinkle over the fish. Often, however, the crumbs are not used in this dish, but they do give a pleasant crisp texture.

To serve: Very hot with sliced lemon, parsley and water-lily shapes of tomato. To make these, insert the tip of a sharp knife into the centre of a tomato and make a small diagonal cut. Continue like this, in a Vandyke pattern, all round the tomato, then pull halves apart.

To vary: Add capers and chopped fresh herbs to butter.

193

Raito provençal
Fish ragoût

Cooking time: 30 min. **Preparation time:** 20 min. **Main cooking utensils:** large deep frying pan/skillet *or* saucepan.

IMPERIAL

For 4 people you need:
1 fish, about 2 lb. use grey* or red mullet, cod *or* haddock (keep whole, or cut into pieces if pan is not large enough)
3–4 tablespoons olive oil

For the sauce:
2 medium-sized onions
1 lb. tomatoes
2–4 oz. mushrooms
2–3 oz. fresh, skinned walnuts**
1 tablespoons mixed herbs (parsley, fennel, thyme, marjoram)
$\frac{1}{2}$ pint white *or* red wine
8–12 black olives
seasoning

AMERICAN

For 4 people you need:
1 fish, about 2 lb., use mullet, cod *or* haddock (keep whole, or cut into pieces if pan is not large enough)
4–5 tablespoons olive oil

For the sauce:
2 medium-sized onions
1 lb. tomatoes
$\frac{1}{2}$–1 cup mushrooms
$\frac{1}{2}$–$\frac{3}{4}$ cup fresh, skinned walnuts**
1 tablespoon mixed herbs (parsley, fennel, thyme, marjoram)
1$\frac{1}{4}$ cups white *or* red wine
8–12 ripe olives
seasoning

*This must be cleaned with great care.
**Walnuts can be easily skinned, but if they have become dry and difficult to peel, heat in the oven for a few minutes, then skin.

1. Fry the fish in oil on either side, then lift out of the pan.
2. Chop the onions very finely.
3. Skin, and chop or slice the tomatoes together with the mushrooms.
4. Cook in the oil for about 5–10 minutes, then add the very finely chopped nuts, chopped herbs, wine, olives and seasoning.
5. Simmer until the onions are nearly tender.
6. Put the fish back in the sauce and continue cooking until tender.

To serve: Either from the pan or put the sauce into a dish and top with the fish. Serve hot.

To vary: Use fried cod (salted or fresh) or eel. If using salted cod, this should be soaked in cold water for 2 days before using.

194

Crêpes farcies aux crevettes
Pancakes filled with shrimps

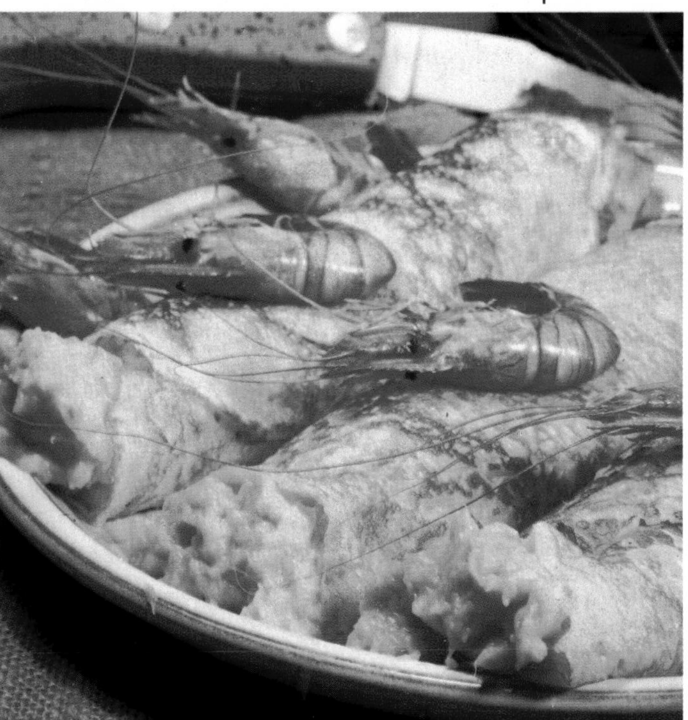

Cooking time: 20 min. **Preparation time:** 20 min. **Main cooking utensils:** 2 saucepans, frying pan/skillet.

IMPERIAL

For 4 people you need:
For the sauce:
$\frac{1}{2}$ pint milk
piece carrot, celery
slice onion
1 oz. butter
1 oz. flour
seasoning

For the pancakes:
4 oz. flour, preferably plain
pinch salt
2 eggs
just under $\frac{1}{2}$ pint milk
2 oz. butter *or* 2 tablespoons oil

For the filling:
6 oz. shelled prawns *or* shrimps
2 oz. butter
2 eggs
seasoning

AMERICAN

For 4 people you need:
For the sauce:
1$\frac{1}{4}$ cups milk
piece carrot, celery
slice onion
2 tablespoons butter
$\frac{1}{4}$ cup all-purpose flour
seasoning

For the pancakes:
1 cup all-purpose flour
dash salt
2 eggs
just under 1$\frac{1}{4}$ cups milk
$\frac{1}{4}$ cup butter *or* 3 tablespoons oil

For the filling:
1 cup shelled prawns *or* shrimps
$\frac{1}{4}$ cup butter
2 eggs
seasoning

1. Heat the milk with the vegetables for 1 minute and stand in a warm place for about 30 minutes to infuse.
2. Heat the butter, stir in flour and cook for 2–3 minutes, then gradually add strained milk and seasoning.
3. Bring to the boil and cook until thickened.
4. Sieve the flour and salt, beat in eggs and half the milk.
5. Whisk hard to aerate the batter, add remaining milk and finally the melted but cooled butter or the oil.
6. Heat some oil in the pan and fry each pancake on both sides until golden brown. Keep hot in a low oven or on a large dish over a pan of boiling water; do not cover the pancakes.
7. Put the shelled prawns or shrimps into the hot sauce.
8. Heat the butter, add beaten egg yolks. Season, scramble lightly, fold into prawn and sauce mixture, together with stiffly beaten egg whites. Do not add the eggs to the sauce until the last minute.
9. Fill the pancakes with the mixture, garnish with prawns or shrimps.

Les merlans à la moutarde
Whiting with mustard sauce

Cooking time: 30 min. **Preparation time:** 15 min. **Main cooking utensils:** ovenproof dish, saucepan. **Oven temperature:** moderate, 350–375°F., 180–190°C., Gas Mark 4–5. **Oven position:** centre.

IMPERIAL

For 4 people you need:
4 whiting
2 oz. butter
seasoning
2 small shallots *or* onions
1 tablespoon French mustard
4 tablespoons dry white wine
juice $\frac{1}{2}$ lemon
1 tablespoon chopped parsley

To garnish:
parsley

AMERICAN

For 4 people you need:
4 whiting
$\frac{1}{4}$ cup butter
seasoning
2 small shallots *or* onions
1 tablespoon French mustard
$\frac{1}{3}$ cup dry white wine
juice $\frac{1}{2}$ lemon
1 tablespoon chopped parsley

To garnish:
parsley

1. Arrange the fish in a buttered ovenproof dish and season well.
2. Peel the shallots, chop finely and scatter over the fish.
3. Blend together the mustard and wine and pour over the fish.
4. Cover with well-buttered paper or foil and bake in the oven until the fish is thoroughly cooked, about 25 minutes.
5. Pour off the cooking liquor into a saucepan, stir in the lemon juice and heat for 2–3 minutes, stirring throughout, to reduce liquid.
6. Stir in remainder of butter and chopped parsley, pour over fish.
7. Garnish with sprigs of parsley.

To serve: Hot as a main dish. This is excellent with fresh peas and new potatoes.

To vary: Use small, fresh trout, tiny, whole codling or herrings.

196

Homard à la crème
Cream lobster

Cooking time: 35 min.* **Preparation time:** 15 min. **Main cooking utensils:** shallow pan, double saucepan/boiler.

IMPERIAL

For 4 people you need:
1 large pre-cooked lobster *or* 2 medium-sized lobsters
little water
pepper
$\frac{1}{2}$ pint thin cream *or* $\frac{1}{4}$ pint thick cream and $\frac{1}{4}$ pint milk
pinch salt
little French mustard
3 egg yolks
1 tablespoon brandy

To garnish:
chopped chervil *or* parsley

AMERICAN

For 4 people you need:
1 large pre-cooked lobster *or* 2 medium-sized lobsters
little water
pepper
$1\frac{1}{4}$ cups coffee cream *or* $\frac{2}{3}$ cup whipping cream and $\frac{2}{3}$ cup milk
dash salt
little French mustard
3 egg yolks
1 tablespoon brandy

To garnish:
chopped chervil *or* parsley

*Shorter time if shells are not simmered.

1. Split the cooked lobster down the centre stomach.
2. Open and remove the long intestinal vein (black thin cord).
3. Remove lobster meat from the body and dice. Crack claws and remove meat, dice neatly.
4. Put the shells into a shallow pan, cover with water and add pepper. Cook for about 15 minutes to extract all the flavour. Strain this liquid and, if necessary, boil in an open pan to reduce to 2 tablespoons (U.S. 3 tablespoons).
5. Put the cream, salt, mustard and well-beaten egg yolks into the top of the double saucepan. Add stock, simmer gently until mixture coats back of spoon.
6. Stir well and do not allow to boil.
7. Add the brandy towards the end of the cooking time.
8. Mix the flesh with this sauce and heat gently for a few minutes.

To serve: Either in a hot entrée dish or back in the shell or shells, which may be polished with a little oil. Garnish. Serve with salad as a main course or fairly substantial hors d'oeuvre.

197

Boeuf en croûte
Steak in pastry

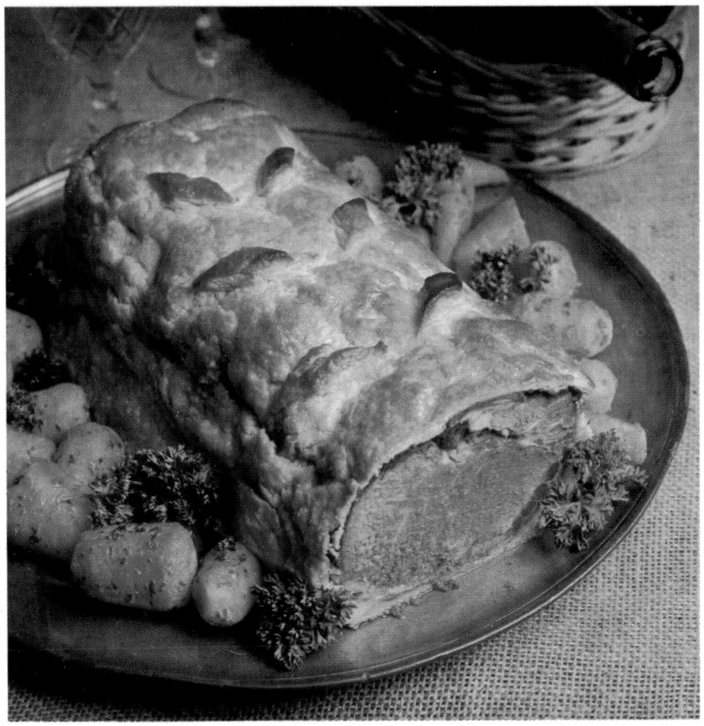

Cooking time: see method. **Preparation time:** 25 min. **Main cooking utensil:** greased baking tray/sheet. **Oven temperature:** hot, 425–450°F., 220–230°C., Gas Mark 6–7, then moderate, 350–375°F., 180–190°C., Gas Mark 4–5. **Oven position:** centre.

IMPERIAL	AMERICAN
For 6–8 people you need:	For 6–8 people you need:
8 oz. short crust pastry	basic pie crust, using 2 cups flour, etc.
4 oz. mushrooms	1 cup mushrooms
2 oz. butter	$\frac{1}{4}$ cup butter
seasoning	seasoning
$1\frac{1}{2}$–2 lb. fillet *or* rump steak, cut in one joint	$1\frac{1}{2}$–2 lb. tenderloin *or* good quality steak, cut in one joint
To garnish:	**To garnish:**
parsley sprigs	parsley sprigs

1. Roll the pastry thinly to an oblong shape.
2. Blend finely chopped mushrooms with butter and seasoning to a paste-like consistency and spread over the centre of the pastry, leaving the ends plain.
3. Put the steak on top, season lightly and wrap pastry round it, sealing edges with water. Glaze with egg, if liked.
4. Cook on a lightly greased baking tray in a hot oven for 20 minutes.
5. 'Rare' steak: lower heat to moderate and cook for a further 20 minutes. Medium 'rare': allow 25–30 minutes extra time in a moderate oven. Well-done: 35–40 minutes extra time in a moderate oven. The pastry will be rather well-cooked with this cooking time, so the steak may be cooked first for 25 minutes, cooled, then put on pastry.

To serve: Hot with vegetables. Garnish with parsley.

To vary: Spread pastry with pâté.

198

Tournedos à la Béarnaise
Steaks with Béarnaise sauce

Cooking time: 5–10 min. for steaks; sauce takes approx. 15–20 min. over very slow heat. **Preparation time:** 15 min. **Main cooking utensils:** double saucepan *or* basin over pan of hot water, frying pan *or* grill pan/skillet *or* broil pan.

IMPERIAL	AMERICAN
For 6–8 people you need:	For 6–8 people you need:
For the sauce:	For the sauce:
1 shallot *or* small onion	1 shallot *or* small onion
sprig fresh tarragon *or* pinch dried tarragon	sprig fresh tarragon *or* pinch dried tarragon
2 tablespoons wine vinegar *or* white malt vinegar *or* use $\frac{1}{4}$ tarragon and $\frac{3}{4}$ wine vinegar	3 tablespoons wine vinegar *or* white malt vinegar *or* use $\frac{1}{4}$ tarragon and $\frac{3}{4}$ wine vinegar
6 peppercorns *or* shake pepper	6 peppercorns *or* dash pepper
3 egg yolks	3 egg yolks
pinch salt, pepper, cayenne	dash salt, pepper, cayenne
1 tablespoon lemon juice	1 tablespoon lemon juice
4 oz. butter (melted *or* softened)	$\frac{1}{2}$ cup melted *or* softened butter
$\frac{1}{2}$ tablespoon chopped parsley	$\frac{1}{2}$ tablespoon chopped parsley
$\frac{1}{2}$ tablespoon chopped chives (optional)	$\frac{1}{2}$ tablespoon chopped chives (optional)
6–8 fillet steaks*	6–8 fillet steaks*
3 oz. butter	6 tablespoons butter
To garnish:	**To garnish:**
matchstick potatoes	matchstick potatoes
lettuce	lettuce

*Ask the butcher to tie the steaks into rounds, known as tournedos.

1. Chop the shallot or onion and tarragon very finely, put into a saucepan with vinegar and peppercorns.
2. Boil steadily for 4–5 minutes, until vinegar has almost evaporated.
3. Pour this into the basin or top of a double saucepan, the shallot and tarragon may be left in vinegar or removed with peppercorns.
4. Add the egg yolks, seasoning and lemon juice.
5. Whisk hard over *hot* but not boiling water until a thick consistency.
6. Remove from the heat, add butter *very gradually*, then parsley and chives (these are not traditional but give a very good flavouring).
7. Fry or grill the steaks in butter to personal taste. Naturally this will be done at the last minute.

To serve: With matchstick potatoes and lettuce, the sauce can be served separately or on top of the steaks as illustrated.

Carré d'agneau aux herbes
Roast lamb with herbs

Cooking time: 25 min. per lb. and 25 min. over. **Main cooking utensil:** roasting tin/pan. **Oven temperature:** 425–450°F., 220–230°C., Gas Mark 6–7. Heat can be reduced after first 30 minutes to be moderately hot 400°F., 200°C., Gas Mark 5–6.

IMPERIAL

For 4–6 people you need:
1 boned loin of lamb, rolled
herbs; marjoram, rosemary *or* a little fresh sage
few thin strips fat pork *or* bacon
about 1 lb. carrots

To garnish:
fresh sprigs herbs

AMERICAN

For 4–6 people you need:
1 boned loin of lamb, rolled
herbs; marjoram, rosemary *or* a little fresh sage
few thin strips salt pork *or* bacon
about 1 lb. carrots

To garnish:
fresh sprigs herbs

1. Insert herbs under the skin of the lamb with the point of a knife.
2. Coat the lean part of the meat with thin strips of fat pork or bacon.
3. Put in a roasting tin in the centre of the preheated oven and cook for the time and temperatures given above.
4. When the meat is partly cooked put par-boiled, sliced carrots into the roasting tin and cook till golden brown.
5. Serve with freshly cooked cabbage and garnish with fresh sprigs of the herbs.

200

Longe de veau aux pruneaux
Loin of veal with prunes

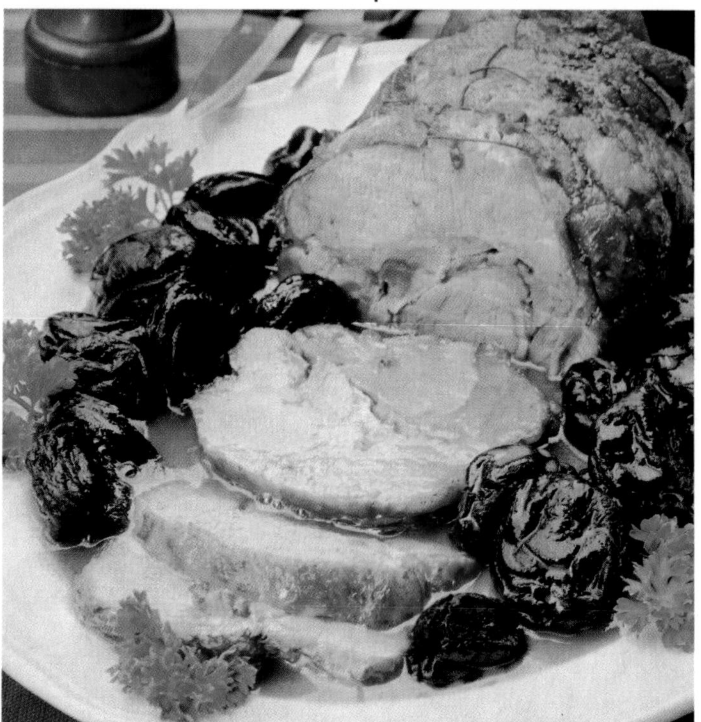

Cooking time: see Stage 4. **Preparation time:** few min. **Main cooking utensils:** roasting tin/pan, saucepan. **Oven temperature:** moderate, 350–375°F., 180–190°C., Gas Mark 4–5. **Oven position:** centre.

IMPERIAL

For 8 people you need:
about 4–5 lb. loin veal (weight before boning)
seasoning
6–8 oz. prunes, unsoaked
little sugar
3 oz. bacon fat, butter *or* dripping
chopped mixed herbs
veal stock (see Stage 1)

For the sauce:
$\frac{1}{4}$ pint prune liquid
1 oz. flour
$\frac{1}{2}$ pint red wine

To garnish:
parsley

AMERICAN

For 8 people you need:
about 4–5 lb. loin veal (weight before boning)
seasoning
1–$1\frac{1}{3}$ cups unsoaked prunes
little sugar
6 tablespoons bacon fat, butter *or* drippings
chopped mixed herbs
veal stock (see Stage 1)

For the sauce:
$\frac{2}{3}$ cup prune liquid
$\frac{1}{4}$ cup all-purpose flour
$1\frac{1}{4}$ cups red wine

To garnish:
parsley

1. Ask the butcher to bone the veal, but keep bones. Simmer these in $\frac{3}{4}$ pint (U.S. 2 cups) water, season.
2. Soak the prunes overnight or for several hours in water to cover. Simmer in water with sugar.
3. Cover the veal with fat or butter, season and top with chopped herbs. Put into a roasting tin, add $\frac{1}{4}$ pint (U.S. $\frac{2}{3}$ cup) veal stock.
4. Cook in a moderate oven, allow 40 minutes per lb. (boned weight) and 40 minutes over.
5. Baste 2–3 times with fat and stock.
6. Blend the prune liquid with the flour, put into the pan. Add red wine and $\frac{1}{4}$ pint (U.S. $\frac{2}{3}$ cup) stock, plus some fat from the roasting tin. Heat gently, stirring until thickened.

To serve: Lift veal on to a dish, top with drained prunes and sauce. Garnish with parsley.

Boeuf à la mode
Pot roast of beef

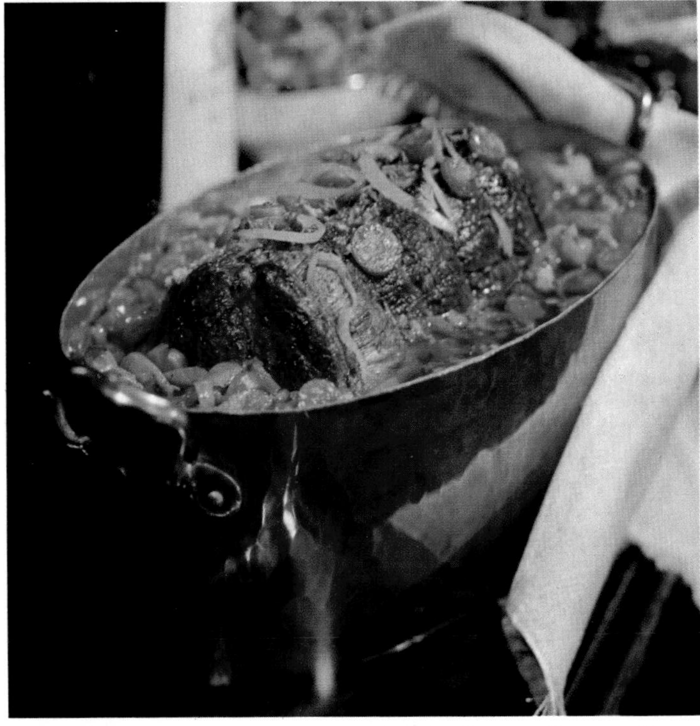

Cooking time: 3–4 hr. **Preparation time:** 25 min. **Main cooking utensils:** large strong pan, sieve.

IMPERIAL

For 8–10 people you need:
4–6 oz. salt pork *or* fat bacon
4–5 lb. beef topside *or* rump*
1 oz. butter
cayenne pepper
paprika pepper
salt
black pepper
1–2 calf's feet
1 lb. onions
$1\frac{1}{2}$ lb. carrots
2–3 cloves
$\frac{3}{4}$ pint white wine
$\frac{3}{4}$ pint brown stock

AMERICAN

For 8–10 people you need:
$\frac{1}{4}$–$\frac{1}{3}$ lb. salt pork *or* bacon
4–5 lb. beef rolled rump
2 tablespoons butter
cayenne pepper
paprika pepper
salt
black pepper
1–2 calf's feet
1 lb. onions
$1\frac{1}{2}$ lb. carrots
2–3 cloves
1 pint white wine
1 pint brown stock

*Fresh brisket could be used but as this contains a high percentage of fat, omit the bacon or pork.

1. Cut the pork into very narrow strips and insert through the beef with a larding needle (large carpet needle could be used).
2. Fry the beef in hot butter until brown on the outside.
3. Season well, adding pinch cayenne and paprika to salt and black pepper. Put in calf's feet, sliced onions, carrots, cloves, white wine and stock. Cover pan, simmer very gently for 3–4 hours.
4. Strain off the stock with half the carrots and onions. Sieve this to use as a sauce.

To serve: Arrange beef with rest of carrots, onions and diced calf's feet; serve sauce separately.

202

Pintade aux légumes
Guinea fowl with vegetables

Cooking time: approx. $2\frac{1}{4}$ hr. see Stages 1 and 4. **Preparation time:** 25 min. plus time for aubergines to stand. **Main cooking utensils:** saucepans, roasting tin/pan. **Oven temperature:** hot, 425–450°F., 220–230°C., Gas Mark 6–7. **Oven position:** centre.

IMPERIAL

For 4 people you need:
1 plump guinea fowl (use chicken when not available)
seasoning
4 oz. bacon
2 onions
1 tablespoon chopped parsley
2 oz. butter

For the vegetable mixture:
1 aubergine
4–6 courgettes *or* 1 young marrow
1 green pepper
6 oz. mushrooms
3–4 sticks celery
1 clove garlic
2 tablespoons oil
$\frac{1}{2}$ oz. flour
1 pint chicken stock

AMERICAN

For 4 people you need:
1 plump guinea fowl (use chicken when not available)
seasoning
$\frac{1}{4}$ lb. bacon
2 onions
1 tablespoon chopped parsley
$\frac{1}{4}$ cup butter

For the vegetable mixture:
1 eggplant
4–6 small zucchini *or* 1 young marrow squash
1 sweet green pepper
$1\frac{1}{2}$ cups mushrooms
3–4 stalks celery
1 clove garlic
3 tablespoons oil
2 tablespoons all-purpose flour
$2\frac{1}{2}$ cups chicken stock

1. Wash and chop the liver of the guinea fowl, put the rest of the giblets into water. Season and simmer for stock for 1 hour.
2. Mix the liver with chopped bacon, chopped onions, parsley, seasoning.
3. Put into guinea fowl, cover bird with butter.
4. Weigh and allow 15 minutes per lb. and 15 minutes over, basting well with butter as this cooks, for guinea fowl can be dry.
5. Meanwhile prepare the vegetables; slice the aubergine, sprinkle with salt, leave for 20 minutes to avoid bitter taste.
6. Slice, but do not peel, courgettes; chop pulp from pepper, discard any seeds and core; wash, do not peel, mushrooms; cut celery into convenient lengths.
7. Crush the clove garlic, toss in oil, then add other vegetables and fry for 5 minutes in a saucepan.
8. Blend in flour, cook for several minutes, then gradually add stock.
9. Season, let vegetables cook gradually, removing lid of pan towards end of cooking time so mixture becomes thick—about 15 minutes.

Coq au vin
Cockerel in wine

Cooking time: $1\frac{1}{4}$ hr. **Preparation time:** 25 min. **Main cooking utensil:** saucepan.

IMPERIAL

For 4–6 people you need:
1 young roasting chicken (preferably a cock bird)
4–6 oz. button mushrooms
about 12–16 small shallots *or* onions
1–2 cloves garlic (optional)
4–6 oz. fat bacon *or* pork
2 oz. butter
1 oz. flour *or* $\frac{1}{2}$ oz. cornflour
seasoning
2 tablespoons brandy
1 pint red wine *or* $\frac{1}{2}$ red wine and $\frac{1}{2}$ chicken stock made by simmering giblets of chicken*

AMERICAN

For 4–6 people you need:
1 young roasting chicken (preferably a cock bird)
$1–1\frac{1}{2}$ cups button mushrooms
about 12–16 small shallots *or* onions
1–2 cloves garlic (optional)
$\frac{1}{4}–\frac{1}{3}$ lb. bacon slices *or* salt pork
$\frac{1}{4}$ cup butter
$\frac{1}{4}$ cup flour *or* 2 tablespoons cornstarch
seasoning
3 tablespoons brandy
$2\frac{1}{2}$ cups red wine *or* $\frac{1}{2}$ red wine and $\frac{1}{2}$ chicken stock, made by simmering giblets of chicken*

*Some recipes use a dry white wine, it is just a matter of personal taste. The mixture of wine and stock is not only more economical, it gives a milder flavour.

1. Joint the chicken, simmer giblets if using stock.
2. Peel the mushrooms or just wash and remove base of stalks.
3. Peel the shallots. Vegetables may be left whole or mushrooms sliced. Garlic should be chopped very finely.
4. Either dice the bacon or pork, or halve rashers, chop some and roll remainder for bacon rolls as in picture.
5. Fry the chopped bacon or pork until crisp, lift out. Toss vegetables in the fat in the pan, remove.
6. Add butter to the bacon fat. Coat the chicken joints in flour or cornflour and seasoning and fry until golden.
7. Pour over brandy and ignite. When the flame has gone out, gradually add the wine.
8. Return vegetables and bacon or pork to the pan, cover tightly and simmer for about 1 hour. Put bacon rolls on top, if using, and cook for a further 15 minutes.

204

Poulet flambé
Chicken legs in brandy

Cooking time: 25 min. **Preparation time:** 15 min. **Main cooking utensil:** frying pan/skillet.

IMPERIAL

For 4 people you need:
2 small frying chickens *or* 4 legs of frying chicken*
1 oz. flour
seasoning
3 oz. butter
1 tablespoon oil
1–2 onions
4 large tomatoes
$\frac{1}{4}$ pint chicken stock
4 tablespoons brandy

To garnish:
2 lemons

AMERICAN

For 4 people you need:
2 small frying chickens or 4 legs of frying chicken*
$\frac{1}{4}$ cup all-purpose flour
seasoning
6 tablespoons butter
1 tablespoon oil
1–2 onions
4 large tomatoes
$\frac{2}{3}$ cup chicken stock
$\frac{1}{3}$ cup brandy

To garnish:
2 lemons

*If using frozen chickens allow to defrost at room temperature before cooking.
If serving at a formal meal then the whole chicken joints can be used. For a more informal occasion, it is easier to handle legs of chicken; wrap paper napkins round these if serving 'barbecue style'.

1. Dry the joints of chicken very well and coat with the flour, mixed with a generous amount of seasoning.
2. Heat the butter and oil, fry the chicken joints for approximately 10 minutes until nearly tender.
3. Lift out of the butter and put on one side.
4. Chop the onions very finely and skin and chop the tomatoes.
5. Simmer with the stock in the pan for about 10 minutes until a thick purée. Season well.
6. Return the chicken joints to the pan and complete cooking.
7. Pour the brandy over the chicken and ignite this if wished.

To serve: Garnished with lemon and with rice or salad.

Caneton à la Bigarade
Duckling with orange sauce

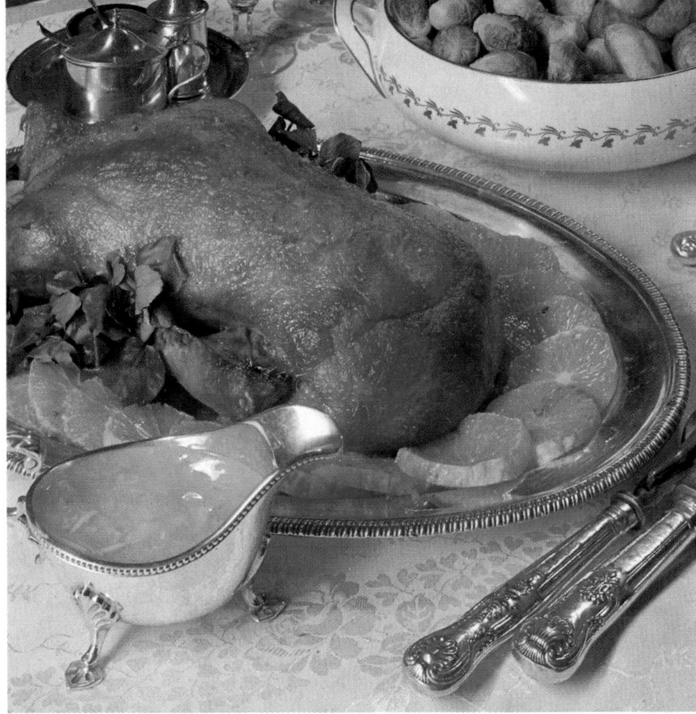

Cooking time: $1\frac{1}{4}$–$1\frac{1}{2}$ hr. Preparation time: 25 min. Main cooking utensils: roasting tin/pan, saucepan. Oven temperature: hot, 425–450°F., 220–230°C., Gas Mark 6–7, then moderately hot, 400°F., 200°C., Gas Mark 5–6.

IMPERIAL

For 4 people you need:
1 young duckling about 4 lb. *or* 2 smaller ducklings
seasoning

For the sauce:
$\frac{1}{2}$ pint giblet stock (see Stage 2) *or* water
3 oranges*
$\frac{1}{2}$–$1\frac{1}{2}$ oz. sugar
1 tablespoon lemon juice
1 tablespoon arrowroot *or* cornflour

To garnish:
2–3 sweet oranges
watercress

AMERICAN

For 4 people you need:
1 young duckling about 4 lb. *or* 2 smaller ducklings
seasoning

For the sauce:
$1\frac{1}{4}$ cups giblet stock (see Stage Stage 2) *or* water
3 oranges*
1–3 tablespoons sugar
1 tablespoon lemon juice
1 tablespoon arrowroot *or* cornstarch

To garnish:
2–3 sweet oranges
watercress

*The real Bigarade sauce is made with bitter oranges, but sweet oranges may be used with smaller amount of sugar.

1. Put the duckling into a tin. Season and roast, allowing 15 minutes per lb. and 15 minutes over, the heat can be reduced after 45 minutes. Half-way through cooking, prick skin *lightly* to allow surplus fat to run out.
2. The giblets may be cooked to give a savoury stock for the sauce.
3. Remove the rind from the oranges, cut away white pith. Cut orange part of peel in thin strips, simmer in stock or water for 30 minutes, covering pan to prevent liquid evaporating.
4. Add the sugar, orange and lemon juices blended with arrowroot or cornflour, cook until thickened and smooth.
5. Taste and season as required.

To serve: Put duck on a dish with sliced oranges and watercress.

To vary: To the sauce add a little brandy; 1 tablespoon redcurrant jelly; or brown the sugar with a little water to give a caramel colour.

206

Faisan aux raisins et noix
Pheasant with grapes and nuts

Cooking time: 1 hr. Preparation time: 25 min. Main cooking utensil: strong saucepan, see Stage 4.

IMPERIAL

For 4 people you need:
12 oz. ripe, white grapes
$1\frac{1}{2}$ oz. butter
1 pheasant*
4 tablespoons soured cream *or* use fresh thin cream and 1 dessertspoon lemon juice
about 24 shelled walnuts *or* walnut halves (if using dried nuts)
2–3 tablespoons brandy
seasoning
2 teaspoons sugar

To garnish:
about 8 oz. white grapes

AMERICAN

For 4 people you need:
$\frac{3}{4}$ lb. ripe, green grapes
3 tablespoons butter
1 pheasant*
$\frac{1}{3}$ cup sour cream *or* use fresh coffee cream and 1 tablespoon lemon juice
about 24 shelled walnuts *or* walnut halves (if using dried nuts)
3–4 tablespoons brandy
seasoning
2 teaspoons sugar

To garnish:
about $\frac{1}{2}$ lb. green grapes

*Other game can be cooked in the same way—e.g. substitute 2 large or 4 small young pigeons.

1. Crush the grapes in a bowl to extract the juice.
2. Heat the butter in a very strong saucepan and add the pheasant. Turn in the butter until golden, then add the soured cream or cream and lemon juice.
3. Put in the juice from the grapes and the nuts.
4. Seal the pan tightly; if you have no well-fitting lid, put foil or paper under the lid or, if preferred, transfer the pheasant to a casserole and cook in a moderately hot oven for 35 minutes.
5. Keep the heat under the pan low so the sauce does not burn.
6. Remove lid of pan or casserole, add brandy, seasoning and stir in sugar.
7. Add about three-quarters of remaining grapes.
8. Continue cooking for approximately 20 minutes, until pheasant is tender.
9. Serve with nuts and grapes, top with extra fresh grapes.

To serve: Boil sauce a little until less in volume, serve with pheasant. This is delicious with small sprouts and creamed potatoes.

207

Soufflé au jambon
Ham soufflé

Cooking time: 40 min. **Preparation time:** 20 min. **Main cooking utensils:** large saucepan, frying pan/skillet, 7-inch soufflé dish. **Oven temperature:** moderately hot, 400°F., 200°C., Gas Mark 5–6. **Oven position:** centre.

IMPERIAL

For 4–8 people you need:*
6 oz. tiny mushrooms *or* chopped mushrooms
2 oz. butter

For the soufflé mixture:
2 oz. butter
$1\frac{1}{2}$ oz. flour
$\frac{1}{2}$ pint milk
$\frac{1}{4}$ teaspoon salt
pinch cayenne pepper
$\frac{1}{2}$ teaspoon made mustard
6 oz. cooked ham
5 egg yolks**
6–7 egg whites**

AMERICAN

For 4–8 people you need:*
$1\frac{1}{2}$ cups tiny mushrooms *or* chopped mushrooms
$\frac{1}{4}$ cup butter

For the soufflé mixture:
$\frac{1}{4}$ cup butter
6 tablespoons all-purpose flour
$1\frac{1}{4}$ cups milk
$\frac{1}{4}$ teaspoon salt
dash cayenne pepper
$\frac{1}{2}$ teaspoon prepared mustard
6 oz. cooked, cured ham
5 egg yolks**
6–7 egg whites**

*4 as a main dish, 8 as an hors d'oeuvre.
**Or equal quantities of egg yolks and whites, but this does not give such a light soufflé.

1. Wash the mushrooms, do not peel unless the skins are very imperfect as they contain a great deal of flavour.
2. Fry the mushrooms in hot butter and keep warm until ready to put the soufflé mixture into the dish.
3. Heat the butter in a saucepan, stir in the flour, cook for several minutes.
4. Gradually blend in the milk, bring to boil and cook until thickened and smooth. Season very well, but do not add too much salt if the ham is fairly salt.
5. Chop or mince the ham finely, put into the sauce.
6. Add the egg yolks, then fold in the stiffly beaten egg whites, do this gently and carefully so the light texture is not lost.
7. Butter the soufflé dish, put in the hot mushrooms and the sauce mixture, level off at the top.
8. Bake until golden coloured and just set. Do not overcook for it should be firm on the outside, but soft in the middle.

To serve: As soon as baked.

208

Vols-au-vent
Pastry cases

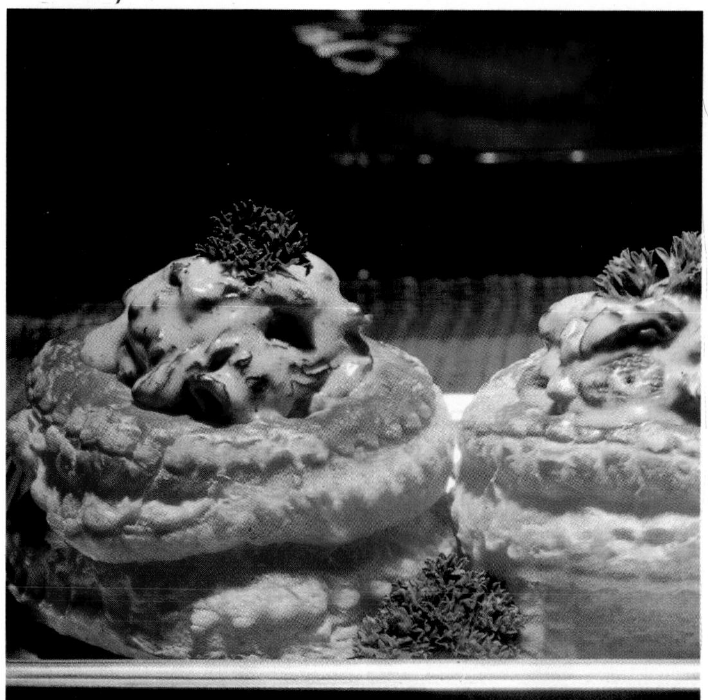

Cooking time: 15–20 min. **Preparation time:** 30 min. plus time for pastry to stand. **Main cooking utensil:** baking tray/sheet. **Oven temperature:** hot to very hot, 450–475°F., 230–240°C., Gas Mark 7–8. **Oven position:** just above centre.

IMPERIAL

For 4–6 people you need:
8 oz. flour, preferably plain
pinch salt
cold water and squeeze lemon juice
8 oz. butter

For the fillings:
(a) cooked chicken in sauce
(b) cooked fish or shellfish in sauce
(c) vegetables in sauce

AMERICAN

For 4–6 people you need:
2 cups all-purpose flour
dash salt
cold water and squeeze lemon juice
1 cup butter

For the fillings:
(a) cooked chicken in sauce
(b) cooked fish or shellfish in sauce
(c) vegetables in sauce

In the picture, 4 oz. (U.S. 1 cup) mushrooms were fried in 1 oz. (U.S. 2 tablespoons) butter and 4 oz. cooked, drained prunes were added to the sauce.

1. Sieve the flour and salt, add sufficient water and lemon juice to make an elastic dough.
2. Roll out to an oblong shape, put the butter in the centre.
3. Fold dough in 3 to cover the butter.
4. Seal ends with a rolling pin, press down at regular intervals i.e. 'rib', turn and roll out.
5. Fold in 3, continue as Stage 4, until dough has 7 rollings and 7 foldings. Put in a cool place between rollings.
6. Roll dough out to about $\frac{1}{3}$–$\frac{1}{2}$ inch thick. Cut into rounds or squares.
7. With a small cutter, mark lids on pastry, cut this to a depth of half the thickness of the pastry. Glaze with egg, if liked.
8. Bake until crisp and brown, reducing heat if necessary.
9. Lift out centre 'lid' and dry case for a few minutes in oven.
10. Make the sauce with 2 oz. (U.S. $\frac{1}{4}$ cup) butter, $1\frac{1}{2}$ oz. (U.S. 6 tablespoons) flour, $\frac{1}{2}$ pint (U.S. $1\frac{1}{4}$ cups) liquid (milk or milk and chicken or fish stock). Thicken well, add a little thick cream, seasoning and put in filling. Fill cases.

Quiche aux champignons
Pastry case with mushrooms

Cooking time: 45 min. **Preparation time:** 30 min. **Main cooking utensils:** frying pan/skillet, saucepan, $7\frac{1}{2}$–8-inch flan ring and baking tray/sheet *or* shallow tin. **Oven temperature:** 400–425°F., 200–220°C., Gas Mark 6 then 350–375°F., 180–190°C., Gas Mark 4. **Oven position:** centre.

IMPERIAL

For 4 people you need:
For the pastry:
6 oz. flour, preferably plain
pinch salt
shake pepper, celery salt, cayenne pepper
2–3 oz. butter
$1\frac{1}{2}$ oz. Parmesan cheese, grated

egg yolk and water to bind

For the filling:
2 oz. butter
6 oz. mushrooms
4 oz. Gruyère cheese, grated
1 oz. Parmesan cheese, grated

2 eggs
2 egg yolks
seasoning
$\frac{1}{4}$ pint thin cream
$\frac{1}{4}$ pint milk

AMERICAN

For 4 people you need:
For the pastry:
$1\frac{1}{2}$ cups all-purpose flour
dash salt
dash pepper, celery salt, cayenne pepper
4–6 tablespoons butter
3 tablespoons grated Parmesan cheese
egg yolk and water to bind

For the filling:
$\frac{1}{4}$ cup butter
$1\frac{1}{2}$ cups mushrooms
1 cup grated Gruyère cheese
$\frac{1}{4}$ cup grated Parmesan cheese
2 eggs
2 egg yolks
seasoning
$\frac{2}{3}$ cup coffee cream
$\frac{2}{3}$ cup milk

1. Sieve together the flour and seasonings.
2. Rub in the butter, use only 2 oz. (U.S. $\frac{1}{4}$ cup) if there is no time to let this pastry stand.
3. Add the cheese, bind with egg yolk and water.
4. If possible let the pastry stand for 30 minutes in a cool place, as it is rather fragile, or see comment Stage 2.
5. Roll out the pastry, line flan ring on upturned baking tray (this makes it easier to remove), or line tin.
6. Bake 'blind' for 15 minutes.
7. Meanwhile, heat the butter and fry sliced mushrooms for 5 minutes, put into the flan with the cheese.
8. Beat the eggs with seasoning and cream. Add hot, but not boiling milk.
9. Strain into pastry flan. Lower oven heat to moderate, bake for approximately 30 minutes until set. Garnish with parsley.

210

Omelette au confiture*
Jam omelette

Cooking time: few min. **Preparation time:** 10 min. **Main cooking utensils:** omelette pan, saucepan.

IMPERIAL

For 2 people you need:
4 eggs
1 oz. sugar
1–2 tablespoons milk, thin cream, rum *or* brandy
$1\frac{1}{2}$ oz. butter
3 tablespoons jam

To decorate:
1–2 oz. sieved icing sugar

AMERICAN

For 2 people you need:
4 eggs
2 tablespoons sugar
1–3 tablespoons milk, coffee cream, rum *or* brandy
3 tablespoons butter
4 tablespoons jam

To decorate:
$\frac{1}{4}$–$\frac{1}{2}$ cup sifted confectioners' sugar

*Often called Omelette sucrée.

1. Separate the egg yolks from whites.
2. Beat the yolks with sugar, milk, cream, rum or brandy.
3. Fold in the stiffly beaten egg whites.
4. Heat the butter in an omelette pan, also heat the jam.
5. Pour the egg mixture into the hot butter, cook for about $\frac{1}{2}$ minute, then tilt pan and sweep the liquid egg down the sides.
6. Continue like this until set *or*, if wished, partially cook the omelette in this way, then put the pan under a hot grill for a few moments—this prevents too slow cooking, which can toughen eggs.
7. Fill with hot jam, fold and sprinkle with sieved icing sugar.

To serve: *At once.*

To vary:
(a) Fill with hot fruit.
(b) Fill with melted chocolate and cream.
(c) Mark icing sugar with hot skewer to caramelize in a lattice pattern.
(d) Blend egg yolk mixture with crumbled macaroons or chopped nuts.

Profiteroles
Cream buns with chocolate sauce

Cooking time: 35 min. **Preparation time:** 20 min. **Main cooking utensils:** 2 saucepans, baking tray/sheet. **Oven temperature:** hot, 425–450°F., 220–230°C., Gas Mark 6–7. **Oven position:** above centre.

IMPERIAL	AMERICAN
To make approximately 12 medium-sized buns you need:	To make approximately 12 medium-sized buns you need:
$\frac{1}{4}$ pint water	$\frac{2}{3}$ cup water
1 oz. butter *or* margarine	2 tablespoons butter *or* margarine
3 oz. plain flour	$\frac{3}{4}$ cup all-purpose flour
pinch salt	dash salt
2 large eggs *or* 2 medium eggs and 1 egg yolk	2 large eggs *or* 2 medium eggs and 1 egg yolk
For the chocolate sauce:	For the chocolate sauce:
6 oz. brown sugar	$\frac{3}{4}$ cup, firmly packed, brown sugar
3 oz. cocoa powder	$\frac{3}{4}$ cup unsweetened cocoa powder
$\frac{1}{2}$ pint milk	$1\frac{1}{4}$ cups milk
few drops vanilla essence	few drops vanilla extract
To serve:	To serve:
$\frac{1}{4}$–$\frac{1}{2}$ pint thick, fresh cream	$\frac{2}{3}$–$1\frac{1}{4}$ cups whipping cream

1. Bring the water and butter slowly to the boil. Add the flour and salt.
2. Draw the pan aside from the heat, and beat until it forms a smooth paste.
3. When cool, beat in the lightly beaten eggs, a little at a time.
4. Pipe or spoon on to a greased baking tray (about a teaspoonful for each profiterole).
5. Bake in a hot oven for 20–25 minutes. For tiny profiteroles, cook for 10–15 minutes only.
6. Chocolate sauce: put all the ingredients into a saucepan. Stir until the sugar has dissolved, and boil for 2 minutes or until a thick pouring sauce is obtained. Allow to cool.

To serve: Slit the profiteroles and allow to cool, then fill with fresh cream. Pile into a dish and cover with the chocolate sauce.

To vary: $\frac{1}{2}$–1 oz. (U.S. 1–2 tablespoons) sugar can be added to the mixture before baking.

212

Babas au rhum
Rum cakes

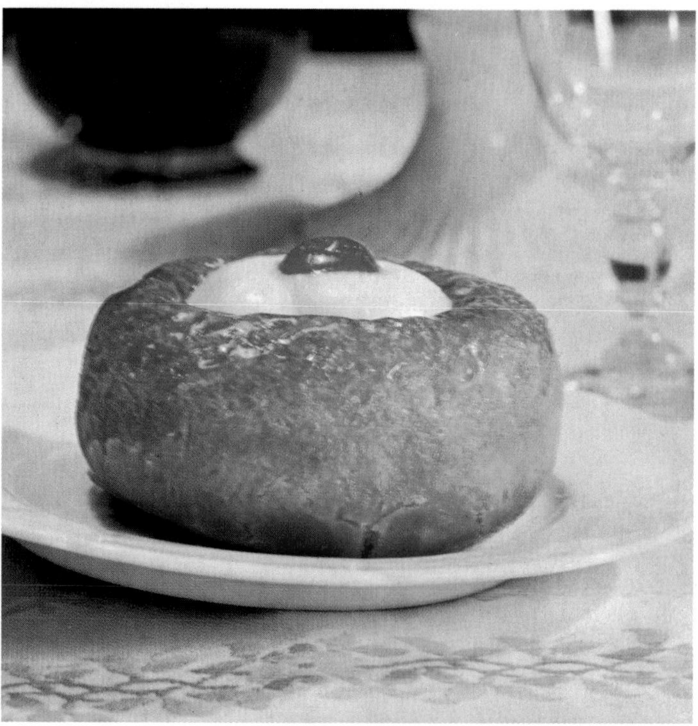

Cooking time: 10–15 min. **Preparation time:** 25 min. plus time for 'proving'. **Main cooking utensils:** 6 baba tins (individual flan *or* patty tins/muffin pans), saucepan. **Oven temperature:** hot to very hot, 450–475°F., 230–240°C., Gas Mark 8. **Oven position:** towards top.

IMPERIAL	AMERICAN
For 6 portions you need:	For 6 portions you need:
$\frac{1}{4}$ oz. fresh yeast	$\frac{1}{4}$ cake compressed yeast
1 teaspoon sugar	1 teaspoon sugar
6 tablespoons tepid milk	about $\frac{1}{2}$ cup tepid milk
4 oz. plain flour	1 cup all-purpose flour
1 oz. currants (optional)	3 tablespoons currants (optional)
2 oz. butter *or* margarine	$\frac{1}{4}$ cup butter *or* margarine
2 eggs	2 eggs
For the syrup:	For the sirup:
$\frac{1}{4}$ pint water	$\frac{2}{3}$ cup water
2–3 oz. sugar	4–6 tablespoons sugar
juice $\frac{1}{2}$ lemon	juice $\frac{1}{2}$ lemon
$1\frac{1}{2}$–2 tablespoons rum	2–3 tablespoons rum
To decorate:	To decorate:
thick cream, with little rum syrup, if liked	whipping cream, with a little rum sirup, if liked
glacé cherries	candied cherries

1. Cream the yeast with the sugar.
2. Add the milk and a sprinkling of flour.
3. Put in a warm place for 20 minutes.
4. Work in the rest of the flour, currants, melted butter or margarine and the beaten eggs.
5. Grease tins and coat lightly with flour. Half-fill with the mixture.
6. Put into warm place to 'prove' for 20–25 minutes.
7. Bake until firm.
8. Turn out of the tins and prick with a steel knitting needle, to allow syrup to soak through.
9. Make the syrup by boiling together water, sugar and lemon juice, add rum. Pour over the babas; allow to cool.
10. Fill with the flavoured cream and decorate with the halved cherries.

To serve: With tea or coffee or as a dessert.

To store: In a cool place for a limited period only.

Clafoutis aux raisins
Grape tart

Cooking time: 45 min. **Preparation time:** 15 min. **Main cooking utensils:** large shallow saucepan, ovenproof dish. **Oven temperature:** moderate, 350–375°F., 180–190°C., Gas Mark 4–5. **Oven position:** centre.

IMPERIAL

For 4–6 portions you need:
12 oz. grapes (preferably black)
3 oz. sugar
$\frac{1}{4}$ pint white wine *or* water

For the batter:
2 oz. butter
4 oz. sugar
2 large eggs
6 oz. flour (plain or self-raising)
scant $\frac{3}{8}$ pint milk

To serve:
sugar *or* vanilla sugar*

AMERICAN

For 4–6 portions you need:
$\frac{3}{4}$ lb. grapes (preferably purple)
6 tablespoons sugar
$\frac{2}{3}$ cup white wine *or* water

For the batter:
$\frac{1}{4}$ cup butter
$\frac{1}{2}$ cup sugar
2 large eggs
$1\frac{1}{2}$ cups all-purpose flour
scant $\frac{3}{4}$ cup milk

To serve:
sugar *or* vanilla sugar*

*Cut a vanilla pod in half, put into a jar of sugar.

1. Remove seeds from the grapes, but keep whole, do not skin.
2. Make a syrup of the sugar and liquid, bring this to the boil.
3. Put in the grapes, simmer gently for a few minutes, then lift out.
4. Cream the butter well, add sugar and beat again, then add the beaten eggs.
5. Stir in the flour and milk to give a smooth thick batter.
6. Blend well-drained grapes with this.
7. Put into a well-greased baking dish and cook until just firm.
8. Towards the end of cooking time, it may be necessary to cover the top to prevent the fruit drying.

To serve: Better served cold topped with plenty of sugar. Equally good as a dessert or for tea.

To vary: Use other fruit, and use less batter ingredients—i.e. $1\frac{1}{2}$ lb. fruit and half the ingredients for the batter—this becomes more suitable for a hot dessert.

214

Melons à la mousse
Melons filled with mousse

Preparation time: 15 min. **Main utensil:** large basin.

IMPERIAL

For 12 people you need:
3 medium-sized ripe melons (all melons except water melons are suitable)
2–3 oz. sugar
$1\frac{1}{2}$ lb. raspberries *or* use equivalent in frozen *or* canned fruit
2 oz. cream cheese
$\frac{1}{2}$ pint thick cream
$1\frac{1}{4}$ tablespoons Ratafia de Framboises (raspberry-flavoured liqueur), Curaçao *or* few drops vanilla essence

AMERICAN

For 12 people you need:
3 medium-sized ripe melons (all melons except water melon are suitable)
4–6 tablespoons sugar
$1\frac{1}{2}$ lb. raspberries, *or* use equivalent in frozen *or* canned fruit
$\frac{1}{4}$ cup cream cheese
$1\frac{1}{4}$ cups whipping cream
2 tablespoons Ratafia de Framboises (raspberry-flavored liqueur), Curaçao *or* few drops vanilla extract

1. Cut the melons into halves and remove all the seeds.
2. Sprinkle with a little sugar if wished, although the filling is a fairly sweet one.
3. Put a few raspberries on one side for decoration and sieve the rest.
4. Blend the raspberry purée with the cream cheese and add sugar to taste.
5. Whip the cream until it just holds its shape. Fold this and the raspberry flavoured liqueur or Curaçao into the fruit purée.
6. If preferred omit this and add a few drops vanilla essence to the cream instead.
7. Put into the melon halves and chill, then decorate with the whole raspberries.

To serve: Cut each melon half downwards to give two portions.

To vary: Use the smaller melons so each half serves one person. As the seed cavities in these are rather large in proportion to the size of the fruit, you will be able to pack more raspberry mixture in; therefore you will need 4 small melons to serve 8 people.

Crème renversée
Caramel cream

Cooking time: $1\frac{1}{4}$ hr.* **Preparation time:** 15 min. **Main cooking utensils:** 1 *strong* saucepan, steamer *or* roasting tin/pan, 6 small moulds/molds. **Oven temperature:** cool, 300°F., 150°C., Gas Mark 1–2. **Oven position:** centre *or* coolest part.

IMPERIAL	AMERICAN
For 6 people you need:	For 6 people you need:
For the caramel:	**For the caramel:**
5 oz. loaf *or* granulated sugar	$\frac{1}{2}$ cup plus 2 tablespoons sugar
$\frac{1}{4}$ pint water	$\frac{2}{3}$ cup water
small piece lemon rind (optional)	small piece lemon rind (optional)
For the custard:	**For the custard:**
3 whole eggs**	3 whole eggs**
yolks 3 eggs**	yolks 3 eggs**
$1\frac{1}{2}$ oz. sugar	3 tablespoons sugar
1 pint milk	$2\frac{1}{2}$ cups milk
$\frac{1}{2}$ pint thin cream	$1\frac{1}{4}$ cups coffee cream

*One 8-inch large mould would take $2–2\frac{1}{2}$ hr.
**All yolks may be used, richer than whole eggs.

1. Put the sugar and 5 tablespoons (U.S. 6 tablespoons) water into a strong pan, stir until sugar has dissolved.
2. Boil steadily until a golden brown caramel, take pan off the heat.
3. Stir in the remaining water, drop in piece of lemon rind. This is not essential but gives a pleasant flavour.
4. Pour into moulds, tilt so it coats the sides, cool. (Rinse out pan immediately.)
5. Beat the eggs, egg yolks and sugar.
6. Warm the milk and cream, stir on to the eggs and sugar.
7. Strain into the moulds, cover with buttered paper.
8. Either steam over *hot* but not boiling water, or bake in oven in a dish of water. If water is put into dish 30 minutes after custard starts cooking, it is always cooler than the custard and prevents it curdling.
9. When set, cool, turn out carefully.

To serve: Really cold.

NOTE: If mould is smeared *very lightly* with oil or butter, the caramel will not stick.

216

Gâteau au vacherin
Meringue gâteau

Cooking time: 2–3 hr. **Preparation time:** 30 min. **Main cooking utensils:** baking trays/sheets, 4 sheets rice paper/wax paper. **Oven temperature:** cool, 200–250°F., 110–130°C., Gas Mark $0–\frac{1}{2}$. **Oven position:** centre or below centre.

IMPERIAL	AMERICAN
For 8–10 portions you need:	For 8–10 portions you need:
5 egg whites	5 egg whites
10 oz. castor sugar	$1\frac{1}{4}$ cups granulated sugar
$1\frac{1}{2}$ oz. cornflour (optional)	6 tablespoons cornstarch (optional)
For the filling:	**For the filling:**
$\frac{1}{2}–\frac{3}{4}$ pint thick cream	$1\frac{1}{4}–2$ cups whipping cream
$\frac{1}{2}–1$ teaspoon vanilla essence	$\frac{1}{2}–1$ teaspoon vanilla extract
1–2 oz. sugar	2–4 tablespoons sugar
For the sauce:	**For the sauce:**
6 oz. plain chocolate	1 cup semi-sweet chocolate pieces
2 teaspoons oil	2 teaspoons oil

1. Cut out four rounds of rice paper; two of 6-inches, one of 8-inches and one of 9–10-inches.
2. Whisk the egg whites until very stiff.
3. Gradually beat in half the sugar, then fold in the remainder of the sugar; for a firmer texture, blend the cornflour with the sugar.
4. Spread over baking sheets lined with the rice paper. Dry out in a cool oven until pale gold on the outside. The inside should be slightly sticky.
5. Whip the cream lightly. Add the vanilla essence and sugar.
6. Sandwich the meringue rounds with this mixture.
7. Melt the chocolate with the oil. Pour the sauce over the meringue. This is more suitable for a dessert.

To vary: To add interest, place an orange or other fruit on top of the gâteau, pour the chocolate sauce over this just before serving.

To store: The rounds of meringue keep well in an airtight tin, before filling.

217

Gâteau de marrons
Chestnut gâteau

Cooking time: 40 min. **Preparation time:** 30 min. **Main cooking utensils:** saucepan, 8–9-inch shallow cake tin/pan, double saucepan. **Oven temperature:** moderate, 350–375°F., 180–190°C., Gas Mark 4–5. **Oven position:** centre.

IMPERIAL

For 8 portions you need:
4 oz. plain chocolate
3 oz. butter
5 oz. castor sugar

½ teaspoon vanilla essence
3 eggs
4 oz. self-raising flour

4 oz. chestnut purée*
½ tablespoon brandy

To decorate:
3 oz. butter
6 oz. icing sugar

1 tablespoon coffee essence
3 oz. chestnut purée*
½ teaspoon vanilla essence

AMERICAN

For 8 portions you need:
4 oz. semi-sweet chocolate
6 tablespoons butter
½ cup plus 2 tablespoons granulated sugar
½ teaspoon vanilla extract
3 eggs
1 cup all-purpose flour, sifted with 1 teaspoon baking powder
¼ lb. chestnut purée*
½ tablespoon brandy

To decorate:
6 tablespoons butter
scant 1½ cups confectioners' sugar
1 tablespoon coffee extract
⅓ cup chestnut purée*
½ teaspoon vanilla extract

*Fresh or canned. To obtain 7 oz. from fresh chestnuts, cook, shell and sieve about 1 lb. Sieve canned purée.

1. Melt and cool the chocolate.
2. Cream the butter and sugar until soft and light, then add chocolate and vanilla essence and beat again.
3. Gradually beat in the eggs, adding a little flour if mixture shows signs of curdling.
4. Add the rest of the sieved flour, chestnut purée and brandy.
5. Put into a well-greased and floured tin, bake until firm. Turn out carefully and cool.
6. Cream the butter, 5 oz. (U.S. generous 1 cup) sieved icing sugar and coffee essence.
7. Add the chestnut purée and vanilla essence.
8. Spread on the cake and mark with knife. Top with sieved icing sugar.

To vary: Put apricot jam under the chestnut topping.

218

Petits moricauds
Little mulattos

Cooking time: 15 min. **Preparation time:** 20 min. **Main cooking utensils:** tiny plain patty tins/muffin pans *or* paper cases, double saucepan. **Oven temperature:** very moderate to moderate, 350–375°F., 180–190°C., Gas Mark 4. **Oven position:** just above centre.

IMPERIAL

To make about 20 cakes you need:
To decorate:
approx. 1½ oz. almonds
1–2 oz. glacé cherries

For the cakes:
2 oz. butter
4 oz. castor sugar
3 oz. plain chocolate

4 oz. ground almonds *or* ground hazelnuts, *or* for economy, use 2 oz. ground nuts and 2 oz. crisp very fine breadcrumbs
3 egg whites

AMERICAN

To make about 20 cakes you need:
To decorate:
generous ⅓ cup almonds
about ¼ cup candied cherries

For the cakes:
¼ cup butter
½ cup granulated sugar
½ cup semi-sweet chocolate pieces
1 cup ground almonds *or* ground hazelnuts, *or* for economy, use ½ cup ground nuts and ½ cup crisp fine bread crumbs
3 egg whites

1. First 'blanch' the almonds; for the very light, fluffy cakes must not be kept waiting before being baked.
2. Cut the almonds into required shape for 'nose' and cherries for 'eyes' and 'mouth'. Keep pieces small, as heavy pieces will sink as mixture cooks.
3. Cream the butter and sugar until soft and light.
4. Melt chocolate in the top of a double saucepan or basin over hot water, or grate very finely. Gradually work into the butter and sugar.
5. Add the ground almonds and finally fold in stiffly whisked egg whites.
6. Grease patty tins well. Do not use fluted shapes, as the cakes will be more difficult to remove when baked.
7. Half fill the patty tins or paper cases.
8. Top with the decoration and bake until just firm to the touch.

Japonaise
Almond cakes

Cooking time: 45–50 min. **Preparation time:** 30 min. **Main cooking utensil:** Swiss roll tin/jelly roll pan. **Oven temperature:** slow to very moderate, 300–325°F., 150–170°C., Gas Mark 2–3. **Oven position:** centre.

IMPERIAL

For about 8 cakes you need:
4 egg whites
8 oz. sugar
8 oz. ground almonds, *or* 6 oz. ground almonds and 2 oz. ground rice, *or* half ground almonds and half fine cake crumbs for economy
few drops almond *or* ratafia essence

To decorate:
4 oz. butter
6 oz. sieved icing sugar

$\frac{1}{2}$–1 tablespoon coffee essence
8 hazelnuts

AMERICAN

For about 8 cakes you need:
4 egg whites
generous 1 cup sugar
2 cups ground almonds, *or* 1$\frac{1}{2}$ cups ground almonds and $\frac{1}{2}$ cup ground rice, *or* half ground almonds and half fine cake crumbs for economy
few drops almond extract

To decorate:
$\frac{1}{2}$ cup butter
scant 1$\frac{1}{2}$ cups confectioners' sugar
$\frac{1}{2}$–1 tablespoon coffee extract
8 hazelnuts

1. Whisk the egg whites until very stiff, gradually whisk in half the sugar, fold in remainder with ground almonds and almond or ratafia essence.
2. Spread the mixture over a greased and lined Swiss roll tin.
3. Bake the mixture for 25–30 minutes, or until almost set and remove from the oven.
4. Cut out about 16 small rounds, return mixture to the oven for a further 10 minutes or until quite firm.
5. Remove once more from the oven, lift out rounds of cake, allow these to cool.
6. Return 'trimmings' to oven to become very brown and crisp, about a further 10 minutes.
7. Crush the trimmings with a rolling pin, placing them between 2 sheets of greaseproof paper.
8. Blend together the butter, icing sugar and coffee essence.
9. Sandwich two rounds together with some coffee icing mixture. Coat sides and roll in crumbs. Spread the icing on top, pipe a rosette in the centre and top with a hazelnut.

220

Brioche
Light rolls

Cooking time: 12 min. **Preparation time:** 20 min. plus time for dough to 'prove'. **Main cooking utensils:** 8–10 fluted tins/individual fluted cake pans. **Oven temperature:** hot, 425–450°F., 220–230°C., Gas Mark 6–7. **Oven position:** just above centre.

IMPERIAL

For 8–10 brioches you need:
$\frac{1}{2}$ oz. fresh yeast
1 oz. sugar
3 tablespoons tepid milk
12 oz. plain flour
pinch salt
5 oz. butter *or* margarine

2 eggs

To glaze:
small egg *or* a little milk

AMERICAN

For 8–10 brioches you need:
$\frac{1}{2}$ cake compressed yeast
2 tablespoons sugar
scant $\frac{1}{4}$ cup tepid milk
3 cups all-purpose flour
dash salt
$\frac{1}{2}$ cup plus 2 tablespoons butter *or* margarine
2 eggs

To glaze:
small egg *or* a little milk

1. Cream the yeast with a teaspoon of the sugar.
2. Add the tepid milk and enough of the flour to make a thick batter.
3. Put into a warm place for 15 minutes to 'prove'.
4. Sieve the remainder of the flour and salt into a warm bowl. Rub in butter or margarine, add the rest of the sugar.
5. Work in yeast mixture and lastly the beaten eggs. Put the dough in a slightly warmer atmosphere to 'prove' for 2 hours. Knead lightly until smooth.
6. Divide the dough into the required number of portions, remembering the dough must only come two-thirds of the way up the tins.
7. Press the brioche dough into the greased and floured, fluted tins.
8. 'Prove' for 10–15 minutes. Brush lightly with a little egg or milk.
9. Bake until firm to the touch.

To serve: At breakfast or tea time, with butter and/or jam.

NOTE: This brioche dough is often used in place of ordinary pastry, to make sweet or savoury flans or tarts. Proceed to Stage 5, roll into the flan shape. Fill, 'prove' and bake as stated.

German cooking is hearty and homely but it is a mistake to think of it as dull or lacking in expertise. Such specialities as dumplings and puddings, although originating in the farmhouse rather than a royal or aristocratic kitchen, require considerable skill to make them light and delicate. Nothing is worse than a heavy, soggy dumpling and the Germans cannot be faulted there. Of course, some famous German inventions that used to be made at home, like sauerkraut, sausages, pickled cucumbers and pumpernickel bread, are now almost always bought ready-made and with these items alone you can have a typical German meal.

But although we are sometimes led to think so, Germans do not live exclusively on beer and sausages. To begin with they make some excellent savouries to serve either as a substantial hors d'oeuvre or a light supper dish. Many of them use potatoes or bacon, both of which are basic ingredients in much German cooking. A particularly unusual and colourful party supper dish is Tomato layer gâteau, a large pastry shell filled with a meat, tomato and cheese mixture and topped with more tomato and cheese.

The Germans love their meat and are never happier than when presented with a beef casserole like Beef in beer served with potatoes or noodles or Beef casserole with dumplings. Game is not as common as it used to be but Venison with fruit and a rich gravy is a popular traditional dish for festive occasions. Fresh-water fish is eaten more than salt-water fish since Germany has more lakes and rivers than coast, but the two fish recipes we have included are suitable for any white fish. An appropriate accompaniment to any of these main dishes would be a cucumber salad, especially one flavoured with dill which is a favourite herb in Germany.

A steamed pudding often concludes a German meal and *Brotkoch*, literally bread cake, is a superb light pudding which proves that a steamed pudding can be an elegant and sophisticated dessert. German bakeries offer an overwhelming array of cakes and biscuits, but housewives continue to bake the old family recipes which have been handed down over the years. Spiced cakes, actually biscuits full of nuts and spices, and the crisp, delicately spiced Christmas butter biscuits never fail to appeal, especially to children.

Brotsuppe
Bread soup

Cooking time: see Stages 2 and 3. **Preparation time:** see Stages 1 and 3.
Main cooking utensils: saucepan, ovenproof soup bowls.

IMPERIAL

For 4–5 people you need:
few beef bones
water
2 onions
2 carrots
1 leek (optional)
seasoning and bouquet garni
Or use instead: 2 pints water and 3–4 beef stock cubes *or* 2 pints canned consommé
2–3 teaspoons soup seasoning
1 teaspoon dried parsley
¼ pint white wine

For the topping:
2–3 small soft bread rolls
1½–2 oz. butter
3 oz. cheese, finely grated
1 teaspoon paprika pepper

AMERICAN

For 4–5 people you need:
few beef bones
water
2 onions
2 carrots
1 leek (optional)
seasoning and bouquet garni
Or use instead: 5 cups water and 3–4 beef bouillon cubes *or* 5 cups canned consommé
2–3 teaspoons soup seasoning
1 teaspoon dried parsley
⅔ cup white wine

For the topping:
2–3 small soft bread rolls
3–4 tablespoons butter
¾ cup finely grated cheese
1 teaspoon paprika pepper

1. If using beef bones put these into a pan with water to cover, the vegetables (they need not be cut as they just provide flavour), seasoning and the herbs.
2. Simmer steadily for 2 hours or allow about 40 minutes at 15 lb. pressure in a pressure cooker; allow pressure to drop to room temperature.
3. Strain the liquid carefully to give 2 pints (U.S. 5 cups) and return to the saucepan. Or use water and stock cubes or canned consommé.
4. Add the soup seasoning and dried parsley, heat for 5 minutes.
5. Pour in the white wine. Heat but do not boil, then pour the liquid into hot soup bowls.
6. Top with fingers of the buttered rolls, sprinkle with the cheese and paprika and put under the grill for a few minutes.

NOTE: If the soup bowls are not suitable to be put under a hot grill, butter and top the split rolls, grill then slice and put on to the hot soup and serve.

222

Ragout mit Nudeln und Fisch
Ragoût of noodles and fish

Cooking time: 30 min. **Preparation time:** 30 min. **Main cooking utensils:** 2 saucepans, large frying pan/large skillet.

IMPERIAL	AMERICAN
For 4–6 people you need:	For 4–6 people you need:
1½ lb. potatoes	1½ lb. potatoes
seasoning	seasoning
6 oz. long ribbon noodles	6 oz. long ribbon noodles
4 oz. butter	½ cup butter
2 onions	2 onions
1 lb. white fish	1 lb. white fish
1½ oz. flour	6 tablespoons all-purpose flour
8–12 oz. German garlic sausage	½–¾ lb. German garlic sausage

1. Peel the potatoes, cut into neat dice and simmer steadily in salted water until just tender. Do not overcook—they must be firm enough to hold their shape.
2. Meanwhile, boil the noodles until tender, drain well.
3. Heat the butter in a frying pan, fry the finely chopped onions.
4. Dice the fish and coat in seasoned flour, fry steadily in butter until soft. Add diced sausage, coated in seasoned flour, when the fish is nearly cooked.
5. Blend in the potatoes and noodles. Season well and heat thoroughly.

To serve: Hot as a main dish.

To vary: Heat 2 oz. (U.S. ¼ cup) butter and toss 2 oz. (U.S. 1 cup) coarse breadcrumbs in this, coat the top of the completed dish with the crisp breadcrumbs.

223

Fisch nach Art Atlanticküste
Fish with tomato and bacon

Cooking time: 20 min. **Preparation time:** 15 min. **Main cooking utensils:** heat-resisting dish with lid *or* frying pan/skillet with lid.

IMPERIAL	AMERICAN
For 4–5 people you need:	For 4–5 people you nee
4–5 rashers streaky bacon	4–5 bacon slices
¼ pint sherry *or* red wine	⅔ cup sherry *or* red wine
1¼–1½ lb. fillet white fish	1¼–1½ lb. fillet white fish
seasoning	seasoning
2 teaspoons mild paprika pepper	2 teaspoons mild paprika pepper
1 onion	1 onion
3–4 tomatoes	3–4 tomatoes
2 tablespoons thin cream *or* evaporated milk	3 tablespoons coffee cream *or* evaporated milk
1–2 tablespoons tomato ketchup	1–3 tablespoons tomato catsup
To garnish:	**To garnish:**
chopped parsley	chopped parsley
paprika pepper	paprika pepper

1. Place bacon rashers in heat resistant dish or frying pan. Fry for a few minutes and moisten with sherry or wine.
2. Divide the fish fillet into 4–5 portions.
3. Season with salt, pepper and paprika and put on the bacon.
4. Add thinly sliced onion and skinned, sliced tomatoes.
5. Add the cream or evaporated milk, blended with the tomato ketchup.
6. Cover the dish or pan and simmer very gently for 12–15 minutes—too quick cooking will cause the cream to curdle.
7. Place the fillets and bacon on a serving plate without allowing them to break.
8. Pour the sauce over the fish. Arrange onion and tomatoes round and garnish with lines of chopped parsley and paprika.

To serve: With boiled rice or boiled potatoes.

224

Rindfleisch in Bier
Beef in beer

Cooking time: $1\frac{3}{4}$ hr. **Preparation time:** 15 min. **Main cooking utensils:** saucepan, casserole. **Oven temperature:** very moderate, 325–350°F., 170–180°C., Gas Mark 3. **Oven position:** centre.

IMPERIAL

For 5–6 people you need:
2 lb. brisket, topside of beef *or* rump steak*
1 oz. flour
seasoning
4–6 oz. fat pork *or* bacon
2 onions
$\frac{1}{2}$ pint brown ale
$\frac{1}{2}$ pint water
pinch powdered cloves and nutmeg
2 tablespoons vinegar
1 oz. brown sugar

To garnish:
chopped parsley

AMERICAN

For 5–6 people you need:
2 lb. rolled rump *or* beef brisket
$\frac{1}{4}$ cup all-purpose flour
seasoning
4–6 oz. salt pork *or* bacon slices
2 onions
$1\frac{1}{4}$ cups dark beer
$1\frac{1}{4}$ cups water
dash powdered cloves and nutmeg
3 tablespoons vinegar
2 tablespoons brown sugar, firmly packed

To garnish:
chopped parsley

*If cooking as a whole joint, roll and tie.

1. Cut the meat into neat pieces, roll in seasoned flour.
2. Heat the fat pork or bacon and add pieces of meat and brown; chop and fry onions.
3. Blend in the beer, water, spices, vinegar, brown sugar and seasoning.
4. Bring to the boil and cook until a thickened sauce. Transfer to a casserole.
5. Cover tightly and cook for about $1\frac{1}{2}$ hours.

To serve: From the casserole, topped with parsley. This is excellent with noodles instead of potatoes.

To vary: Use a rolled brisket or topside of beef—allow twice as much liquid, which gives a thinner sauce and cook for $2\frac{1}{2}$ hours in the oven.

225

Rinderschmorbraten
Beef casserole with dumplings

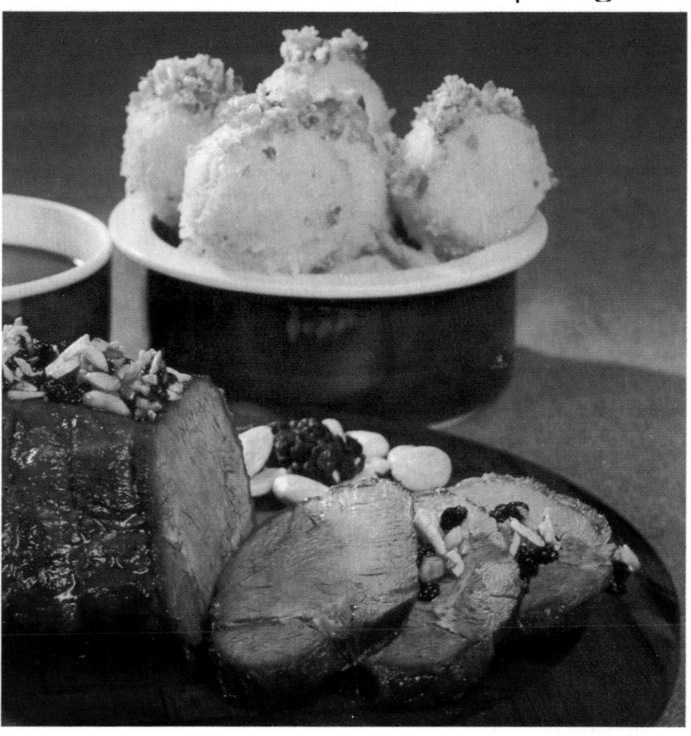

Cooking time: 2 hr. 20 min. **Preparation time:** 30 min. **Main cooking utensils:** 2 saucepans, casserole, ovenproof dish. **Oven temperature:** slow to very moderate, 300–325°F., 150–170°C., Gas Mark 2–3 (see also Stage 6). **Oven position:** centre.

IMPERIAL

For 6 people you need:
seasoning
$2\frac{1}{2}$ lb. topside beef
potato dumplings (Stage 5)

For the marinade:
$\frac{1}{2}$ pint white wine
1 liqueur glass Echte Kroatzbeere

For the casserole:
$1\frac{1}{2}$ oz. flour
2 oz. fat
2 onions, 2 carrots
$\frac{3}{4}$ pint stock, bouquet garni
1 tablespoon tomato purée
peel 1 orange and 1 lemon

To garnish:
4 oz. sultanas
2 oz. almonds
2 liqueur glasses Echte Kroatzbeere

AMERICAN

For 6 people you need:
seasoning
$2\frac{1}{2}$ lb. rolled rump
potato dumplings (Stage 5)

For the marinade:
$1\frac{1}{4}$ cups white wine
1 liqueur glass Echte Kroatzbeere

For the casserole:
6 tablespoons all-purpose flour
$\frac{1}{4}$ cup fat
2 onions, 2 carrots
2 cups stock, bouquet garni
1 tablespoon tomato paste
peel 1 orange and 1 lemon

To garnish:
$\frac{2}{3}$ cup seedless white raisins
$\frac{1}{2}$ cup almonds
2 liqueur glasses Echte Kroatzbeere

1. Season the meat, put in marinade for 1 hour. Lift out, dry and coat in seasoned flour. Brown in hot fat and put in the casserole with remaining ingredients for casserole, chopping vegetables. Add marinade.
2. Cover tightly and cook gently for 2 hours.
3. Plump sultanas--pour on boiling water, leave for a while; drain.
4. Blanch almonds, keep some whole and shred rest. Mix half sultanas with shredded almonds, rest with whole ones, moisten with liqueur.
5. Mash 1 lb. old potatoes, blend with 2 oz. (U.S. $\frac{1}{2}$ cup plus $\frac{1}{2}$ teaspoon B.P.) self-raising flour, 2 oz. (U.S. $\frac{1}{2}$ cup) potato flour, seasoning and an egg. Form into balls with floured hands. Lower into boiling salted water, simmer for 15 minutes. Drain, top with breadcrumbs fried in hot butter.
6. Lift meat from sauce, put on to an ovenproof dish. Top with sultanas and shredded almonds, either brown for 10 minutes in the oven, raising heat to moderately hot, or put under the grill. Serve with whole almonds, sultanas, dumplings and the sauce.

226

Rehkotelett 'Cleopatra'
Venison with fruit

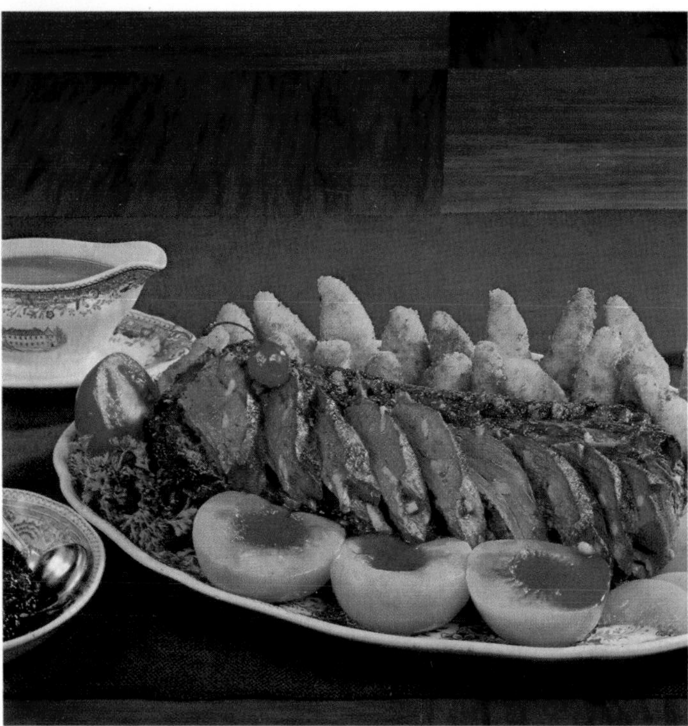

Cooking time: 1½ hr. **Preparation time:** 15 min. **Main cooking utensils:** roasting tin/pan, saucepan, pan for frying croquettes. **Oven temperature:** moderate, 375°F., 190°C., Gas Mark 4–5. **Oven position:** towards top.

IMPERIAL

For 4–6 people you need:
2 lb. back of venison (use mutton when venison unavailable)
seasoning
4 oz. butter
2–3 sticks celery
3 liqueur glasses Echte Kroatzbeere*
½ oz. flour
¼ pint soured cream

To garnish:
1 oz. butter
2–3 liqueur glasses Echte Kroatzbeere*
about 6 halved peaches
little cherry jam, canned Morello *or* red cherries
tomato
parsley
potato croquettes

AMERICAN

For 4–6 people you need:
2 lb. back of venison (use mutton when venison unavailable)
seasoning
½ cup butter
2–3 stalks celery
3 liqueur glasses Echte Kroatzbeere*
2 tablespoons all-purpose flour
⅔ cup sour cream

To garnish:
2 tablespoons butter
2–3 liqueur glasses Echte Kroatzbeere*
about 6 halved peaches
little cherry jam, canned Morello *or* red cherries
tomato
parsley
potato croquettes

*Echte Kroatzbeere is a liqueur made from wild blackberries.

1. Strip the skin from venison, season well. (If liked, lard venison with fat pork or bacon before roasting.)
2. Heat the butter in a roasting tin, add chopped celery, then venison.
3. Pour over the liqueur and roast for about 1½ hours in moderate oven, basting from time to time with butter.
4. Meanwhile, heat the garnish butter in a saucepan, add the liqueur.
5. Slice some of the peaches. Heat thoroughly in butter and liqueur.
6. Lift the venison on to a hot dish and slice thickly.
7. Blend the flour with the fat remaining in the roasting tin (or transfer fat to a saucepan), cook for several minutes, then blend in soured cream and heat gently. Serve as a sauce.

To serve: Arrange sliced and halved peaches round meat, top with jam or cherries. Garnish with parsley, tomato and potato croquettes.

227

Sauerkraut mit Wurst
Sauerkraut and sausage

Cooking time: 40 min. **Preparation time:** 15 min. **Main cooking utensils:** large saucepan, frying pan/skillet.

IMPERIAL

For 4–6 people you need:
For the cabbage mixture:
1 can *or* 1½ lb. prepared sauerkraut*
2 oz. butter
2 onions
½ pint beer
seasoning
pinch mustard
good pinch sugar

For the sausage topping:
12 oz.–1 lb. garlic sausage
2 oz. butter
little mustard
seasoning

To garnish:
cooked carrot balls (optional)

AMERICAN

For 4–6 people you need:
For the cabbage mixture:
1 can *or* 1½ lb. prepared sauerkraut*
¼ cup butter
2 onions
1¼ cups beer
seasoning
dash mustard
dash sugar

For the sausage topping:
¾–1 lb. garlic sausage
¼ cup butter
little mustard
seasoning

To garnish:
cooked carrot balls (optional)

*When preparing sauerkraut always keep top layer covered with salt and little water.

1. Open the can of sauerkraut, drain away liquid well; or drain other sauerkraut.
2. Heat the butter and fry chopped onions until transparent.
3. Add the beer, seasoning, then sauerkraut. Cover the pan and simmer for about 20 minutes. Taste, add extra seasoning and the sugar.
4. Lower the heat, stir well, cover tightly and continue cooking.
5. Meanwhile, slice the sausage and heat in hot butter.
6. Season to taste.

To serve: Arrange the hot sauerkraut, which should have absorbed the liquid, in a hot shallow dish. Top with the sausage and garnish with cooked carrot balls.

228

Nadziewane Papryki
Meat stuffed peppers

Cooking time: 45 min. **Preparation time:** 20 min. plus 30 min. for rolls to stand. **Main cooking utensils:** 2 saucepans, grill/broiler (optional).

IMPERIAL

For 4 people you need:
¼ pint milk
2 medium-sized bread rolls
4 large green peppers
seasoning
1 lb. minced, uncooked meat (all pork *or* all beef *or* a mixture of beef, pork and veal)
1 egg
¼ teaspoon mild paprika pepper
¼–½ teaspoon onion seasoning
good pinch garlic seasoning
1 tablespoon oil

For the sauce:
1 onion
1 oz. butter
1 lb. ripe tomatoes
½ teaspoon mild paprika pepper
small bunch parsley, pinch thyme
¼ pint water
1 oz. flour

AMERICAN

For 4 people you need:
⅔ cup milk
2 medium-sized bread rolls
4 large sweet green peppers
seasoning
1 lb. ground, uncooked meat (all pork *or* beef, *or* a mixture of beef, pork and veal)
1 egg
¼ teaspoon mild paprika pepper
¼–½ teaspoon onion seasoning
dash garlic seasoning
1 tablespoon oil

For the sauce:
1 onion
2 tablespoons butter
1 lb. ripe tomatoes
½ teaspoon mild paprika pepper
small bunch parsley, dash thyme
⅔ cup water
¼ cup all-purpose flour

1. Pour milk over rolls, leave for 30 minutes, mash well.
2. Cut tops off peppers, remove centre core and seeds, wipe carefully.
3. Blend soaked rolls with minced meat, beaten egg and seasonings, put into peppers.
4. Put about ½ pint (U.S. 1¼ cups) salted water and a tablespoon oil in pan, put in peppers, cover tightly, cook for approximately 40 minutes, turn during cooking, then put under grill for 5 minutes to crisp meat stuffing.
5. Meanwhile make sauce: fry chopped onion in butter, add skinned tomatoes, seasoning, paprika, herbs and water.
6. Simmer until soft purée, remove parsley. Sieve, blend with flour, return to pan and thicken; stir well, add water if too thick.

Garnish with lettuce, fresh tomato and parsley. Serve with sauce and cooked rice or potatoes.

229

Hamburger im Stehkragen
Meat patties in a collar

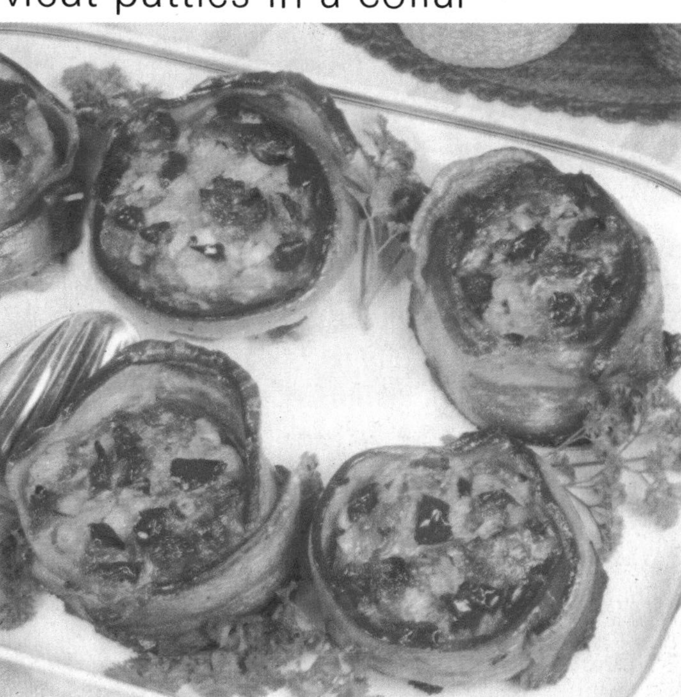

Cooking time: 25 min. **Preparation time:** 20 min. **Main cooking utensils:** frying pan/skillet, roasting tin/pan *or* ovenproof dish. **Oven temperature:** hot, 425–450°F., 220–230°C., Gas Mark 6–7. **Oven position:** above centre.

IMPERIAL

For 6 people you need:
12 oz.–1 lb. beef, good quality topside, rump, point *or* sirloin steak
pinch salt
1 teaspoon mixed spice
1 teaspoon dried parsley
½ large lemon
1 large onion
1 oz. butter
2 large tomatoes
few chives
½–1 teaspoon onion seasoning, onion salt *or* pinch garlic salt
1 teaspoon mild paprika pepper
1½ oz. soft breadcrumbs
1 egg
6 long rashers streaky bacon

To garnish:
sprigs parsley

AMERICAN

For 6 people you need:
¾–1 lb. beef, good quality rolled rump *or* sirloin
dash salt
1 teaspoon mixed spice
1 teaspoon dried parsley
½ large lemon
1 large onion
2 tablespoons butter
2 large tomatoes
few chives
½–1 teaspoon onion seasoning, onion salt *or* dash garlic salt
1 teaspoon mild paprika pepper
¾ cup soft bread crumbs
1 egg
6 long bacon slices

To garnish:
sprigs parsley

1. Mince the beef, blend with salt, spice, parsley, grated lemon rind and 2 teaspoons lemon juice.
2. Chop or grate the onion, fry in the hot butter for a few minutes.
3. Add to the meat with diced (uncooked) tomatoes, finely chopped chives, onion seasoning and paprika.
4. Add the breadcrumbs and egg, bind thoroughly.
5. Form into 6 round flat cakes.
6. Remove rinds from the bacon rashers and wrap each rasher round a meat cake.
7. Secure each with a wooden cocktail stick.
8. Bake until crisp and golden; remove cocktail sticks.
9. Garnish with parsley, which could be fried for a few seconds in very hot fat.

NOTE: This is an excellent way of serving canned corned beef or other meat. Veal or lamb could be used in place of beef in these meat patties.

230

Gefüllte Zwiebel
Stuffed barbecued onions

Cooking time: 1½ hr. **Preparation time:** 20 min. **Main cooking utensils:** 2 saucepans.

IMPERIAL

For 6 people you need:
6 large firm onions
seasoning

For the filling:
1 lb. minced beef
1 green pepper
4 oz. fairly coarse breadcrumbs, preferably brown
3 tablespoons tomato ketchup
seasoning
good pinch cayenne pepper and/*or* chilli powder
few drops Worcestershire sauce
2 oz. butter

For the sauce:
8 oz. cranberries
3 oz. sugar
½ pint water
3–4 tablespoons red cabbage *or* 1 *large* cooking apple

2 oz. Gruyère *or* processed cheese

AMERICAN

For 6 people you need:
6 large firm onions
seasoning

For the filling:
1 lb. ground beef
1 sweet green pepper
1 cup fairly coarse bread crumbs, preferably brown
¼ cup tomato catsup
seasoning
dash cayenne pepper and/*or* chili powder
few drops Worcestershire sauce
¼ cup butter

For the sauce:
½ lb. cranberries
6 tablespoons sugar
1¼ cups water
¼–⅓ cup red cabbage, *or* 1 *large* baking apple

2 oz. Gruyère *or* processed cheese

1. Peel the onions, put in a pan with seasoning and water to cover.
2. Cook steadily for 30 minutes. Drain, take out centres and chop finely.
3. Mix with beef, chopped pepper, crumbs, ketchup, seasoning, cayenne and/or chilli powder, Worcestershire sauce and half of the butter.
4. Press this mixture into the onion cases, put back into pan.
5. Put remaining butter and ½ pint (U.S. 1¼ cups) onion stock into saucepan, cover tightly. Cook gently for 1 hour or until tender.
6. Meanwhile, cook cranberries with sugar and water until a thick sauce. Blend with red cabbage or peel and cut apple into thick slices and add to the sauce. Cook until just tender but unbroken. Turn into the centre of a serving dish.
7. Arrange the onions round the sauce and top with portions of cheese.

231

Früchtehähnchen Amoretti
Fruited chicken

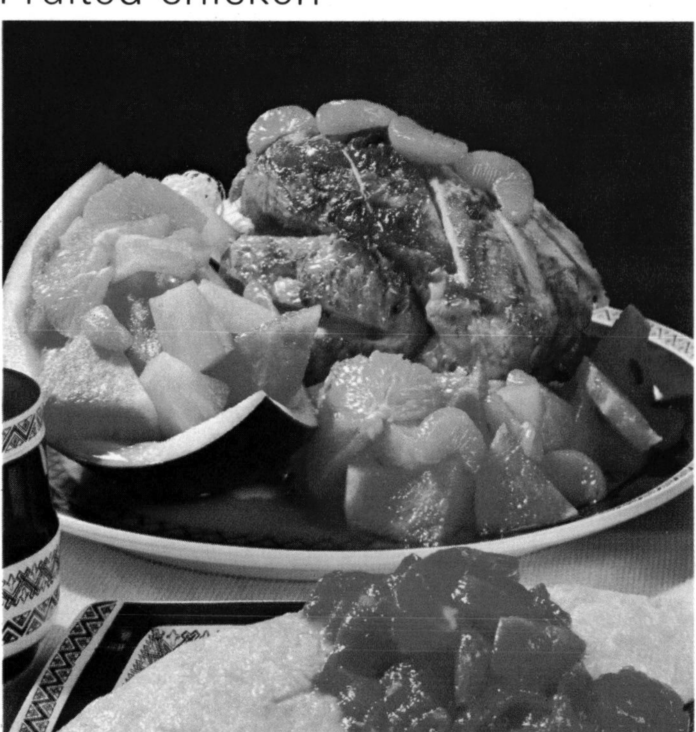

Cooking time: approx. 1¼ hr. see Stage 4. **Preparation time:** 20 min. **Main cooking utensils:** roasting tin/pan, saucepan. **Oven temperature:** hot, 425–450°F., 220–230°C., Gas Mark 6–7 then moderately hot, 400°F., 200°C., Gas Mark 5–6. **Oven position:** centre.

IMPERIAL

For 4–6 people you need:
1 roasting chicken, about 4 lb. when trussed
seasoning
2 oz. butter
3 tablespoons oil

For the fruit topping:
small segment melon
2 bananas
2 apples
1 orange
1 peach
juice ½ lemon
2–3 liqueur glasses Echte Kroatzbeere*
1 can mandarin oranges
slice fresh *or* canned pineapple

AMERICAN

For 4–6 people you need:
1 roasting chicken, about 4 lb. when trussed
seasoning
¼ cup butter
scant ¼ cup oil

For the fruit topping:
small segment melon
2 bananas
2 apples
1 orange
1 peach
juice ½ lemon
2–3 liqueur glasses Echte Kroatzbeere*
1 can mandarin oranges
slice fresh *or* canned pineapple

*Liqueur made from wild blackberries.

1. Wash and dry the chicken. Giblets could be simmered to make a gravy, but as the fruit mixture gives a moist texture it is not really necessary.
2. Season the chicken, blend ½ oz. (U.S. 1 tablespoon) butter with plenty of seasoning, put into body of the bird.
3. Heat the oil in a roasting tin, turn bird in this, roasting first on breast, then on back.
4. This sized bird should take 1¼ hours cooking time; after 45 minutes heat may be reduced to moderately hot.
5. Towards end of cooking time, turn bird breast-side uppermost and cut the breast skin and flesh in a definite pattern as shown in picture.
6. Heat remaining butter in a pan, add diced melon flesh, sliced bananas, apples, orange and peach together with lemon juice and liqueur. Heat for a few minutes.

To serve: Garnish with segments of mandarin oranges. Pile the rest of the fruit round the chicken and into the melon skin.

232

Schinkenkartoffeltorteletts
Bacon in potato cases

Cooking time: 40 min. **Preparation time:** 25 min. **Main cooking utensils:** 2 saucepans, 4 large patty tins/muffin pans *or* individual flan rings. **Oven temperature:** hot, 425–450°F., 220–230°C., Gas Mark 6–7. **Oven position:** above centre.

IMPERIAL

For 4 people you need:*
For the potato cases:
$1\frac{1}{2}$ lb. old potatoes (weight when peeled)
seasoning
2 oz. self-raising *or* plain flour
$\frac{1}{2}$ oz. cornflour
pinch each salt, grated nutmeg, dry *or* chopped marjoram
2 eggs

For the filling:
1 large onion
$1\frac{1}{2}$ oz. cooking fat *or* butter
1 can sauerkraut
8 oz. cooked ham *or* bacon
pepper
2 oz. cheese, grated (optional)

To garnish:
lettuce

AMERICAN

For 4 people you need:*
For the potato cases:
$1\frac{1}{2}$ lb. old potatoes (weight when peeled)
seasoning
$\frac{1}{2}$ cup all-purpose flour
2 tablespoons cornstarch
dash salt, grated nutmeg, dry *or* chopped marjoram
2 eggs

For the filling:
1 large onion
3 tablespoons lard *or* butter
1 can sauerkraut
$\frac{1}{2}$ lb. cooked, cured ham
pepper
$\frac{1}{2}$ cup grated cheese (optional)

To garnish:
lettuce

*This amount can be made into 8 cases and served as an hors d'oeuvre.

1. Boil the potatoes *steadily* in well seasoned water.
2. Strain and mash very carefully, sieve if at all lumpy. Cool.
3. Sieve flour, cornflour, salt and nutmeg, add potatoes and marjoram.
4. Bind with the beaten eggs, adding these gradually.
5. Knead until a smooth dough, then roll lightly and line large patty tins or individual flan rings. Pinch edges or mark with a fork and brush with any remaining egg.
6. Bake for 15 minutes until golden.
7. Meanwhile chop and cook onion in fat until tender, add well-drained sauerkraut, thin strips of ham and plenty of pepper.
8. Heat thoroughly. Put into potato cases and top with grated cheese, if wished. Garnish with lettuce.

To vary: Use diced, cooked poultry or other meat instead of the ham.

233

Lauch-Schinkenauflauf
Leek and bacon savoury

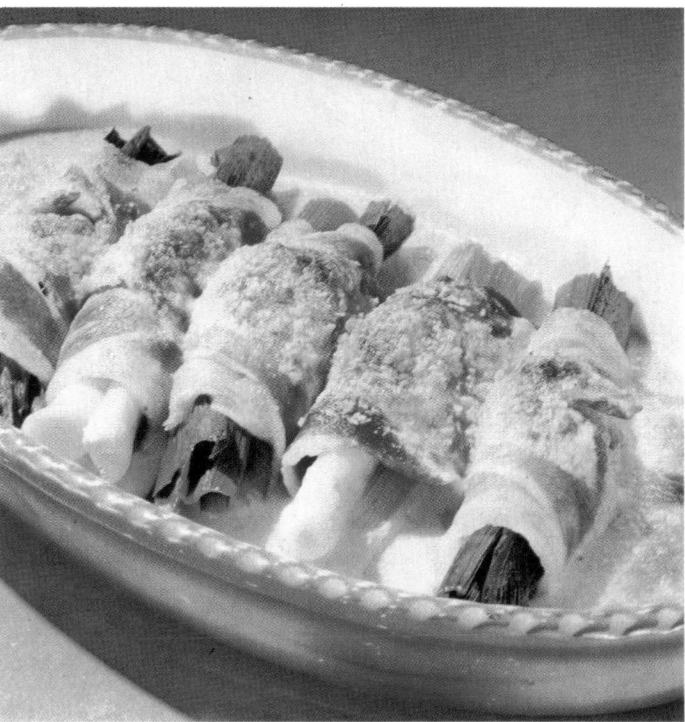

Cooking time: 30 min. **Preparation time:** 15 min. **Main cooking utensils:** saucepan, ovenproof dish. **Oven temperature:** moderate to moderately hot, 375–400°F., 190–200°C., Gas Mark 5. **Oven position:** centre.

IMPERIAL

For 5 people you need:
5 large *or* 10 smaller leeks
seasoning
5 rashers back bacon

1 oz. butter
1 oz. flour
$\frac{1}{4}$ pint milk *or* thin cream
$\frac{1}{4}$ pint leek stock
little grated nutmeg
2 oz. Cheddar *or* Parmesan cheese, finely grated

AMERICAN

For 5 people you need:
5 large *or* 10 smaller leeks
seasoning
5 slices bacon *or* Canadian style bacon
2 tablespoons butter
$\frac{1}{4}$ cup all-purpose flour
$\frac{2}{3}$ cup milk *or* coffee cream
$\frac{2}{3}$ cup leek stock
little grated nutmeg
$\frac{1}{2}$ cup finely grated Cheddar *or* Parmesan cheese

1. Cut tops off the leeks, pull away outer leaves.
2. Wash carefully, simmer in well-seasoned water for 10 minutes until half-cooked.
3. Drain carefully, cool sufficiently to handle.
4. Wrap each leek or pair of smaller leeks in a slice of bacon. Put into the dish.
5. Heat butter, stir in flour and cook for several minutes.
6. Gradually blend in milk or cream, bring to boil. Cook until thickened, adding $\frac{1}{4}$ pint (U.S. $\frac{2}{3}$ cup) leek stock.
7. Season well and add nutmeg. Pour round the bacon and leek rolls.
8. Top with grated cheese and bake for about 20 minutes until the bacon is crisp and leeks are quite tender.

234

Weiss Bohnen Topf

Hot-pot of beans

Cooking time: 2–2½ hr. **Preparation time:** 15 min. plus overnight soaking. **Main cooking utensils:** 2 large saucepans.

IMPERIAL

For 4–5 people you need:
8 oz. haricot beans
2 onions
1 oz. fat
1–2 tablespoons oil
¾–1 pint water
2 tablespoons concentrated tomato purée *or* 4 tomatoes
1 tablespoon green pepper purée *or* ½ green pepper
1–1¼ lb. diced beef *or* mutton
2–3 carrots
2–3 leeks
3–4 sticks celery
2 teaspoons soup seasoning
1 teaspoon mild paprika pepper
pepper
shake garlic powder

To garnish:
dried *or* freshly chopped parsley
cress

AMERICAN

For 4–5 people you need:
½ lb. navy beans
2 onions
2 tablespoons fat
1–3 tablespoons oil
2–2½ cups water
3 tablespoons concentrated tomato paste *or* 4 tomatoes
1 tablespoon sweet green pepper purée *or* ½ sweet green pepper
1–1¼ lb. diced beef *or* mutton
2–3 carrots
2–3 leeks
3–4 stalks celery
2 teaspoons soup seasoning
1 teaspoon mild paprika pepper
pepper
dash garlic powder

To garnish:
dried *or* freshly chopped parsley
cress

1. Cover the beans with cold water and soak overnight.
2. Cook in the water in which they were soaked until tender, about 2 hours; do not season.
3. Meanwhile dice the onions, fry in hot fat and oil until tender, but do not allow to brown.
4. Add the water, tomato purée, green pepper purée or diced green pepper, with diced meat and vegetables.
5. Season with the soup seasoning, paprika, pepper and garlic powder. Do not over-season, for it is better to taste later and adjust this.
6. Cover pan tightly and allow stew to cook gently until the meat and vegetables are tender.
7. Drain the beans and blend with meat mixture. Taste, add more seasoning if necessary.
8. Garnish with the parsley and cress.

235

Spinazie mit Eieren in Nestjes

Eggs and spinach nests

Cooking time: 35 min. **Preparation time:** 35 min. **Main cooking utensils:** 4 saucepans, ovenproof dish. **Oven temperature:** hot, 425–450°F., 220–230°C., Gas Mark 6–7. **Oven position:** above centre.

IMPERIAL

For 4 people you need:
1½ lb. potatoes
1 lb. spinach *or* equivalent in frozen spinach
seasoning
4 eggs

For the sauce:
1 oz. butter
1 oz. flour
12 tablespoons milk
seasoning
little grated nutmeg
3 oz. Edam cheese, grated

To mash potatoes:
1½ oz. butter (save a little for greasing dish)
3 tablespoons milk
little grated nutmeg
tomato ketchup

AMERICAN

For 4 people you need:
1½ lb. potatoes
1 lb. spinach *or* equivalent in frozen spinach
seasoning
4 eggs

For the sauce:
2 tablespoons butter
¼ cup all-purpose flour
1 cup milk
seasoning
little grated nutmeg
¾ cup grated Edam cheese

To mash potatoes:
3 tablespoons butter (save a little for greasing dish)
scant ¼ cup milk
little grated nutmeg
tomato catsup

1. Cook the potatoes steadily.
2. Meanwhile, wash the spinach and cook without additional water, season well.
3. Hard-boil the eggs.
4. Make the sauce, heat the butter in a saucepan, stir in the flour and cook for 2–3 minutes.
5. Gradually blend in the milk and bring to the boil, cook until thickened. Add seasoning and grated nutmeg, finally add the cheese.
6. Mash the potatoes with butter and milk, taste and re-season if necessary, add a little grated nutmeg.
7. Butter an ovenproof dish, either pipe or form potatoes into nest shapes.
8. Brown for 10 minutes in oven.
9. Strain and chop or sieve the spinach.
10. Fill the 'nests' with the sauce, top with the spinach, halved, hard-boiled eggs and a little tomato ketchup.

Kartoffelpuffer
Potato pancakes

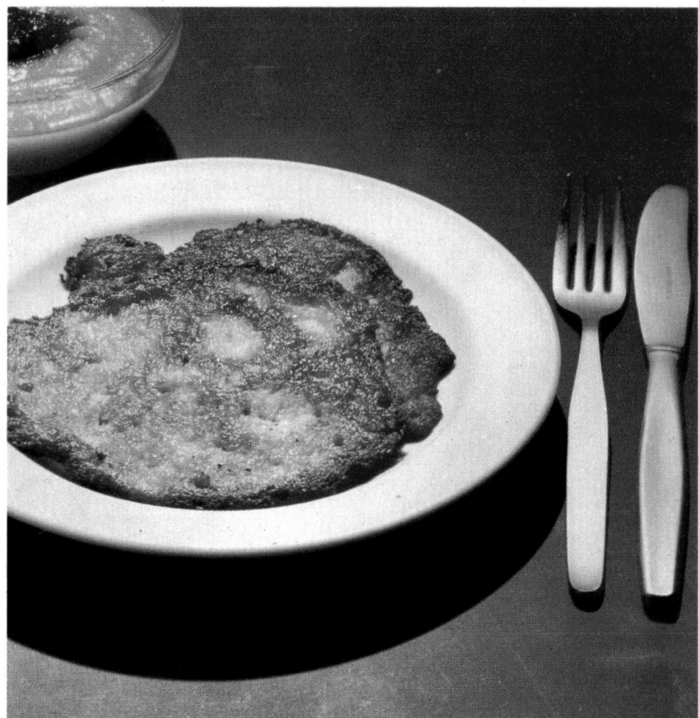

Cooking time: 20 min. **Preparation time:** 15 min. **Main cooking utensils:** frying pan/skillet, 2 saucepans.

IMPERIAL

For 4–6 people you need:
2 lb. raw potatoes
2 large eggs
1 oz. flour *or* use fine breadcrumbs
seasoning
good pinch powdered nutmeg
$\frac{1}{2}$ teaspoon onion seasoning
$\frac{1}{2}$ teaspoon dried parsley

To fry:
4 oz. fat

For the apple sauce:
1 lb. apples
3 oz. sugar
little water
pinch powdered nutmeg

For the cranberry sauce:
8 oz. cranberries
3 oz. sugar
$\frac{1}{4}$ pint water

AMERICAN

For 4–6 people you need:
2 lb. raw potatoes
2 large eggs
$\frac{1}{4}$ cup flour *or* use soft, fine breadcrumbs
seasoning
dash powdered nutmeg
$\frac{1}{2}$ teaspoon onion seasoning
$\frac{1}{2}$ teaspoon dried parsley

To fry:
$\frac{1}{2}$ cup fat

For the apple sauce:
1 lb. apples
6 tablespoons sugar
little water
dash powdered nutmeg

For the cranberry sauce:
$\frac{1}{2}$ lb. cranberries
6 tablespoons sugar
$\frac{2}{3}$ cup water

1. Peel the potatoes and grate coarsely into a bowl.
2. Add the eggs, flour and remaining ingredients.
3. Heat the fat, spoon in enough potato mixture to give a thin coating over pan.
4. Cook steadily on each side until brown and crisp, and the potatoes are cooked; continue in this way.
5. Meanwhile make one or both of the sauces.
6. Peel the apples, simmer with sugar and water. Sieve or beat until a smooth purée; flavour with nutmeg.
7. Put the cranberries into a pan with sugar and water, simmer steadily; it is advisable to keep a lid on the pan as the fruit 'explodes' almost as the skins break. Taste and add more sugar if wished.

To serve: Serve as soon as cooked, as a light dish.

237

Tomaten Torte
Tomato layer gâteau

Cooking time: 1 hr. 10 min. **Preparation time:** 30 min. **Main cooking utensils:** 10–11-inch flan ring and baking tray/sheet, saucepan. **Oven temperature:** hot, 425–450°F., 220–230°C., Gas Mark 6–7 then moderate, 375°F., 190°C., Gas Mark 4–5. **Oven position:** centre.

IMPERIAL

For 8–10 people you need:
For the pastry case:
10 oz. plain flour
good pinch salt, pepper, cayenne pepper, dry mustard and celery salt
5 oz. butter
$1\frac{1}{2}$ oz. Parmesan cheese, grated

2 egg yolks and whites

For the filling:
2 onions
2 oz. butter
$1\frac{1}{4}$ lb. tomatoes
1 lb. finely minced beef
8 oz. Gruyère *or* Emmental cheese
12 oz. tomatoes
8 oz. cheese, sliced

To garnish:
5 medium-sized tomatoes
2–3 oz. cheese
parsley, lettuce

AMERICAN

For 8–10 people you need:
For the pastry case:
$2\frac{1}{2}$ cups all-purpose flour
dash salt, pepper, cayenne pepper, dry mustard and celery salt
$\frac{1}{2}$ cup plus 2 tablespoons butter
3 tablespoons grated Parmesan cheese
2 egg yolks and whites

For the filling:
2 onions
$\frac{1}{4}$ cup butter
$1\frac{1}{4}$ lb. tomatoes
1 lb. finely ground beef
$\frac{1}{2}$ lb. Gruyère *or* Emmental cheese
$\frac{3}{4}$ lb. tomatoes
$\frac{1}{2}$ lb. cheese, sliced

To garnish:
5 medium-sized tomatoes
2–3 oz. cheese
parsley, lettuce

1. Sieve flour with all the seasonings. Rub in butter until mixture resembles fine breadcrumbs, add cheese and bind with yolks and water.
2. Roll out very thinly and line flan ring with pastry.
3. Chop onions very finely and fry until soft in the butter. Add the skinned, chopped tomatoes, meat, diced cheese and season well.
4. Put into the pastry case and bake in a hot oven for approximately 25 minutes to set the pastry, then lower the heat and cook for 25 minutes.
5. Remove flan ring, then brush sides of pastry with egg whites. Top with the sliced tomatoes and cheese and reheat for 10 minutes.
6. Skin and halve remaining tomatoes, arrange on the gâteau with diced cheese and parsley. Serve with lettuce.

238

Gurkensalats

Cucumber salads

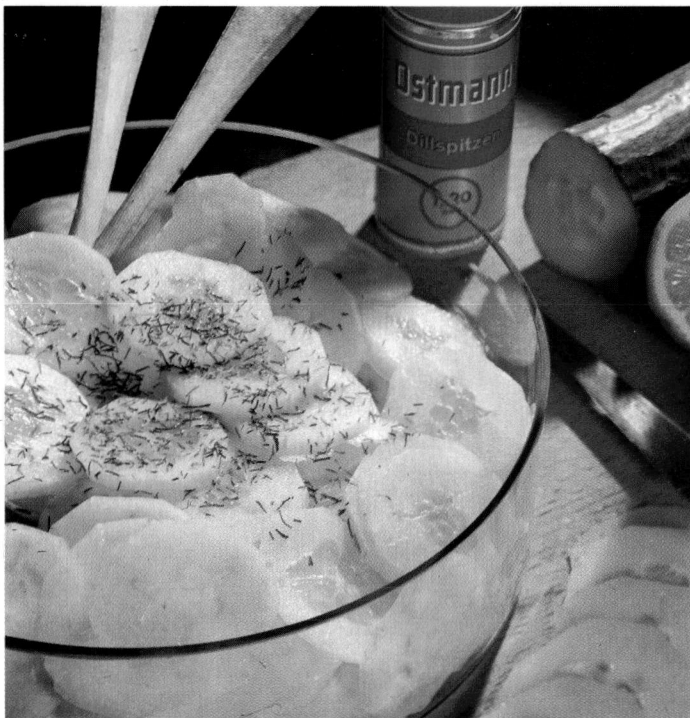

Preparation time: 15 min. each. **Main cooking utensils: A** and **B:** mixing bowl.

IMPERIAL

For 6–8 people you need:

A:
1 cucumber
1½ tablespoons oil
juice 1 lemon
pinch salt
pinch sugar
½ teaspoon onion seasoning *or* finely chopped onion
pinch pepper and paprika pepper
½ teaspoon dried dill
½ teaspoon dried parsley (*or* use fresh herbs)
pinch summer seasoning *or* mixed herbs
extra dried dill

B:
1 cucumber
3 cooked potatoes
1 cooked beetroot
¼ pint soured cream
pinch pepper
¼–½ teaspoon caraway seeds

AMERICAN

For 6–8 people you need:

A:
1 cucumber
2 tablespoons oil
juice 1 lemon
dash salt
dash sugar
½ teaspoon onion seasoning *or* finely chopped onion
dash pepper and paprika pepper
½ teaspoon dried dill
½ teaspoon dried parsley (*or* use fresh herbs)
pinch summer seasoning *or* mixed herbs
extra dried dill

B:
1 cucumber
3 cooked potatoes
1 cooked beet
⅔ cup sour cream
dash pepper
¼–½ teaspoons caraway seeds

A:
1. Peel the cucumber and cut into thin slices.
2. Blend the oil, lemon juice, salt, sugar and various other seasonings.
3. Turn the cucumber in this dressing, allow to stand for at least 30 minutes. Top with more dill.

To serve: With most dishes, hot or cold. Excellent with fish.

B:
1. Peel the cucumber and cut into very thin slices.
2. Slice the cold potatoes thinly, slice or dice the beetroot.
3. Blend with the soured cream, pepper and a few caraway seeds.

To serve: Excellent with pork, duck or other cold meats.

239

Brotkoch

Light breadcrumb mould

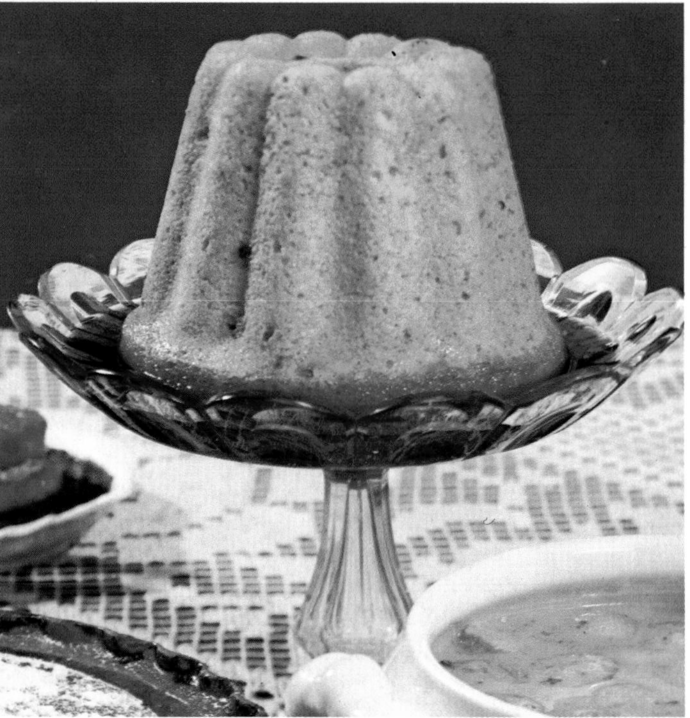

Cooking time: 1½ hr. **Preparation time:** 20 min. **Main cooking utensils:** 2-pint/2½-pint basin *or* heat-resistant mould, steamer, saucepan, greaseproof paper *or* foil.

IMPERIAL

For 6–8 people you need:
3 oz. fine soft breadcrumbs
4 tablespoons thin cream
4 eggs
4 oz. castor sugar
2 oz. self-raising flour
2 oz. blanched almonds
3 oz. dried fruit *or* chopped candied peel
1 oz. butter, melted
2 tablespoons brandy *or* orange juice

For the sauce:
8 oz. jam *or* jelly *or* ½ pint thick fruit purée
1 tablespoon brandy
¼ pint water
1 teaspoon cornflour *or* potato flour

AMERICAN

For 6–8 people you need:
1½ cups fine soft bread crumbs
⅓ cup coffee cream
4 eggs
½ cup granulated sugar
½ cup all-purpose flour sifted with ½ teaspoon baking powder
scant ½ cup blanched almonds
½ cup dried fruit *or* chopped candied peel
2 tablespoons melted butter
3 tablespoons brandy *or* orange juice

For the sauce:
½ lb. jam *or* jelly *or* 1¼ cups thick fruit pulp
1 tablespoon brandy
⅔ cup water
1 teaspoon cornstarch *or* potato flour

1. Put crumbs into a basin with the cream. Leave for 10 minutes, then beat with a fork until soft.
2. Separate egg yolks from whites, beat the yolks with half the sugar until thick and creamy.
3. Blend the flour into the crumb mixture, together with chopped nuts, fruit or peel, melted butter and brandy. Blend with egg yolk mixture.
4. Whisk egg whites until very stiff, then beat in half the remaining sugar, fold in the rest.
5. Add the meringue mixture gently and carefully to remainder of the ingredients.
6. Put into a very well greased mould and cover with greased paper or foil, allow room for the pudding to rise. Steam until firm.

To serve: Hot with the sauce, made by blending all the ingredients together in a pan and simmering until smooth and thickened.

240

Gewurz Kekse
Spiced cakes

Cooking time: 15–20 min. **Preparation time:** 25 min. **Main cooking utensils:** baking trays/sheets, double saucepan. **Oven temperature:** very moderate to moderate, 350–375°F., 180–190°C., Gas Mark 4. **Oven position:** above centre.

IMPERIAL

For about 12 biscuit-like cakes you need:
8 oz. flour, preferably plain
1 teaspoon baking powder
6 oz. butter
4 oz. nuts; almonds, walnuts, pine nuts *or* hazelnuts
3 oz. sugar
pinch paprika pepper, powdered ginger, cloves and coriander
$\frac{1}{4}$–$\frac{1}{2}$ teaspoon powdered aniseed
2 oz. vanilla sugar *or* use 2 oz. sugar and $\frac{1}{2}$ teaspoon vanilla essence
$\frac{1}{2}$ large *or* small lemon

To glaze and decorate:
1 egg
1–2 oz. granulated sugar
2–3 oz. plain chocolate

honeycake spices

AMERICAN

For about 12 biscuit-like cakes you need:
2 cups all-purpose flour
1 teaspoon baking powder
$\frac{3}{4}$ cup butter
1 cup nuts; almonds, walnuts, pine nuts *or* hazelnuts
6 tablespoons sugar
dash paprika pepper, powdered ginger, cloves, and coriander
$\frac{1}{4}$–$\frac{1}{2}$ teaspoon anise seed
$\frac{1}{4}$ cup vanilla sugar *or* use $\frac{1}{4}$ cup sugar and $\frac{1}{2}$ teaspoon vanilla extract
$\frac{1}{2}$ large *or* small lemon

To glaze and decorate:
1 egg
2–4 tablespoons sugar
$\frac{1}{3}$–$\frac{1}{2}$ cup semi-sweet chocolate pieces
honeycake spices

1. Sieve the flour and baking powder into a bowl.
2. Rub in the butter, do this lightly as there is a high percentage of fat in this recipe.
3. Roughly chop the nuts, then add with sugar, spices, vanilla sugar and grated lemon rind and juice. If lemon is very juicy, do not use it all. Dough should be soft enough to form into a roll 2 inches in diameter. If too soft to cut, put into a cold place for 1 hour.
4. Cut into slices about $\frac{1}{3}$-inch thick. Place on lightly greased trays, allowing room for mixture to spread slightly in cooking.
5. Brush with beaten egg or egg yolk and sprinkle with sugar.
6. Bake until firm round the edges and allow to cool thoroughly.
7. Melt chocolate, a pinch of German honeycake spices could be added to the chocolate.
8. Put into a piping bag with fine writing pipe, No. 1 or 2. Pipe lines on part of the cakes.

241

Weihnacht Plätzchen
Christmas butter biscuits

Cooking time: 15 min. **Preparation time:** 35 min. **Main cooking utensils:** baking trays/sheets, wire rack. **Oven temperature:** very moderate to moderate, 350–375°F., 180–190°C., Gas Mark 4. **Oven position:** centre.

IMPERIAL

For approx. 36–48 biscuits you need:
8 oz. butter
8 oz. sugar
2 eggs
1 lb. flour, preferably plain
pinch salt
good pinch powdered pimento, coriander, aniseed
grated rind and juice $\frac{1}{2}$ lemon

To decorate:
little jam
8 oz. icing sugar

few drops rum
little lemon juice
currants
raisins
chocolate

AMERICAN

For approx. 36–48 biscuits you need:
1 cup butter
generous 1 cup sugar
2 eggs
1 lb. all-purpose flour
dash salt
dash powdered pimento, coriander, anise seed
grated rind and juice $\frac{1}{2}$ lemon

To decorate:
little jam
scant 2 cups sifted confectioners' sugar
few drops rum
little lemon juice
currants
raisins
chocolate

1. Cream the butter and sugar until soft.
2. Beat in the eggs, then add flour sieved with salt and spices, the finely grated lemon rind and juice.
3. Knead the mixture very well, then take portions of the dough, roll thinly (this is easier than trying to roll out all the dough at once).
4. Cut into required shapes, those shown in the picture are various animals, birds, rounds and some rings.
5. Bake on ungreased baking trays until just firm. Leave on the trays until nearly cold. Cool on a rack.
6. When quite cold, store in airtight tins until ready to decorate and fill.
7. Spread some plain rounds with jam.
8. Blend half the sieved icing sugar with rum, and half with lemon juice. Spread over ring biscuits, allow to set.
9. Lift iced rings over jam-covered biscuits. Complete decoration of other biscuits by pressing on currants and raisins and piping tiny dots and lines of melted chocolate.

The flat scenery of Holland, crisscrossed with canals and tree-lined avenues, has a prosperous, restful atmosphere. Life in the cities is always bustling, but apart from the modern farms, much of the countryside has remained virtually unchanged for centuries.

The Dutch are a friendly and hospitable people, always ready to invite you into their neat, cosy homes—you would never guess from it's invariably spotless condition how much the Dutch housewife uses her kitchen. Dutch women are exemplary in the domestic arts, not only in looking after their houses so beautifully but also in providing their families with good balanced meals. The day begins with a substantial breakfast of brown and white bread with slices of cheese and cold meat, jam and grated chocolate or chocolate vermicelli. Coffee or tea is served, tea being drunk more often in Holland than in most continental countries, usually sweetened and without milk.

Lunch is similar to breakfast with the addition of a salad or vegetable dish. Dairy farming is central to the Dutch economy and eggs and cheese, particularly the famous Edam and Gouda, feature in much of the cooking. Cheese complements many other ingredients; Mussels with cheese, for example, is an unusual and tasty combination. Stuffed vegetables with cheese, like Meat and cheese stuffed peppers and Stuffed cucumbers, are particularly good and different when entertaining.

The Dutch enjoy German sausages and dumplings and such Scandinavian specialities as pickled fish and Danish open sandwiches. Thus it is not surprising to find dishes like Rollmop herring salad and Savoury meats and sauerkraut on a typical Dutch menu.

Pies and pastries are often eaten in Holland, either for dessert or later in the evening at about nine, when it is the custom to serve tea. Apple pastries are particular favourites, like the Apple lattice tarts resembling dainty apple dumplings and the attractive Apple cake with an apricot glaze. Cherry flan, using dark Morello cherries, is made with a crumbly pastry base and decorated with piped whipped cream. Finally, *Boterletter*, a rich pastry with an almond filling, is traditionally served on December 6th, St. Nicholas' Day, which marks the beginning of the Christmas season in Holland.

Appel-bieten slaatje
Apple beetroot salad

Cooking time: 10 min. **Preparation time:** 15 min. **Main cooking utensil:** saucepan.

IMPERIAL

For 4 people you need:
4 eggs
1 lettuce
1 large cooked beetroot
2 dessert apples
juice 1 lemon

For the dressing:
seasoning
pinch sugar
little made mustard
2 tablespoons oil
2 tablespoons lemon juice

To garnish:
1 lemon
chopped parsley

AMERICAN

For 4 people you need:
4 eggs
1 lettuce
1 large cooked beet
2 eating apples
juice 1 lemon

For the dressing:
seasoning
dash sugar
little prepared mustard
3 tablespoons oil
3 tablespoons lemon juice

To garnish:
1 lemon
chopped parsley

1. Boil the eggs for 10 minutes, until firm. Crack the shells and plunge them into cold water to prevent a dark line forming round the yolks.
2. Wash the lettuce, shake dry in a salad shaker, or dry in a tea cloth—do not press hard or you will bruise it.
3. Skin the beetroot, cut into neat pieces or grate coarsely.
4. Peel the apples, cut into neat fingers, toss in lemon juice to prevent them turning brown.
5. Put the beetroot into a bowl, toss in the dressing. To make dressing, blend all ingredients together.
6. Cut the eggs into halves, remove yolks from 3 eggs, sieve or chop these. Cut a neat slice from the fourth egg and sieve or chop the rest of the yolk.
7. Chop the whites of the eggs fairly coarsely.

To serve: Put the lettuce on a dish, arrange the beetroot and apple, then the egg yolks and whites. Garnish with a slice of egg, lemon and parsley. Excellent as a light first course.

Kaas snacks
Cheese bites

It is possible to make very speedy appetizers with cheese and the picture gives suggestions for some of these together with an attractive way of serving them. Allow 4–6 per person. Always choose a firm cheese if putting it on to cocktail sticks. Edam and Gouda cheeses are ideal.

CHEESE AND FRUIT

Cut neat shapes in the cheese and spear with **a)** cubes *or* balls of melon; **b)** slices of banana dipped in lemon juice to keep them white; **c)** banana as b) but then rolled in finely chopped nuts; **d)** pieces of well-drained canned *or* fresh pineapple; **e)** segments of fresh *or* canned oranges; **f)** small *or* halved de-seeded grapes; **g)** glacé/candied *or* maraschino cherries—either by themselves or with other fruits.

CHEESE AND MEAT

Spear the cheese with **a)** cubes of ham; **b)** tongue; **c)** chicken, dipped in mayonnaise then rolled in chopped nuts; **d)** sliced, cooked sausages and pieces of salami.

CHEESE AND FISH

a) Top whirls of smoked salmon with the cheese. Mix cheese with **b)** prawns; **c)** smoked egg balls made with smoked, cooked haddock blended with a little mayonnaise and rolled in chopped, hard-boiled egg and parsley; **d)** neat pieces of smoked eel lightly dipped in horseradish cream then topped with chopped parsley and paprika pepper.

CHEESE AND PRESERVES

Blend the cheese with **a)** slices of preserved ginger; **b)** crystallized fruits such as pineapple and apricots; **c)** well-drained pickled onions and/*or* gherkins; **d)** black, green (stoned) *or* stuffed olives; **e)** nuts (these must be speared carefully with the cocktail stick so they do not break).

To keep appetizers moist

Prepare the food, put into the dish or press into a cabbage covered with foil as shown. Cover loosely with foil or slip the food inside large polythene bags or cover with damp kitchen paper.

NOTE: Not all the suggestions given are shown in the picture.

244

Haring kaassla
Rollmop herring salad

Cooking time: dependent on vegetables, approx. 15 min. **Preparation time:** 15 min. **Main cooking utensil:** saucepan.

IMPERIAL

For 6 people you need:
6 oz. diced root vegetables *or* small packet frozen, mixed vegetables
6 oz. fresh, frozen *or* canned peas

6 oz. Gouda cheese
1 apple
small head *or* part larger head celery
6 large *or* 12 small gherkins
seasoning
5 tablespoons mayonnaise
6 rollmop herrings

To garnish:
6 oz. black grapes
parsley

AMERICAN

For 6 people you need:
1 cup diced root vegetables *or* small package frozen, mixed vegetables
1 cup fresh, frozen *or* canned peas
6 oz. Gouda cheese
1 apple
small bunch *or* part larger bunch celery
6 large *or* 12 sweet dill pickles
seasoning
6 tablespoons mayonnaise
6 rollmop herrings

To garnish:
1 cup purple grapes
parsley

1. Cook the vegetables until tender, strain carefully. If using canned peas, heat gently, strain and then blend with the cooked, diced root vegetables.
2. Dice the cheese, apple, celery and gherkins.
3. Mix with the peas, mixed vegetables and seasoning.
4. Blend with the mayonnaise and pile on a long dish.
5. Arrange well-drained rollmops over the top.
6. Garnish with halved, stoned grapes and parsley.

To serve: As an hors d'oeuvre or light dish for luncheon or supper.

To make your own rollmops: Clean 6–8 herrings, fillet if large. Soak for 2–4 hours, dependent upon size, in brine made from 2 oz. (U.S. $\frac{1}{4}$ cup) salt and 1 pint (U.S. $2\frac{1}{2}$ cups) water. Drain well, put into dish and cover with malt vinegar. Boil more vinegar with pickling spice. Pack herrings in jars with spiced vinegar, bay leaves, chilli pepper and gherkins/sweet dill pickles.

245

Mosselen met kaas
Mussels with cheese

Cooking time: 20 min. **Preparation time:** 20 min. **Main cooking utensils:** large saucepan, ovenproof dish.

IMPERIAL

For 4–6 people you need:
2 pints mussels
1 onion
6 sticks celery
salt
8 oz. tomatoes
4 oz. Gouda cheese

To garnish:
parsley

AMERICAN

For 4–6 people you need:
$2\frac{1}{2}$ pints mussels
1 onion
6 stalks celery
salt
$\frac{1}{2}$ lb. tomatoes
$\frac{1}{4}$ lb. Gouda cheese

To garnish:
parsley

1. Clean the mussels in cold water, discard any that will not close when tapped sharply.
2. Place the mussels in a pan with chopped onion, celery and salt.
3. Cover, bring to the boil and simmer until all the shells are open.
4. Remove from the heat and drain. When cool, remove mussels from shells and discard half the shells and weed from the mussels.
5. Skin the tomatoes, remove pips and chop fleshy part finely.
6. Place each mussel in one half of a shell and arrange on a dish.
7. Blend the chopped tomatoes, seasoning and finely grated cheese.
8. Spread the tomato mixture over the mussels.
9. Brown under the grill and garnish with parsley.

To serve: Hot as a light luncheon or supper dish with green salad.

To vary: Canned mussels could be used. Heat, then drain and put in a dish, top with tomato mixture and brown under the grill.

Another way of serving the ingredients above is to omit the onion and celery when cooking the mussels. Then fry the celery and 2 onions. Put this cooked vegetable purée with tomatoes on to the mussels, then add the cheese and brown under grill.

246

Spaghetti met varkensvlees
Spaghetti with pork chops

Cooking time: 30 min. **Preparation time:** 25 min. **Main cooking utensils:** large frying pan/skillet, 2 saucepans, ovenproof dish. **Oven temperature:** hot, 425–450°F., 220–230°C., Gas Mark 6–7. **Oven position:** above centre.

IMPERIAL

For 5 people you need:
5 good-sized pork chops
seasoning
1 oz. flour
4 oz. butter *or* margarine
1 lb. small onions
3 tablespoons concentrated tomato purée
2 teaspoons paprika pepper
$\frac{1}{2}$ pint water *or* stock
$1\frac{1}{2}$ lb. Brussels sprouts*
8 oz. spaghetti
extra 2 oz. butter

To garnish:
paprika pepper

AMERICAN

For 5 people you need:
5 good-sized pork chops
seasoning
$\frac{1}{4}$ cup all-purpose flour
$\frac{1}{2}$ cup butter *or* margarine
1 lb. small onions
$\frac{1}{4}$ cup concentrated tomato paste
2 teaspoons paprika pepper
$1\frac{1}{4}$ cups water *or* stock
$1\frac{1}{2}$ lb. Brussels sprouts*
$\frac{1}{2}$ lb. spaghetti
extra $\frac{1}{4}$ cup butter

To garnish:
paprika pepper

*Instead of serving sprouts with this dish, cook sauerkraut. Wash sauerkraut well in cold water, simmer in seasoned water for about 1 hour, drain and toss in melted butter.

1. Trim the pork chops, if necessary cut off excess fat.
2. Coat in seasoned flour.
3. Heat the butter or margarine with any pieces of pork fat.
4. Fry the chops in this until golden brown. Lift out and transfer to oven and cook for about 20 minutes.
5. Put the peeled onions in butter remaining in pan, turn until golden coloured. Add tomato purée and paprika pepper blended with water or stock.
6. Simmer gently until tender, about 20 minutes, season well.
7. Meanwhile, cook the sprouts and spaghetti until tender, drain and toss both sprouts and spaghetti in butter. Sprinkle spaghetti with paprika.

247

Zuurkool met rookworst

Savoury meats and sauerkraut

Cooking time: 1 hr. 5 min. **Preparation time:** 20 min. **Main cooking utensils:** saucepan, frying pan/skillet.

IMPERIAL

For 4 people you need:
1½ lb. sauerkraut *or* use ordinary cabbage
seasoning
2 medium-sized onions
1 medium-sized apple
4 oz. butter
nutmeg
about 8 oz. salami *or* garlic sausage, *or* 4 oz. piece bacon and 4 oz. salami
about 8 oz. small sausages *or* frankfurters
about 12 oz. veal *or* pork, cut from top of leg
¼ pint soured cream *or* thin cream with 2 teaspoons lemon juice

2 teaspoons peppercorns
1–2 teaspoons French mustard

AMERICAN

For 4 people you need:
1½ lb. sauerkraut *or* use ordinary cabbage
seasoning
2 medium-sized onions
1 medium-sized apple
½ cup butter
nutmeg
about ½ lb. salami *or* garlic sausage, *or* ¼ lb. bacon and ¼ lb. salami
about ½ lb. small sausages *or* frankfurters
about ¾ lb. veal *or* pork, cut from top of leg
⅔ cup sour cream *or* coffee cream with 2 teaspoons lemon juice
2 teaspoons peppercorns
1–2 teaspoons French mustard

1. Rinse the sauerkraut in fresh cold water. Put into a pan with fresh water and seasoning to taste. Simmer until tender, about 1 hour, or cook shredded cabbage in the usual way.
2. Drain, blend with chopped onions and finely chopped apple, both fried in half the hot butter in the pan, a little extra pepper and light sprinkling of grated nutmeg.
3. Meanwhile slice the salami and bacon, if used, prick sausages, cut veal or pork into neat pieces.
4. Fry the veal, sausages and bacon in butter until tender, turning to brown evenly. Add sliced salami and frankfurters, if used, near end of cooking time.
5. Put the sauerkraut on a hot dish, top with meats.
6. Stir soured cream into the frying pan together with a few peppercorns and mustard. Heat.

To serve: Pour cream sauce over meat and sauerkraut or serve separately.

248

Gevulde paprika's

Meat and cheese stuffed peppers

Cooking time: 1 hr. **Preparation time:** 20 min. **Main cooking utensils:** 2 saucepans, ovenproof dish. **Oven temperature:** moderate, 375°F., 190°C., Gas Mark 4–5. **Oven position:** centre.

IMPERIAL

For 6 people you need:
6 large firm green peppers
seasoning
2 onions
8 oz. carrots
1–2 cloves garlic
1 lb. raw good quality minced steak *or* roasting meat
1 tablespoon oil

For the topping:
1 oz. butter
1 oz. Gouda cheese, grated

For the sauce:
2 oz. butter
2 oz. flour
1 pint milk
4 oz. Gouda cheese, grated

AMERICAN

For 6 people you need:
6 large firm sweet green peppers
seasoning
2 onions
½ lb. carrots
1–2 cloves garlic
1 lb. raw, good quality ground beef *or* roasting meat
1 tablespoon oil

For the topping:
2 tablespoons butter
¼ cup grated Gouda cheese

For the sauce:
¼ cup butter
½ cup all-purpose flour
2½ cups milk
1 cup grated Gouda cheese

1. Cut tops off the peppers and remove cores and seeds.
2. Boil the peppers in salted water for 5 minutes.
3. Remove from the water and drain well.
4. Chop the peeled onions and carrots and crush the garlic, then fry slowly with the beef in the hot oil for 20 minutes.
5. Season well and press this mixture into the peppers.
6. Put into a buttered dish and top each pepper with a little butter and cheese.
7. Heat butter for the sauce in a pan, stir in the flour, cook for several minutes.
8. Gradually blend in the milk, bring to the boil. Cook until thickened then add the grated cheese and seasoning.
9. Pour round peppers, bake for 30–40 minutes.

To serve: With boiled rice. Garnish with tomato.

249

Knolselderij met ham

Celery hearts with ham

Cooking time: 15–20 min. **Preparation time:** 20 min. plus time for celery and salad dressing to cool. **Main cooking utensils:** 2 saucepans.

IMPERIAL

For 4 people you need:
2 medium-sized heads celery

For the cooked mayonnaise:
2 oz. butter
1 oz. flour
$\frac{1}{4}$ pint celery stock
$\frac{1}{4}$ pint thin cream
1 teaspoon French mustard
seasoning, pinch sugar
2 egg yolks
$\frac{1}{2}$ teaspoon finely grated lemon rind
2 tablespoons lemon juice *or* vinegar

For the topping:
6–8 oz. cooked ham, cut in 2 thick slices
3 gherkins (optional)

To garnish:
chopped parsley
2–3 tomatoes

AMERICAN

For 4 people you need:
2 medium-sized bunches celery

For the cooked mayonnaise:
$\frac{1}{4}$ cup butter
$\frac{1}{4}$ cup all-purpose flour
$\frac{2}{3}$ cup celery stock
$\frac{2}{3}$ cup coffee cream
1 teaspoon French mustard
seasoning, dash sugar
2 egg yolks
$\frac{1}{2}$ teaspoon finely grated lemon rind
3 tablespoons lemon juice *or* vinegar

For the topping:
$\frac{1}{3}$–$\frac{1}{2}$ lb. cooked ham, cut in 2 thick slices
3 sweet dill pickles (optional)

To garnish:
chopped parsley
2–3 tomatoes

1. Wash the celery and cut away tops of stalks.
2. Divide each head to give 4 portions of celery.
3. Cook in well-seasoned, boiling water until tender, drain.
4. To make the mayonnaise sauce, heat the butter, stir in the flour and cook for several minutes.
5. Gradually add stock and cream. Stir, cook until thickened.
6. Stir in mustard, seasoning, sugar, beaten yolks, rind and juice.
7. Cook for a few minutes *without boiling*, then cover with damp paper to prevent skin forming and cool.
8. Dice ham and gherkins, blend with mayonnaise.

To serve: Arrange celery in a serving dish, top with ham mixture; garnish. This makes an excellent hors d'oeuvre or light dish.

250

Gevulde komkommer

Stuffed cucumbers

Cooking time: 10–15 min. **Preparation time:** 15 min. **Main cooking utensils:** 2 saucepans.

IMPERIAL

For 6 people you need:
2 medium-sized young cucumbers*
seasoning
1 oz. butter

For the filling:
1 oz. butter
1 oz. flour
just under $\frac{1}{2}$ pint milk
seasoning
pinch paprika pepper
squeeze lemon juice
2 tablespoons thick cream
5–6 oz. Gouda *or* Edam cheese

To garnish:
parsley

AMERICAN

For 6 people you need:
2 medium-sized young cucumbers*
seasoning
2 tablespoons butter

For the filling:
2 tablespoons butter
$\frac{1}{4}$ cup all-purpose flour
just under $1\frac{1}{4}$ cups milk
seasoning
dash paprika pepper
squeeze lemon juice
3 tablespoons whipping cream
5–6 oz. Gouda *or* Edam cheese

To garnish:
parsley

*If the skin is tough, either remove or simmer cucumber for a short time to soften. Sprinkle with lemon juice, if wished, before filling.

This unusual method of serving cucumber makes a delicious hors d'oeuvre.

1. Wash the cucumber, do not peel. Cut into 3–4-inch lengths, then cut these in halves.
2. Scoop out the centre pulp, chop finely.
3. Simmer for 5–8 minutes in salted water, do not over-cook as it should still be fairly firm.
4. Melt the butter in a pan, stir in flour and cook for several minutes.
5. Blend in milk, bring to the boil, cook until thickened. Add seasoning, paprika, lemon juice, cucumber pulp, cream and diced cheese.

To serve: Toss drained cucumber in well-seasoned butter, pile cheese mixture on top. Serve hot garnished with a little chopped parsley, and a few sprigs.

To vary: Fry crushed clove garlic in butter when making sauce.
Add shelled prawns or shrimps as well as the diced cheese.
Add flaked, cooked fish or diced, cooked ham or chicken.

251

Appelen in zandtaartdeeg
Apple lattice tarts

Cooking time: 40 min. **Preparation time:** 20 min. **Main cooking utensil:** baking tray/sheet *or* ovenproof dish. **Oven temperature:** moderately hot, 400°F., 200°C., Gas Mark 5–6, then very moderate, 350°F., 180°C., Gas Mark 3–4. **Oven position:** centre.

IMPERIAL

For 4 people you need:
4 medium-sized good cooking apples
lemon juice
2 tablespoons apricot jam
2 oz. chopped candied peel

For the pastry:
6 oz. flour, preferably plain
pinch salt
3 oz. butter
1 oz. sugar
water to mix

For the glaze:
1 egg
little sugar
1–2 tablespoons sieved apricot jam
1 tablespoon water

AMERICAN

For 4 people you need:
4 medium-sized good baking apples
lemon juice
3 tablespoons apricot jam
$\frac{1}{3}$ cup chopped candied peel

For the pastry:
$1\frac{1}{2}$ cups all-purpose flour
dash salt
6 tablespoons butter
2 tablespoons sugar
water to mix

For the glaze:
1 egg
little sugar
1–3 tablespoons sieved apricot jam
1 tablespoon water

1. Peel and core the apples, sprinkle with lemon juice to keep them a good colour.
2. Fill centres with apricot jam and peel (other dried fruit may also be added).
3. To make the pastry, sieve flour with the salt, rub in butter. Add sugar and enough water to bind.
4. Roll out the pastry and cut into 12 long strips.
5. Put the apples on to a well-greased baking tray or dish, top with the lattice of pastry. Brush with beaten egg and sprinkle very lightly with the sugar.
6. Bake for approximately 20 minutes in a moderately hot oven to set the pastry, then lower the heat to very moderate to make sure the apples are tender.
7. Dissolve jam in hot water, brush over apples. Serve with cream or custard.

252

Limburgse vlaai
Cherry flan

Cooking time: 40 min. **Preparation time:** 20 min. **Main cooking utensils:** 10-inch sandwich tin/layer cake pan, saucepan. **Oven temperature:** moderate, 375°F., 190°C., Gas Mark 4–5. **Oven position:** centre.

IMPERIAL

For 6–8 portions you need:
For the pastry:
4 oz. butter
6 oz. plain flour
pinch salt
2 oz. castor sugar
1 egg yolk

For the filling:
1 (1 lb. 2 oz.) can black *or* Morello cherries*
$1\frac{1}{2}$ teaspoons arrowroot
$\frac{1}{4}$ pint cherry juice from can
1 tablespoon cherry brandy

To decorate:
$\frac{1}{2}$ pint thick cream

AMERICAN

For 6–8 portions you need:
For the pastry:
$\frac{1}{2}$ cup butter
$1\frac{1}{2}$ cups all-purpose flour
dash salt
$\frac{1}{4}$ cup granulated sugar
1 egg yolk

For the filling:
1 (1 lb.2 oz.) can Bing *or* Morello cherries*
$1\frac{1}{2}$ teaspoons cornstarch
$\frac{2}{3}$ cup cherry juice from can
1 tablespoon cherry brandy

To decorate:
$1\frac{1}{4}$ cups whipping cream

*Or use 1 lb. fresh black or Morello cherries—cook gently in syrup of $\frac{1}{2}$ pint (U.S. $1\frac{1}{4}$ cups) water and 3–5 oz. (U.S. 6–10 tablespoons) sugar.

1. Make the pastry base by rubbing the butter into sieved flour and salt until mixture resembles breadcrumbs.
2. Add the sugar, bind with egg yolk; use no liquid.
3. Press into a well-buttered tin, prick bottom with fork.
4. Bake for 30 minutes in a moderate oven.
5. Leave for 10 minutes to cool slightly before removing from tin.
6. Drain and stone the cherries: this may be done with a proper cherry stoner or the bent end of a fine new hairpin.
7. Arrange over the cold pastry base to within about 1 inch of the edge.
8. Blend the arrowroot with cherry juice and heat until the glaze thickens, stirring well.
9. Stir in the cherry brandy when thickened.
10. Cool slightly, then spread with a spoon, knife or brush over the cherries.
11. When quite cold, decorate with a border of piped, whipped cream.

Appelkoek
Apple cake

Cooking time: 40–45 min. **Preparation time:** 20 min. **Main cooking utensils:** Swiss roll tin/jelly roll pan, greaseproof paper/wax paper, saucepan. **Oven temperature:** moderate, 375°F., 190°C., Gas Mark 4–5. **Oven position:** just above centre.

IMPERIAL	AMERICAN
For 6–8 people you need:	**For 6–8 people you need:**
5 oz. butter *or* margarine	$\frac{1}{2}$ cup plus 2 tablespoons butter *or* margarine
5 oz. castor sugar	$\frac{1}{2}$ cup plus 2 tablespoons sugar
grated rind 1 lemon	grated rind 1 lemon
2 eggs	2 eggs
10 oz. self-raising flour	$2\frac{1}{2}$ cups all-purpose flour, sifted with 3 teaspoons baking powder
little milk	little milk
For the topping:	**For the topping:**
about $1\frac{1}{2}$ lb. apples	about $1\frac{1}{2}$ lb. apples
lemon juice	lemon juice
1 oz. icing sugar	$\frac{1}{4}$ cup sifted confectioners' sugar
4 tablespoons sieved apricot jam	$\frac{1}{3}$ cup sieved apricot jam

1. Cream the butter and sugar with lemon rind, until soft and light.
2. Gradually beat in the eggs, then fold in sieved flour.
3. Add a little milk to make a sticky consistency—*do not make too wet.*
4. Spread the mixture into a tin lined with greased greaseproof paper.
5. Peel and slice the apples, arrange in neat lines on the cake mixture. This allows cake to rise higher on either side of apple slices, as shown in the picture.
6. Sprinkle with lemon juice and sieved icing sugar.
7. Bake until golden brown and firm, reducing heat if necessary.
8. Heat sieved jam and spread over the cake.

To serve: Slice neatly. Excellent with hot vanilla sauce made by blending $\frac{1}{2}$ oz. (U.S. 2 tablespoons) cornflour, $\frac{1}{2}$ pint (U.S. $1\frac{1}{4}$ cups) milk, 1–2 oz. (U.S. 2–4 tablespoons) sugar and $\frac{1}{2}$ teaspoon vanilla essence. Cook until thickened and smooth, add $\frac{1}{2}$ oz. (U.S. 1 tablespoon) butter and 2 tablespoons (U.S. 3 tablespoons) thick cream.

To vary: Add grated nutmeg and/or powdered cinnamon at Stage 6.

254

Boterletter
Dutch celebration cake

Cooking time: 30 min. **Preparation time:** 30 min. plus time for pastry to stand. **Main cooking utensil:** baking tray/sheet. **Oven temperature:** hot, 425–450°F., 220–230°C., Gas Mark 6–7. **Oven position:** centre.

IMPERIAL	AMERICAN
For 6–8 people you need:	**For 6–8 people you need:**
For the flaky pastry:	**For the flaky pastry:**
6 oz. plain flour	$1\frac{1}{2}$ cups all-purpose flour
pinch salt	dash salt
4 oz. unsalted butter	$\frac{1}{2}$ cup sweet butter
water to mix	water to mix
For the almond paste:	**For the almond paste:**
6 oz. ground almonds	$1\frac{1}{2}$ cups ground almonds
6 oz. castor sugar	$\frac{3}{4}$ cup granulated sugar
1 egg	1 egg
juice $\frac{1}{2}$ lemon	juice $\frac{1}{2}$ lemon
few drops almond essence (to taste)	few drops almond extract (to taste)
To seal and glaze:	**To seal and glaze:**
1 egg	1 egg

There are parties all over Holland on St. Nicholas Day, and the traditional food includes Boterletter, a cake made in the shape of a letter; usually 'M' for Mother.

1. Sieve the flour and salt; rub in just over 1 oz. (U.S. 2 tablespoons) butter. Bind to an elastic dough with water.
2. Roll to an oblong, cover two-thirds of dough with half remaining butter, fold in three, turn, seal edges.
3. Re-roll into oblong, repeat Stage 2 with remaining butter. Put into cool place. Roll pastry into a long strip, about 4 inches wide.
4. Mix all the ingredients for the almond paste together. Form into long sausage shape, a little shorter than the length of pastry.
5. Place on top of the pastry strip.
6. Wrap pastry round the paste, seal edge and ends with beaten egg. Form into the shape of the letter 'M'. Glaze.
7. Bake in hot oven for 30 minutes until golden brown, allow to cool.

To vary: Form into a circle. Glaze with apricot jam, diluted with a little sherry and decorate with glacé cherries, almonds and angelica.

Jhal farzi
Cooked meat curry

Indian food is always assumed to be very hot and spicy and many people are afraid to try it. But many Indian dishes are delicious and not too spicy to a Western palate.

India, of course, is the home of curry which varies enormously from one region to another, depending on the ingredients and spices used. The Indian housewife never uses curry powder but grinds and mixes her own fresh spices. In the West, most Indian spices are easily found in good grocers and Oriental shops, although you may find it convenient to buy them already ground. Many Indian curries are vegetarian because several religious groups are vegetarian and meat is often scarce, especially in the south. Beef is never eaten by the Hindus to whom cows are sacred but it is found in some areas. The most common meats are goat and mutton or lamb, our Curried lamb being a typical curry thickened with lentils.

India is a poverty stricken country and a curry often consists only of a sauce with a few vegetables to be eaten with large quantities of rice. Because rice is such an important staple, the Indians are expert at cooking it. The best way is to wash the rice thoroughly and then place it in a saucepan with twice its volume of water (i.e. 2 cups of water to 1 cup of rice) and a little salt. Cover tightly and bring to the boil; then turn the heat down to very low and leave for about 15 minutes. The other way is to cook the rice in a large quantity of salted water until tender, rinse and then reheat before serving. Indians tend to prefer the first method because it retains all the food value of the rice.

In prosperous families, curry is a substantial dish and rice is only one of many side dishes. An assortment of pickles and chutneys are served as well as shredded coconut and other nuts like peanuts and cashews. A cooked vegetable is not essential but aubergines, okra and crisply fried sliced onions are typical Indian choices. Diced fresh vegetables and fruits are colourful accompaniments which provide a refreshing contrast to the hot curry. Yoghurt is usually served in some form, either on its own or in a *raitha* with vegetables or fruit and seasoning. Finally, some sort of Indian bread is provided; there are several varieties, most of them unleavened and made with wholemeal flour. Puris are a popular fried bread which are easy to make; the secret with all Indian breads being to knead them thoroughly and fry them in a good heavy frying pan.

Cooking time: 1½–2 hr. **Preparation time:** 25 min. **Main cooking utensil:** strong saucepan with tightly fitting lid.

IMPERIAL

For 5–6 people you need:
1½ lb. cooked beef—topside *or* good quality stewing steak
2 onions
1–2 cloves garlic
1 teaspoon powdered ginger
1 teaspoon coriander powder
½ teaspoon turmeric
¼–1 teaspoon chilli powder
½–1 teaspoon garam masala*
1 oz. flour
3 oz. butter
1 pint stock
grated rind and juice 1 lemon
1 tablespoon chutney and jam
2 oz. sultanas
coconut milk *or* 2 oz. desiccated coconut and boiling water
seasoning
2 oz. blanched almonds

AMERICAN

For 5–6 people you need:
1½ lb. cooked beef—good quality stewing steak
2 onions
1–2 cloves garlic
1 teaspoon powdered ginger
1 teaspoon coriander powder
½ teaspoon turmeric
¼–1 teaspoon chili powder
½–1 teaspoon garam masala*
¼ cup all-purpose flour
6 tablespoons butter
2½ cups stock
grated rind and juice 1 lemon
1 tablespoon chutney and jam
⅓ cup seedless white raisins
coconut milk *or* ⅔ cup shredded coconut and boiling water
seasoning
scant ½ cup blanched almonds

*A mixture of spices. 1–2 tablespoons curry powder may be used.

1. Cut the meat into neat pieces.
2. Blend chopped onions, crushed garlic with all the spices and flour.
3. Fry the onion mixture in butter for 10 minutes, stirring well.
4. Blend in stock, lemon rind and juice, chutney, jam and sultanas.
5. If using fresh coconut, add the milk. If using desiccated coconut, pour a little boiling water over this, stand for 10 minutes. Add liquid to the curry with coconut if wished. Season mixture.
6. Add the meat. Cover the pan tightly. Simmer gently for 1½–2 hours, stirring from time to time. Stir in the nuts.

Side dishes:
a) Cooked rice. **b)** Saffron rice—add pinch saffron to rice. **c)** Popadums—buy ready-made, fry for less than a minute in hot fat, turn frequently so they keep flat. **d)** Raitha—blend grated or finely diced cucumber with yoghurt. Other side dishes—chutney, nuts, fruit, vegetables.

Curried lamb

Cooking time: $2\frac{1}{2}$ hr. **Preparation time:** 25 min. plus 1 hr. to stand. **Main cooking utensils:** 2 saucepans.

IMPERIAL

For 4–5 people you need:
2 oz. lentils
1 pint water
$1\frac{1}{2}$ lb. lamb, cut from leg
2 onions
1 clove garlic
$\frac{1}{2}$ small green pepper
4 tomatoes
3 oz. ghee (clarified butter)

2 small potatoes (optional)
$\frac{1}{2}$–1 teaspoon powdered chilli
$\frac{1}{2}$ teaspoon powdered ginger
pinch cinnamon, cloves
$\frac{1}{2}$ teaspoon turmeric
salt
$\frac{1}{2}$ lemon
little sugar
2 dessert apples

To serve:
8 oz. long grain rice
side dishes

AMERICAN

For 4–5 people you need:
$\frac{1}{4}$ cup lentils
$2\frac{1}{2}$ cups water
$1\frac{1}{2}$ lb. lamb, cut from leg
2 onions
1 clove garlic
$\frac{1}{2}$ small sweet green pepper
4 tomatoes
6 tablespoons ghee (clarified butter)
2 small potatoes (optional)
$\frac{1}{2}$–1 teaspoon powdered chili
$\frac{1}{2}$ teaspoon powdered ginger
dash cinnamon, cloves
$\frac{1}{2}$ teaspoon turmeric
salt
$\frac{1}{2}$ lemon
little sugar
2 eating apples

To serve:
generous 1 cup long grain rice
sides dishes

1. Cover lentils with the boiling water, put on one side for 1 hour.
2. Cut meat into neat pieces, chop onions finely, crush garlic.
3. Cut flesh of pepper into neat strips, skin and chop tomatoes.
4. Toss meat and vegetables in hot ghee. Add peeled, diced potatoes when the remainder of the vegetables have been cooking for 10 minutes.
5. Stir in lentils, water, spices, adding chilli powder gradually to taste as this is very hot, little salt and lemon juice.
6. Cover the pan, simmer for $1\frac{3}{4}$ hours, stirring from time to time.
7. Taste, add sugar, with cored and sliced apple. Finish cooking.
8. Meanwhile cook the rice in 3–4 pints (U.S. $7\frac{1}{2}$–10 cups) boiling, salted water for 12–15 minutes until just tender.

To serve: On a bed of rice with side dishes. These usually include chutney, Bombay duck, sliced peppers, bananas, lemon, apple, grated coconut.

257

Puris

Fried bread puffs

Cooking time: 5 min. **Preparation time:** 10 min. **Main cooking utensil:** large frying pan/skillet *or* griddle.

IMPERIAL

To make about 16 rounds of light bread you need:
8 oz. flour, preferably wholemeal *or* use half wholemeal and half white flour, plain *or* self-raising
$\frac{1}{2}$–1 teaspoon salt
shake pepper
$1\frac{1}{2}$ oz. butter *or* margarine

water to bind (slightly warm water helps in mixing rather than cold water)

To fry:
butter, oil *or* fat

To garnish:
parsley (optional)

AMERICAN

To make about 16 rounds of light bread you need:
2 cups flour, preferably wholewheat *or* use half wholewheat and half white all-purpose flour
$\frac{1}{2}$–1 teaspoon salt
dash pepper
3 tablespoons butter *or* margarine
water to bind (slightly warm water helps in mixing rather than cold water)

To fry:
butter, oil *or* fat

To garnish:
parsley (optional)

1. Sieve the flour and seasoning.
2. Rub in the butter or margarine, blend with enough water to give firm dough.
3. Knead well then roll out at once, or better still, leave for about 30 minutes then knead and roll.
4. Roll out until mixture is well under $\frac{1}{4}$ inch in thickness, cut into rounds or squares to fit into frying pan or on the griddle. To make a convenient size for turning, do not exceed about 4 inches in diameter.
5. Heat enough butter or fat in pan to coat bottom, or grease griddle very thoroughly.
6. To test if fat is correct heat, shake on a little flour, it should turn golden brown within 1 minute. Put the rounds or squares of puris into pan or on hot griddle.
7. Cook for about $1\frac{1}{2}$ minutes until nearly set on underside, then press firmly with a palette knife or fish slice, this will make the dough 'puff' up.
8. Turn and cook on the second side.
9. Remove from the pan or griddle, drain and serve with butter, in place of bread. Garnish with parsley if liked.

Proscuitto di Parma
Parma ham and figs

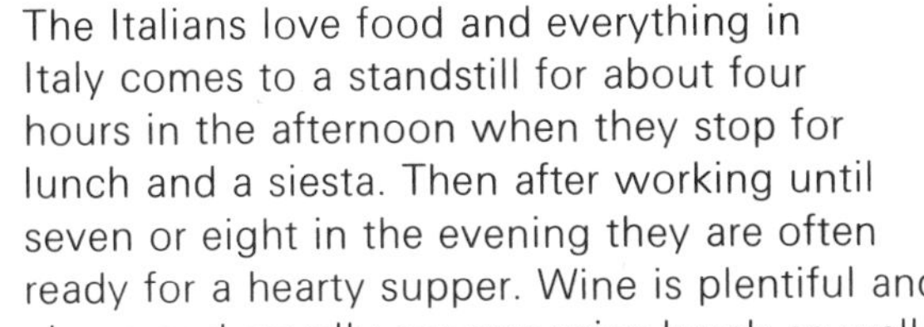

The Italians love food and everything in Italy comes to a standstill for about four hours in the afternoon when they stop for lunch and a siesta. Then after working until seven or eight in the evening they are often ready for a hearty supper. Wine is plentiful and cheap and usually accompanies lunch as well as supper.

Most Italians begin their meal with a pasta dish which we would often consider substantial enough for a main course. Spaghetti is only one of the innumerable types of Italian pasta, from the tubular or rolled cannelloni to narrow tagliatelle noodles, wide lasagne noodles, and stuffed pasta in all different shapes and sizes.

For the main course you could choose fish, usually grilled or fried and served with a sauce as in Fish and spinach cream and Grilled fish and cheese. Beef is popular but expensive and Steak with tomato sauce is an excellent Neapolitan speciality for entertaining. Veal, on the other hand, is comparitively inexpensive and eaten a great deal, Veal and ham cooked Roman style being an original and delicious way of preparing it.

Stuffed vegetables often accompany the main dish and also make good light dishes on their own. Anchovies, olives and pine nuts feature in Stuffed peppers. There are several distinctive Italian cheeses that are excellent in cooking. Mozzarella being a mild, semi-soft cheese often used in baked pasta dishes, while the famous Parmesan is a sharp, hard cheese which is grated for use in countless dishes and is always on the table for sprinkling over pasta. Cheese and tomatoes are the essential ingredients in the ubiquitous pizza of which there are numerous regional variations, like Sicilian pizza with anchovies, olives and fennel. Pizza is sold everywhere, as a snack at pizza stalls and in restaurants it is served instead of the pasta course.

After a hearty Italian meal, fruit or one of the incomparable ice creams or sorbets is a perfect dessert. For a more substantial pudding, Peach tart is ideal, but of course the most famous Italian sweet is Zabaglione, a superb whipped egg custard flavoured with wine. To conclude you will be served a small cup of the strong, distinctively flavoured Espresso coffee or, if you prefer, Capuccino which is made with frothy, hot milk.

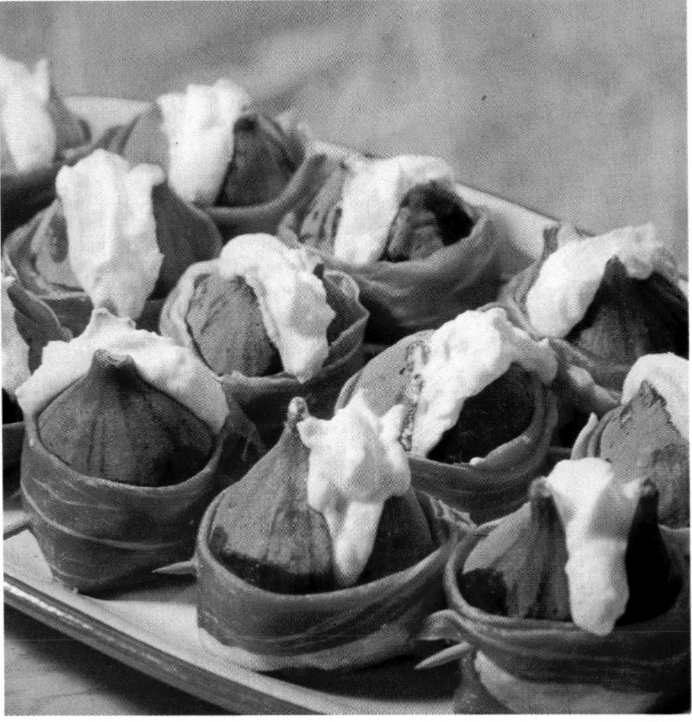

Preparation time: few min. **Main cooking utensil:** mixing bowl.

IMPERIAL

For 8 portions you need:
8 large *or* 16 smaller ripe fresh dessert figs
6–8 oz. Parma ham (smoked raw)

For the mayonnaise:
2 egg yolks
good pinch salt
shake pepper
$\frac{1}{2}$ teaspoon made mustard
pinch sugar
1 tablespoon lemon juice
$\frac{1}{4}$ pint olive oil
2 teaspoons boiling water

AMERICAN

For 8 portions you need:
8 large *or* 16 smaller ripe, fresh dessert figs
$\frac{1}{3}$–$\frac{1}{2}$ lb. Parma ham (smoked raw)

For the mayonnaise:
2 egg yolks
dash salt
dash pepper
$\frac{1}{2}$ teaspoon prepared mustard
dash sugar
1 tablespoon lemon juice
$\frac{2}{3}$ cup olive oil
2 teaspoons boiling water

1. Wash and dry the figs.
2. Cut the ham into thin strips (this is generally sold cut into wafer-thin slices or in cans, ready sliced).
3. Twist strips of ham round the figs and secure with cocktail sticks.
4. Coat the tops with a ribbon of mayonnaise.
5. To make this, put the egg yolks into a dry basin with seasonings and sugar.
6. Whisk in lemon juice and beat until egg yolks thicken slightly.
7. Add the oil very gradually and continue beating until very thick.
8. This mayonnaise is not as 'oily' as some—more oil could be added.
9. Finally beat in boiling water; this gives an extra creamy taste.

To serve: Always served as an hors d'oeuvre.

To vary: Serve ripe slices of melon with ham instead of figs, and omit mayonnaise. Garnish with lemon, serve with cayenne or paprika pepper and a little sugar for the melon.

259

Zuppa di zucchini
Courgette and vegetable soup

Cooking time: 1 hr. 50 min. **Preparation time:** 25 min. plus overnight soaking of beans. **Main cooking utensil:** large saucepan.

IMPERIAL

For 4–6 people you need:
4–6 oz. haricot beans *or*
1 medium-sized can beans
4 medium-sized potatoes (new potatoes are excellent)
3–4 courgettes
1–2 leeks
2 tablespoons olive oil
1–2 cloves garlic
2 pints water *or* white stock (2 chicken stock cubes could be added to water)
seasoning
2 teaspoons chopped basil *or* $\frac{1}{2}$–1 teaspoon dried basil

To serve:
4 oz. Parmesan *or* Cheddar cheese, grated

AMERICAN

For 4–6 people you need:
$\frac{1}{4}$–$\frac{1}{3}$ lb. navy beans *or*
1 medium-sized can beans
4 medium-sized potatoes (new potatoes are excellent)
3–4 small zucchini
1–2 leeks
3 tablespoons olive oil
1–2 cloves garlic
5 cups water *or* white stock (2 chicken bouillon cubes could be added to water)
seasoning
2 teaspoons chopped basil *or* $\frac{1}{2}$–1 teaspoon dried basil

To serve:
1 cup grated Parmesan *or* Cheddar cheese

1. Soak the haricot beans in cold water to cover overnight, then simmer in the water for $1\frac{1}{2}$ hours, season lightly while cooking, drain well. Or use canned haricot beans and just add these at Stage 4.
2. Peel and dice the potatoes and wash and slice the courgettes. Chop the leeks very finely.
3. Heat the oil, fry the finely crushed garlic, then add the other vegetables and cook gently in the oil for 5 minutes.
4. Cover with boiling water or stock, add the seasoning, the finely chopped fresh basil or dried herb.
5. Simmer steadily for 15–20 minutes until the vegetables are tender; they should be unbroken.

To serve: Either sprinkle the cheese on top of each serving, or hand separately. This is a sustaining kind of soup that is almost a meal.

260

Cannelloni di mortadella
Cannelloni filled with Mortadella

Cooking time: 30 min. **Preparation time:** 25 min. **Main cooking utensils:** frying pan/ skillet, grill pan/broil pan.

IMPERIAL

For 4–8 people you need:
For the cannelloni batter:
2 spring onions
6 oz. flour, preferably plain
pinch salt
shake pepper
$\frac{1}{2}$ teaspoon French mustard
2 eggs
$\frac{1}{2}$ pint milk and water mixed

To fry:
2 oz. butter
2 tablespoons oil

For the filling:
6–8 oz. Mortadella di Bologna (8 slices, one for each cannelloni)
4 oz. Gruyère *or* Cheddar cheese, finely grated
1 tablespoon brandy (optional)
little grated lemon rind
1 teaspoon French mustard
2 tablespoons mayonnaise

To garnish:
green olives
tomatoes
lettuce

AMERICAN

For 4–8 people you need:
For the cannelloni batter:
2 scallions
$1\frac{1}{2}$ cups all-purpose flour
dash salt
dash pepper
$\frac{1}{2}$ teaspoon French mustard
2 eggs
$1\frac{1}{4}$ cups milk and water mixed

To fry:
$\frac{1}{4}$ cup butter
3 tablespoons oil

For the filling:
$\frac{1}{3}$–$\frac{1}{2}$ lb. Mortadella di Bologna (8 slices, one for each cannelloni)
1 cup finely grated Gruyère *or* Cheddar cheese
1 tablespoon brandy (optional)
little grated lemon rind
1 teaspoon French mustard
3 tablespoons mayonnaise

To garnish:
green olives
tomatoes
lettuce

1. Chop the white part of the onions very finely, then mix with the flour.
2. Add all the other ingredients for the batter and fry in a mixture of butter and oil to give 8 pancakes.
3. Cover each one with a slice of sausage. Blend cheese and all the other ingredients for filling together. Spread just over half on the sausage. Roll up pancakes and cover with the remaining mixture.
4. Put under a hot grill and brown. Serve hot or cold, garnished with olives, tomatoes and lettuce.

Rotoli di lasagne verdi
Green lasagna roll

Cooking time: 1 hr. 25 min. **Preparation time:** 25 min. if buying lasagna. **Main cooking utensils:** 2 saucepans, casserole. **Oven temperature:** very moderate, 350–375°F., 180–190°C., Gas Mark 4. **Oven position:** centre.

IMPERIAL

For 4 people you need:
8 oz. green lasagna
seasoning
3 medium-sized onions
2 oz. butter
12 oz. minced beef
4 chicken livers *or* use more minced beef
2 teaspoons chopped parsley
$\frac{1}{2}$ pint stock

For the sauce:
onions (see Stages 2 and 6)
3 medium-sized tomatoes
$\frac{1}{4}$ pint stock
$\frac{1}{4}$ pint white wine *or* use all stock

To garnish:
cooked tomato
cooked peas

AMERICAN

For 4 people you need:
$\frac{1}{2}$ lb. green lasagna
seasoning
3 medium-sized onions
$\frac{1}{4}$ cup butter
$\frac{3}{4}$ lb. ground beef
4 chicken livers *or* use more ground beef
2 teaspoons chopped parsley
$1\frac{1}{4}$ cups stock

For the sauce:
onions (see Stages 2 and 6)
3 medium-sized tomatoes
$\frac{2}{3}$ cup stock
$\frac{2}{3}$ cup white wine *or* use all stock

To garnish:
cooked tomato
cooked peas

1. Cook the lasagna in boiling, salted water until tender. Strain and drape over a colander to dry.
2. Chop the onions, fry one in butter. Add the minced beef, minced or chopped chicken livers, parsley, seasoning and stock.
3. Simmer steadily until a thick purée, about 30 minutes, stirring well as liquid evaporates to prevent mixture sticking to pan.
4. Put a layer of lasagna on a board, spread with meat mixture. Cover with lasagna, more meat, lasagna, meat and a final layer of lasagna.
5. Form into a neat roll.
6. Put remaining chopped onions, skinned, chopped tomatoes, stock, wine and seasoning into casserole with lasagna roll. Cover and cook for 45 minutes.
7. Garnish with baked tomato and peas.

262

Ravioli
Stuffed pasta

Cooking time: 40–45 min. **Preparation time:** 40 min. plus time to stand. **Main cooking utensils:** 3 saucepans.

IMPERIAL

For 4–6 people you need:
For the pasta:
1 lb. flour
$\frac{1}{2}$ teaspoon salt
2 eggs

For the filling:
8 oz. veal
1 onion
seasoning
$\frac{1}{2}$ pint stock
2 oz. Parmesan cheese, grated
2 oz. soft breadcrumbs

For the tomato sauce:
2 tablespoons oil
1 onion
$\frac{1}{2}$ oz. cornflour
1 lb. tomatoes
$\frac{3}{4}$ pint water
seasoning

AMERICAN

For 4–6 people you need:
For the pasta:
1 lb. all-purpose flour
$\frac{1}{2}$ teaspoon salt
2 eggs

For the filling:
$\frac{1}{2}$ lb. veal
1 onion
seasoning
$1\frac{1}{4}$ cups stock
$\frac{1}{2}$ cup grated Parmesan cheese
1 cup soft bread crumbs

For the tomato sauce:
3 tablespoons oil
1 onion
2 tablespoons cornstarch
1 lb. tomatoes
scant 2 cups water
seasoning

1. Sieve the flour and salt, add eggs and enough water to make a pliable dough. Knead well, then stand for 30 minutes.
2. Roll out to paper thinness and cut into half. Leave to dry for a short time.
3. To make filling, chop meat and onion and simmer in the well-seasoned stock for 25–35 minutes. Drain well, add cheese and crumbs; add liquid to the sauce, see Stage 8.
4. Put teaspoonfuls of the filling on one half of the pasta, lay other half on top, press very firmly round filling. Cut into $1\frac{1}{2}$-inch squares, making sure each ravioli is firmly sealed.
5. Drop into a pan of rapidly boiling salted water, cook for 8 minutes.
6. Remove carefully.
7. To make sauce: heat oil, fry chopped onion, then stir in cornflour.
8. Cook for several minutes. Add skinned chopped tomatoes, water, seasoning and veal liquid. Simmer until tender, sieve and reheat. Serve at once with grated cheese and tomato sauce; garnish with parsley.

Tagliatelle alla finanziera
Pasta with chicken livers

Cooking time: $1\frac{1}{4}$ hr. **Preparation time:** 20 min. **Main cooking utensils:** 2 saucepans.

IMPERIAL

For 4 people you need:
For the sauce:
2 tablespoons oil
3 oz. butter
3 medium-sized onions
4 large tomatoes
6 chicken livers *or* 12 oz. diced rump steak*
1 pint chicken stock
seasoning
2 tablespoons tomato purée
4 oz. mushrooms
$\frac{1}{4}$ teaspoon each chopped thyme, sage and parsley
$\frac{1}{2}$ pint red wine

6 oz. Tagliatelle (noodles)
little chopped parsley and/*or* chopped oregano

To serve:
2–3 oz. Mozzarella *or* Cheddar cheese, grated

AMERICAN

For 4 people you need:
For the sauce:
3 tablespoons oil
6 tablespoons butter
3 medium-sized onions
4 large tomatoes
6 chicken livers *or* $\frac{3}{4}$ lb. diced round *or* rump steak*
$2\frac{1}{2}$ cups chicken stock
seasoning
3 tablespoons tomato paste
1 cup mushrooms
$\frac{1}{4}$ teaspoon each chopped thyme, sage and parsley
$1\frac{1}{4}$ cups red wine

6 oz. Tagliatelle (noodles)
little chopped parsley and/*or* chopped oregano

To serve:
$\frac{1}{2}$–$\frac{3}{4}$ cup grated Mozzarella *or* Cheddar cheese

*If using cheaper stewing meat, cook for a longer period.

1. Heat the oil and half the butter, fry the fairly coarsely sliced onions in this. Add the skinned, chopped tomatoes, chopped chicken livers or steak and cook for about 5 minutes.
2. Stir in the stock, seasoning, tomato purée and chopped mushrooms, together with the chopped herbs and wine.
3. Cook steadily for approximately 45 minutes–1 hour, until the sauce thickens.
4. Meanwhile, cook the noodles in 3 pints (U.S. $7\frac{1}{2}$ cups) boiling, salted water until just tender.
5. Strain, toss in remaining butter and chopped parsley and/or oregano.
6. Arrange round the edge of a dish and fill the centre with the savoury mixture. Serve with the grated cheese.

264

Tonno agli spinaci
Fish and spinach cream

Cooking time: 25 min. **Preparation time:** 25 min. **Main cooking utensils:** 2 saucepans, frying pan/skillet.

IMPERIAL

For 4 people you need:
$1\frac{1}{2}$ lb. fresh spinach
seasoning

For the sauce:
$1\frac{1}{2}$ oz. butter *or* margarine

$1\frac{1}{2}$ oz. flour
$\frac{1}{2}$ pint milk
2 tablespoons thin cream
grated nutmeg

3 oz. butter
1–2 cloves garlic (optional)
1 small onion
4 portions fresh tunny fish *or* skate* or other fairly firm-fleshed fish
$\frac{1}{2}$ oz. flour
seasoning

For the topping:
1–2 oz. cheese, grated

AMERICAN

For 4 people you need:
$1\frac{1}{2}$ lb. fresh spinach
seasoning

For the sauce:
3 tablespoons butter *or* margarine
6 tablespoons all-purpose flour
$1\frac{1}{4}$ cups milk
3 tablespoons coffee cream
grated nutmeg

6 tablespoons butter
1–2 cloves garlic (optional)
1 small onion
4 portions fresh swordfish *or* skate*, or other fairly firm-fleshed fish
2 tablespoons all-purpose flour
seasoning

For the topping:
$\frac{1}{4}$–$\frac{1}{2}$ cup grated cheese

*If using skate, steam for about 10 minutes before frying.

1. Wash the spinach, cook without water until tender, season lightly.
2. Sieve, or remove from pan and chop until very fine.
3. Heat the butter in a pan, stir in flour, cook for several minutes. Add the milk and cook until a very thick sauce.
4. Stir in the cream and nutmeg to taste.
5. Blend the spinach with the sauce and put into a very hot dish.
6. Meanwhile heat 2 oz. (U.S. $\frac{1}{4}$ cup) butter, fry crushed garlic then the onion for a few minutes. Add fish, coated with flour and seasoning. Cook until tender.
7. Lift fish on to the spinach cream, top with remaining butter and the cheese and heat for a few minutes only under the grill. Serve with a crisp green salad.

Pesce spada al forno
Grilled fish and cheese

Cooking time: 25–30 min. **Preparation time:** 20 min. **Main cooking utensils:** saucepan *or* frying pan/skillet, grill pan/broil pan, ovenproof dish.

IMPERIAL

For 5 people you need:
4 medium-sized tomatoes
4 oz. mushrooms
2–3 cloves garlic
3 tablespoons oil
seasoning
¼ pint red *or* white wine
2 teaspoons chopped parsley, chervil *or* fennel (*or* mixture)
5 fish, use red mullet, whiting *or* trout
2 oz. cheese, grated*

To garnish:
chervil *or* parsley

AMERICAN

For 5 people you need:
4 medium-sized tomatoes
1 cup mushrooms
2–3 cloves garlic
scant ¼ cup oil
seasoning
⅔ cup red *or* white wine
2 teaspoons chopped parsley, chervil *or* fennel (*or* mixture)
5 fish, use mullet, whiting *or* trout
½ cup grated cheese*

To garnish:
chervil *or* parsley

*Use Parmesan, Gruyère, Cheddar or Mozzarella.

1. Skin and chop the tomatoes, slice mushrooms fairly thinly.
2. Crush 1–2 cloves of garlic.
3. Heat 2 tablespoons (U.S. 3 tablespoons) oil, fry mushrooms for a few minutes.
4. Remove half to use as garnish and keep hot. Add tomatoes, garlic and seasoning to the remainder, simmer until tender.
5. Add the wine and chopped herbs. Keep mixture hot.
6. Clean the fish but keep heads on. Season well and flavour with a cut clove garlic (rub this along skin if wished).
7. Brush with oil and grill until tender.
8. Arrange the tomato mixture in a heat-resistant dish. Top with cooked fish, turn them in the mixture to moisten.
9. Sprinkle with a band of cheese down the centre and add mushrooms. Replace under the grill for a few minutes.

To serve: Garnish with chervil or parsley and serve with green salad.

266

Bistecca alla pizzaiola
Steak with tomato sauce

Cooking time: approx. 15 min. (see Stage 2). **Preparation time:** 15 min. **Main cooking utensils:** 1 or 2 frying pans/skillets, saucepan.

IMPERIAL

For 4 people you need:
4 steaks—fillet, rump *or* entrecôte
salt, black pepper
2 tablespoons oil

For the sauce:
2–3 shallots *or* small onions
1–2 cloves garlic
2 tablespoons oil
good pinch oregano *or* marjoram
good pinch basil
1 medium-sized can Italian tomatoes
seasoning
pinch sugar

To garnish:
3–4 oz. mushrooms
little oil
parsley

AMERICAN

For 4 people you need:
4 steaks—fillet, rump *or* entrecôte
salt, black pepper
3 tablespoons oil

For the sauce:
2–3 shallots *or* small onions
1–2 cloves garlic
3 tablespoons oil
dash oregano *or* marjoram
dash basil
1 medium-sized can Italian tomatoes
seasoning
dash sugar

To garnish:
¾–1 cup mushrooms
little oil
parsley

1. Beat the steaks and season.
2. Heat the oil in a pan and fry steaks on both sides until cooked to personal taste, i.e. about 2–3 minutes each side, underdone; 3–4 minutes each side, medium cooked; 4–6 minutes each side, well done.
3. To make the sauce, slice shallots, crush garlic and fry in oil. Add oregano or marjoram together with a little basil.
4. Add canned tomatoes with seasoning and sugar. Simmer gently for 5–10 minutes.
5. Fry sliced mushrooms in oil.

To serve: Arrange steaks on serving dish, top with sauce and chopped parsley. Arrange mushrooms round.

To vary: Add a little red pepper to the sauce.

Tournedos di fegato
Liver tournedos

Cooking time: 15 min. **Preparation time:** 10 min. **Main cooking utensil:** large frying pan/skillet.

IMPERIAL

For 6 people you need:
$1\frac{1}{2}$ lb. calf's liver, cut into 2–3 slices
seasoning
pinch dried sage
grated rind 1 lemon
$\frac{1}{2}$ oz. flour
1 large onion
3 oz. butter
2 large tomatoes

To garnish:
6 sage leaves

For the sauce (optional):
$\frac{1}{4}$ pint thin cream
$\frac{1}{4}$ pint stock
squeeze lemon juice

AMERICAN

For 6 people you need:
$1\frac{1}{2}$ lb. calf liver, cut into 2–3 slices
seasoning
dash dried sage
grated rind 1 lemon
2 tablespoons all-purpose flour
1 large onion
6 tablespoons butter
2 large tomatoes

To garnish:
6 sage leaves

For the sauce (optional):
$\frac{2}{3}$ cup coffee cream
$\frac{2}{3}$ cup stock
squeeze lemon juice

1. Cut the liver into 12 rounds or neat portions, tie these into a round shape with cotton or fine string.
4. Mix seasoning, dried sage, finely grated lemon rind and flour.
3. Coat the liver with this mixture.
4. Peel and cut onion into 6 slices.
5. Fry in the hot butter until just tender.
6. Take 6 large slices from the tomatoes. Fry for 1–2 minutes only, so they are still very firm.
7. Keep the onion and tomato slices hot while cooking the liver. Fry this until just tender, do not over-cook.

To serve: Put a slice of tomato on the dish, top with liver tournedo, slice of onion, liver and sage leaf. If wishing to serve as a more formal dish, heat cream and stock in pan. Remove from heat and stir in squeeze lemon juice.

268

Saltimbocca alla romana
Veal and ham cooked Roman style

Cooking time: 15 min. plus time to cook carrots. **Preparation time:** 10 min. **Main cooking utensils:** frying pan/skillet.

IMPERIAL

For 4 people you need:
8 small thin slices veal (cut from top of leg)
seasoning
grated rind 1 lemon
8 sage leaves
8 slices ham (same size as veal)

To coat:
$\frac{1}{2}$–1 oz. seasoned flour
1 egg
2 oz. crisp breadcrumbs

To fry:
3 oz. butter and 1 tablespoon oil *or* 4 oz. butter

6 tablespoons red *or* white wine

To garnish:
cooked carrots
parsley
lemon

AMERICAN

For 4 people you need:
8 small thin slices veal (cut from top of leg)
seasoning
grated rind 1 lemon
8 sage leaves
8 slices cured ham (same size as veal)

To coat:
2–4 tablespoons seasoned flour
1 egg
$\frac{1}{2}$ cup crisp dry bread crumbs

To fry:
6 tablespoons butter and 1 tablespoon oil *or* $\frac{1}{2}$ cup butter
$\frac{1}{2}$ cup red *or* white wine

To garnish:
cooked carrots
parsley
lemon

1. If the veal slices are not very thin, beat with a rolling pin.
2. Season lightly, add a little grated lemon rind. Put a sage leaf on each piece of veal.
3. Lay a slice of ham on each piece of veal.
4. Put wooden cocktail sticks through pieces of meat to hold together.
5. Coat with seasoned flour, then beaten egg and crumbs.
6. Heat butter and oil or butter, fry meat until golden brown on each side. Lower heat, cook for further 10 minutes to make sure veal is tender. Remove cocktail sticks.
7. Lift on to a serving dish; add wine to fat, etc., in pan and heat.

To serve: Pour the liquid over the meat just before serving. Garnish with cooked carrots, parsley, lemon.

269

Sformato di mortadella
Salami mould

Cooking time: 50 min. **Preparation time:** 25 min. **Main cooking utensils:** 2 saucepans, basin *or* mould, ovenproof dish. **Oven temperature:** moderately hot, 400°F., 200°C., Gas Mark 5–6. **Oven position:** just above centre.

IMPERIAL

For 5–6 people you need:
1½ lb. fresh spinach *or* equivalent in frozen leaf spinach
2 lb. potatoes, weight when unpeeled
seasoning
3 oz. butter
3 tablespoons thin cream
5 oz. cheese, grated, Gruyère, *or* mixture of Gruyère and Parmesan
little grated nutmeg
8 oz. Mortadella *or* other salami
3 oz. Gruyère cheese, sliced

To serve:
cooked tomatoes *or* mushrooms

AMERICAN

For 5–6 people you need:
1½ lb. fresh spinach *or* equivalent in frozen leaf spinach
2 lb. potatoes, weight when unpeeled
seasoning
6 tablespoons butter
scant ¼ cup coffee cream
1¼ cups grated cheese, Gruyère, *or* mixture of Gruyère and Parmesan
little grated nutmeg
½ lb. Mortadella *or* other salami
¾ cup sliced Gruyère cheese

To serve:
cooked tomatoes *or* mushrooms

1. Wash and cook the spinach until tender. Peel and cook potatoes steadily, taking care they do not become overcooked and 'watery'.
2. Season both vegetables very well when cooked, strain carefully.
3. Mash the potatoes with 2 oz. (U.S. ¼ cup) butter, 2 tablespoons (U.S. 3 tablespoons) cream and half the grated cheese.
4. Blend remaining butter, cream and cheese with the nutmeg and spinach.
5. Put half the potato into a buttered plain mould or basin with the spinach spread over this.
6. Cover with the remaining potato mixture and bake in a hot oven for approximately 15 minutes.
7. Remove from the basin or mould on to an ovenproof dish.
8. Cut the sliced Mortadella into pieces. Press half against the mould, cover with sliced cheese.
9. Return the mould to the oven, heat for further 10 minutes until cheese is thoroughly melted. Garnish with remaining slices of Mortadella.

To serve: Hot with cooked tomatoes or mushrooms.

270

Pollo alla romana
Chicken with peppers

Cooking time: 40 min. **Preparation time:** 25 min. **Main cooking utensils:** large frying pan/skillet (with lid) or saucepan, small saucepan.

IMPERIAL

For 4 people you need:
2 young frying chickens *or* 1 young but larger chicken
seasoning
½ oz. flour
3 oz. butter
2 tablespoons oil
1 clove garlic (optional)
1 medium-sized onion
3–4 oz. bacon
pinch powdered rosemary *or* little chopped fresh herb
2–4 oz. mushrooms
4 large skinned tomatoes
½ pint red wine
1–2 green peppers
1 red pepper (optional)

AMERICAN

For 4 people you need:
2 young frying chickens *or* 1 young but larger chicken
seasoning
2 tablespoons all-purpose flour
6 tablespoons butter
3 tablespoons oil
1 clove garlic (optional)
1 medium-sized onion
about ¼ lb. bacon *or* cured ham
dash powdered rosemary *or* little chopped fresh herb
½–1 cup mushrooms
4 large skinned tomatoes
1¼ cups red wine
1–2 sweet green peppers
1 sweet red pepper

1. Cut the chicken into 4 joints, coat in seasoned flour.
2. Heat 2 oz. (U.S. ¼ cup) butter and 1 tablespoon oil, cook chicken until brown on both sides. Lift out of the pan.
3. Heat the remainder of the butter and oil, add crushed garlic, chopped onion and diced bacon and fry for 5 minutes.
4. Sprinkle with rosemary, then add sliced mushrooms, sliced tomatoes and wine. Simmer for a few minutes, season well.
5. Return the chicken to the sauce, cover tightly and cook for a further 20–25 minutes.
6. Meanwhile cut the peppers into neat pieces, blanch in boiling salted water for 5 minutes. Add to ingredients in pan towards the end of the cooking time.

To serve: Put chicken joints on dish, top with vegetables.

To vary: Toss pepper in butter without blanching for crisper texture.

271

Peperoni ripieni
Stuffed peppers

Cooking time: 45 min. **Preparation time:** 15 min. **Main cooking utensils:** saucepan, ovenproof dish, frying pan/skillet. **Oven temperature:** moderate, 375°F., 190°C., Gas Mark 4–5. **Oven position:** centre.

IMPERIAL

For 4 people you need:
4 medium-sized green peppers
seasoning
2 medium-sized onions
2 oz. butter
6 oz. pancetta* *or* bacon
1 can anchovy fillets
½ teaspoon oregano
about 12 black olives, stoned
3 oz. fresh fine breadcrumbs
2 oz. pine nuts

For the sauce:
1 lb. ripe tomatoes
1 onion
1 clove garlic
¼ pint stock *or* water
1–2 oz. pine nuts

To garnish:
4 black olives
4 anchovy fillets

*Cured belly of pork.

AMERICAN

For 4 people you need:
4 medium sweet green peppers
seasoning
2 medium-sized onions
¼ cup butter
⅓ lb. pancetta* *or* bacon
1 can anchovy fillets
½ teaspoon oregano
about 12 ripe olives, pitted
1½ cups fresh fine bread crumbs
about ⅓ cup pine nuts

For the sauce:
1 lb. ripe tomatoes
1 onion
1 clove garlic
⅔ cup stock *or* water
¼–½ cup pine nuts

To garnish:
4 ripe olives
4 anchovy fillets

1. Cut tops off the peppers and remove centre cores and seeds.
2. Chop the tops very finely to use in the stuffing.
3. Blanch the peppers for 5 minutes in boiling salted water, drain.
4. Chop the onions finely, toss in hot butter together with diced pancetta or bacon.
5. Add diced peppers, anchovy fillets, oregano and olives (these can be chopped if wished). Stir well and add crumbs and nuts.
6. Season if necessary, and pack into pepper cases. Put into greased dish and bake for 35 minutes until peppers are soft.
7. To make sauce, skin and chop tomatoes, put into pan with rest of ingredients and simmer.

To serve: Garnish with olives and anchovy fillets and pour sauce round.

272

Pizza siciliana
Sicilian pizza

Cooking time: 35 min. **Preparation time:** 15 min. **Main cooking utensil:** baking tray/sheet. **Oven temperature:** hot, 425–450°F., 220–230°C., Gas Mark 6–7. **Oven position:** centre.

IMPERIAL

For 4 people you need:
10 oz. self-raising flour

good pinch salt
black pepper and dry mustard
1 oz. butter *or* fat
water to mix

For the topping:
1–2 tablespoons olive oil
1 tablespoon fennel root
1 small onion
1–2 cloves garlic
2–3 tomatoes
seasoning
1 small can anchovies *or* about
8 anchovy fillets
about 10 black olives
2 oz. Parmesan cheese, grated

AMERICAN

For 4 people you need:
2½ cups flour, sifted with
2¾ teaspoons baking powder
dash salt
black pepper and dry mustard
2 tablespoons butter *or* fat
water to mix

For the topping:
1–3 tablespoons olive oil
1 tablespoon fennel root
1 small onion
1–2 cloves garlic
2–3 tomatoes
seasoning
1 small can anchovies *or* about
8 anchovy fillets
about 10 ripe olives
½ cup grated Parmesan cheese

1. Sieve the flour and seasonings.
2. Rub in the butter or add the fat.
3. Blend with water to make a sticky dough that can just be formed into a round, do not make it too dry.
4. Put on to an ungreased baking tray.
5. Heat the oil, fry finely chopped fennel, onion and crushed garlic until tender. Spread over the dough. Top with sliced tomatoes, seasoning, anchovy fillets and chopped olives, saving four for garnishing.
6. Bake for 25 minutes, then sprinkle over the cheese, top with remaining olives and return to the oven to finish baking.

To serve: Hot or cold.

Formaggio in carrozza
Cheese in a carriage

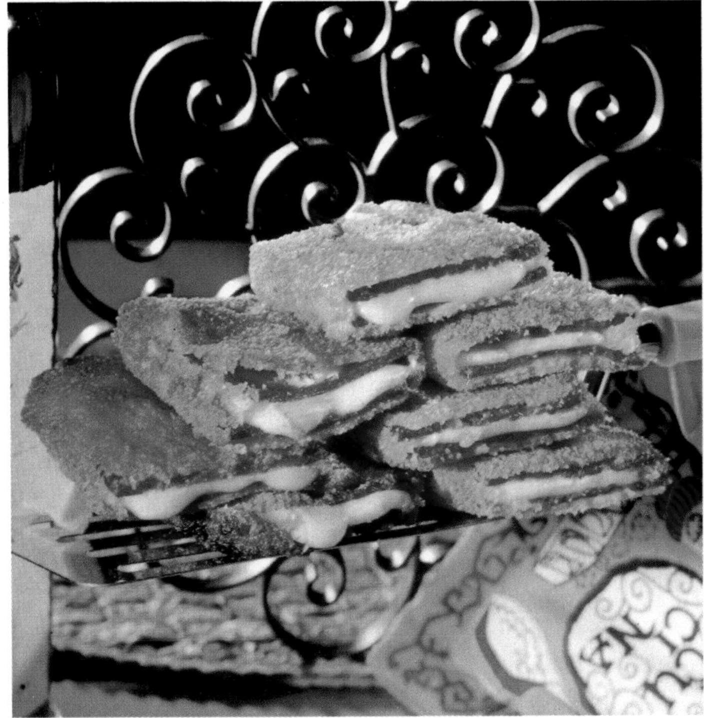

Cooking time: few min. **Preparation time:** 10–15 min. **Main cooking utensils:** large frying pan/skillet, absorbent paper/paper towels.

IMPERIAL	AMERICAN
For 4 people you need:	**For 4 people you need:**
bread	bread
butter	butter
4–6 oz. Mozzarella cheese	4–6 oz. Mozzarella cheese
4 thin slices Parma ham	4 thin slices Parma ham
To coat:	**To coat:**
$\frac{1}{2}$ oz. flour	2 tablespoons all-purpose flour
1–2 eggs	1–2 eggs
2 oz. very fine, soft breadcrumbs	1 cup very fine soft bread crumbs
To fry:	**To fry:**
oil *or* fat	oil *or* fat

1. Cut the bread into 4 large or 8 smaller wafer-thin slices, remove crusts.
2. Butter, then cover half the bread and butter with cheese and Parma ham. Fold bread and butter over to make a sandwich, or put second slice on top.
3. Dip in the flour, then well-beaten egg, finally in very fine crumbs.
4. Heat the oil or fat in frying pan. Put in sandwiches, fry until golden brown, turn and fry on second side. Drain on absorbent paper and serve.

To serve: Hot as a light supper savoury, or tiny sandwiches for a cocktail savoury.

To vary: Just coat cheese and ham with flour, egg and crumbs, fry.

274

Zucchini ripieni
Stuffed courgettes

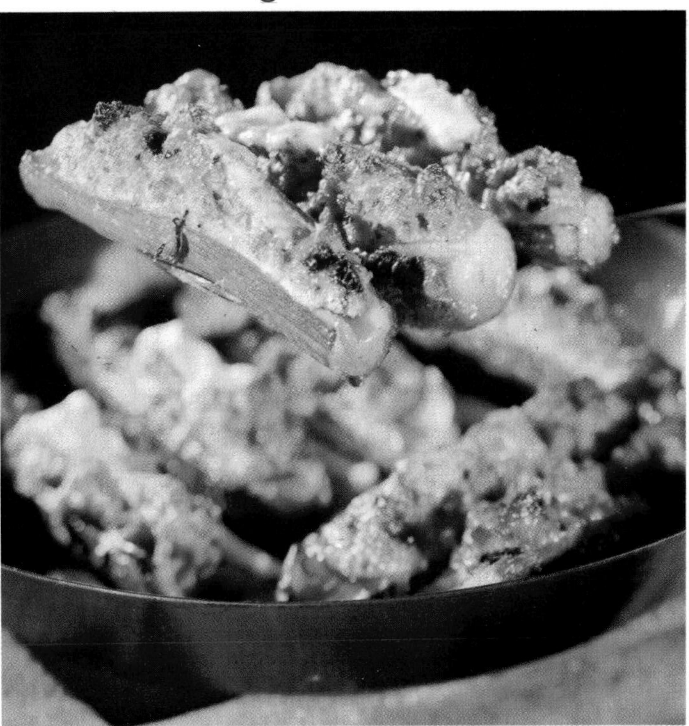

Cooking time: 20–30 min. (see Stages 1 and 6). **Preparation time:** 20 min. **Main cooking utensils:** saucepan, frying pan/skillet, and ovenproof dish *or* 2 frying pans/skillets. **Oven temperature:** moderately hot, 400°F., 200°C., Gas Mark 5–6. **Oven position:** above centre.

IMPERIAL	AMERICAN
For 4–8 people you need:*	**For 4–8 people you need:***
8 courgettes	8 small zucchini
seasoning	seasoning
2 oz. *or* 6 oz. butter (see Stages 1 and 4)	$\frac{1}{4}$ *or* $\frac{3}{4}$ cup butter (see Stages 1 and 4)
8 oz. mushrooms (stalks could be used)	2 cups mushrooms (stems could be used)
2 medium-sized onions	2 medium-sized onions
4 oz. soft breadcrumbs	2 cups soft bread crumbs
1 teaspoon mixed fresh herbs (rosemary, parsley, marjoram) *or* pinch dried herbs	1 teaspoon mixed fresh herbs (rosemary, parsley, marjoram) *or* dash dried herbs
3 oz. cheese, grated, either all Parmesan *or* $\frac{1}{2}$ Parmesan, $\frac{1}{2}$ Gruyère *or* Cheddar	$\frac{3}{4}$ cup grated cheese, either all Parmesan *or* $\frac{1}{2}$ Parmesan, $\frac{1}{2}$ Gruyère *or* Cheddar
For the topping:	**For the topping:**
1–2 oz. cheese, grated	$\frac{1}{4}$–$\frac{1}{2}$ cup grated cheese

*Serves 4 as main dish or 8 as hors d'oeuvre.

1. Wash the courgettes, cut into halves lengthways. Either simmer steadily in well-seasoned water until half-cooked or, better still, cook very gently in a large frying pan with plenty of butter, turning once or twice.
2. Which ever method of cooking is used, the courgettes should be fairly firm ready to stuff.
3. Lift out of the pan, if using the water method, drain well. Scoop out centre pulp, chop finely.
4. Meanwhile, fry the chopped mushrooms and onions in hot butter until soft. Add to breadcrumbs with chopped fresh herbs or dried herbs, cheese and courgette pulp. Season well.
5. Pack this mixture into the cavities of the courgettes and sprinkle the tops with grated cheese.
6. Either put back into the frying pan (if using the sauté method at Stage 1), and reheat in remaining butter then put pan under hot grill to brown, or put stuffed marrows into well-buttered dish and bake for 25 minutes until crisp and brown.

275

Fritelle ripiene
Stuffed vegetable fritters

Cooking time: 15–20 min. **Preparation time:** 20 min. **Main cooking utensils:** saucepan, deep fat pan, frying basket.

IMPERIAL

For 4 people you need:
2 very large onions
1 oz. lard
1 medium-sized bread roll
1 can anchovy fillets
seasoning

For the batter:
6 oz. flour
seasoning
2 eggs
4 oz. Parmesan cheese, finely grated
little grated nutmeg
½ pint light beer *or* milk and water

To fry:
oil

To garnish:
parsley *or* chervil

AMERICAN

For 4 people you need:
2 very large onions
2 tablespoons lard
1 medium-sized bread roll
1 can anchovy fillets
seasoning

For the batter:
1½ cups all-purpose flour
seasoning
2 eggs
1 cup finely grated Parmesan cheese
little grated nutmeg
1¼ cups light beer *or* milk and water

To fry:
oil

To garnish:
parsley *or* chervil

1. Peel and cut the onions into rings, then fry in the hot lard until soft, but only pale golden brown.
2. Break the roll into fine crumbs and blend with onions, together with chopped anchovies and seasoning to taste; use only a little salt.
3. Press together to make a filling for the fritters.
4. Sieve the flour into a bowl and season well.
5. Beat in the eggs, cheese and nutmeg and gradually add the beer, or milk and water to give a light batter. If wished, the egg yolks may be beaten into the flour and the stiffly beaten egg whites folded into the batter just before cooking.
6. Heat the oil, a cube of day-old bread should turn golden within 30 seconds.
7. Gather up spoonfuls of the onion mixture and dip into the batter. Fry until crisp and golden brown, drain on absorbent paper.
8. Garnish with parsley or chervil and serve at once.

276

Torta di pesche
Peach tart

Cooking time: 45 min. **Preparation time:** 25 min. **Main cooking utensils:** ovenproof shallow dish *or* pie dish, saucepan. **Oven temperature:** moderately hot to hot, 400–425°F., 200–220°C., Gas Mark 6, then very moderate, 325–350°F., 170–180°C., Gas Mark 3. **Oven position:** centre.

IMPERIAL

For 5–6 people you need:
For the pastry:
4 oz. butter
2 oz. sugar
6 oz. flour, preferably plain
1 oz. cornflour
1 egg yolk
cold water

To glaze pastry:
1 egg white

For the filling:
4–5 large peaches *or* equivalent in smaller fruit
2 eggs
3 oz. sugar
½ pint milk
2 oz. fine cake crumbs
2 oz. blanched almonds

AMERICAN

For 5–6 people you need:
For the pastry:
½ cup butter
¼ cup sugar
1½ cups all-purpose flour
¼ cup cornstarch
1 egg yolk
cold water

To glaze pastry:
1 egg white

For the filling:
4–5 large peaches *or* equivalent in smaller fruit
2 eggs
6 tablespoons sugar
1¼ cups milk
1 cup fine cake crumbs
about ½ cup blanched almonds

1. Cream the butter and sugar.
2. Work in the flour, cornflour, egg yolk and water to bind.
3. Roll out and line the dish—this tart is very fragile, due to the rather heavy filling, so it is better to cook and serve in the same dish.
4. Brush the pastry with egg white and bake 'blind' in hot oven for 15 minutes.
5. Loosen skin of peaches by lowering carefully into boiling water for 30 seconds, then into cold water.
6. Halve or divide into portions and put into pastry case.
7. Beat the eggs, 2 oz. (U.S. ¼ cup) sugar, add hot milk, crumbs and chopped nuts.
8. Spoon into the pastry case, sprinkle with the rest of the sugar.
9. Return to the oven, lowering heat; bake until set.

To serve: Hot with cream, or it is delicious with soft cream cheese.

To vary: Use ripe apricots instead of peaches.

277

Zabaglione
Egg dessert

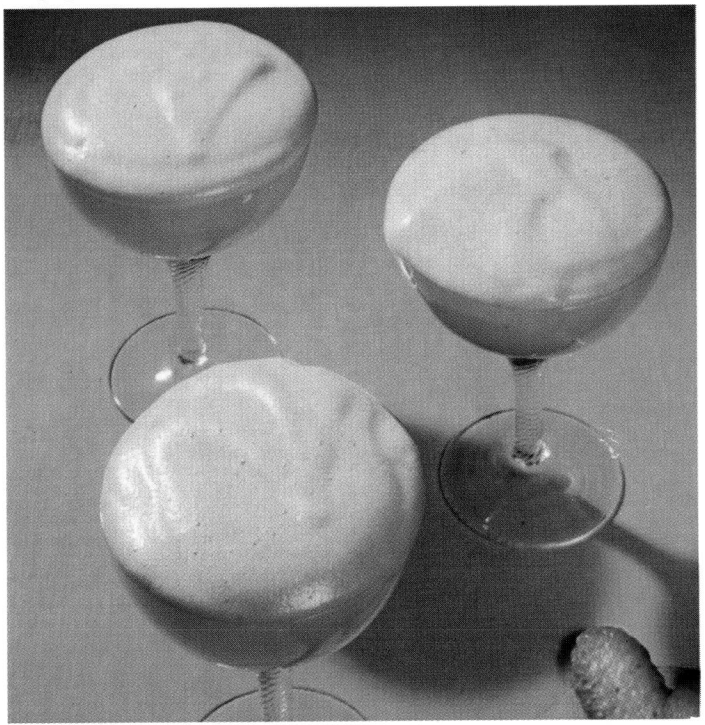

Cooking time: 10–15 min. **Preparation time:** 10 min. **Main cooking utensil:** saucepan.

IMPERIAL	**AMERICAN**
For 3 people you need:	For 3 people you need:
2 oz. castor sugar	$\frac{1}{4}$ cup granulated sugar
1 tablespoon water	1 tablespoon water
1 egg, separated	1 egg, separated
2 egg yolks	2 egg yolks
1 tablespoon Marsala*	1 tablespoon Marsala*
Or: (see Stage 5)	**Or:** (see Stage 5)
3 egg yolks	3 egg yolks
2 oz. castor sugar	$\frac{1}{4}$ cup granulated sugar
2–3 tablespoons Marsala*	3–4 tablespoons Marsala*
2 tablespoons sweet white wine	3 tablespoons sweet white wine

*This is a heavy sweet wine from Sicily, ideal in this recipe. If not available, use a sweet Madeira wine.

1. Put the sugar and water into a small pan and stir until the sugar has dissolved. Then boil quickly to 260°F. (until a firm ball when tested in cold water).
2. Beat the egg white until stiff, add the sugar syrup and mix quickly with a whisk.
3. Place the yolks and Marsala in a basin and whisk over a pan of hot water until thick and mousse-like, being careful not to overheat the eggs.
4. Combine the Marsala mixture with the meringue mixture and pour into glasses.
5. **Or** whisk yolks and castor sugar, as above, until thick and light in colour. Gradually beat in the Marsala and the white wine. This is a lighter dessert.

To serve: At once. Zabaglione is also delicious as a topping on poached black cherries.

278

Torta di nocciola
Hazelnut slices

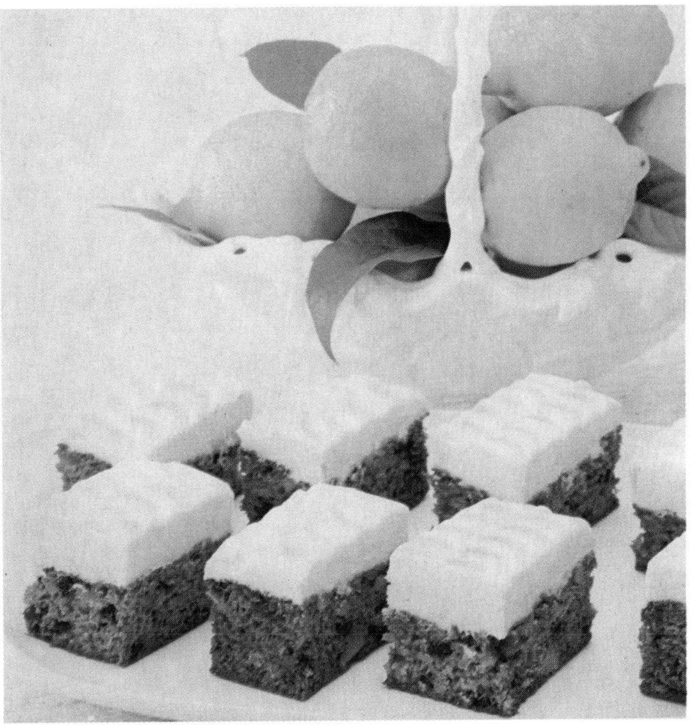

Cooking time: 15–20 min. **Preparation time:** 25 min. **Main cooking utensil:** Swiss roll tin/jelly roll pan, greaseproof paper/wax paper. **Oven temperature:** moderate to moderately hot, 375–400°F., 190–200°C., Gas Mark 5–6. **Oven position:** just above centre.

IMPERIAL	**AMERICAN**
For 12–18 cakes you need:	For 12–18 cakes you need:
4 oz. hazelnuts *or* almonds	$\frac{1}{4}$ lb. hazelnuts *or* almonds
4 eggs	4 eggs
5 oz. castor sugar	$\frac{1}{2}$ cup plus 2 tablespoons sugar
2 oz. self-raising flour	$\frac{1}{2}$ cup all-purpose flour, sifted with $\frac{1}{2}$ teaspoon baking powder
2 oz. crisp breadcrumbs	$\frac{1}{2}$ cup fine dry bread crumbs
little water	little water
To decorate:	To decorate:
5 oz. butter	$\frac{1}{2}$ cup plus 2 tablespoons butter
8 oz. sieved icing sugar	scant 2 cups sifted confectioners sugar
grated rind 2 lemons	grated rind 2 lemons
1–2 tablespoons lemon juice	1–3 tablespoons lemon juice

1. Roast the nuts in the oven for a few minutes. Grind in an electric blender or chop finely. (There is no need to skin.)
2. Put the eggs and sugar into a mixing bowl, whisk until thick.
3. Fold in the sieved flour, nuts and crumbs. The mixture should be soft enough to spread, but if a little stiff, add small quantity of warm water.
4. Put into a tin lined with greased greaseproof paper—allow this to stand above the rim of the tin. Bake until firm to the touch.
5. Allow to cool—handle very carefully.
6. Cream the butter and icing sugar until soft and light, then add lemon rind and juice.
7. Spread very carefully over the cake. Mark as picture and cut into portions.

To vary: (as picture)—add 2 oz. (U.S. $\frac{1}{2}$ cup) coarsely chopped nuts, 2 oz. (U.S. $\frac{1}{3}$ cup) dried fruit and 1 teaspoon cinnamon.

SCANDINAVIA

The countries of Scandinavia have certain similarities which tend to unify their cooking. They all have long coast-lines, bitter winters, and largely rural populations. But at the same time there is considerable diversity between them; the people are proud of their respective nationalities and are eager to preserve their traditions, which naturally include their national cuisines.

Norway, one-third of which extends beyond the Arctic circle, has the most rugged terrain and climate. Being so mountainous, few areas are suitable for crops or cattle and the Norwegians depend a great deal on their fishing industry. A terrific amount of herring is caught: Baked herrings with tomatoes and Herring in pastry cases are only two of the many delicious recipes for this versatile fish. To see them through the hard winter months, the Norwegians eat salted fish which can often be seen hanging outside to dry; some fish is cured and pickled in brine to be kept for months in large wooden tubs. Goats thrive in the mountains and are important for providing milk and cheese; Norwegian bannocks, a homely quick bread made on a griddle, are often served with goat's cheese as well as jam. The Norwegians make superb sponge cakes and Light fruit and nut cake or the more elegant Light layer cake with jam and cream are guaranteed to brighten any dark winter's day.

Finland is a land of forests, beautiful and awe-inspiring, in the midst of which the cities are isolated pockets of civilisation. The influence of neighbouring Russia is seen especially in the popularity of many types of pasties which are frequently eaten by lumberjacks. They can be carried easily for some time and even allowed to freeze before being reheated. *Kalakukko,* stuffed with fish, is one of the most well-known pasties originating in Savo, a central province of Finland. Berries of all kinds, especially cranberries and lingonberries, grow in profusion and are often the only fresh item available when no fruit or vegetables can be obtained; they are made into jam or used as a sauce over pancakes and puddings.

Sweden, reaching from above the Arctic Circle almost to Northern Germany, has greater differences in its weather and land conditions than the other Scandinavian countries. Consequently its cooking is more varied, as is demonstrated in the famous Swedish *smörgåsbord.* This popular way of giving a dinner party is not just an ordinary buffet but is presented according to long established traditions. To begin with there are several fish dishes, always including some cold pickled fish and perhaps a dish like the attractive Creamed fish mould. The guests are then given clean plates for assorted cold meats and salads and one or two hot dishes such as Veal birds or Chicken balls. Several different cheeses and fruit or a simple fruit dessert usually conclude the meal. Plenty of white and rye bread as well as Swedish crispbread should be provided with a *smörgåsbord* and the standard drinks are schnapps and beer. Schnapps, drunk ice cold in small glasses, should never be served beforehand as an aperitif because it goes best with food and beer.

Denmark is different from the rest of Scandinavia in that it is largely made up of rolling farmland. Renowned for their dairy products and their bacon and ham, the Danes have evolved some delicious recipes using these products. There are two specialities for which Denmark is internationally famous: their *smørrebrød,* or open-faced sandwiches, and Danish pastries. The preparation of open-faced sandwiches is an art in itself, for they must look as beautiful as they taste. The main topping, be it meat, cheese or egg, should cover the bread completely, while the garnish should add colour and height to the sandwich. They are designed to be eaten with a knife and fork and are ideal for a light luncheon party. The Danes wrap them carefully in polythene or foil and take them to school and the office for lunch. Everyone is familiar with Danish pastries, the rich, flaky yeast pastries made in various shapes, iced with a glacé icing, and served with morning coffee or as an afternoon snack.

Christmas is a time of great family celebrations in Scandinavia and elaborate preparations go on in the kitchen for weeks in advance. The Scandinavians are superb cookie makers but particularly so at this season when homes are filled with the aroma of baking. Mother Monsen cookies and Berlin garlands are served at a Norwegian Christmas. A Swedish speciality is Brandy cookies and the Finns make pretty Checkerboard and jelly cookies. Needless to say, these tempting biscuits, so popular with children, are enjoyed all year round as well as at Christmas.

Sild med tomater
Baked herrings with tomatoes

Cooking time: 35–40 min. **Preparation time:** 20 min. **Main cooking utensils:** frying pan/skillet *or* saucepan, ovenproof baking dish. **Oven temperature:** moderate, 375°F., 190°C., Gas Mark 4–5. **Oven position:** just above centre.

IMPERIAL

For 4 people you need:
- 4 good-sized herrings (with roes if possible)
- seasoning
- 2 teaspoons chopped dill *or* parsley
- 2–3 medium-sized onions
- 2 oz. butter
- 1–2 teaspoons French mustard
- 1–2 teaspoons sugar
- $\frac{1}{4}$ pint white *or* brown malt *or* wine vinegar
- 2–3 bay leaves
- 12 oz.–1 lb. ripe tomatoes

AMERICAN

For 4 people you need:
- 4 good-sized herring (with roe if possible)
- seasoning
- 2 teaspoons chopped dill *or* parsley
- 2–3 medium-sized onions
- $\frac{1}{4}$ cup butter
- 1–2 teaspoons French mustard
- 1–2 teaspoons sugar
- $\frac{2}{3}$ cup white *or* brown malt *or* wine vinegar
- 2–3 bay leaves
- $\frac{3}{4}$–1 lb. ripe tomatoes

1. Remove the heads and backbones from the herrings.
2. To bone, split the fish along the stomach. Lay fish on a board, slit side downwards, press firmly along backbone with your thumb.
3. Turn over, all the bones can then be removed.
4. Season inside of each fish. Sprinkle with a little chopped dill, fold and season. Return roes to the fish, seasoning these well.
5. Cut the onions into wafer-thin slices.
6. Fry in the butter for a few minutes only.
7. Blend the mustard, sugar, seasoning and vinegar with the onions.
8. Transfer to a baking dish, top with herrings and bay leaves, cover.
9. Bake for 10 minutes; add tomatoes cut in wedges, continue cooking until fish is tender.
10. Remove bay leaves before serving.

To vary: Use wafer-thin slices of raw potato as well as the onion. When nearly cooked, top the fish with crisp breadcrumbs.

280

Sild i skjell
Herring in pastry cases

Cooking time: 12–15 min. **Preparation time:** 30 min. **Main cooking utensils:** patty tins/muffin pans, saucepan. **Oven temperature:** hot, 425–450°F., 220–230°C., Gas Mark 6–7. **Oven position:** above centre.

IMPERIAL

For 8 people you need:
- 1–2 cans sild *or* 2 rollmop *or* Bismarck herrings
- 1 tablespoon chives
- 1 small beetroot

For the pastry:
- 4 oz. butter
- 8 oz. flour, plain *or* self-raising
- pinch salt
- 1 egg
- little water

For the egg mixture:
- 4–6 eggs
- 2 oz. butter
- seasoning
- 2 tablespoons thin cream
- little chopped dill *or* parsley

To garnish:
- herring tit-bits *or* anchovies
- black olives (optional)

AMERICAN

For 8 people you need:
- 2 rollmop herrings
- 1 tablespoon chives
- 1 small beet

For the pastry:
- $\frac{1}{2}$ cup butter
- 2 cups all-purpose flour
- dash salt
- 1 egg
- little water

For the egg mixture:
- 4–6 eggs
- $\frac{1}{4}$ cup butter
- seasoning
- 3 tablespoons coffee cream
- little chopped dill *or* parsley

To garnish:
- herring tit-bits *or* anchovies
- ripe olives (optional)

1. If using the canned sild, cut fish into tiny pieces. If preferred, use rollmop or Bismarck herrings and dice, draining well; save some for garnish.
2. Blend with finely chopped chives and diced beetroot.
3. To make the pastry, rub the butter into the flour, sieved with salt. Bind with egg and water.
4. Roll out and line about 8 fairly deep patty tins, measuring about $2\frac{1}{2}$–3 inches in diameter. Bake 'blind' until crisp and golden.
5. Scramble eggs in the butter, adding seasoning, cream and chopped dill or parsley. Do not allow to become too stiff.

To serve: Put herring mixture into hot or cold pastry, top with the scrambled eggs, herring pieces or anchovies and olives. Serve at once.

281

Fiskfars
Creamed fish mould

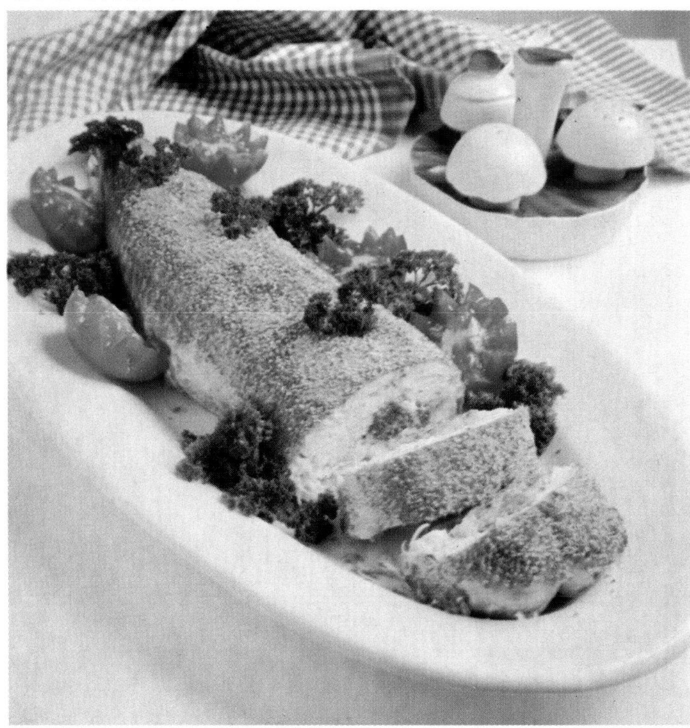

Cooking time: $1\frac{1}{2}$ hr. **Preparation time:** 30 min. **Main cooking utensils:** baking tray/sheet *or* 2-pint/$2\frac{1}{2}$-pint fish mould. **Oven temperature:** slow to very moderate, 300–325°F., 150–170°C., Gas Mark 2–3. **Oven position:** centre.

IMPERIAL	AMERICAN
For 6 people you need:	For 6 people you need:
2 lb. white fish	2 lb. white fish
4 oz. butter	$\frac{1}{2}$ cup butter
2 eggs	2 eggs
$1\frac{1}{2}$ oz. flour	6 tablespoons all-purpose flour
4 tablespoons thin cream	$\frac{1}{3}$ cup coffee cream
seasoning	seasoning
$\frac{1}{4}$ pint thick cream	$\frac{2}{3}$ cup whipping cream
1 oz. butter	2 tablespoons butter
2 oz. crisp breadcrumbs	$\frac{1}{2}$ cup crisp bread crumbs
For the stuffing:	For the stuffing:
4–6 oz. mushrooms	1–$1\frac{1}{2}$ cups mushrooms
2 oz. butter	$\frac{1}{4}$ cup butter
2 oz. soft breadcrumbs	1 cup soft bread crumbs
1 egg	1 egg
To garnish:	To garnish:
tomatoes, parsley	tomatoes, parsley

1. Remove all bones and skin from the fish and put this twice through a fine mincer. If it is not possible to mince the fish, then chop and pound well. Gradually work the butter into the fish.
2. Add egg yolks, flour and thin cream gradually to the fish mixture.
3. If the mixture shows signs of curdling, place the bowl of mixture over hot water and beat until smooth, season well.
4. Fold in the lightly whipped cream and the stiffly beaten egg whites.
5. Butter a 2-pint (U.S. $2\frac{1}{2}$-pint) fish mould and coat with crumbs.
6. Put part of the mixture into the mould. Add the stuffing made by frying finely chopped mushrooms in the butter, adding crumbs, egg and seasoning.
7. Cover with the rest of the fish mixture and bake until firm.
8. Garnish with tomatoes and parsley. Serve hot with mixed vegetables. Cold with various salads.

NOTE: If preferred fish mixture may be formed into roll shape with stuffing in the centre, put on to well-buttered baking tray and coated with melted butter and crumbs.

282

Kalakukko
Fish in a dough case

Cooking time: 1–$1\frac{1}{4}$ hr. **Preparation time:** 30 min. **Main cooking utensil:** flat baking tray/sheet. **Oven temperature:** moderate to moderately hot, 375–400°F., 190–200°C., Gas Mark 5–6, then very moderate, 325–350°F., 170–180°C., Gas Mark 3. **Oven position:** centre.

IMPERIAL	AMERICAN
For 4–5 portions you need:	For 4–5 portions you need:
8 oz. flour, preferably plain	2 cups all-purpose flour
$\frac{1}{2}$ teaspoon salt	$\frac{1}{2}$ teaspoon salt
2 teaspoons sugar	2 teaspoons sugar
3 oz. rye flour*	$\frac{3}{4}$ cup rye flour*
4 oz. butter *or* fat	$\frac{1}{2}$ cup butter *or* fat
milk and water to mix	milk and water to mix
For the filling:	For the filling:
$1\frac{1}{4}$ lb. raw white fish	$1\frac{1}{4}$ lb. raw white fish
4 oz. fat bacon *or* salt pork	$\frac{1}{4}$ lb. salt pork
seasoning	seasoning
little milk *or* egg	little milk *or* egg
To glaze:	To glaze:
melted bacon *or* pork fat	melted pork fat

*Or use fine oatmeal.

1. Sieve together the flour, salt and sugar. Add rye flour.
2. Rub in the butter or fat.
3. Add enough liquid to make a rolling consistency.
4. Roll out to a large round and make edges neat.
5. Cut the fish into small neat strips and bacon or pork fat into tiny pieces. Mix together, season well and moisten with milk or egg.
6. Put over half the pastry, fold rest to make a 'pasty' shape, brushing edges well. Brush top with melted fat.
7. Seal and flute edges, then lift on to a baking tray and cook for about 25 minutes at the higher temperature, then lower heat and continue cooking until very firm.

To serve: Hot or cold with salad. Ideal for a picnic.

To vary: Reduce amount of fish to 12 oz., add 1–2 oz. (U.S. $\frac{1}{4}$–$\frac{1}{3}$ cup) cooked rice, chopped hard-boiled eggs, skinned slice tomato, beaten egg or milk to moisten. Make into small shapes and bake for 40 minutes only.

Rakefisk
Corned or salted fish

Cooking time: none, but see Stage 3. **Preparation time:** 5 min. **Main utensils:** large bowl, see Stage 1; if cooking, a large pan, see Stage 3.

IMPERIAL

For 4 people you need:
1 whole fish *or* 2 fillets
salt to cover
sugar to flavour
water

When cooking:
mixed dried pickling spices
to taste
2–3 bay leaves
$\frac{1}{4}$ pint malt vinegar
1 onion

AMERICAN

For 4 people you need:
1 whole fish *or* 2 fillets
salt to cover
sugar to flavor
water

When cooking:
mixed dried pickling spices
to taste
2–3 bay leaves
$\frac{2}{3}$ cup malt vinegar
1 onion

1. Clean the fish well. If not filleting, salt inside very thoroughly. Pack into a container; in Norway, wooden ones are used but a strong earthenware bowl could be used.
2. Sprinkle a good layer of salt and sprinkling of sugar between the layers. Press down with a good weight and cover with water. In Norway this is stored in a cold place for 3 months, but can be used earlier.
3. The fish can be lifted from the brine and served raw. But, as shown in the picture, it can be sliced and filleted, covered with pickling spices, bay leaves, little vinegar and rings of raw onion, then simmered gently until tender. Remove pickling spices before serving.

284

Laxmajonas
Salmon mayonnaise

Preparation time: 15 min. **Main utensils:** 2 mixing bowls.

IMPERIAL

For 4 people you need:
10 oz. cooked *or* well-drained
canned salmon
3 medium-sized firm tomatoes
piece cucumber (3 inches)
4 oz. cooked peas
4 oz. cooked potatoes (preferably
new)

For the dressing:
2 tablespoons mayonnaise
1 tablespoon lemon juice
pinch sugar
pinch salt
shake pepper
2 teaspoons chopped dill

To garnish:
1 lettuce
1 hard-boiled egg

AMERICAN

For 4 people you need:
scant $\frac{3}{4}$ lb. cooked *or*
well-drained canned salmon
3 medium-sized firm tomatoes
piece cucumber (3 inches)
$\frac{1}{4}$ lb. cooked peas
$\frac{1}{4}$ lb. cooked potatoes (preferably
new)

For the dressing:
3 tablespoons mayonnaise
1 tablespoon lemon juice
dash sugar
dash salt
dash pepper
2 teaspoons chopped dill

To garnish:
1 lettuce
1 hard-cooked egg

1. Flake the fish and put into a bowl.
2. Skin the tomatoes and dice neatly, blend with the salmon.
3. Peel and dice the cucumber finely, add to the fish together with the peas and the diced potatoes.
4. Blend the mayonnaise with the other ingredients for the dressing.
5. Spoon over the fish mixture, mixing gently until moist.
6. Shred most of the lettuce in a bowl. Pile the fish mixture on top of this and garnish with a ring of shredded lettuce, then a flower design of quartered hard-boiled egg.

To vary: Add a little chopped chive to the dressing.
Mix salmon with prawns or other shellfish.
Blend chopped hard-boiled egg into the salad with the fish.

Bacon oliven
Bacon olives

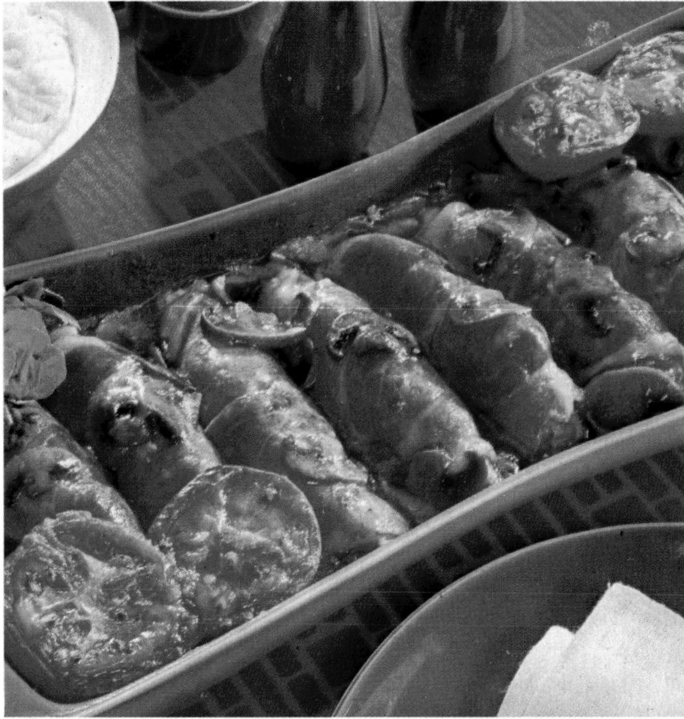

Cooking time: 35 min. **Preparation time:** 20 min. **Main cooking utensils:** frying pan/skillet, ovenproof dish, cotton *or* wooden cocktail sticks/toothpicks. **Oven temperature:** moderately hot, 400°F., 200°C., Gas Mark 5–6. **Oven position:** above centre.

IMPERIAL

For 4–8 people you need:*
3 oz. butter
4 oz. mushrooms
1 medium-sized onion
3 oz. soft breadcrumbs
1 tablespoon chopped parsley
1 egg
seasoning
8 thin uncooked gammon rashers *or* long back rashers
2–4 tomatoes

To garnish:
watercress

AMERICAN

For 4–8 people you need:*
6 tablespoons butter
1 cup mushrooms
1 medium-sized onion
$1\frac{1}{2}$ cups soft bread crumbs
1 tablespoon chopped parsley
1 egg
seasoning
8 thin slices Canadian bacon

2–4 tomatoes

To garnish:
watercress

*4 as a main meal, 8 as a snack.

1. Heat half the butter and fry half the sliced mushrooms and finely chopped onion in this until soft.
2. Mix with the breadcrumbs and parsley, bind with egg.
3. Season well. (Most Danish bacon is mild in flavour so a reasonable amount of salt could be used.)
4. Form the stuffing into 8 finger shapes.
5. Remove rinds from the bacon, roll round stuffing, tie with cotton or secure with cocktail sticks.
6. Put into a dish, cook for approximately 25 minutes until bacon is tender. Very lean gammon could be brushed with a little melted butter before cooking.
7. Meanwhile, slice remaining mushrooms and halve tomatoes. Fry in remaining butter and add to the dish just before serving.

To serve: Garnish with watercress and serve with creamed potatoes.

To vary: (As in picture) – blend $\frac{1}{2}$ oz. (U.S. 2 tablespoons) flour with $\frac{1}{2}$ pint (U.S. $1\frac{1}{4}$ cups) good brown stock. Use 1 oz. (U.S. $\frac{1}{4}$ cup) flour for a thicker sauce. Put into the pan after removing stuffing ingredients, cook until thickened, add to bacon near end of cooking time.

286

Lever med skinke ruller
Liver and bacon roll

Cooking time: 1 hr. **Preparation time:** 35 min. **Main cooking utensils:** frying pan/skillet, baking tray/sheet. **Oven temperature:** moderately hot, 400°F., 200°C., Gas Mark 5–6. **Oven position:** centre.

IMPERIAL

For 4–6 people you need:
8–10 oz. streaky bacon
1 oz. fat
1–2 onions
8–10 oz. calf's, lamb's *or* pig's liver
seasoning
$\frac{1}{2}$–1 teaspoon chopped parsley
1 teaspoon sugar (optional)

For the pastry:
10 oz. self-raising flour

seasoning
4 oz. shredded suet *or* 4 oz. butter
water to mix

To garnish:
4 tomatoes
chopped parsley

AMERICAN

For 4–6 people you need:
$\frac{1}{2}$–$\frac{2}{3}$ lb. bacon slices
2 tablespoons fat
1–2 onions
$\frac{1}{2}$–$\frac{2}{3}$ lb. calf, lamb *or* pork liver

seasoning
$\frac{1}{2}$–1 teaspoon chopped parsley
1 teaspoon sugar (optional)

For the pastry:
$2\frac{1}{2}$ cups all-purpose flour, sifted with 3 teaspoons baking powder
seasoning
scant 1 cup shredded suet *or* $\frac{1}{2}$ cup butter
water to mix

To garnish:
4 tomatoes
chopped parsley

1. Remove rinds from the bacon, cut bacon into small pieces.
2. Put the bacon rinds and fat into a pan. Heat, then fry finely chopped onion until tender, do not allow to brown.
3. Blend the bacon with onion and finely diced liver, heat in pan for a few minutes only. Remove bacon rinds.
4. Season well, flavour with parsley and sugar.
5. Sieve the flour and seasoning, add suet or rub in butter, bind with water.
6. Roll out thinly to form an oblong. Spread with the bacon mixture.
7. Roll firmly, lift on to a baking tray. Brush with milk.
8. Bake until crisp and golden; reduce heat after 35–40 minutes to moderate if necessary. Halve and bake tomatoes, top with parsley.

To serve: With thickened gravy; make this in the frying pan to retain flavour of liver.

Kalv järpar
Veal birds (Mock chicken)

Cooking time: 45–55 min. **Preparation time:** 25 min. **Main cooking utensil:** large frying pan/skillet with lid *or* shallow saucepan.

IMPERIAL

For 6 people you need:
6 thin slices fillet of veal, cut from top of leg
2 oz. flour
2 oz. margarine

For the stuffing:
8 oz. pork *or* pork sausage meat
2 medium-sized onions
1 oz. margarine
2 oz. soft breadcrumbs
1 tablespoon chopped parsley
seasoning

For the sauce:
4 medium-sized onions
4 medium-sized carrots
1 pint white stock

AMERICAN

For 6 people you need:
6 thin slices boned veal cutlets
$\frac{1}{2}$ cup all-purpose flour
$\frac{1}{4}$ cup margarine

For the stuffing:
$\frac{1}{2}$ lb. pork *or* pork sausage meat
2 medium-sized onions
2 tablespoons margarine
1 cup soft bread crumbs
1 tablespoon chopped parsley
seasoning

For the sauce:
4 medium-sized onions
4 medium-sized carrots
$2\frac{1}{2}$ cups white stock

1. Beat the veal slices until very thin, if preferred, each slice may be cut into half to make smaller rolls.
2. Prepare the stuffing: mince pork or use pork sausage meat.
3. Chop the onions finely, fry in hot margarine until just soft.
4. Blend with pork or sausage meat, crumbs, parsley and seasoning.
5. Spread stuffing over the meat, roll up firmly, secure with cotton or wooden cocktail sticks.
6. Season the flour, coat meat and fry in margarine.
7. Lift out meat. Toss peeled, sliced onions and carrots in remaining margarine.
8. Gradually blend in the stock. Bring to the boil, cook until thickened, stirring well.
9. Replace meat, cover pan and simmer for 30–35 minutes until tender.

To serve: Arrange meat rolls on dish with broccoli, carrots, onions or other vegetables and Duchesse potatoes. Serve sauce separately.

288

Buitenpostej
Danish country pie

Cooking time: $1\frac{1}{4}$ hr. **Preparation time:** 30 min. **Main cooking utensils:** frying pan/skillet *or* saucepan, 2-pint/$2\frac{1}{2}$-pint pie dish. **Oven temperature:** hot, 425–450°F., 220–230°C., Gas Mark 6–7, then moderate, 375°F., 190°C., Gas Mark 4–5. **Oven position:** centre.

IMPERIAL

For 4–5 people you need:
For the pastry:
6 oz. plain flour
pinch salt
2 oz. lard
2 oz. butter
water to mix
$1\frac{1}{4}$ lb. Danish back bacon *or* gammon cut into thick slices
1–2 oz. butter *or* lard
2 onions
4 oz. mushrooms
8 oz. cooked green beans
1 oz. flour
$\frac{1}{2}$ pint white stock
seasoning

To glaze:
1 egg

AMERICAN

For 4–5 people you need:
For the pastry:
$1\frac{1}{2}$ cups all-purpose flour
dash salt
$\frac{1}{4}$ cup lard
$\frac{1}{4}$ cup butter
water to mix
$1\frac{1}{4}$ lb. Canadian bacon, cut into thick slices
2–4 tablespoons butter *or* lard
2 onions
1 cup mushrooms
$\frac{1}{2}$ lb. cooked green beans
$\frac{1}{4}$ cup all-purpose flour
$1\frac{1}{4}$ cups white stock
seasoning

To glaze:
1 egg

1. First make the pastry; sieve the flour and salt.
2. Mix the lard and butter, rub in third, bind with water.
3. Roll to an oblong, then put half remaining fat over two-thirds of dough, fold like an envelope.
4. Turn, re-roll and repeat Stage 3. Put in a cool place before final rolling.
5. Remove bacon rind if necessary, cut bacon into dice. Fry in a pan for approximately 5 minutes, remove on to a plate.
6. Add enough butter or lard to fry very finely chopped onions and mushrooms until tender.
7. Mix with bacon and green beans, then put into a dish.
8. Blend flour with fat in the pan, stir in stock. Bring to the boil and cook until thickened. Season and pour over bacon.
9. Cover with pastry and brush with beaten egg.
10. Cook for 25 minutes in hot oven, then lower heat for further 20 minutes.

289

Smørrebrød
Open-faced sandwiches

These open sandwiches are used for most occasions in Scandinavia, particularly in Denmark.
Never cut the bread too thick. Cut thin slices of brown, white, rye or crispbread, butter lavishly then put on the toppings.

TOPPINGS

1) Slices of liver pâté topped with salad and slices of cucumber, tomato and sprig of parsley.
2) Liver pâté topped with crisp slice of fried or grilled bacon, fried mushrooms and curl of beetroot.
3) Lettuce topped with potato salad, tomato, crisp slice of fried or grilled bacon and gherkin fan.
4) Lettuce topped with sliced hard-boiled egg, pieces of crisp bacon and twist of tomato, sprig of parsley.
5) Curls of luncheon meat or cooked ham, potato salad, prune, twist of sliced orange and sprig of parsley.
6) Lettuce, pieces of Danish Camembert cheese, halved slices of fried or grilled bacon and sprig of parsley.
7) Thin overlapping slices of Esrom or Havarti (Danish cheeses), slice of fried or grilled bacon, twist tomato and sprigs of parsley.
8) Thin slices smoked ham, sliced raw mushrooms, twist of orange, twist of tomato and sprig of parsley.
9) Lettuce, sliced hard-boiled egg, curled slice of fried or grilled bacon, twist tomato and sprig of parsley.
10) Prawns in thick mayonnaise.
11) Smoked salmon, mackerel or eel with scrambled egg and chopped dill or chives.
12) Tongue with prunes and salad.
13) Beef with red cabbage and horseradish.

290

Svinesylte
Brawn

Cooking time: $2\frac{1}{2}$–3 hr. **Preparation time:** 30 min. plus overnight soaking of pig's head and setting time. **Main cooking utensils:** large saucepan, 3–4-pint/$3\frac{1}{2}$–$4\frac{1}{2}$-pint basin *or* mould.

IMPERIAL

For 8 people you need:
1 pig's head
salt
2 lb. pork (shoulder is generally used)
3 bay leaves
2–3 cloves
$\frac{1}{2}$–1 teaspoon black pepper
$\frac{1}{2}$ teaspoon allspice
good pinch curry powder

To garnish:
parsley

AMERICAN

For 8 people you need:
1 pig's head
salt
2 lb. fresh picnic shoulder of pork
3 bay leaves
2–3 cloves
$\frac{1}{2}$–1 teaspoon black pepper
$\frac{1}{2}$ teaspoon allspice
dash curry powder

To garnish:
parsley

1. Wash the pig's head, dry all over and rub with salt.
2. Put into a bowl, cover with cold water and soak overnight.
3. Lift the pig's head out of the water, put into a large saucepan with the pork. Cover with fresh cold water, add bay leaves and cloves.
4. Cover and simmer steadily for $2\frac{1}{2}$ hours or until meat is tender.
5. Lift pig's head and pork out of liquid. Boil liquid rapidly in open pan until reduced to $\frac{1}{2}$ pint (U.S. $1\frac{1}{4}$ cups).
6. Meanwhile cut all meat from head and shoulder, put into a basin or mould. Add a sprinkling of pepper, allspice and curry powder to each layer of meat (mix lean and fat together as you pack.)
7. Pour sufficient concentrated liquid over the meat to cover. Put a plate on top with a light weight. Leave until set.

To serve: Remove surplus fat from top and turn out. Serve with pickled beetroot and garnish with parsley.

Skinke à la Tivolii

Ham in Tivoli style

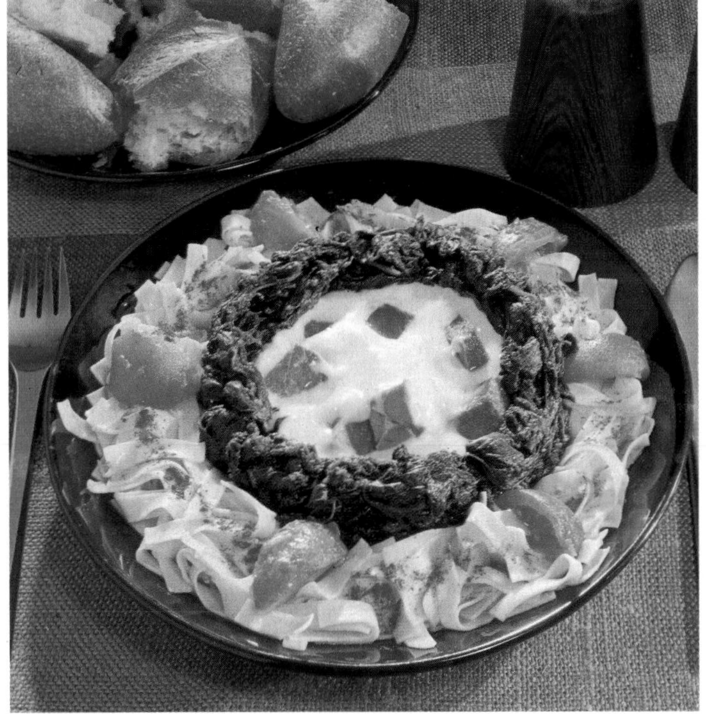

Cooking time: 20 min. **Preparation time:** 30 min. **Main cooking utensils:** 2 saucepans and 1 double saucepan if serving ham hot.

IMPERIAL

For 4–5 people you need:
2 lb. spinach
seasoning
3 oz. butter
6 oz. pasta (can be any type)
1 can Danish ham *or* about 12 oz. cooked ham

For the sauce:
$\frac{1}{2}$ pint soured cream
1–2 tablespoons freshly grated horseradish *or* equivalent in horseradish cream
1–2 teaspoons sugar
1–2 teaspoons lemon juice *or* white vinegar

For the creamy sauce: (optional)
$1\frac{1}{2}$ oz. butter
1 oz. flour
$\frac{1}{4}$ pint milk
$\frac{1}{4}$ pint thin cream
seasoning

AMERICAN

For 4–5 people you need:
2 lb. spinach
seasoning
6 tablespoons butter
1 cup pasta (can be any type)
1 can Danish ham *or* about $\frac{3}{4}$ lb. cooked cured ham

For the sauce:
$1\frac{1}{4}$ cups sour cream
1–3 tablespoons freshly grated horseradish *or* equivalent in horseradish cream
1–2 teaspoons sugar
1–2 teaspoons lemon juice *or* white vinegar

For the creamy sauce: (optional)
3 tablespoons butter
$\frac{1}{4}$ cup all-purpose flour
$\frac{2}{3}$ cup milk
$\frac{2}{3}$ cup coffee cream
seasoning

1. Wash and cook the spinach with seasoning and little water until tender. Strain, chop or sieve and reheat with half the butter.
2. Cook the noodles in 4 pints (U.S. 5 pints) boiling, salted water until tender. Toss in remaining butter, strain.
3. Dice the ham. Blend soured cream with grated fresh horseradish or horseradish cream, add sugar and lemon juice or vinegar. Mix ham with this. Serve sauce cold. If preferred the sauce and ham could be heated together in double pan in a creamy white sauce.
4. To make sauce, melt butter and add flour. Stir in milk, bring to boil. Remove from heat, add cream and reheat without boiling. Season.

To serve: Arrange noodles round edge of dish, top with paprika and segments of skinned tomato. Form spinach into a neat ring, fill with the ham mixture.

292

Kyckling kroketter

Chicken balls

Cooking time: A: 15 min., B: 5 min. **Preparation time:** A: 20 min., B: 10 min. **Main cooking utensils:** 2 saucepans, pan for oil, absorbent paper/paper towels.

IMPERIAL

To make about 12 balls you need:
A: KYCKLING KROKETTER
1 oz. butter
1 oz. flour
$\frac{1}{4}$ pint milk
seasoning
8 oz. cooked chicken
3 oz. gherkins
1 egg
2 oz. plain biscuit crumbs

To coat:
2 oz. biscuit crumbs

B: KYCKLINGLEVER KROKETTER
2 oz. butter
6 oz. chicken livers
2 oz. gherkins
1 tablespoon mayonnaise
$\frac{1}{2}$ teaspoon paprika pepper
2 hard-boiled eggs
dill *or* parsley

AMERICAN

To make about 12 balls you need:
A: KYCKLING KROKETTER
2 tablespoons butter
$\frac{1}{4}$ cup all-purpose flour
$\frac{2}{3}$ cup milk
seasoning
$\frac{1}{2}$ lb. cooked chicken
about 6 sweet dill pickles
1 egg
$\frac{3}{4}$ cup Graham cracker crumbs

To coat:
$\frac{3}{4}$ cup cracker crumbs

B: KYCKLINGLEVER KROKETTER
$\frac{1}{4}$ cup butter
about $\frac{1}{3}$ lb. chicken liver
about 4 sweet dill pickles
1 tablespoon mayonnaise
$\frac{1}{2}$ teaspoon paprika pepper
2 hard-cooked eggs
dill *or* parsley

A: KYCKLING KROKETTER
1. Make a thick sauce of butter, flour and milk; season well.
2. Add finely chopped or minced chicken, chopped gherkins, egg and crumbs. Allow to cool and stiffen.
3. Roll into balls, then turn in the fine biscuit crumbs.
4. Fry in hot oil or butter until crisp and golden, about 1 minute, then drain well. Put a cocktail stick through each.

To serve: With stuffed tomatoes.

B: KYCKLINGLEVER KROKETTER
1. Heat butter, fry liver until tender, mash and cool. Blend with chopped gherkins, mayonnaise and paprika.
2. Roll into balls and turn in chopped hard-boiled egg and dill or parsley.

Ohukaiset
Pancakes

Cooking time: 15 min. **Preparation time:** 10 min. **Main cooking utensil:** griddle *or* frying pan/skillet.

IMPERIAL

For 4 people you need:
4 oz. flour, plain *or* self-raising
pinch salt
1 egg
$\frac{1}{2}$ pint milk
2 teaspoons sugar
$\frac{1}{4}$ teaspoon powdered nutmeg
$\frac{1}{2}$–1 oz. butter for griddle *or* 2–3 oz. butter for frying pan

To serve:
jam *or* jelly

AMERICAN

For 4 people you need:
1 cup all-purpose flour
dash salt
1 egg
$1\frac{1}{4}$ cups milk
2 teaspoons sugar
$\frac{1}{4}$ teaspoon powdered nutmeg
1–2 tablespoons butter for griddle *or* 4–6 tablespoons butter for skillet

To serve:
jam *or* jelly

1. Sieve the flour and salt.
2. Add the egg and milk and beat hard to a smooth batter. Add the sugar and nutmeg.
3. Most Scandinavian pancakes are cooked on a griddle but these may be cooked in hot butter in a frying pan.
4. If using a griddle, grease and heat. Test to see if right temperature by shaking on a little dry flour, this should turn golden brown in 1 minute.
5. Pour a spoonful of batter on to the griddle to give a neat round.
6. Cook steadily for 2 minutes, until golden on underside and bubbling on top. Turn, cook on second side.

To serve: With a rather sharp-flavoured jam. Although sweet, these are often served in generous quantities as a light lunch with coffee.

294

Rombudding
Rum pudding with cherry sauce

Cooking time: 5 min. **Preparation time:** 15 min. plus time for mould to set. **Main cooking utensils:** saucepans, mould.

IMPERIAL

For 6 people you need:
$\frac{1}{2}$ pint thick cream *or* 1 (10 oz.) can Danish cream
3 teaspoons powder gelatine*
3 tablespoons water
4 large egg yolks
5 oz. sugar
$\frac{1}{4}$ pint milk
$\frac{1}{4}$ pint thin cream
3 tablespoons rum
$\frac{1}{2}$ teaspoon vanilla essence

For the cherry sauce:
8 oz. Morello cherries
5 tablespoons water
1–2 oz. sugar
2 teaspoons cornflour

*Or 5 thin leaves gelatine.

AMERICAN

For 6 people you need:
$1\frac{1}{4}$ cups whipping cream *or* 1 (10 oz.) can cream
3 teaspoons powder gelatin
scant $\frac{1}{4}$ cup water
4 large egg yolks
$\frac{1}{2}$ cup plus 2 tablespoons sugar
$\frac{2}{3}$ cup milk
$\frac{2}{3}$ cup coffee cream
scant $\frac{1}{4}$ cup rum
$\frac{1}{2}$ teaspoon vanilla extract

For the cherry sauce:
$\frac{1}{2}$ lb. Morello cherries
6 tablespoons water
2–4 tablespoons sugar
2 teaspoons cornstarch

1. Chill the thick cream thoroughly.
2. Put the powder gelatine blended with water in a basin over hot water: leave until dissolved.
3. Whisk the egg yolks and sugar until really thick.
4. Bring the milk and thin cream just to the boil.
5. Remove from the heat, then add gelatine when thoroughly dissolved, and stir very well.
6. Stir the milk and gelatine mixture into beaten eggs and sugar, with rum and vanilla essence.
7. Chill until thick, but not set, then fold in lightly whipped cream.
8. Put into a mould, rinsed out in cold water, and leave to set.
9. Put the cherries, with half water, and sugar, in a pan. Cook for a few minutes.
10. Blend the cornflour with the rest of the water, stir into cherry mixture and cook until smooth and clear.

To serve: Unmould the rum pudding, serve with very hot cherry sauce. This sauce should not be too sweet.

295

Saftkräm
Fruit whip

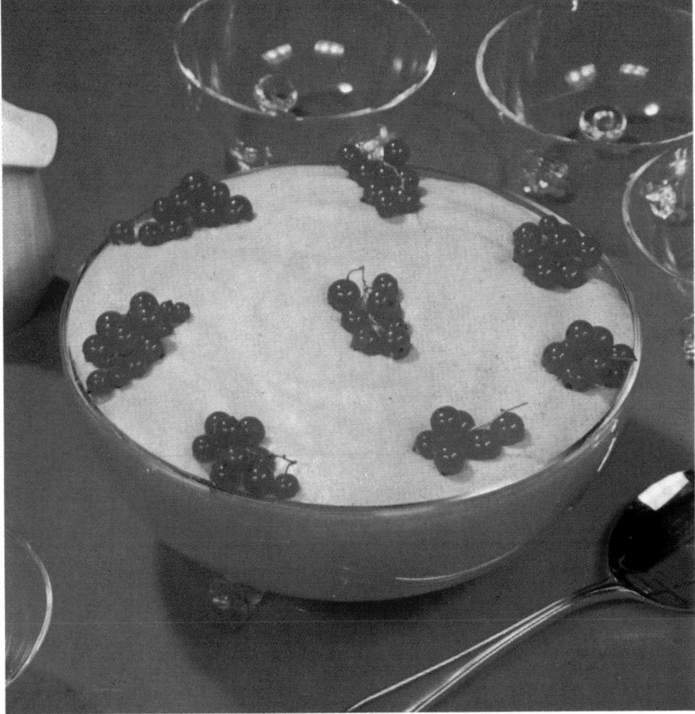

Cooking time: 35 min. **Preparation time:** 15 min. **Main cooking utensils:** large saucepan, sieve.

IMPERIAL

For 6–8 people you need:
$2\frac{1}{2}$ lb. redcurrants*
$1\frac{1}{2}$ pints water
4 oz. sugar
3 oz. semolina
$\frac{1}{4}$ pint thick cream
2 egg whites

To decorate:
about 8 oz. redcurrants in neat bunches
little sugar, preferably vanilla sugar

AMERICAN

For 6–8 people you need:
$2\frac{1}{2}$ lb. red currants*
$3\frac{3}{4}$ cups water
$\frac{1}{2}$ cup sugar
$\frac{1}{2}$ cup semolina flour
$\frac{2}{3}$ cup whipping cream
2 egg whites

To decorate:
about $\frac{1}{2}$ lb. red currants in neat bunches
little sugar, preferably vanilla sugar

*For a more economical and less strongly-flavoured juice, use $1\frac{1}{2}$ lb. redcurrants only and add extra water at Stage 2. Other juicy fruits can be used instead.

1. Put the redcurrants with water and sugar into a saucepan and simmer gently until the fruit is very soft.
2. Strain through fine muslin or a fine sieve or strainer. Make liquid up to $1\frac{1}{2}$ pints (U.S. $3\frac{3}{4}$ cups) again if necessary.
3. Return the liquid to the washed saucepan, bring to the boil. Shower in the semolina gradually. Cook until thickened, stirring from time to time.
4. Allow the mixture to cool, stirring as it does.
5. Fold in the lightly whipped cream and stiffly whisked egg whites.
6. Put into a serving bowl and top with the bunches of redcurrants. These should be dusted with sugar or vanilla sugar and left to stand for a while.

NOTE: Potato flour is often used in Sweden to thicken the fruit juice, but semolina gives a very pleasant texture to the mixture. If using potato flour however, blend with some of the cold liquid, then stir into the hot liquid and cook until thickened.

296

Biskopskake
Light fruit and nut cake

Cooking time: 50 min.–1 hr. **Preparation time:** 20 min. **Main cooking utensils:** 8 or 9-inch round cake tin/layer cake pan, wire rack. **Oven temperature:** very moderate, 325–350°F., 170–180°C., Gas Mark 3. **Oven position:** centre.

IMPERIAL

For 8–10 portions you need:
5 eggs
7 oz. castor sugar
8 oz. self-raising flour
4 oz. seedless raisins
2–3 oz. blanched almonds
pinch salt

To top:
few blanched almonds (optional)

AMERICAN

For 8–10 portions you need:
5 eggs
scant 1 cup granulated sugar
2 cups all-purpose flour, sifted with $2\frac{1}{4}$ teaspoons baking powder
$\frac{2}{3}$ cup seedless raisins
about $\frac{1}{2}$ cup blanched almonds
dash salt

To top:
few blanched almonds (optional)

1. Separate the egg yolks and whites, then whisk yolks with sugar until very thick.
2. Sieve the flour at least twice to make sure it is very fine.
3. Add the raisins and very finely chopped almonds to the egg yolk mixture, then fold in the flour.
4. Finally fold in the stiffly beaten egg whites, whisked with the salt.
5. Spoon carefully into the tin, tap this lightly when filled to make sure the mixture settles down evenly.
6. Bake until firm to the touch.
7. Cool the cake on a wire rack.
8. Top with a few almonds if wished.

To store: In an airtight tin for 2–3 days.

297

Bløtkake
Light layer cake

Cooking time: 25 min. **Preparation time:** 20 min. **Main cooking utensil:** 8–9-inch cake tin/spring form pan. **Oven temperature:** moderate, 350–375°F., 180–190°C., Gas Mark 4–5. **Oven position:** just above centre.

IMPERIAL	AMERICAN
For 8–10 portions you need:	For 8–10 portions you need:
4 eggs	4 eggs
5 oz. castor sugar	$\frac{1}{2}$ cup plus 2 tablespoons granulated sugar
3 oz. self-raising flour	$\frac{3}{4}$ cup all-purpose flour, sifted with $\frac{3}{4}$ tablespoon baking powder
1 oz. potato flour *or* cornflour	$\frac{1}{4}$ cup cornstarch *or* potato flour
1 tablespoon hot water	1 tablespoon hot water
To fill and decorate:	To fill and decorate:
either fresh fruit, jam *or* lemon curd	either fresh fruit, jam *or* lemon cheese
$\frac{1}{2}$ pint thick cream	$1\frac{1}{4}$ cups whipping cream
2–3 oz. almonds, flaked and browned	about $\frac{1}{2}$ cup flaked and browned almonds

1. Whisk the eggs and sugar until thick enough to hold the mark of the whisk. This can be done over hot water if wished, but care must be taken that the eggs do not set.
2. Sieve the flour and potato flour or cornflour at least once, put into a warm place while whisking the eggs.
3. Fold the flour into the egg mixture, then fold in hot water.
4. Put into the well-greased and floured tin and bake until just firm to the touch.
5. Split and fill with fruit, jam or curd and some of the whipped cream and flaked, browned almonds. Decorate top with fruit, jam or curd and pipe top with whipped cream.

To serve: This is served in Norway as a special gâteau with coffee in the evening, or as a dessert.

To store: For a limited period in a really cool place.

298

Mandelkubbar
Almond buns

Cooking time: 30 min. **Preparation time:** 30 min. plus time for the dough to 'prove'. **Main cooking utensils:** saucepan, flat baking tray/sheet. **Oven temperature:** moderately hot to hot, 400–425°F., 200–220°C., Gas Mark 6. **Oven position:** centre.

IMPERIAL	AMERICAN
For 6–8 people you need:	For 6–8 people you need:
For the dough:	For the dough:
12 oz. flour, preferably plain	3 cups all-purpose flour
1 teaspoon powdered cinnamon	1 teaspoon powdered cinnamon
$\frac{1}{2}$ teaspoon powdered cardamom	$\frac{1}{2}$ teaspoon powdered cardamom
pinch salt	dash salt
2 oz. butter	$\frac{1}{4}$ cup butter
just over $\frac{1}{4}$ pint milk	just over $\frac{2}{3}$ cup milk
scant $\frac{1}{2}$ oz. yeast	scant $\frac{1}{2}$ cake compressed yeast
3 oz. sugar	6 tablespoons sugar
2 oz. blanched almonds	about $\frac{1}{2}$ cup blanched almonds
1 egg yolk	1 egg yolk
For the filling:	For the filling:
2 oz. ground almonds	$\frac{1}{2}$ cup ground almonds
2 oz. fine bread *or* cake crumbs	1 cup fine bread *or* cake crumbs
2 oz. sugar	$\frac{1}{4}$ cup sugar
1 egg white	1 egg white
For the topping:	For the topping:
1 oz. sugar	2 tablespoons sugar
4 oz. icing sugar	scant 1 cup confectioners' sugar

1. Sieve the flour, spices and salt into a bowl, rub in butter.
2. Warm $\frac{1}{4}$ pint (U.S. $\frac{2}{3}$ cup) milk until tepid. Cream yeast and 1 teaspoon sugar, add milk and sprinkling of flour. Leave in warm place until surface is covered with bubbles.
3. Add to the flour with remaining sugar, finely chopped almonds, egg yolk and extra milk to give a *soft* rolling consistency.
4. Knead, cover and allow to 'prove' for about 1 hour until nearly double its original size.
5. Knead until smooth. Remove one-third, form into a round and put on a greased baking tray. Roll out remainder into an oblong $\frac{1}{4}$-inch thick.
6. Blend ingredients for the filling, moistening with little milk.
7. Spread over dough. Roll as Swiss roll and cut into 6 portions.
8. Put on top of round, 'prove' for 25 minutes, sprinkle with sugar.
9. Bake until brown. Cool, top with icing.

299

Mor Monsen
Mother Monsen cookies

Cooking time: 30 min. **Preparation time:** 20 min. **Main cooking utensil:** 10-inch square shallow cake tin/square layer cake pan. **Oven temperature:** very moderate, 325°F., 170°C., Gas Mark 3. **Oven position:** just above centre.

IMPERIAL

To make about 24 cookies you need:
4 oz. almonds
3 oz. currants
8 oz. butter
8 oz. castor *or* brown sugar

1 oz. vanilla sugar* *or* extra ordinary sugar
8 oz. flour, preferably plain
4 eggs

For the topping:
some of the almonds and currants
1 oz. vanilla *or* ordinary sugar

AMERICAN

To make about 24 cookies you need:
scant 1 cup almonds
$\frac{1}{2}$ cup currants
1 cup butter
1 cup granulated *or* soft brown sugar
2 tablespoons vanilla sugar* *or* extra granulated sugar
2 cups all-purpose flour
4 eggs

For the topping:
some of the almonds and currants
2 tablespoons vanilla *or* granulated sugar

*To make vanilla sugar, cut 1 or 2 vanilla pods/beans into halves, stand with cut ends downwards in a jar of sugar. Use as required.

1. Blanch the almonds in boiling water. Lift out, dry well after removing the skins.
2. Chop half of them and shred the remainder.
3. Make sure the currants are well dried, if they have been washed.
4. Cream the butter and sugar until soft and light, add ordinary or vanilla sugar. Add the *chopped* almonds and 1 oz. (U.S. 3 tablespoons) currants.
5. Stir in the sieved flour and the beaten eggs alternately.
6. Put into a tin, lined with greased greaseproof paper and top the cake with the remaining currants and the shredded almonds, sprinkle with the sugar.*
7. Cook this rather more slowly than an ordinary light cake, so it becomes a little browner and more dry and crumbly in texture.
8. Remove paper and when cold, cut into fancy shapes i.e. diamonds, fingers or rounds.

*For lightly cooked currants and almonds, add sugar after 10 minutes' baking.

300

Wienerbrød
Danish pastries

Cooking time: 12 min. **Preparation time:** 35 min. **Main cooking utensil:** flat baking tray/sheet. **Oven temperature:** hot, 425–450°F., 220–230°C., Gas Mark 6–7. **Oven position:** above centre.

IMPERIAL

For 12–16 portions you need:
generous $\frac{3}{4}$ oz. fresh yeast

2 oz. sugar
$\frac{1}{4}$ pint milk
nearly $\frac{1}{4}$ pint water (or use milk)
1 lb. plain flour
6 oz. butter
1 egg

For the marzipan:
4 oz. ground almonds
2 oz. icing sugar
1 egg yolk

For the glacé icing:
4 oz. icing sugar
little warm water

To decorate:
few glacé cherries
flaked and browned almonds

AMERICAN

For 12–16 portions you need:
generous $\frac{3}{4}$ cake compressed yeast
$\frac{1}{4}$ cup sugar
$\frac{2}{3}$ cup milk
nearly $\frac{2}{3}$ cup water (or use milk)
1 lb. all-purpose flour
$\frac{3}{4}$ cup butter
1 egg

For the marzipan:
1 cup ground almonds
$\frac{1}{2}$ cup confectioners' sugar
1 egg yolk

For the glacé icing:
1 cup confectioners' sugar
little warm water

To decorate:
few candied cherries
flaked and browned almonds

1. Cream the yeast with 1 teaspoon sugar.
2. Add three-quarters of the milk and a sprinkling of flour. Leave in warm place for 20 minutes, until the surface bubbles.
3. Add the rest of the sugar to the flour, rub in 2 oz. (U.S. $\frac{1}{4}$ cup) butter. Add the yeast mixture and beaten egg.
4. Knead well, add rest of liquid to make a soft elastic dough. Knead on floured board until smooth; return to basin, cover with a cloth.
5. Leave in a warm place for about 1 hour, until double in size.
6. Turn on to a floured board. Knead lightly until no impression is left.
7. Roll out to a neat oblong, $\frac{1}{2}$-inch thick. Spread with half remaining butter, fold in 3, turn.
8. Repeat Stage 7 with rest of butter. Mix marzipan ingredients together.
9. Cut dough into squares, put marzipan in centre. Fold over 2 corners to cover it or make into croissant shapes. 'Prove' pastries for 15 minutes and bake until golden. Top with icing and decorate.

Konjakskransar
Brandy cookies

Cooking time: 10 min. **Preparation time:** 20 min. **Main cooking utensils:** ½-inch pipe and piping bag/½-inch nozzle and pastry bag, flat baking trays/sheets, wire rack. **Oven temperature:** very moderate to moderate, 350–375°F., 180–190°C., Gas Mark 4. **Oven position:** just above centre.

IMPERIAL	**AMERICAN**
For about 12–15 cookies you need:	For about 12–15 cookies you need:
8 oz. butter	1 cup butter
4 oz. sugar, preferably icing sugar	½ cup sugar *or* scant 1 cup confectioners' sugar
1 tablespoon brandy	1 tablespoon brandy
12 oz. flour, preferably plain	3 cups all-purpose flour
1 oz. cocoa powder	¼ cup unsweetened cocoa powder
To decorate:	To decorate:
1–2 oz. blanched almonds	about ⅓ cup blanched almonds

1. Cream the butter and sugar together, then beat in the brandy.
2. Work in the sieved flour and cocoa.
3. Put the mixture into a piping bag with a ½-inch pipe and press out into rings on greased trays.
4. Chop the almonds very coarsely and sprinkle on the rings.
5. Bake until just firm to the touch. Allow to stand on trays until nearly cold, as they are rather fragile, then transfer to a wire rack.

To vary: Another recipe for these Brandy cookies omits the cocoa and uses 2 tablespoons (U.S. 3 tablespoons) brandy instead of 1. Chill the dough, roll out and cut into very thin strips about 2½–3 inches long. Two strips are twisted together and baked until golden coloured.

Shakkiruudut and Hillokakut
Checkerboard and jelly cookies

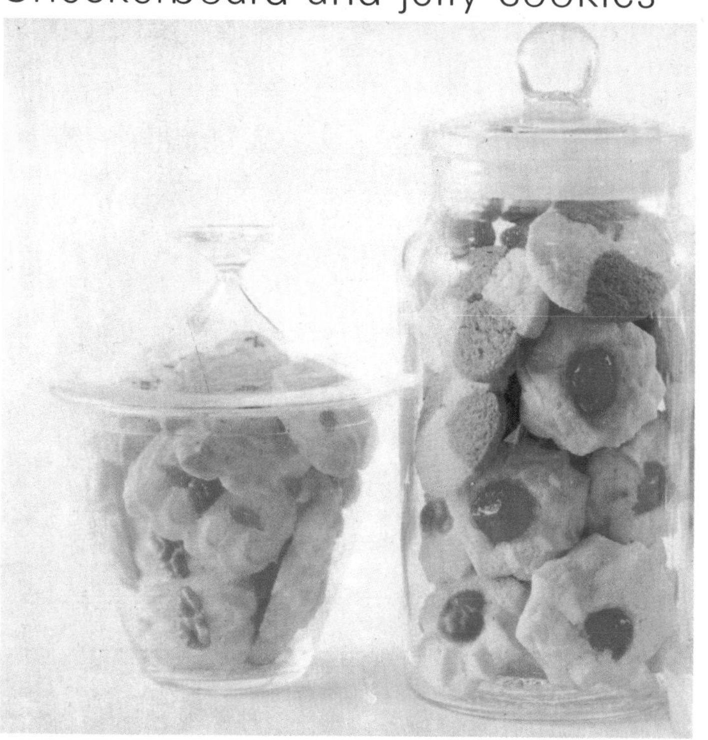

SHAKKIRUUDUT

Makes about 30 biscuits: Cream 6 oz. (U.S. ¾ cup) butter and 4 oz. (U.S. ½ cup) castor or (U.S. 1 cup) sieved icing sugar. Work in 9 oz. (U.S. 2¼ cups) plain flour. Divide dough in half, work ½ teaspoon vanilla essence into one half, and 1½ tablespoons (U.S. 2 tablespoons) sieved cocoa into the other. Form dough into 4 long, thin rolls, about ½–¾ inch in diameter. Put 1 vanilla and 1 chocolate roll side by side. Top vanilla roll with second chocolate roll and chocolate roll with remaining vanilla roll. Press firmly together to shape into a complete roll again. Wrap in greaseproof or wax paper and leave in cool place for at least 1 hour.

Cut into slices, about ¼–⅓ inch thick, put on lightly greased baking trays. Bake for about 15 minutes in centre of a very moderate to moderate oven, 350–375°F., 180–190°C., Gas Mark 4. Handle carefully when cold.

HILLOKAKUT

Makes about 24–30 biscuits: Make basic dough as above, but use 3 oz. (U.S. ¾ cup) icing sugar. Work in ½ beaten egg to make a dough that can be piped or formed into soft balls. Flatten these slightly. Bake as above.
These biscuits can be varied in many ways:
1. Brush with remaining beaten egg, sprinkle with sugar and chopped almonds.
2. Top with jam or jelly after baking; if storing in a jar as picture, use ½ glacé cherry instead.
3. Thinly roll out dough, cut half into plain rounds and half into rings. Brush rings with egg, sprinkle with almonds and sugar. When baked, sandwich together with jam or jelly.
4. Decorate with angelica or walnut halves.

Berlinerkranser

Berlin garlands

Cooking time: 25 min. **Preparation time:** 30 min. plus time for the dough to stand.* **Main cooking utensils:** saucepan, flat baking tray/sheet. **Oven temperature:** moderate, 350–375°F., 180–190°C., Gas Mark 4–5. **Oven position:** centre.

IMPERIAL

For about 16 garlands you need:
4 eggs
6 oz. sieved icing sugar

8 oz. flour, preferably plain
6 oz. butter, preferably unsalted

For the topping:
2 egg whites (see Stage 3)
2–3 oz. loaf sugar

AMERICAN

For about 16 garlands you need:
4 eggs
scant $1\frac{1}{2}$ cups sifted confectioners' sugar
2 cups all-purpose flour
$\frac{3}{4}$ cup butter, preferably sweet

For the topping:
2 egg whites (see Stage 3)
4–6 tablespoons lump sugar

*It is important to allow these to stand for they will spread badly in cooking if this is not done.

One of the many biscuit-type small cakes served in Norway, on special occasions such as Christmas.

1. Boil 2 eggs for 10 minutes, cool and shell at once; take great care not to over-cook these.
2. Chop them coarsely in a bowl, so there is no waste.
3. Separate the remaining egg yolks and whites, use the whites for the topping and blend the yolks with the hard-boiled eggs.
4. Cream thoroughly, adding the sugar.
5. Gradually incorporate sieved flour and soft butter into egg mixture; the easiest way is to add a little flour, then a little butter and continue until all is mixed.
6. *Leave in a cool place overnight.*
7. Roll out dough until $\frac{1}{2}$ inch thick, cut into thin strips and plait into garlands.
8. Brush lavishly with unbeaten egg white and sprinkle with crushed loaf sugar.
9. Put on a greased tray and bake for approximately 15 minutes.

To store: In an airtight tin when cold.

304

Lefse

Norwegian bannocks

Cooking time: few min. **Preparation time:** 10 min. **Main cooking utensil:** solid hot plate, griddle *or* strong frying pan/skillet.

IMPERIAL

For about 18 bannocks you need:
12 oz. self-raising flour

pinch salt
2 eggs
approx. $\frac{3}{4}$ pint thin cream *or* use partly cream and partly milk

little fat for greasing hot plate

AMERICAN

For about 18 bannocks you need:
3 cups all-purpose flour, sifted with $3\frac{1}{2}$ teaspoons baking powder
dash salt
2 eggs
approx. 2 cups coffee cream *or* use partly cream and partly milk
little fat for greasing hot plate

1. Sieve the flour and salt, add the eggs and gradually add enough cream to make a soft rolling consistency.
2. Roll out the dough very thinly and cut into rounds.
3. Grease the hot plate, griddle or frying pan and heat steadily.
4. To test if sufficiently hot, shake on a little dry flour, this should turn golden brown within 1 minute. It is important that this is the correct temperature.
5. Put the pancakes on to the hot plate, cook until golden, turn and brown on the other side.
6. To test, press firmly on top and if firm, they are cooked.

To serve: With jam or sugar and butter, or with any sweet or savoury filling; goat's cheese being a particular favourite in Norway.

NOTE: To prevent the bannocks from hardening on the outside, wrap in a clean tea cloth when cooked.

SPAIN & PORTUGAL

Spanish cooking, like the country and its people, is colourful, lively and robust. It owes much to the influences of various peoples and countries that have played a part in their history. Garlic and olive oil, two of the most commonly used ingredients, were introduced long ago by the Romans. Arab invaders brought saffron, spices like nutmeg and pepper and, even more important, sugar. The discovery of America by Columbus, in 1492, changed cooking immeasurably, bringing new ingredients like potatoes, tomatoes, peppers, chillies and chocolate, which have all become endemic to the Spanish cuisine. There has been considerable give and take between Spain and France. The Spanish have learnt subtlety and refinement from French cooking while the French, although they tend to look down on Spanish cooking as rather crude, owe more to Spain than is usually realised. Alioli, the famous Spanish garlic sauce, was the inspiration for the French Aioli, and the tortilla, the hearty Spanish omelette, preceded the more delicate French omelette.

If you go to Spain you will soon fall in with their daily routine which, like the Italian, allows for a long break in the middle of the day. Breakfast usually consists of coffee or chocolate and probably *Churros*, choux pastry fried in long thin strips and sprinkled with icing sugar. The main meal of the day is lunch, a good three course meal with wine, and most shops and offices shut for several hours for lunch and a siesta. They then stay open until quite late in the evening and supper, sometimes almost as substantial as lunch, is served at about nine or ten.

The midday meal may begin with *entremeses*, a small hors d'oeuvre; in the south they have *tapas*, various snacks of vegetables, nuts and fish that are served with drinks and often make almost a meal in themselves. An everyday meal may not have *entremeses* but begin straight away with soup or a fish or egg dish. Fish of all sorts are prolific on the Spanish coast, some of them, like swordfish and bonito, unfortunately not being available away from the Mediterranean. There are many local fish specialities: Spiced fish and peppers, from the southern provinces known as Andalusia, is typical of the region in its use of tomatoes and peppers. Shellfish is excellent and of the many delicious shellfish recipes the most famous is undoubtedly paella. This is a rice dish which always includes saffron and shellfish, and various combinations of poultry, meat and vegetables are added in different regions. *Paella a la vasca* is a particularly hearty version from the Basque country in the north which uses ham and chorizo, the famous Spanish smoked sausage.

Valencia, on the east coast, is in the centre of the citrus fruit area and here you are likely to have Liver with orange and Casserole of pork with wine, usually served with rice which is also grown here. It is fascinating to travel round Spain trying the local specialities and to conclude in Madrid where one can sample some of each. Madrid is situated on a plateau surrounded by arid plains of wheat and sheep-grazing land—to the south east is La Mancha, the home of Don Quixote. The region around Madrid isn't particularly fertile, but produce from all parts of the country is brought in and contributes to the sophisticated and varied cuisine of this lively capitol city.

Spanish wine is plentiful, very cheap, but rather unpredictable in quality, the best being the Riojan wines from the area around Logrono. But it is sherry, the fortified wine from Andalusia, for which Spain is really famous. Sherry is always a popular aperitif and sweet sherry can accompany or follow a dessert. It is rivalled by port and Madeira, however, the former from Oporto on the west coast of Portugal and the latter from Madeira, 500 miles south west of Lisbon. These are also fortified wines; although one still tends to associate them with Victorian and Edwardian England, they have recently regained popularity, occasionally as aperitifs but more often as dessert wines.

As one would expect, Portuguese cooking is similar to the Spanish in many ways. There is an abundance of fish and sardines, and anchovies especially are eaten and exported in vast quantities. Sardine salad, a sort of sardine pâté in lemon cases, makes an unusual and attractive hors d'oeuvre. Madeira, a delightful island with lush vegetation, has originated many recipes including Beef pot roast, using dry Madeira wine.

Neither Spain nor Portugal serve desserts very often, preferring to have hearty first courses and finish off with fruit. However, you may be treated to a Spanish Fruit tart with a custard filling which makes a delicious and elegant dessert. Doughnuts are popular in Portugal and are frequently served as a snack or for breakfast.

305

Sopa de tomate

Tomato vegetable broth

Cooking time: 30 min. **Preparation time:** 20 min. **Main cooking utensil:** saucepan.

IMPERIAL

For 6 people you need:
2 lb. tomatoes, choose 8 oz. very small ones
4 medium-sized onions
2 cloves garlic (optional)
4 tablespoons oil
water and 2 chicken stock cubes
seasoning
3-inch piece cucumber
1 green pepper
about $\frac{1}{4}$ small cabbage

AMERICAN

For 6 people you need:
2 lb. tomatoes, choose $\frac{1}{2}$ lb. very small ones
4 medium-sized onions
2 cloves garlic (optional)
$\frac{1}{3}$ cup oil
water and 2 chicken bouillon cubes
seasoning
3-inch piece cucumber
1 sweet green pepper
about $\frac{1}{4}$ small cabbage

Tomato soup is a favourite in Portugal, and tomatoes are used in soups with a variety of ingredients.

1. Chop $1\frac{1}{2}$ lb. large tomatoes, do not skin, for the soup is generally sieved.
2. Peel and chop 3 of the onions and crush the garlic cloves.
3. Heat 3 tablespoons oil and toss the tomatoes and onions in this, then add the stock, or water and stock cubes. Season well and simmer for 15–20 minutes, sieve and put on one side.
4. Slice the remaining onion, the cucumber and the pepper, discarding core and seeds, and shred the cabbage.
5. Toss in remaining oil for a few minutes, add remaining skinned tomatoes, heat for a few minutes only.
6. Add the sieved mixture and heat together gently until soup is very hot.

To serve: With crusty bread.

To vary: Add sliced hard-boiled eggs.

306

Salada en cangrejo

Salad with crab

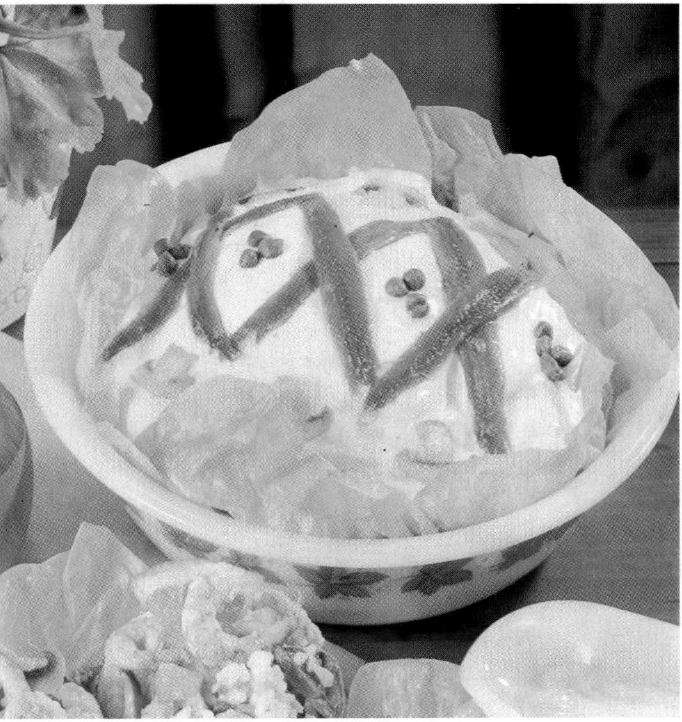

Preparation time: 15 min. **Main utensil:** large bowl.

IMPERIAL

For 4–6 people you need:
1 large lettuce
1 large cooked crab *or* 1 can crab meat
2 hard-boiled eggs
1–2 oz. mushrooms
1 clove garlic
$\frac{1}{4}$–$\frac{1}{2}$ pint thick mayonnaise
$\frac{1}{2}$–1 teaspoon chilli sauce
few capers
few anchovy fillets

To garnish:
mayonnaise
anchovy fillets
few mushrooms
capers

AMERICAN

For 4–6 people you need:
1 large lettuce
1 large cooked crab *or* 1 can crab meat
2 hard-cooked eggs
$\frac{1}{4}$–$\frac{1}{2}$ cup mushrooms
1 clove garlic
$\frac{2}{3}$–$1\frac{1}{4}$ cups thick mayonnaise
$\frac{1}{2}$–1 teaspoon chili sauce
few capers
few anchovy fillets

To garnish:
mayonnaise
anchovy fillets
few mushrooms
capers

1. Wash and drain the lettuce, dry carefully; this salad needs lots of lettuce.
2. Remove all the crab meat from the shell or can. Flake well, discarding any bones.
3. Chop the shelled, hard-boiled eggs and mushrooms, these need not be skinned if well washed.
4. Rub a salad bowl with a cut clove garlic, put in the lettuce.
5. Blend the crab, eggs, mushrooms with mayonnaise, chilli sauce, capers and finely chopped anchovy fillets.
6. Pile over the lettuce, top with more mayonnaise, anchovy fillets, neatly sliced mushrooms and capers.

To serve: As an hors d'oeuvre or light main dish.

To vary: To make a more economical dish, use little crab meat and cooked white fish. The Spanish bacalao (cooked salt cod) is excellent for this.

Salada de sardinhas
Sardine salad

Cooking time: if using fresh fish about 5 min. **Preparation time:** 15 min. **Main cooking utensils:** frying pan/skillet.

IMPERIAL

For 4 people you need:
4 firm lemons
1–$1\frac{1}{2}$ lb. fresh sardines *or* sprats and oil for frying *or* 1 large can sardines in oil
1 medium-sized onion
4 medium-sized tomatoes
1 tablespoon oil
2 teaspoons vinegar
about 12 black olives
seasoning

To garnish:
4 black olives

AMERICAN

For 4 people you need:
4 firm lemons
1–$1\frac{1}{2}$ lb. fresh sardines *or* sprats and oil for frying *or* 1 large can sardines in oil
1 medium-sized onion
4 medium-sized tomatoes
1 tablespoon oil
2 teaspoons vinegar
about 12 ripe olives
seasoning

To garnish:
4 ripe olives

1. Cut a slice from lemons, scoop out centre pulp.
2. Discard any pith, skin and pips, but chop the pulp very finely.
3. In Portugal and other Mediterranean countries, fresh sardines would be used, fried in oil, then treated as canned sardines. Where fresh sardines are not available, use sprats or canned fish.
4. Remove heads and bones from the cooked fish, mash well. Add tiny pieces of lemon and grated or very finely chopped onion.
5. Put a layer of freshly chopped tomatoes at bottom of each lemon case, topped with a little oil, vinegar and chopped olives; season well.
6. Top with well-mashed sardine mixture, use any oil from can or from frying the fish to give a moist texture; season well.
7. Garnish with black olives.

To serve: As an interesting hors d'oeuvre; serve with a small fork or spoon.

308

Cozido a portuguesa
Portuguese pot-au-feu

Cooking time: 3 hr. plus overnight soaking of peas. **Preparation time:** 25 min. **Main cooking utensil:** very large saucepan.

IMPERIAL

For 8 people you need:
8–10 oz. chick peas *or* ordinary dried peas
bay leaf
2 cloves
sprig thyme *or* $\frac{1}{2}$ teaspoon dried thyme
3 lb. fowl (see Stage 2)
$1\frac{1}{2}$–2 lb. fresh brisket of beef
seasoning
8 oz. salt pork, ham *or* a ham bone
2–3 very large onions *or* equivalent in small ones
2–3 crushed cloves garlic
2–3 leeks (*or* more)
2–3 carrots (*or* more)
1 medium-sized cabbage
1 large smoked sausage *or* about 8–10 oz. frankfurters
4–8 tomatoes

AMERICAN

For 8 people you need:
1–$1\frac{1}{2}$ cups chick peas *or* ordinary dried peas
bay leaf
2 cloves
sprig thyme *or* $\frac{1}{2}$ teaspoon dried thyme
3 lb. fowl (see Stage 2)
$1\frac{1}{2}$–2 lb. fresh brisket of beef
seasoning
$\frac{1}{2}$ lb. lean salt pork, cured ham *or* a ham bone
2–3 very large onions *or* equivalent in small ones
2–3 crushed cloves garlic
2–3 leeks (*or* more)
2–3 carrots (*or* more)
1 medium-sized cabbage
1 large smoked sausage *or* about $\frac{1}{2}$–$\frac{2}{3}$ lb. frankfurters
4–8 tomatoes

1. Soak the peas overnight in water to cover. Put peas, soaking liquid, the bay leaf, cloves and thyme into the saucepan and simmer for 1 hour.
2. Add the fowl (if this is a young bird do not add until Stage 4) and the diced beef (or keep in one piece if meat is good quality). Season lightly, then put in the pork, ham or ham bone and onions.
3. Simmer for a further hour.
4. Put in the crushed garlic, leeks, carrots, cabbage and sausage and continue cooking for a further hour. The tomatoes should be added towards the end of the time.

To serve: Either as picture, i.e. as a main course, with meats all on one dish, vegetables on another, strained stock in a sauce-boat and peas in a dish *or* put the stock and peas in a bowl, add chopped vegetables, and serve meat as a separate meal or separate course.

NOTE: At each stage, check there is adequate liquid.

309

Camarones fritos
Fried prawns

Cooking time: 10 min. plus time to cook potatoes. **Preparation time:** 20 min. **Main cooking utensils:** saucepan, frying pan/skillet.

IMPERIAL

For 4 people you need:
about 16–20 large prawns

8 oz. potatoes, peeled
2 large onions
2 oz. butter*
1–2 tablespoons oil*
1–2 tablespoons chopped parsley

AMERICAN

For 4 people you need:
about 16–20 large prawns *or* jumbo shrimp
$\frac{1}{2}$ lb. potatoes, peeled
2 large onions
$\frac{1}{4}$ lb. butter*
1–3 tablespoons oil*
1–3 tablespoons chopped parsley

*By using both butter and oil, one has the combination of a good 'buttery' flavour. The mixture is less likely to overheat and discolour than when using butter alone.

1. Shell the prawns but keep them whole. Boil the potatoes until just soft.
2. Dice the cooked potatoes and raw onions very finely.
3. Heat the butter and oil, fry onions and potatoes very gently until they are tender—do not allow to brown.
4. Remove from the pan. If necessary, heat a little more butter and oil in the pan then toss prawns in this until just heated well, do not overcook.
5. Return the onion and potato mixture to the pan, toss for 1 minute with prawns, adding finely chopped parsley.

To serve: As hot as possible with crusty, fresh bread and butter as an hors d'oeuvre or light main dish.

To vary: Fry chopped, diced green and red peppers, skinned, chopped tomatoes with onions instead of potato.

310

Sardinhas con salada
Salad with sardines and rice

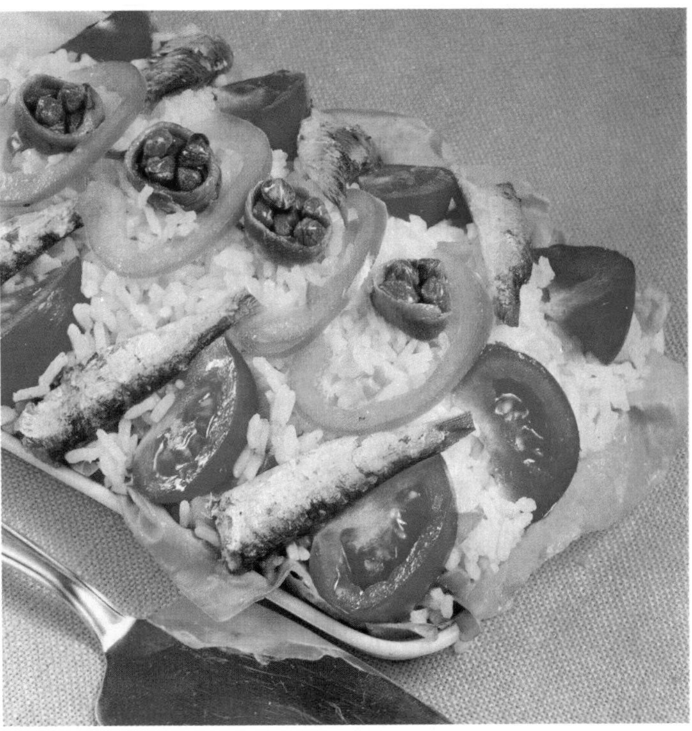

Cooking time: 20 min. **Preparation time:** 15 min. **Main cooking utensil:** saucepan.

IMPERIAL

For 6 people you need:
6 oz. long grain rice
1 can sardines in oil
2 tablespoons olive oil
2 tablespoons lemon juice
seasoning
lettuce
4 large tomatoes
1 can anchovy fillets
2 tablespoons capers
1 green pepper

AMERICAN

For 6 people you need:
scant 1 cup long grain rice
1 can sardines in oil
3 tablespoons olive oil
3 tablespoons lemon juice
seasoning
lettuce
4 large tomatoes
1 can anchovy fillets
3 tablespoons capers
1 sweet green pepper

1. Put the rice into boiling, salted water. Cook until tender, strain.
2. Pour out the oil from can of sardines, blend oil with olive oil, lemon juice and seasoning.
3. Toss the rice in this, allow to cool.
4. Arrange the rice on a bed of lettuce. Top with quartered tomatoes, sardines and anchovy fillets twisted into rings and filled with capers.
5. Cut the flesh from the green pepper into neat pieces. Arrange on the salad.

To serve: As a light main dish.

311

Pescado con guindilla
Chilli flavoured fish

Cooking time: 25–30 min. **Preparation time:** 20 min. **Main cooking utensils:** heat-resistant serving dish, if possible (suitable for using on cooker) *or* frying pan/skillet, piece of muslin/cheesecloth.

IMPERIAL

For 6 people you need:
6 portions cod *or* fresh haddock weighing about 2 lb. (*or* 6 small portions cod *or* fresh haddock and 6 small portions smoked haddock)
1–2 onions
1–2 cloves garlic
2 tablespoons olive oil
2 oz. concentrated tomato purée
few drops Tabasco sauce
2–4 red chillis
seasoning
$\frac{1}{2}$ pint dry white wine

To garnish:
green olives

AMERICAN

For 6 people you need:
6 portions cod *or* fresh haddock, weighing about 2 lb. (*or* use 6 small portions cod *or* fresh haddock and 6 small portions smoked haddock)
1–2 onions
1–2 cloves garlic
3 tablespoons olive oil
scant $\frac{1}{4}$ cup concentrated tomato paste
few drops Tabasco sauce
2–4 red chilis
seasoning
$1\frac{1}{4}$ cups dry white wine

To garnish:
green olives

1. Trim the fish neatly.
2. Chop and fry the onions and crushed garlic in the hot oil until just tender. Stir in the tomato purée, the sauce, chillis (tied securely in a piece of muslin) and seasoning.
3. Put the fish into the tomato mixture together with a little wine, and cook gently until tender.
4. Remove the bag of chilli peppers.
5. Stir in the wine and heat gently, do not break the fish.
6. Taste the sauce and add extra seasoning if necessary.
7. Garnish with green olives and serve.

To serve: Hot. This dish is excellent with rice or new potatoes. Serve with a really cold white wine to 'counteract' the hot sauce.

To vary: Add large prawns, shelled mussels, slices of lobster, if wished at Stage 4; or use a mixture of white fish, cutting this into neat portions.

312

Pescado a la malagueña
Fish and onion savoury pie

Cooking time: 1 hr. **Preparation time:** 30 min. **Main cooking utensils:** saucepan, flat baking tray/sheet. **Oven temperature:** hot, 425–450°F., 220–230°C., Gas Mark 6–7, then moderate, 375°F., 190°C., Gas Mark 5. **Oven position:** centre.

IMPERIAL

For 4–6 people you need:
2 lb. white fish, turbot, cod *or* fresh haddock
$\frac{1}{2}$ pint water
grated rind and juice 1 lemon
seasoning
about 8 spring onions
1 clove garlic
2 tablespoons oil
1 green and red chilli pepper
1 egg

For the pastry:
12 oz. flour, preferably plain
pinch salt
6 oz. butter
juice 1 lemon
egg to glaze

To garnish:
tomatoes
small pieces lemon rind

AMERICAN

For 4–6 people you need:
2 lb. white fish, cod *or* fresh haddock
$1\frac{1}{4}$ cups water
grated rind and juice 1 lemon
seasoning
about 8 scallions
1 clove garlic
3 tablespoons oil
1 green and red chili pepper
1 egg

For the pastry:
3 cups all-purpose flour
dash salt
$\frac{3}{4}$ cup butter
juice 1 lemon
egg to glaze

To garnish:
tomatoes
small pieces lemon rind

1. Put fish into water with lemon juice, seasoning and poach gently for 10 minutes or until *just* cooked but firm. Drain well and flake.
2. Chop spring onions, using some of the green, crush clove garlic.
3. Fry in hot oil until tender. Blend with grated lemon rind and 2 teaspoons each of chopped green and red chilli peppers. Add fish. Season, cool and bind with egg.
4. Sieve flour and salt. Rub in butter, bind with lemon juice and water.
5. Roll out to a neat oblong shape.
6. Form fish mixture into a roll, 1 inch shorter than pastry, put on pastry. Fold in either end to protect filling. Make into a roll round fish and put on to tray with the joined side on base.
7. Make 3 'funnels' with remaining pastry, put piece of lemon rind in each. Place on top of pie with a few pastry 'leaves'. Brush with beaten egg, bake until pastry is crisp and brown, 30–35 minutes, lower heat for further 10–15 minutes. Garnish with tomato segments.

313

Paella a la vasca

Rice with fish

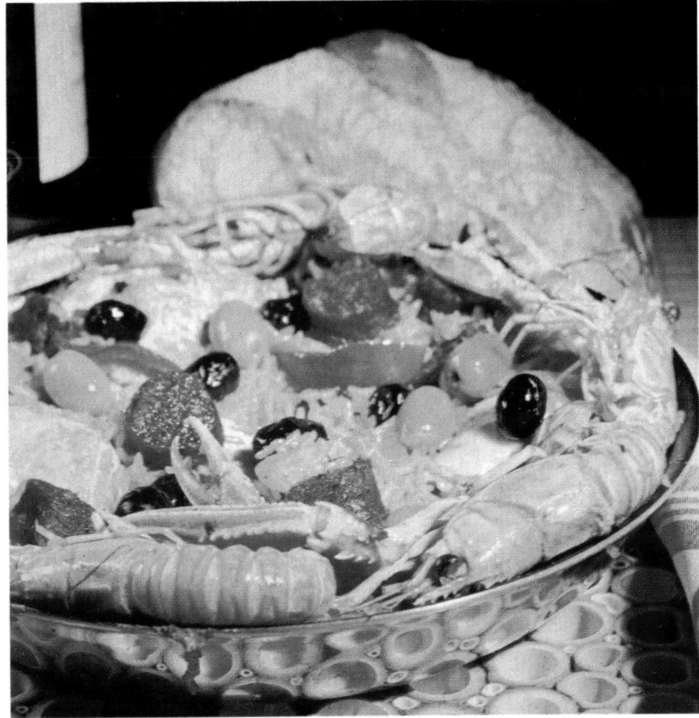

Cooking time: 35 min. **Preparation time:** 20 min. plus time to soak saffron. **Main cooking utensil:** large shallow pan, see below.*

IMPERIAL

For 6 people you need:

$\frac{1}{2}$ teaspoon saffron
$1\frac{1}{2}$ pints chicken stock
4 tablespoons olive oil
1 large onion
4 pieces uncooked, young chicken
seasoning
8 oz. long grain rice
6–8 oz. smoked sausage (chorizo)
6–8 oz. smoked ham
1 red pepper
about 12 langoustine *or* large prawns

To garnish:
black and green olives

AMERICAN

For 6 people you need:

$\frac{1}{2}$ teaspoon saffron
$3\frac{3}{4}$ cups chicken stock
$\frac{1}{3}$ cup olive oil
1 large onion
4 pieces uncooked, young chicken
seasoning
generous 1 cup long grain rice
$\frac{1}{3}$–$\frac{1}{2}$ lb. smoked sausage (chorizo)
$\frac{1}{4}$–$\frac{1}{2}$ lb. smoked cured ham
1 sweet red pepper
about 12 jumbo shrimp *or* large prawns

To garnish:
ripe and green olives

*There are special paella copper pans in which the dish may be cooked and served—paella means pan dish.

1. Put saffron in a basin, add a little chicken stock, soak for 1 hour.
2. Heat the olive oil in a large pan.
3. Fry the chopped onion in oil for several minutes, then fry diced chicken until golden.
4. Add the rice and toss in the oil.
5. Pour in rest of chicken stock and the strained saffron liquid.
6. Season well, simmer gently until rice starts to absorb the liquid and soften.
7. Add the sliced smoked sausage, ham and strips of de-seeded red pepper. Continue cooking for about 15 minutes, stirring well as mixture thickens.
8. Add shelled langoustine tails or prawns and heat thoroughly.
9. Garnish with unshelled langoustine or prawns, black and green olives.

To serve: From the pan—with finger bowls, because of shelling fish.

To vary: The flavourings in paella vary throughout Spain and the Mediterranean—cooked peas, mussels, small prawns may be added and the sausage and ham omitted.

314

Pescado a la andaluza

Spiced fish and peppers

Cooking time: 30–35 min. **Preparation time:** 25 min. **Main cooking utensil:** large frying pan/skillet.

IMPERIAL

For 4–6 people you need:

1–3 cloves garlic (depending on personal taste)
3 good-sized onions
3 tablespoons oil
$1\frac{1}{4}$ lb. tomatoes
2 tablespoons chopped parsley
1–2 oz. walnuts
grated rind and juice 1 lemon
3–4 canned pimentos *or* use fresh red peppers
$1\frac{1}{2}$–2 lb. white fish; cod, haddock *or* turbot, weight without bones
about 4–6 oz. shelled shrimps, prawns *or* other shellfish
seasoning

To serve:
3–4 slices bread, cut into croûtons
3–4 oz. butter

AMERICAN

For 4–6 people you need:

1–3 cloves garlic (depending on personal taste)
3 good-sized onions
scant $\frac{1}{4}$ cup oil
$1\frac{1}{4}$ lb. tomatoes
3 tablespoons chopped parsley
$\frac{1}{4}$–$\frac{1}{2}$ cup walnuts
grated rind and juice 1 lemon
3–4 canned pimentos *or* use fresh sweet red peppers
$1\frac{1}{2}$–2 lb. white fish; cod *or* haddock, weight without bones
about $\frac{2}{3}$–1 cup shelled shrimp, prawns *or* other shellfish
seasoning

To serve:
3–4 slices bread, cut into croûtons
6–8 tablespoons butter

1. Crush the garlic and chop onions.
2. Heat the oil, fry with skinned, chopped tomatoes for 10 minutes.
3. Add half the parsley, finely chopped walnuts (unusual, but interesting flavour with fish), grated lemon rind and juice and sliced peppers. Cook for 10 minutes. (If using fresh peppers, blanch for 5 minutes in boiling, salted water.)
4. Cut the white fish into small neat pieces, making sure there are no bones or pieces of skin.
5. Heat in the tomato and pepper mixture for 5 minutes until beginning to soften, then add shellfish. Complete cooking for a further 5–10 minutes, season. Top with remaining parsley.

To serve: Very hot. An interesting accompaniment is to fry croûtons of bread in hot butter and top fish with this.

315

Cocktail de marisco
Shellfish party

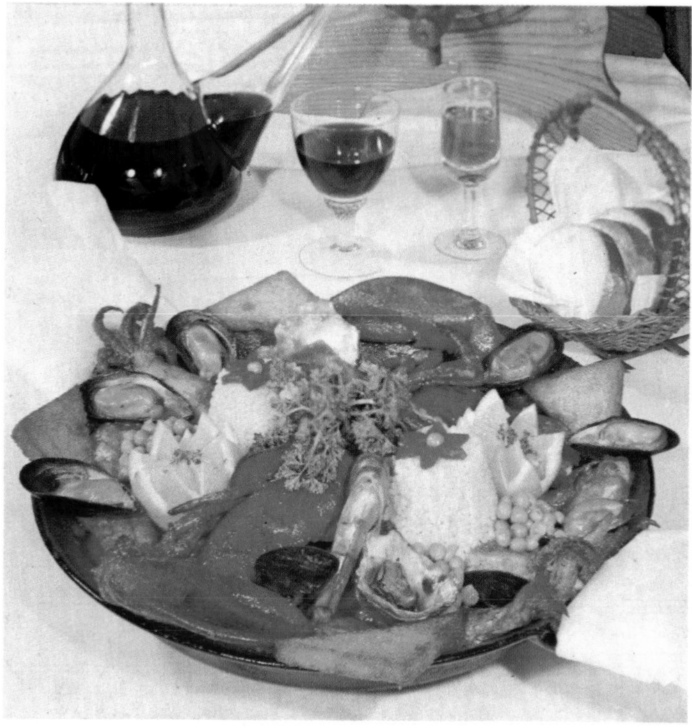

Spanish fish dishes are world-famous and the Spaniards enjoy an abundance of shellfish. In the picture a meal of various fish is served with moulds of well-flavoured rice, crisply fried bread, peas, lemon, parsley, French bread and wine.

CRAB AND LOBSTER

Either plunge them live into boiling water or put in warm water and bring to the boil. Cook steadily for approximately 20–25 minutes until the shells are bright red. *Cool*, split and remove stomach and grey fingers from the crab (these form where small claws join the body); remove intestinal vein and fingers from lobster.

MUSSELS

Scrub the mussels well, discard any that do not close when tapped. Put in pan with crushed clove garlic, parsley, seasoning and either little water or white wine. Heat until the mussels open, remove beards (weed-like growth). Serve on halved shells with a little of the liquid if wished.

EEL

Cut the eel in pieces unless very tiny, when it could be cooked whole. Toss for a few minutes in a little hot oil. Cover with a few tablespoons vinegar, chopped onions and seasoning, then simmer for about 45 minutes.

OCTOPUS AND SMALL SQUID

Remove ink bag from the squid. Toss chopped onions in little oil, add few skinned, chopped tomatoes, then fish; season. Cover with water, simmer until tender, about 1–$1\frac{1}{2}$ hours. Thicken liquid with breadcrumbs. Add ink (if wished) at the end.

316

Peixe com molho de tomate
Bacon and fish in tomato sauce

Cooking time: 20 min. **Preparation time:** 15 min. (see also Stage 1). **Main cooking utensils:** saucepan, pan and frying basket for oil, absorbent paper/paper towels.

IMPERIAL

For 4 people you need:
1 lb. salted cod *or* about $1\frac{1}{2}$ lb. smoked cod*
1 onion
1 lb. cooked potatoes

For the batter:
4 oz. plain *or* self-raising flour
seasoning
1 egg
$\frac{1}{4}$ pint milk
2–3 oz. bacon, finely chopped

For the sauce:
2 onions
2 tablespoons oil
4 large tomatoes
1 tablespoon tomato purée

To serve:
bread and butter, jam

AMERICAN

For 4 people you need:
1 lb. salt cod *or* about $1\frac{1}{2}$ lb. smoked cod*
1 onion
1 lb. cooked potatoes

For the batter:
1 cup all-purpose flour
seasoning
1 egg
$\frac{2}{3}$ cup milk
about $\frac{1}{4}$ cup finely chopped bacon

For the sauce:
2 onions
3 tablespoons oil
4 large tomatoes
1 tablespoon tomato paste

To serve:
bread and butter, jam

*If using smoked cod, omit Stage 1.

1. Cut the fish into neat pieces, soak for 24 or even 48 hours in cold water, changing the water several times.
2. Put into a pan with whole onion and simmer until tender but unbroken.
3. Drain well, discard onion. Dip fish pieces in the batter made by mixing flour, seasoning, egg, milk and chopped bacon.
4. Fry in hot oil until crisp and golden, drain well.
5. Dice cooked potatoes, heat for 2–3 minutes only in the oil, drain.
6. Meanwhile, fry chopped onions in oil, add chopped, skinned tomatoes purée and seasoning. Cook until thick.

To serve: Arrange fish and potatoes on hot dish with bread and butter and sharp-flavoured jam or jelly (cranberry is ideal). Either top with sauce or serve separately. Garnish with parsley.

318

Portuguese special party

In Portugal, shellfish, sardines and cod, which is often dried and salted, are some of the most usual foods.

The following menu would serve 4–6 people.
Choose either Shellfish with mayonnaise or the Stuffed lobster dish, or serve smaller portions of each.

ALMOND SOUP (not shown)

Blanch and mince 4 oz. (U.S. 1 cup) almonds, or use ground almonds. Put in pan with 2 oz. (U.S. $\frac{1}{4}$ cup) butter, $1\frac{1}{2}$ pints (U.S. $3\frac{3}{4}$ cups) milk, blended with 1 oz. (U.S. $\frac{1}{4}$ cup) flour, seasoning, pinch spice and cinnamon. Cook gently until thickened. Whisk in $\frac{1}{4}$ pint (U.S. $\frac{2}{3}$ cup) white wine, *do not boil*. Serve with croûtons of fried bread.

LOBSTER ROE PATE

Pound coral from a hen lobster with crushed clove garlic, little grated lemon rind and juice, and butter. Season. In the picture, this is canned.

SHELLFISH WITH MAYONNAISE

Serve cooked shellfish with salad and Portuguese mayonnaise sauce. Blend each $\frac{1}{4}$ pint (U.S. $\frac{2}{3}$ cup) mayonnaise with 1 tablespoon chopped olives, 1–2 teaspoons capers, good pinch cayenne pepper and 2–3 chopped anchovy fillets.

STUFFED LOBSTERS OR LANGOUSTINES

Halve 3 medium cooked fish, remove flesh and chop. Fry 2 crushed cloves garlic and 2 medium chopped onions in 3 tablespoons (U.S. $\frac{1}{4}$ cup) oil. Add 4 skinned, chopped tomatoes, 3 oz. (U.S. $1\frac{1}{2}$ cups) soft brown breadcrumbs, seasoning and lobster meat. Pile into halved body shells. Put a thick layer of sliced tomatoes, onions and green peppers into a dish. Moisten with red wine, season well. Cover and cook until tender. Put shellfish on top with claws to garnish, return to moderately hot oven for about 25 minutes.

SAVOURY RICE

Cook 8 oz. (U.S. generous 1 cup) rice in $1\frac{1}{2}$ pints (U.S. $3\frac{3}{4}$ cups) chicken stock; add crushed clove garlic and whole onion, if wished. Remove onion before serving.

Cerdo a la cacerola
Casserole of pork with wine

Cooking time: $1\frac{1}{4}$ hr. **Preparation time:** 25 min. **Main cooking utensils:** saucepan, frying pan/skillet, casserole. **Oven temperature:** very moderate to moderate, 350–375°F., 180–190°C., Gas Mark 4. **Oven position:** centre.

IMPERIAL	AMERICAN
For 6 people you need:	For 6 people you need:
6 thick loin chops *or* 12 thin chops *or* slices of pork cut from leg	6 thick loin pork chops *or* 12 thin chops *or* slices of pork cut from leg
6–8 oz. young carrots	$\frac{1}{3}$–$\frac{1}{2}$ lb. young carrots
8 oz. small onions	$\frac{1}{2}$ lb. small onions
seasoning	seasoning
3 oz. butter	6 tablespoons butter
good pinch saffron powder	dash saffron powder
$\frac{1}{2}$ pint white stock *or* use partly white stock and partly vegetable stock	$1\frac{1}{4}$ cups white stock *or* use partly white stock and partly vegetable stock
1 oz. flour *or* $\frac{1}{2}$ oz. cornflour	$\frac{1}{4}$ cup all-purpose flour *or* 2 tablespoons cornstarch
juice 1 large orange	juice 1 large orange
$\frac{1}{4}$ pint white wine	$\frac{2}{3}$ cup white wine
1–2 dessert apples	1–2 eating apples
To garnish:	**To garnish:**
parsley	parsley

1. Remove any bones possible from the meat if using loin.
2. Cook peeled, halved or whole carrots and halved or whole onions for 10 minutes only in boiling, salted water, strain.
3. Heat the butter in a large pan, fry meat for 5 minutes, turning so it does not become too brown, put into a casserole.
4. Toss the carrots and onions in fat in pan, put into the casserole.
5. Soak the saffron in a little stock; saffron powder will dissolve, but saffron strands need straining after about 15 minutes. Blend flour or cornflour with remaining stock.
6. Stir stock, orange juice and wine into fat and meat juices remaining in the frying pan. Bring to the boil and cook until thickened. Add saffron liquid.
7. Pour over meat and vegetables, cover with a lid and cook for 1 hour.
8. Add the cored sliced apple (there is no need to peel this) after about 30 minutes. Garnish with parsley before serving.

319

Filete de lomo con coñac
Fillet steaks and brandy

Cooking time: 40–55 min. **Preparation time:** 15 min. **Main cooking utensils:** large frying pan/skillet with lid *or* saucepan, casserole (optional, see Stage 5). **Oven temperature:** moderate, 375°F., 190°C., Gas Mark 4–5. **Oven position:** centre.

IMPERIAL

For 4 people you need:
8 small, thin slices fillet steak
$\frac{1}{2}$ oz. flour
seasoning
3 oz. butter
4–8 very small onions
3 tablespoons brandy
$\frac{1}{2}$ pint stock
2 tablespoons concentrated tomato purée
4–6 oz. button mushrooms
1 teaspoon paprika pepper
4 tablespoons thin cream

To garnish:
chopped parsley
baked tomatoes

AMERICAN

For 4 people you need:
8 small, thin slices tenderloin steak
2 tablespoons all-purpose flour
seasoning
6 tablespoons butter
4–8 very small onions
scant $\frac{1}{4}$ cup brandy
$1\frac{1}{4}$ cups stock
3 tablespoons concentrated tomato paste
1–$1\frac{1}{2}$ cups button mushrooms
1 teaspoon paprika pepper
$\frac{1}{3}$ cup coffee cream

To garnish:
chopped parsley
baked tomatoes

1. Coat the fillets of beef in seasoned flour.
2. Heat the butter in a pan and toss halved or whole peeled onions and coated fillets of beef until just sealed on the outside.
3. Add the brandy, set light to this but shake pan to prevent meat becoming too dark on outside.
4. Blend in the stock, tomato purée, whole mushrooms, seasoning, including paprika.
5. Cover the pan, lower heat and cook for about 30 minutes, or if preferred, transfer to shallow casserole in the oven and leave for about 45 minutes.
6. Just before serving, stir in cream. Do not boil sauce.

To serve: Lift meat out of the sauce, arrange on a dish with the vegetables round. Top with sauce, and garnish with parsley and baked tomatoes.

320

Chuletas de cordero payesa
Loin chops in a savoury sauce

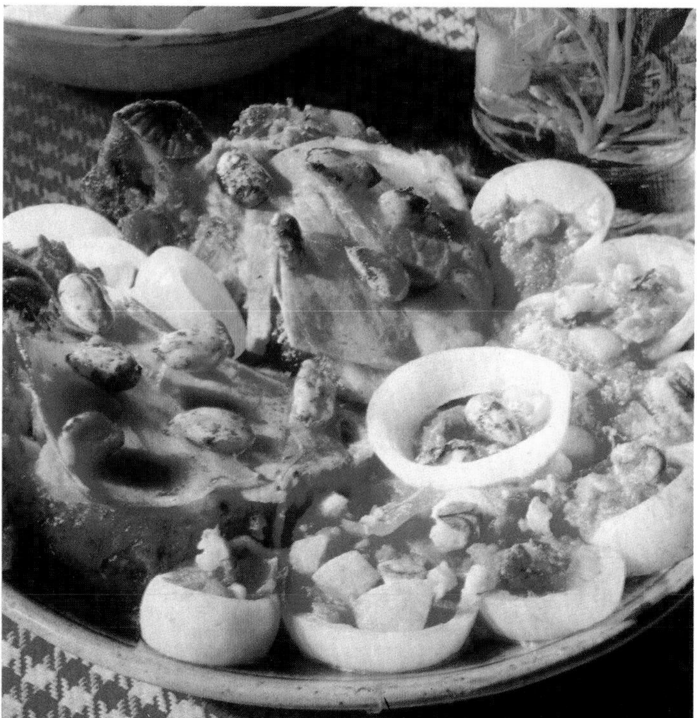

Cooking time: 30 min. **Preparation time:** 25 min. **Main cooking utensils:** frying pan/skillet, saucepan.

IMPERIAL

For 4 people you need:
4 good-sized loin chops, lamb *or* veal
$2\frac{1}{2}$–3 tablespoons olive oil
$\frac{1}{4}$ pint white wine
2 oz. plain chocolate pieces
2–3 oz. almonds
4 slices smoked ham
2 medium-sized onions
4 tablespoons concentrated tomato purée
seasoning
2–3 sage leaves
little stock *or* more white wine
about 1 oz. potato crisps

AMERICAN

For 4 people you need:
4 good-sized loin chops, lamb *or* veal
3–4 tablespoons olive oil
$\frac{2}{3}$ cup white wine
$\frac{1}{3}$ cup semi-sweet chocolate pieces
$\frac{1}{2}$–$\frac{3}{4}$ cup almonds
4 slices smoked ham
2 medium-sized onions
$\frac{1}{3}$ cup concentrated tomato paste
seasoning
2–3 sage leaves
little stock *or* more white wine
about 1 cup potato chips

1. Fry the chops on both sides in pan until nearly cooked. If using veal which is lean, you will need about $1\frac{1}{2}$ tablespoons (U.S. 2 tablespoons) oil, use rather less for lamb unless very lean.
2. Add the wine and grated chocolate to pan, heat gently until a thick mixture. This may sound very unusual, but it gives an excellent flavour to the meat. Add almonds and top chops with the ham just before serving.
3. Meanwhile, heat the remaining oil, fry very finely chopped onions, saving a few rings for garnish; these should be very lightly fried only and kept hot, or served raw.
4. Stir in the tomato purée, seasoning, very finely chopped sage, and enough wine or stock to make a thick sauce-like consistency.

To serve: Arrange chops, ham, almonds and any chocolate mixture on a dish. Put tomato sauce round with onions rings and crumbled potato crisps.

321

Hígado con naranja
Liver with orange

Cooking time: 10–15 min. **Preparation time:** 15 min. **Main cooking utensil:** large frying pan/skillet.

IMPERIAL

For 5–6 people you need:
$1\frac{1}{4}$–$1\frac{1}{2}$ lb. calf's *or* lamb's liver
1 oz. flour
seasoning
grated rind 1 orange
3 tablespoons oil
1–2 cloves garlic (optional)
$\frac{1}{4}$ pint red wine
$\frac{1}{4}$ pint orange juice
1 tablespoon sugar

To garnish:
1–2 sliced oranges
little powdered cinnamon
$\frac{1}{2}$–1 oz. butter
little smooth pâté *or* Continental mustard

AMERICAN

For 5–6 people you need:
$1\frac{1}{4}$–$1\frac{1}{2}$ lb. calf *or* lamb liver
$\frac{1}{4}$ cup all-purpose flour
seasoning
grated rind 1 orange
scant $\frac{1}{4}$ cup oil
1–2 cloves garlic (optional)
$\frac{2}{3}$ cup red wine
$\frac{2}{3}$ cup orange juice
1 tablespoon sugar

To garnish:
1–2 sliced oranges
little powdered cinnamon
1–2 tablespoons butter
little smooth pâté *or* Continental mustard

1. Cut the liver into neat slices and coat with flour, mixed with seasoning and finely grated orange rind.
2. Fry steadily in hot oil until brown and tender on one side, adding the crushed garlic if wished.
3. Turn and brown on second side, lift out of the pan.
4. Stir in the wine, orange juice and sugar, heat until sauce thickens. Return the liver to the pan and cook for a further 2–3 minutes. Heat orange slices in pan, sprinkle with cinnamon.
5. Blend butter with the pâté.

To serve: Arrange liver on hot dish, pour over sauce remaining in pan, or serve separately. Garnish with slices of orange and top with soft pâté mixture or with mustard just before serving. Excellent with green beans and a mixed salad.

322

Carne estufada
Beef pot roast

Cooking time: 1 hr. **Preparation time:** 25 min. **Main cooking utensil:** large saucepan with tightly-fitting lid *or* put foil under lid.

IMPERIAL

For 5–6 people you need:
seasoning
5–6 portions rump steak *or* thick slices topside *or* sirloin beef*
$\frac{1}{4}$ teaspoon mixed dried herbs
3 tablespoons oil *or* $2\frac{1}{2}$ oz. fat

1 clove garlic
4 large onions
6 medium-sized tomatoes
4 carrots
3–4 sticks celery
$1\frac{1}{2}$ lb. medium-sized potatoes
$\frac{1}{2}$ pint stock *or* water and stock cube *or* half stock and half dry Madeira wine
1 lemon

To garnish:
parsley

AMERICAN

For 5–6 people you need:
seasoning
5–6 slices sirloin steak *or* thick slices from the round*
$\frac{1}{4}$ teaspoon mixed dried herbs
scant $\frac{1}{4}$ cup oil *or* 5 tablespoons fat
1 clove garlic
4 large onions
6 medium-sized tomatoes
4 carrots
3–4 stalks celery
$1\frac{1}{2}$ lb. medium-sized potatoes
$1\frac{1}{4}$ cups stock *or* water and bouillon cube *or* half stock and half dry Madeira wine
1 lemon

To garnish:
parsley

*This recipe can be used with lamb chops.

1. Season the meat well, press herbs in this.
2. Brown the meat lightly in the hot oil or fat, but do not harden. Lift out of the pan and put on a plate.
3. Crush the garlic, chop half the onions and all the tomatoes and cook in the oil or fat remaining in the pan, until soft. Lift out and put on the meat.
4. Slice the carrots, remaining onions and celery.
5. Peel the potatoes, put into the pan with the stock, season well.
6. Put the carrots, onions and celery on top of this, season again.
7. Finally add the pieces of meat and tomato mixture, grated lemon rind and little juice. Cover pan tightly and cook for approximately 45 minutes.

To serve: Often served with saffron-flavoured rice, but as potatoes are included in this version, rice may be omitted. Serve with salad or green vegetable. Garnish with parsley.

Lentejas guisadas con chorizo
Sausages and lentils

Cooking time: $1\frac{1}{2}$ hr. **Preparation time:** 20 min. plus time for lentils to soak. **Main cooking utensil:** saucepan.

IMPERIAL

For 4–5 people you need:
12 oz. lentils
seasoning
2 pints stock
1 bay leaf
1 teaspoon mixed fresh herbs
4–6 onions
4–6 carrots
about 12 oz. well-flavoured piece sausage *or* sausages

AMERICAN

For 4–5 people you need:
$1\frac{1}{2}$ cups lentils
seasoning
5 cups stock
1 bay leaf
1 teaspoon mixed fresh herbs
4–6 onions
4–6 carrots
about $\frac{3}{4}$ lb. well-flavored piece sausage *or* sausages

1. Soak the lentils overnight or for several hours in well-seasoned stock. Then simmer for about 30 minutes, adding bay leaf and herbs.
2. Peel and cut the onions and carrots into thick slices, or good-sized portions. Add to lentils, continue cooking until vegetables and lentils are tender.
3. Any stock remaining can be served separately, or the lid removed from the pan so this is gradually absorbed by the lentils.
4. Slice sausage or half the sausages, put into the pan about 25 minutes before the lentils and other vegetables are cooked.

To serve: Hot with a green salad or vegetable.

To vary: Add sliced, skinned tomatoes to the dish; use diced fat pork instead of sausage, and cook pork for about $1–1\frac{1}{4}$ hours. When lentils are served in Austria with pork, they are flavoured with a little lemon or vinegar, and a good pinch sugar, for a piquant 'sweet-sour' taste.

324

Tortilla con pimientos
Omelette with peppers

Cooking time: 15 min. **Preparation time:** 10 min. **Main cooking utensils:** frying pan/skillet, omelette pan.

IMPERIAL

For 6–8 people you need:*
2 cloves garlic (optional)
1 large onion
8 large tomatoes
2 large *or* 4 smaller green peppers**
1 large *or* 2 smaller red peppers**
4 tablespoons oil
seasoning

For the omelettes:
8 large *or* 10 medium eggs
seasoning
3 oz. butter *or* 3 tablespoons oil

AMERICAN

For 6–8 people you need:*
2 cloves garlic (optional)
1 large onion
8 large tomatoes
2 large *or* 4 smaller sweet green peppers**
1 large *or* 2 smaller sweet red peppers**
$\frac{1}{3}$ cup oil
seasoning

For the omelettes:
8 large *or* 10 medium eggs
seasoning
6 tablespoons butter *or* scant $\frac{1}{4}$ cup oil

*As an hors d'oeuvre, 4 people as a main dish.
**To blanch peppers: simmer for about 5–10 minutes in salted water to give a softened texture.

1. Crush the cloves of garlic very finely.
2. Chop the onion very finely; skin tomatoes.
3. Cut the flesh from the green and red peppers into strips, discard core and seeds.
4. Heat the oil in the pan, fry the vegetables until as soft as wished. Some people prefer the peppers to be firm, so add when onion and tomatoes are nearly soft. If wished, 'blanch' peppers for softer texture. Season well.
5. Beat the eggs with seasoning. For a slightly lighter, less rich omelette, add 2–4 tablespoons (U.S. 3–5 tablespoons) water.
6. Heat half butter or oil in omelette pan. Pour in half the egg mixture, allow to set on bottom, then tilt pan to allow liquid egg on top to flow down sides.
7. When lightly set, tip on to a serving dish; do not fold. Make second omelette.

To serve: Top with very hot vegetable mixture.

 325

Rollo de sangayna
Vegetable rolls

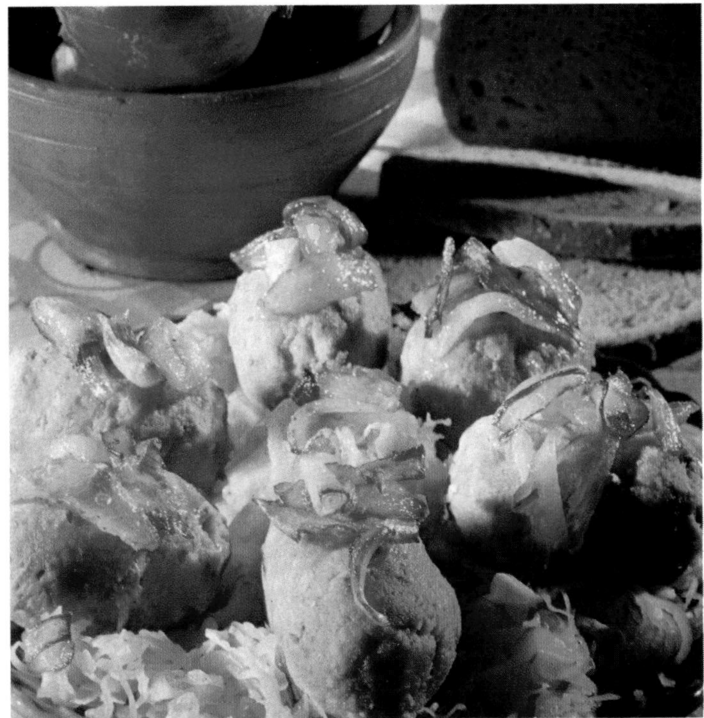

Cooking time: 45 min. **Preparation time:** 30 min. **Main cooking utensils:** saucepan, frying pan/skillet, flat baking tray/sheet. **Oven temperature:** hot, 425–450°F., 220–230°C., Gas Mark 6–7. **Oven position:** just above centre.

IMPERIAL

For 6 people you need:
For the pastry:
4 oz. potatoes, weight when peeled and cooked
8 oz. flour
pinch salt
4 oz. butter *or* margarine

For the filling:
3–4 large onions
2 red peppers, *or* 1 green and 1 red
4 large tomatoes
2–3 oz. mushrooms
small portion marrow *or* 2–3 courgettes
1 crushed clove garlic
3 tablespoons oil
4–5 tablespoons thick mayonnaise

To garnish:
small white cabbage
little butter
1 clove garlic (optional)

AMERICAN

For 6 people you need:
For the pastry:
$\frac{1}{4}$ lb. potatoes, weight when peeled and cooked
2 cups all-purpose flour
dash salt
$\frac{1}{2}$ cup butter *or* margarine

For the filling:
3–4 large onions
2 sweet red peppers, *or* 1 green and 1 red
4 large tomatoes
$\frac{1}{2}$–$\frac{3}{4}$ cup mushrooms
small portion marrow squash *or* 2–3 small zucchini
1 crushed clove garlic
scant $\frac{1}{4}$ cup oil
5–6 tablespoons thick mayonnaise

To garnish:
small white cabbage
little butter
1 clove garlic (optional)

1. Cook and mash the potatoes, do not add milk or fat to them.
2. Sieve the flour and salt, rub in butter or margarine. Add cool potatoes and bind with water.
3. Meanwhile peel vegetables and cut into neat slices, mix with garlic.
4. Fry in hot oil until tender, allowing onions to become crisp.
5. Lift out enough onion for garnish, and blend remainder of vegetables with the mayonnaise.
6. Roll out pastry, cut into 6 rectangles. Put a little vegetable mixture on each, tuck in ends, roll up and seal edges. Bake until crisp and golden.
7. Top with fried onions. Serve with the finely shredded white cabbage; cooked until tender, drained, then tossed in hot butter, flavoured with little crushed garlic if wished.

326

Tortilla
Spanish omelette

Cooking time: 10 min. **Preparation time:** 10 min. **Main cooking utensils:** omelette pan, palette knife *or* fork.

IMPERIAL

For 1 person you need:
1 tablespoon olive oil
4 oz. onion, chopped
6 oz. cooked potato
$\frac{1}{2}$ small green pepper
3 eggs
3 teaspoons cold water
seasoning

AMERICAN

For 1 person you need:
1 tablespoon olive oil
1 cup chopped onion
1 cup diced, cooked potato
$\frac{1}{2}$ small sweet green pepper
3 eggs
3 teaspoons cold water
seasoning

1. Heat the oil in omelette pan, add the chopped onion and cook slowly until soft.
2. Add the diced potato and green pepper and heat through. (The pepper could be 'blanched' in a little salted water if wished.)
3. Meanwhile prepare the omelette mixture: beat the eggs with the water and seasoning just sufficiently to break up the eggs.
4. Pour this on to the hot onion mixture. With a fork or palette knife, stir mixture from sides to the middle of the pan, so allowing underside to cook.
5. When this is firm, but the top still runny, put the pan under a hot grill for about $\frac{1}{2}$ minute until just set.

To serve: Do not fold the omelette, slide it out flat on to a hot plate.

To vary: Add 2 oz. (U.S. $\frac{1}{4}$ cup) chopped cooked ham or 1–2 oz. (U.S. $\frac{1}{4}$–$\frac{1}{3}$ cup) shelled prawns or shrimps to the onion mixture, and/or a crushed clove garlic.

327

Ensalada a la bohemia
Ham and bean salad

Cooking time: 20–25 min. **Preparation time:** 15 min. **Main cooking utensil:** saucepan.

IMPERIAL

For 4 people you need:
For the sauce:
2 tablespoons Continental (French) mustard
1 egg yolk
pinch salt
shake pepper
1 teaspoon sugar
1 tablespoon lemon juice
$\frac{1}{4}$ pint olive oil
1 clove garlic

1 lb. green beans
8–10 oz. lean ham *or* cooked Spanish spiced sausage

To garnish:
chopped parsley

AMERICAN

For 4 people you need:
For the sauce:
3 tablespoons Continental (French) mustard
1 egg yolk
dash salt
dash pepper
1 teaspoon sugar
1 tablespoon lemon juice
$\frac{2}{3}$ cup olive oil
1 clove garlic

1 lb. green beans
$\frac{1}{2}$–$\frac{2}{3}$ lb. lean cured ham *or* cooked Spanish spiced sausage

To garnish:
chopped parsley

1. Put the mustard into a bowl, add egg yolk and beat well. Stir in the seasonings, sugar and half the lemon juice.
2. Gradually beat in the oil then add remaining lemon juice and crushed clove garlic.
3. Prepare and cook the beans in seasoned water.
4. Drain, blend with diced ham or sausage. Top with some of the dressing while the beans are hot.

To serve: Add remaining dressing and garnish with parsley when beans are cold. This is excellent for a light supper or luncheon dish.

To vary: Blend the cooked beans with oil, lemon juice to taste and seasoning together with 1–2 crushed cloves garlic.

328

Churros
Fried choux pastry

Cooking time: 8–10 min. **Preparation time:** 20 min. **Main cooking utensils:** saucepan, pan of oil *or* fat for frying, piping bag/pastry bag with plain nozzle.

IMPERIAL

To make 20–24 churros you need:*
For the choux pastry:
$\frac{1}{4}$ pint water
1 oz. butter *or* margarine

pinch sugar
3 oz. flour, plain *or* self-raising
1 egg yolk
2 eggs

For frying:
oil *or* fat

For coating:
icing sugar

AMERICAN

To make 20–24 churros you need:*
For the choux pastry:
$\frac{2}{3}$ cup water
2 tablespoons butter *or* margarine
dash sugar
$\frac{3}{4}$ cup all-purpose flour
1 egg yolk
2 eggs

For frying:
oil *or* fat

For coating:
sifted confectioners' sugar

*Where it is difficult to fry the traditional long churros, make shorter lengths as picture. Quantity refers to smaller size.

These are sold in the streets, and made in the homes, for all special occasions.

1. Put the water, butter or margarine and sugar in saucepan.
2. Heat gently until the butter or margarine and sugar have melted. Stir in the flour.
3. Return the pan to a low heat, cook very gently but thoroughly, stirring all the time, until mixture is dry enough to form a ball, leaving the sides of the pan clean.
4. Remove the pan from the heat, gradually beat in well-beaten eggs. Do this slowly to produce a perfectly smooth mixture.
5. When cool, put into a piping bag with a plain nozzle. This should be no wider than a $\frac{1}{2}$ inch.
6. Squeeze the nozzle with the left hand, and cut into 12-inch sticks with a pair of scissors in the right hand.
7. Fry in the hot oil until crisp and golden brown.
8. Drain and sprinkle with sieved icing sugar. Serve hot or cold.

329

Pastel de frutas
Fruit tarts

Cooking time: 35 min. **Preparation time:** 35 min. **Main cooking utensils:** deep patty tins/deep muffin pans, double saucepan. **Oven temperature:** hot, 425–450°F., 220–230°C., Gas Mark 6–7. **Oven position:** centre.

IMPERIAL

For 9–10 tarts you need:
For the pastry:
8 oz. flour, preferably plain
pinch salt
4 oz. butter *or* margarine
2 teaspoons sugar
cold water to mix

For the custard base:
2 egg yolks
$\frac{1}{2}$ pint milk
1 oz. sugar
$\frac{1}{4}$ teaspoon vanilla essence

For the fruit topping:
4–6 dessert apples*
9–10 grapes
4 tablespoons apricot jam
4 tablespoons water

AMERICAN

For 9–10 tarts you need:
For the pastry:
2 cups all-purpose flour
dash salt
$\frac{1}{2}$ cup butter *or* margarine
2 teaspoons sugar
cold water to mix

For the custard base:
2 egg yolks
$1\frac{1}{4}$ cups milk
2 tablespoons sugar
$\frac{1}{4}$ teaspoon vanilla extract

For the fruit topping:
4–6 eating apples*
9–10 grapes
$\frac{1}{3}$ cup apricot jam
$\frac{1}{3}$ cup water

*Or use mixture of fruit.

1. Sieve the flour and salt, rub in the butter or margarine. Add the sugar and bind with the water.
2. Roll out thinly and line the patty tins.
3. Prick the pastry well and bake 'blind', until golden brown, about 7–10 minutes. Cool.
4. Blend all the ingredients for the custard. Put into the double saucepan (or basin over a pan of hot water) and cook steadily, stirring well until thickened. Allow to cool, stirring from time to time.
5. Spoon the custard into the pastry cases.
6. Core, but do not peel the apples when the skin is perfect. Cut in thin slices and arrange over the custard, with a de-seeded grape in the centre.
7. Meanwhile heat the jam and water (in the double saucepan if wished). Cool slightly, brush over the top of the fruit, allow to cool.

To serve: As a dessert, or with coffee or tea.

330

Bolas de berlim
Doughnuts

Cooking time: 5–8 min. **Preparation time:** 20 min. plus time for dough to 'prove'. **Main cooking utensils:** saucepan, deep pan of lard.

IMPERIAL

To make 12–18 doughnuts you need:
$\frac{1}{4}$ pint warmed milk
3 oz. sugar
$\frac{3}{4}$ oz. fresh yeast *or* 3 teaspoons dried yeast
12 oz. flour, preferably plain
pinch salt
2 oz. butter
1 egg
1 egg yolk
little soured cream *or* milk (approx. 4 tablespoons)
jam *or* jelly
lard

To coat:
castor *or* icing sugar

AMERICAN

To make 12–18 doughnuts you need:
$\frac{2}{3}$ cup warmed milk
6 tablespoons sugar
$\frac{3}{4}$ cake compressed yeast *or* 3 teaspoons dried yeast
3 cups all-purpose flour
dash salt
$\frac{1}{4}$ cup butter
1 egg
1 egg yolk
little sour cream *or* milk (approx. $\frac{1}{3}$ cup)
jam *or* jelly
lard

To coat:
granulated *or* sifted confectioners' sugar

1. Mix tepid milk with 2 teaspoons sugar, pour over yeast in a basin and blend. Sprinkle with a little flour, leave until mixture 'bubbles', about 15 minutes, or cream yeast and sugar, then add milk and sprinkling of flour.
2. Sieve the flour and salt into a basin.
3. Cream the butter and remaining sugar, beat in whole egg and yolk. Add the yeast mixture, flour and enough soured cream or milk to give a soft elastic dough.
4. Knead lightly but firmly until smooth, then cover and leave to 'prove' for about $1\frac{1}{4}$–$1\frac{1}{2}$ hours until double in size.
5. Knead again, either roll out until about $\frac{3}{4}$–1-inch thick and cut into rounds or rings, or form into balls enclosing a little jam in the centre of each.
6. Put on to a lightly greased tray. Leave until well risen again, approximately 15–20 minutes.
7. Meanwhile heat lard until a cube of bread turns golden in 1 minute. Fry a few doughnuts until crisp and golden. Drain on absorbent paper and roll in sugar. Reheat lard, cook rest in batches.

To serve: Top ring doughnuts with jam or jelly.

Visitors to Switzerland are always impressed not only by the spectacular scenery, but by the peaceful atmosphere and the clear mountain air. Whether you go for the skiing or for a restful holiday, you will soon feel healthy and invigorated in this picturesque country. Springtime is particularly lovely when the snow-capped mountains are the background for lush green fields full of colourful Alpine flowers. Often the only sound to be heard is the mellow clank of cowbells as one drives over the mountain passes and looks down on the quiet valleys below.

Dairy farming is crucial to the Swiss economy and dairy products naturally play an important part in Swiss cookery. Emmental and Gruyère are the internationally renowned nutty-flavoured cheeses which form the basis of Swiss fondue. This famous dish is made with cheese and wine, ideally the dry white Neuchâtel wine, cooked until blended and smooth. It is kept hot on a spirit burner and accompanied by a chilled white wine and cubes of crusty bread which everyone dips into the fondue. In their use of milk and cheese for all sorts of dishes from appetisers and soups to main dishes and desserts, the Swiss are aware that dairy products are an excellent economical source of protein. They are a health conscious people and, next to fondue, their best-known invention is muesli, the cereal made with rolled oats, wheat germ, fruit and nuts. It is full of vitamins and protein and, served with milk or yoghurt, makes a well-balanced breakfast in itself.

Germany, Austria, Italy and France, the four countries surrounding Switzerland, have all had their effects on the country as one realises immediately from the languages spoken. The majority of people speak German but in the west French is spoken and the southern part extending into Italy is Italian speaking. Many Swiss dishes show one or more of these influences. Cheese flans, for example, are a cross between a French quiche and an Italian pizza. Geneva, on the border of France, has a very French character and cuisine and *Malakoff à la genèvoise* are made of French choux pastry fried in oil. The German and Austrian influence is especially evident in the Swiss fondness for soups and their delicious rich cakes of which Coffee and chocolate gâteau is an excellent example.

Betasuppe

Chicken broth and pot-au-feu

Cooking time: approx. 2 hr. **Preparation time:** 20 min. **Main cooking utensil:** saucepan.

IMPERIAL

For 4–6 people you need:
1 medium-sized boiling fowl
2 cloves garlic (optional)
1 lb. carrots
12 oz. leeks
seasoning
bouquet garni
1 swede and/*or* turnip
any other vegetables liked

To garnish:
chopped parsley

Sauce to serve with chicken:
$1\frac{1}{2}$ oz. butter
$1\frac{1}{2}$ oz. flour
$\frac{1}{2}$ pint chicken stock
$\frac{1}{2}$ pint milk
2 egg yolks
4 tablespoons thin cream
chopped parsley *or* other herbs

AMERICAN

For 4–6 people you need:
1 medium-sized stewing chicken
2 cloves garlic (optional)
1 lb. carrots
$\frac{3}{4}$ lb. leeks
seasoning
bouquet garni
1 rutabaga and/*or* turnip
any other vegetables liked

To garnish:
chopped parsley

Sauce to serve with chicken:
3 tablespoons butter
6 tablespoons all-purpose flour
$1\frac{1}{4}$ cups chicken stock
$1\frac{1}{4}$ cups milk
2 egg yolks
$\frac{1}{3}$ cup coffee cream
chopped parsley *or* other herbs

1. Wash the fowl and giblets well; make quite sure there is no green gall on liver, as this would give a bitter taste to the stock.
2. Put the chicken, giblets and crushed cloves of garlic into pan, with water to cover.
3. Add most of the peeled, whole carrots and whole or halved leeks; save one carrot and part of one leek for cutting into smaller pieces, add seasoning and bouquet garni.
4. Simmer steadily for $1\frac{1}{4}$ hours, add diced carrots, swede or turnip and shredded leek. Continue cooking until the fowl is tender.
5. Strain most of liquid into hot serving bowl, add all the vegetables. Top with parsley or other herbs.

To serve: This is the first course of the meal. The chicken can be served hot with a sauce made by heating butter in a pan. Stir in flour, add stock and milk, bring to boil, cook until thickened, season well. Blend egg yolks with cream and stir into sauce with parsley or other herbs.

332

Salade aux champignons
Mushroom salad

Cooking time: 10 min. **Preparation time:** 15–20 min. **Main cooking utensil:** saucepan.

IMPERIAL

For 4 people you need:
1 good-sized potato
seasoning
small portion cauliflower
about 1 pint prawns *or* 2–3 oz. shelled prawns

3–4 oz. button mushrooms

For the mayonnaise:
2 hard-boiled egg yolks
good pinch salt, pepper, dry mustard and sugar
1 egg yolk
$\frac{1}{4}$ pint olive oil
1 tablespoon white *or* wine vinegar *or* lemon juice
1 tablespoon thick cream (optional)

AMERICAN

For 4 people you need:
1 good-sized potato
seasoning
small portion cauliflower
about $2\frac{1}{2}$ cups prawns *or* shrimp *or* $\frac{1}{3}$–$\frac{1}{2}$ cup peeled prawns *or* shrimp
about 1 cup button mushrooms

For the mayonnaise:
2 hard-cooked egg yolks
dash salt, pepper, dry mustard and sugar
1 egg yolk
$\frac{2}{3}$ cup olive oil
1 tablespoon white *or* wine vinegar *or* lemon juice
1 tablespoon whipping cream (optional)

1. Peel or scrape the potato, dice neatly and cook in boiling, salted water for 5–6 minutes.
2. Divide the cauliflower into neat flowerets (sprigs) and cook in the same pan for about 4–5 minutes. Strain.
3. Shell and chop the prawns, keeping 4 (unshelled) for garnish, or allow frozen prawns to defrost at room temperature.
4. Wash the mushrooms, if they are perfect there is no need to peel them, just cut a slice from bottom of each.
5. Slice or chop neatly, keeping 4 good slices for garnish.
6. To make the mayonnaise, sieve the egg yolks, blend with seasonings, then sugar and fresh egg yolk.
7. Gradually add the oil, beating hard as you do so, until a thick mixture.
8. Whisk in the vinegar or lemon juice, then add cream, beating well.
9. Put the vegetables, prawns and mushrooms in basin, blend with mayonnaise.

To serve: Arrange lettuce leaves on scallop shells or plates. Top with salad, garnish with prawns and mushrooms.

333

Savouries au fromage
Cheese savouries

Cooking time: approximately 10 min. **Oven temperature:** hot to very hot, 450–475°F., 230–240°C., Gas Mark 8. **Oven position:** centre.

CHEESE SAVOURIES

Basic recipe for Sbrinz* puff pastry: Sprinkle 1 oz. (U.S. $\frac{1}{4}$ cup) grated Sbrinz on pastry board. Place puff pastry (made with 8 oz. (U.S. 2 cups) flour etc.) on board and roll out to about $\frac{1}{8}$ inch in thickness. Sprinkle with 1 oz. (U.S. $\frac{1}{4}$ cup) grated cheese and a little cayenne pepper and/or cumin. Repeat this operation 2–3 times, folding pastry, re-rolling and sprinkling with cheese and seasoning. Place in refrigerator before using. Roll out to $\frac{1}{4}$ inch thick, cut into required shapes, glaze with egg before sprinkling with selected seasonings and bake until golden brown. This makes about 48 savouries.

Cheese straws: Cut pastry into thin sticks about $2\frac{1}{2}$ inches thick and sprinkle with poppy seeds.

Horseshoes: Cut horseshoe shapes out of the pastry and sprinkle with finely grated Sbrinz and cumin seeds. Use the ovals from inside the horseshoe as other shapes.

Spirals: Cut strips about $4\frac{1}{2}$ inches long and $\frac{3}{4}$ inch wide. Sprinkle with chopped almonds, twist into spirals.

Stars: Cut small strips of pastry. For each star, take 4 strips of pastry, pinch them in the middle and twist them once. Place the 4 strips on top of each other, forming a star-shape. Sprinkle with Sbrinz.

Bretzels: Cut the pastry into strips and twist into bretzels (like a figure of 8). Sprinkle with salt, paprika pepper and Sbrinz.

Plaits: Plait the pastry and sprinkle with Sbrinz.

Hearts: Cut a rectangular piece of pastry, slightly less than $\frac{1}{2}$ inch thick, 8 inches wide and as long as you require. Take the long sides and fold them twice round towards the centre to achieve a heart-shape; slice.

*Sbrinz is a hard cheese, use Parmesan cheese if unobtainable.

Consommé au fromage
Clear soup with cheese

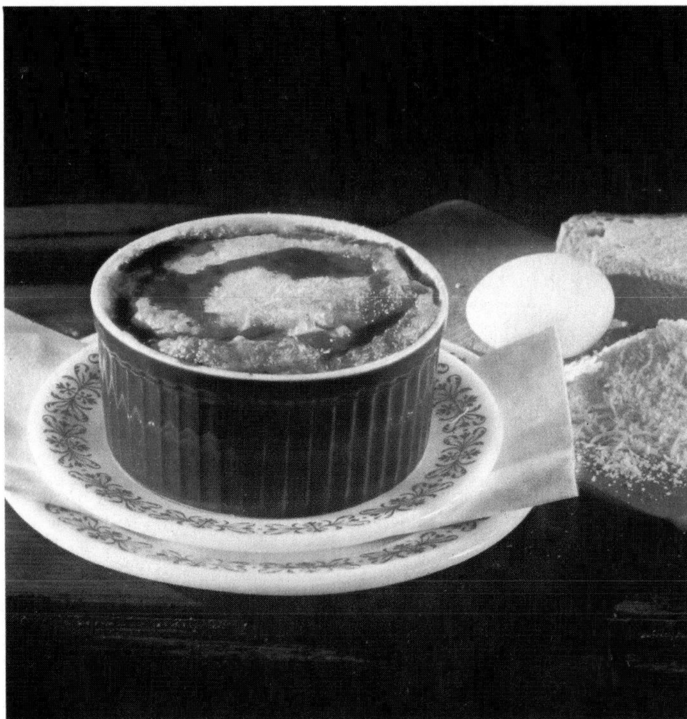

Cooking time: see Stage 1. **Preparation time:** see Stages 1 and 3. **Main cooking utensils:** saucepan, ovenproof soup bowls.

IMPERIAL

For 4–5 people you need:
beef bones *or* 12 oz. shin of beef
water
2 onions
2 carrots
1 leek (optional)
seasoning and bouquet garni
or use 2 pints water and 3–4 beef stock cubes *or* use 2 pints canned consommé
4–5 slices bread
4–5 eggs
2–3 oz. Sbrinz cheese*, grated

*If unavailable, use Parmesan cheese.

AMERICAN

For 4–5 people you need:
beef bones *or* $\frac{3}{4}$ lb. shank knuckle of beef
water
2 onions
2 carrots
1 leek (optional)
seasoning and bouquet garni
or use 5 cups water and 3–4 beef bouillon cubes *or* 5 cups canned consommé
4–5 slices bread
4–5 eggs
$\frac{1}{2}$–$\frac{3}{4}$ cup grated Sbrinz cheese*

1. If using beef bones, put these into a pan with water to cover. Add vegetables, seasoning and herbs, simmer steadily for 2 hours or allow 40 minutes at 15 lb. pressure in a pressure cooker. Allow pressure to drop at room temperature. If using shin of beef, cook for same time, or use water and stock cubes or canned consommé.
2. Strain the liquid giving 2 pints (U.S. 5 cups), from the bones or meat, reheat.
3. Toast the slices of bread on both sides until crisp and golden.
4. Pour the soup into very hot soup bowls and break an egg into each bowl.
5. Top with the toast and a liberal grating of cheese.
6. Put into the oven for 5–8 minutes to brown the cheese and to set the egg very lightly, do not over-heat.

To vary: Flavour the soup with red wine, sherry or a little brandy. Spread toast lightly with butter, top with cheese, brown under the grill; meanwhile poach eggs lightly, put into soup, top with toast.

To store: If using homemade stock or consommé, this *MUST* be stored with great care in a refrigerator and heated regularly.

335

Malakoff à la genèvoise
Cheese choux pastry

Cooking time: 10–12 min. **Preparation time:** 15 min. **Main cooking utensils:** saucepan, pan for oil, large piping bag/pastry bag, $\frac{1}{4}$-inch pipe/nozzle.

IMPERIAL

For 3–4 people you need:*
1 oz. butter *or* fat
$\frac{1}{4}$ pint water
seasoning (including pinch cayenne pepper and celery salt)
$2\frac{1}{2}$ oz. plain flour
2 eggs
3 oz. cheese, finely grated (Gruyère, Emmenthal *or* Parmesan)
oil for frying

To coat:
extra grated Parmesan cheese, if liked

AMERICAN

For 3–4 people you need:*
2 tablespoons butter *or* fat
$\frac{2}{3}$ cup water
seasoning (including dash cayenne pepper and celery salt)
$\frac{1}{2}$ cup plus 2 tablespoons all-purpose flour
2 eggs
$\frac{3}{4}$ cup finely grated cheese (Gruyère, Emmenthal *or* Parmesan)
oil for frying

To coat:
extra grated Parmesan cheese, if liked

*This will serve more people if other appetisers are also served.

1. Put the butter into a pan with the water.
2. Heat steadily until the butter has melted, add seasoning.
3. Take pan off the heat and gradually beat in the flour until mixture is smooth.
4. Return to the heat and continue cooking over a very low heat until flour mixture forms a dry-looking ball and leaves the saucepan quite clean. Take care it does not burn the bottom of the pan, you should stir well all the time.
5. Remove from the heat and gradually incorporate the well-beaten eggs.
6. For twists, shown in picture, the mixture should be fairly soft so it will flow from the piping bag. If eggs are very small, you may need a little extra.
7. Add the cheese, do not heat again.
8. Put into a piping bag and pipe long strips into very hot oil.
9. Fry for few minutes until crisp and brown. Lift out and drain on absorbent paper.

To serve: Hot, topped with more cheese if wished.

Souffléesaux tomates

Soufflé tomatoes

Cooking time: 10–15 min. **Preparation time:** 15 min. **Main cooking utensil:** flat ovenproof dish. **Oven temperature:** hot, 425–450°F., 220–230°C., Gas Mark 6–7. **Oven position:** above centre.

IMPERIAL

For 4–8 people you need:
4 good-sized firm, ripe tomatoes
$1\frac{1}{2}$ oz. butter
seasoning
$\frac{1}{4}$ teaspoon paprika pepper
$\frac{1}{2}$ oz. flour
3 eggs, separated
6 oz. Emmenthal *or* Gruyère cheese
$\frac{1}{4}$ pint thin cream *or* milk

AMERICAN

For 4–8 people you need:
4 good-sized firm, ripe tomatoes
3 tablespoons butter
seasoning
$\frac{1}{4}$ teaspoon paprika pepper
2 tablespoons all-purpose flour
3 eggs, separated
$\frac{1}{3}$ lb. Emmenthal *or* Gruyère cheese
$\frac{2}{3}$ cup coffee cream *or* milk

1. Cut a slice from the tomatoes, make sure they stand firmly.
2. Scoop out the centre pulp, strain off the juice; this may be added to salads or served with soufflés.
3. Chop the pulp finely, blend with butter, seasonings, flour, egg yolks and finely grated cheese.
4. Work in the cream or milk gradually so you have a soft paste-like consistency. There is no need to cook the mixture; the flour will be cooked in the baking.
5. Lastly fold in the stiffly beaten egg whites.
6. Pack into seasoned tomato cases, bake until golden brown.

To serve: Hot, as soon as cooked.

337

Fondue

Cheese dip

Cooking time: varies—can be 20 min. before ready. **Preparation time:** few min. **Main cooking utensil:** see method.

IMPERIAL

For 4–6 people you need:
1 oz. butter (preferably unsalted) *or* little oil
8 oz. Gruyère cheese
8 oz. Emmenthal cheese
seasoning
$\frac{1}{2}$ pint dry white wine
1–2 tablespoons brandy *or* Curaçao (optional)
1–2 teaspoons cornflour (optional)
little paprika pepper

AMERICAN

For 4–6 people you need:
2 tablespoons butter (preferably sweet) *or* little oil
$\frac{1}{2}$ lb. Gruyère cheese
$\frac{1}{2}$ lb. Emmenthal cheese
seasoning
$1\frac{1}{4}$ cups dry white wine
1–3 tablespoons brandy *or* Curaçao (optional)
1–2 teaspoons cornstarch (optional)
little paprika pepper

1. Butter or oil the bottom and sides of a dish that may be used on top of the cooker or fondue pan over the special heater.
2. Add the grated cheese, seasoning and wine.
3. Heat gently and stir from time to time. Do not let the mixture boil, or the cheese becomes tough.
4. Add brandy or Curaçao.
5. Blend the cornflour with a little of the wine and add to the mixture to prevent it curdling—this is not essential if a special heater is available to prevent any possibility of the mixture boiling.

To serve: Sprinkle with paprika. With squares of toast or bread. Use a fork, roll the toast or bread quickly in the cheese mixture and eat while hot.

To vary: Cubes of fillet beef may be fried in hot oil or butter, then dipped in the fondue, or even cooked for a moment in the cheese mixture.

Gâteaux au fromage

Cheese flans

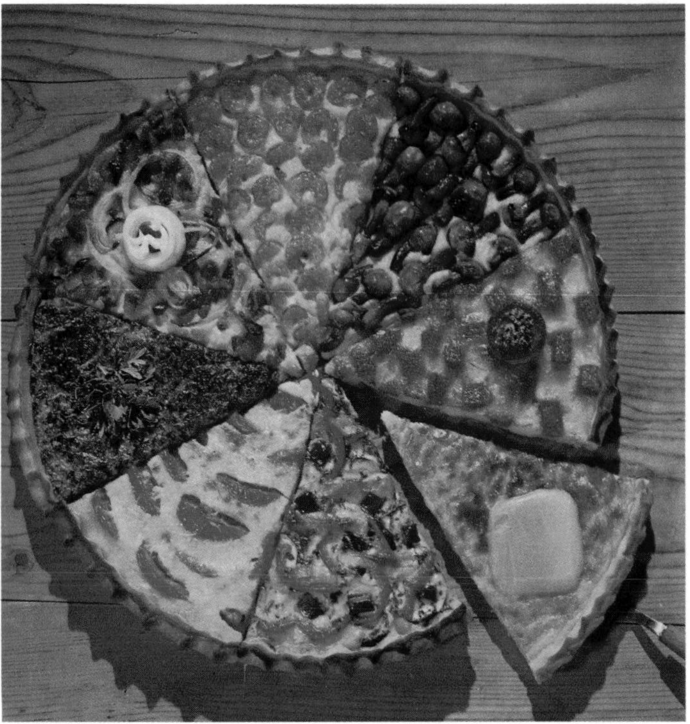

Cooking time: 40 min. **Preparation time:** 25 min. **Main cooking utensils:** 12-inch large shallow flan ring and baking tray/sheet. **Oven temperature:** moderately hot, 400°F., 200°C., Gas Mark 5–6, then very moderate, 350°F., 180°C., Gas Mark 3–4. **Oven position:** centre.

IMPERIAL

For about 8 people you need:
10 oz. short crust pastry

For the basic cheese mixture:
3 oz. Gruyère cheese, grated
3 oz. Emmenthal cheese, grated
$1\frac{1}{2}$ oz. flour
$\frac{1}{4}$ pint milk
$\frac{1}{4}$ pint thick cream
seasoning
paprika pepper
nutmeg

AMERICAN

For about 8 people you need:
basic pie crust using $2\frac{1}{2}$ cups all-purpose flour etc.

For the basic cheese mixture:
$\frac{3}{4}$ cup grated Gruyère cheese
$\frac{3}{4}$ cup grated Emmenthal cheese
6 tablespoons all-purpose flour
$\frac{2}{3}$ cup milk
$\frac{2}{3}$ cup whipping cream
seasoning
paprika pepper
nutmeg

Variations are all shown in picture for interest, but quantities will give one flan with ANY of these.

1. Roll out the pastry, line tin then bake 'blind' for 15 minutes.
2. Prepare the basic mixture by blending all ingredients together.
3. Put the mixture into the pastry and then put on topping.

The toppings are set by returning flan to very moderate oven until mixture is firm.

A. Top with 8 oz. sliced cheese, set until firm.
B. Heat 2 tablespoons butter. Thinly slice 2 courgettes, 1 red pepper and a small aubergine. Toss vegetables in butter. Top basic mixture and set.
C. Top basic mixture with 8 sliced tomatoes, set.
D. Cut 4 oz. bacon finely and 8 oz. onions thinly, top basic mixture and set.
E. Cover basic mixture with 8 oz. prawns, set.
F. Cook 6 oz. (U.S. $1\frac{1}{2}$ cups) mushrooms in 2 oz. (U.S. $\frac{1}{4}$ cup) butter, add 2 oz. (U.S. $\frac{1}{2}$ cup) raw mushrooms and cover basic mixture, set.
G. Dice 4 oz. bacon, fry, then fry 8 oz. finely diced leeks, cook until soft. Add 1 oz. (U.S. $\frac{1}{2}$ cup) breadcrumbs and 1 oz. (U.S. $\frac{1}{4}$ cup) grated cheese, season and top basic mixture, set.

339

Roulade aux cerises

Cherry sponge roll

Cooking time: 10 min. **Preparation time:** 15 min. **Main cooking utensils:** saucepans, Swiss roll tin/jelly roll pan, approximately 11 × 8 inches, greaseproof paper/wax paper. **Oven temperature:** moderately hot, 400°F., 200°C., Gas Mark 5–6. **Oven position:** towards top.

IMPERIAL

For 6–8 portions you need:
$1\frac{1}{2}$ oz. lard
3 eggs
3 oz. castor sugar
$\frac{1}{2}$–1 teaspoon almond essence
3 oz. self-raising flour

$\frac{1}{2}$–1 oz. castor sugar

For the filling:
2 oz. butter
3 oz. icing sugar
$\frac{1}{4}$ teaspoon almond essence

For the cherry sauce:
4–6 tablespoons cherry jam
4 tablespoons water
1 teaspoon arrowroot

To decorate:
icing sugar

AMERICAN

For 6–8 portions you need:
3 tablespoons lard
3 eggs
6 tablespoons granulated sugar
$\frac{1}{2}$–1 teaspoon almond extract
$\frac{3}{4}$ cup all-purpose flour, sifted with $\frac{3}{4}$ teaspoon baking powder
1–2 tablespoons sugar

For the filling:
$\frac{1}{4}$ cup butter
$\frac{3}{4}$ cup sifted confectioners' sugar
$\frac{1}{4}$ teaspoon almond extract

For the cherry sauce:
$\frac{1}{3}$–$\frac{1}{2}$ cup cherry jam
$\frac{1}{3}$ cup water
1 teaspoon arrowroot

To decorate:
sifted confectioners' sugar

1. Line a Swiss roll tin with greased greaseproof paper.
2. Melt the lard, allow to cool.
3. Whisk the eggs, sugar and almond essence over hot water until thick and creamy. Carefully fold in sieved flour and melted lard.
4. Spread mixture into Swiss roll tin, bake until firm to the touch.
5. Turn on to a sugared sheet of greaseproof paper, or roll on paper on damp cloth. Remove backing paper from sponge, carefully roll up with a fresh sheet of greaseproof in the centre. Allow to cool.
6. Make filling by creaming butter, sieved icing sugar and essence.
7. Unroll the sponge carefully, spread on filling and re-roll.
8. Heat the cherry jam with water blended with arrowroot or cornflour, stir until clear.
9. Sprinkle the sponge with icing sugar and top with the sauce.

To serve: With hot sauce as a dessert; with cold sauce as a cake.

Mousse aux pruneaux
Prune mousse

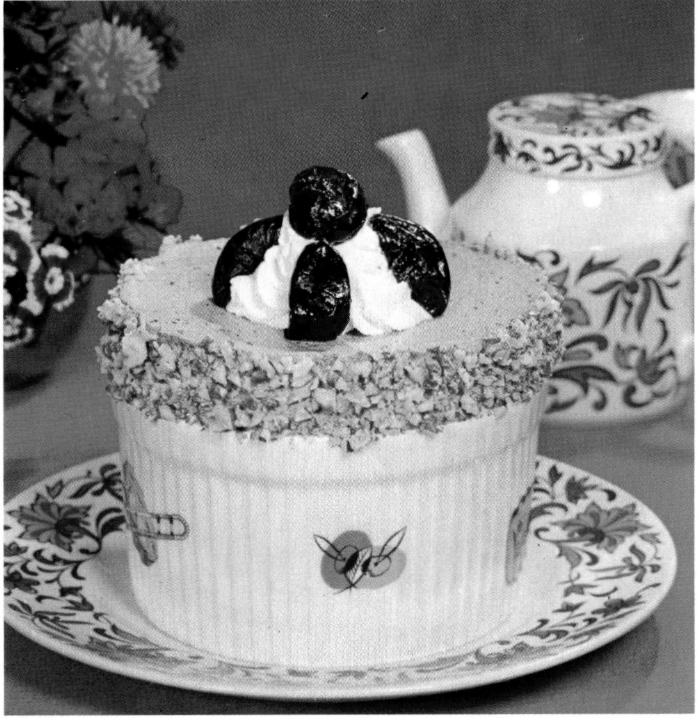

Cooking time: see Stage 2. **Preparation time:** 20–25 min. plus overnight soaking of prunes (see Stage 2). **Main cooking utensils:** buttered greaseproof paper/wax paper and 6–7-inch soufflé dish *or* serving dish, saucepan.

IMPERIAL

For 4 people you need:
- 1 can prunes, 8 oz. dried prunes (with stones) *or* 6 oz. tenderised prunes (stoned)
- syrup from can *or* $\frac{1}{2}$ pint water and 1 oz. sugar
- 1 tablespoon powdered gelatine
- 2 tablespoons cold water
- $\frac{1}{4}$ pint thick cream
- $\frac{1}{4}$ pint thin cream
- squeeze lemon juice
- 3 egg whites
- 2 teaspoons sugar

To decorate:
- 2 oz. walnuts
- little thick cream
- few cooked, stoned prunes

AMERICAN

For 4 people you need:
- 1 can prunes, $1\frac{1}{3}$ cups dried prunes (with pits) *or* $\frac{1}{3}$ lb. tenderized prunes (pitted)
- sirup from can *or* $1\frac{1}{4}$ cups water and 2 tablespoons sugar
- 1 tablespoon powdered gelatin
- 3 tablespoons cold water
- $\frac{2}{3}$ cup whipping cream
- $\frac{2}{3}$ cup coffee cream
- squeeze lemon juice
- 3 egg whites
- 2 teaspoons sugar

To decorate:
- about $\frac{1}{2}$ cup walnuts
- little whipping cream
- few cooked, pitted prunes

1. If using a soufflé dish, tie a band of buttered greaseproof, 3 inches deeper than the soufflé dish, round the outside of the dish.
2. Strain the juice from canned prunes or soak prunes overnight then cook with water and sugar until tender. Add extra water as necessary, you need approximately $\frac{1}{2}$ pint (U.S. $1\frac{1}{4}$ cups) syrup. If using tenderised prunes, do not soak, just simmer with water and sugar until very tender (about 5 minutes).
3. Soften the gelatine in cold water.
4. Sieve the prunes with liquid. Heat, add softened gelatine. Stir until dissolved then cool.
5. Whisk the thick cream until it *begins* to hold a shape then gradually add the thin cream and whisk again. When firm, fold into the prune mixture with lemon juice.
6. Allow to stiffen slightly. Whisk the egg whites until very stiff, beat in sugar, then fold meringue into prune and cream purée.
7. Turn into a prepared soufflé dish, leave until quite firm.
8. Remove the band of greaseproof paper. Decorate with chopped nuts, whipped cream and whole prunes.

341

Gâteau moka
Coffee and chocolate gâteau

Cooking time: 1–$1\frac{1}{2}$ hr. **Preparation time:** 30 min. **Main cooking utensils:** double saucepan, 8-inch cake tin/spring form cake pan, greaseproof paper/wax paper. **Oven temperature:** slow to very moderate, 300–325°F., 150–170°C., Gas Mark 2–3. **Oven position:** centre.

IMPERIAL

For 8 portions you need:
- 4 oz. plain chocolate
- 1 tablespoon coffee essence
- 6 oz. butter *or* margarine
- 6 oz. castor sugar
- 4 eggs
- 8 oz. self-raising flour

To decorate:
- 10 oz. plain chocolate pieces
- 1 tablespoon coffee essence
- 1 oz. butter
- 4 oz. icing sugar
- 2 tablespoons hot water
- 3 oz. halved walnuts

AMERICAN

For 8 portions you need:
- $\frac{1}{4}$ lb. semi-sweet chocolate
- 1 tablespoon coffee extract
- $\frac{3}{4}$ cup butter *or* margarine
- $\frac{3}{4}$ cup granulated sugar
- 4 eggs
- 2 cups all-purpose flour, sifted with $2\frac{1}{4}$ teaspoons baking powder

To decorate:
- $1\frac{2}{3}$ cups semi-sweet chocolate pieces
- 1 tablespoon coffee extract
- 2 tablespoons butter
- 1 cup sifted confectioners' sugar
- 3 tablespoons hot water
- $\frac{3}{4}$ cup halved walnuts

1. Put the chocolate and coffee essence in the top of a double saucepan (or basin over hot but not boiling water) and heat until chocolate has melted; allow to cool.
2. Cream the butter or margarine and sugar until soft and light. Gradually beat in the chocolate and coffee mixture and then the eggs.
3. Fold in the well-sieved flour and put into the tin, lined with greased greaseproof paper.
4. Bake in a slow to very moderate oven—this is important in view of the chocolate content—until firm to the touch.
5. Allow to cool, then split into 4 layers.
6. Sandwich together with some of the icing. To make this, melt the chocolate in a double saucepan with the coffee essence and butter.
7. Work in the sieved icing sugar and hot water.
8. Coat the sides of the cake with icing, then coat with chopped walnuts.
9. Spread the remaining icing on top of the gâteau.

All references are to recipe numbers